The Eskimos of Bering Strait, 1650–1898

THE ESKIMOS
OF BERING STRAIT,
1650–1898

BY

Dorothy Jean Ray

UNIVERSITY OF WASHINGTON PRESS

SEATTLE AND LONDON

Library of Congress Cataloging in Publication Data

Ray, Dorothy Jean.
  The Eskimos of Bering Strait, 1650–1898.

  Bibliography: p.
  Includes index.
  1. Eskimos—Alaska. 2. Bering Strait—History.
I. Title.
E99.E7R29   979.8'004'97   75-17819
ISBN 0-295-95435-3

Procedure and Acknowledgments

THIS study is based upon the examination of documentary and bibliographical materials in numerous repositories, and is thus a history derived mainly from written sources. All of the data, however, are interpreted within a thorough knowledge of the ethnography of the area obtained from extensive field researches at Bering Strait.

Field and archival researches go hand in hand, and if I ever publish the field material in ethnographic form, the archival work will be as valuable in its interpretation as is the field work for this study. The ethnographic information is used herein mainly for various interpretations needed for the archival data, and in a chapter that summarizes Bering Strait tribes and intertribal relations. The main outline of the history of the Eskimos around Bering Strait is taken from eyewitness, firsthand accounts during the many decades before Eskimos had learned to communicate with a written language.

The organizations and libraries where I made use of all pertinent manuscript materials include: the Smithsonian Institution libraries, Washington, D.C., especially the archives of the Office of Anthropology; the Alaska State Library, Juneau; the Bancroft Library of the University of California, Berkeley; the Oregon Historical Society, Portland; the Presbyterian Historical Society, Philadelphia, Pennsylvania; Sheldon Jackson College library, Sitka, Alaska; the University of Alaska library, College, Alaska; the University of Oregon library, Eugene; the Henry Suzzallo Library, University of Washington, Seattle; and Whittier College library, Whittier, California.

In the National Archives of the United States I worked mainly with Record Group 75 (records of the Bureau of Indian Affairs), which contains teachers' reports and correspondence of the Bureau of Education under whose auspices the first public schools in northern Alaska were established in 1890; and Record Group 36 (records of the United States Coast Guard).

During the course of many years of study of Eskimo art in many museums, I obtained information from catalogue and accession records, and sometimes from the artifacts themselves, which has contributed significantly to the present study. Among these museums are the Alaska State Museum, Juneau; Thomas Burke Memorial Washington State Museum, Seattle; Robert H. Lowie Museum of Anthropology, Berkeley; Museum of Primitive Art, New York; Museum of History and Industry, Seattle; Mystic Museum, Mystic Seaport, Connecticut; Peabody Museum of Archaeology and Ethnology, Cambridge, Massachusetts; Sheldon Jackson Museum, Sitka, Alaska; National Museum of Natural History, Smithsonian Institution, Washington, D.C.; University Museum, University of Pennsylvania, Philadelphia; University of Alaska Museum, Fairbanks; and Washington State Historical Society Museum, Tacoma. I have also made use of the catalogue files of the Indian Arts and Crafts Board of the United States Department of the Interior, Washington, D.C.

My field work in the Bering Strait area has extended over almost two decades, but work on the specific study of political organization, land tenure, and historical events did not begin until 1961. Some of the information recorded during field sessions in 1954 and 1955, under the sponsorship of the Department of Anthropology, University of Washington, while obtained primarily for analysis of the ivory carving industry and contemporary attitudes toward art, has also found a place in this study.

In 1961, after a wilderness canoeing trip on the Reed and Kobuk rivers at the southern edge of the Brooks Range, I embarked on my first research into Eskimo settlement and subsistence patterns, and land tenure of the Bering Strait region, starting with the villages on the Kobuk. After leaving Kotzebue, I went to Nome, where the largest and most varied representation of tribal membership is to be found in any one present-day locality. There I sought out the oldest men and women from the various Seward Peninsula tribes, fortunately locating several older persons who had been especially interested in aboriginal tribal political patterns. I continued my research with the tribes situated in Nome in 1964 in conjunction with the gathering of material for a study of Eskimo masks. At that time, I returned to Unalakleet and Saint Michael for a more complete understanding of the joint occupancy in Norton Sound by the Unalit, Malemiut, and Kauweramiut in the nineteenth century. I published my findings as "Nineteenth Century Settlement and Subsistence Patterns in Bering Strait," in *Arctic Anthropology* and "Land Tenure and Polity of the Bering Strait Eskimos," in *Journal of the West*.

In 1968, with the support of a grant from the Penrose Fund of the American Philosophical Society, I spent two months on Seward Peninsula and in Unalakleet and Saint Michael carrying further my study of tribal relations in Norton Sound. I also obtained more data on settlement and subsistence patterns and mapped nineteenth-century villages and camps between Koyuk and Pastolik. I carried out field investigations at Egavik, Shaktoolik, Wales, and Stebbins for the first time, and revisited Kotzebue, Teller, Golovin, Marys Igloo, Koyuk, and White Mountain. As a supplement to my field work on tribal relations in the Norton Sound area, I obtained genealogies that represented the principal lineages of the three related tribes in Unalit territory, tracing their connections with the North.

My informants, almost without exception, cooperated eagerly and generously, partly as a consequence of their own deep interest in the history of their people. These informants were carefully selected persons who had taken care during their younger years to listen to the older people and to learn as much as they could about the history of their tribe. Such persons were difficult to find. Before the Alaska Native Claims Settlement Act of 1971, the Eskimo had relatively little feeling for history as a systematic area of knowledge and had only a rudimentary concept of chronology, dating, and the anecdotal aspects of historical events. Among the Eskimo there were specialists—musicians, sled makers, mask makers, story tellers—but no historians. To most Eskimos, specific dates meant nothing; genealogical depth extended only two or three generations; and knowledge was meager even on events occurring relatively recently. From most informants, the answers I received concerning such matters as establishment of the first schools in the Bering Strait area or the landing of reindeer at the first reindeer station, or details of government transactions such as those involved in the reindeer industry, were often quite inaccurate. (Because of this, the habit of journalists and popular writers to accept stories of the past from Eskimo spokesmen with the assumption that dating and sequence of events are correct has led to an abundance of erroneous writing.) Although I found, as expected, that informants in their seventies and older were best suited for providing general ethnographic information, it was persons in their fifties or sixties who, with a special interest in history, were most valuable for providing information with a chronological dimension. They drew upon the information that they had obtained from their parents and grandparents, whereas the remaining very old people, who had actually lived the lives that the younger ones were recalling at secondhand, were often too deaf, feeble, or withdrawn to be of assistance.

Therefore, I relied almost exclusively upon the published primary sources and original manuscript journals, diaries, and correspondence in all those instances where chronology is significant. Fortunately these sources proved to be sufficient in number and scope to permit reconstruction of events in an almost unbroken sequence. Many of the printed sources are in the Russian and German languages, which I have translated, but the majority of them are in English. In transliteration of Russian names I have followed a modified form of Library of Congress system with a few exceptions, namely, Ignatiev, Muraviev, and Vasiliev.

Many of the Eskimo men and women who have provided me with information over the many years of my research are my good personal friends and my thanks go to them, first of all and most gratefully, for all of the precious information that they have supplied. We often worked very hard during our interviews, and the nature of the work was unusually tiring for my friends, but they did not complain.

Some of my new informants I had known for a long time through reading about them in early writings. I was delighted to find that some persons whose names I had encountered in publications dating back to the 1890s were still alive. I had the opportunity of meeting two of the early reindeer herders, Simon Sagoonik and George Ootenna. Sagoonik had lived in a small village near Cape Nome before the gold rush, and his father was the first Eskimo to have a glass window in his dwelling.

I had read about Ootenna of Cape Prince of Wales in a reindeer report of 1894, when he was about seventeen years of age. The report noted that he had searched all night for a reindeer herd lost in a blinding blizzard, and as a reward had received not only high praise but powder for his gun.[1] In 1968 Ootenna lived alone in Wales in a sturdy old house built for reindeer herders. Although blind and almost deaf, he still had a strong voice, and through an interpreter he told me that his big, old-fashioned wire bedstead had once belonged to Harrison Thornton, the Wales schoolteacher who was murdered in 1893.

In the Bureau of Education reports for 1904 and 1905 I had read about a bright young lad, Nagozruk, who became one of the first Eskimo career teachers in the Bureau of Indian Affairs schools. He and his wife, Lucy, were living in Nome in 1968, leading busy lives, although retired from teaching.

In Unalakleet I met the gracious, dignified Shafter Toshavik, a Saint Michael orphan, who had been the messenger boy for the last "Inviting-in" feast, held in Saint Michael for the people of Unalakleet in 1912.[2]

It is a pleasure to extend my thanks to several of my hostesses. The oldest and the sprightliest was Mrs. Marion Gonangan of Unalakleet, who is now dead. I stayed with her in 1968, but I had first met her in 1964. Born in 1891, she was the daughter of the last chief of Unalakleet.[3] Mrs. Myles, as she was called after her late husband's first name, was known as the queen mother of Unalakleet. In her widow's household she provided me with a room where I could do serious scholarly work while engaged in the study of her people's history. As an illustration of the manner in which most of the Alaskan Eskimos live today, I may mention that she had prepared one-half of a huge room as a living room–study–bedroom for me. I had a bed with an inner-spring mattress, eiderdown comforter, and two big pillows; a stove and freshly split wood for the occasional touch of summer coolness; a bedside table,

1. Fourth reindeer report (1895), p. 73.
2. Hawkes 1913. Hawkes, however, did not identify a single person by name who had taken part in this important ceremony. With the help of Unalakleet people, I learned that Kachatak and Tungun were the Unalakleet headmen and Anauruk and Anakasuk (also known as Saxy or Saxo) were the Saint Michael headmen. Their descendants now carry the surnames Katchatag, Tomron, Anawrok, and Soxie.
3. Mrs. Gonangan's father was Nashoaluk (now the surname Nashalook), son of Alluyianuk, a well-known man who helped members of the Western Union Telegraph Expedition.

chairs, and a desk cleared of all ornaments, on which, she declared, I was to write up all my notes and make my maps.

Her daughter, Mrs. Peter Nanouk, also served as an informant in my work. Martha was one of those exceptional persons with a keen interest in the history of her people. She was always hard-working, warm-hearted, and generous, and during my stay, was constantly concerned with the success of my work, serving as informant, liaison, and confidante.

In the Kauwerak area, John E. and Ruth Kakaruk not only provided me with information but took me, in 1964, over historic ground: from their fishing camp, Titkaok, on the Tuksuk Channel to their house in Marys Igloo on the Kuzitrin River. The Kakaruks' large reindeer herd, estimated in 1971 to be the largest private herd in Alaska with 4,878 reindeer,[4] roamed the hills where caribou (the wild reindeer) had lived in the nineteenth century. I was able to visit their corralling camp, Ipnuk, on Canyon Creek on the southwest shore of Imuruk Basin, and to see another of their camps on the southeast shore. Mr. Kakaruk died in 1965.

Also in 1964, I traveled up the Unalakleet River to the fishing camp, Chauiyak ("Eskimo drum"), belonging to Thora Katchatag, whose generosity extends to a guest tent for her visitors. Four years later I made another trip to the same locality, and was also able to go to Egavik by boat where Thora's sister, Hazel Kotongan, and husband, John, spend part of their summers.

Most of my informants lived in the villages of the west coast of Alaska, but because of the extensive travel undertaken by many during the 1960s, some lived throughout Alaska and other states. The Alaska Medical Center Hospital in Anchorage draws Eskimos from all over for free medical care, and I talked to several persons who were hospitalized there. Many former villagers now live in Nome and Seattle; for example, all of my conversations with Margaret Johnsson were in Mukilteo or Edmonds, Washington. I have also carried on an active correspondence with my numerous friends and informants from which I have often clarified various data. My informants, totaling seventy-five persons, are listed in the appendix. To each, I give my thanks for his or her contributions in the reconstruction of their own history.

All of my field research has been conducted in the English language. Most of the Eskimos are bilingual, and I have found that the best informants, with the exception of some King and Diomede islanders, are those who speak and write English. I made use of interpreters, however, upon a number of occasions, even when my informant was bilingual, in order to deal more adequately with complicated material, or with an informant with hearing difficulties. For a few hours, during the later phases of my work, I made use of a tape recorder. In all of my other field work over the years I have recorded the information directly from informants by writing in longhand in a notebook. As I have explained, my best informants were those in the fifty-

4. Bureau of Indian Affairs 1971, p. 4.

and sixty-year age range. Two of my informants were over ninety years old, and twenty-five were in their seventies or eighties; only a few were less than forty years of age. The Eskimos of Seward Peninsula and Norton Sound appear to be enjoying a longer span of life than ever before, and they live a very active life even during their later years. Several of my women informants in their seventies were active on every bright day in picking berries in the hills, sometimes venturing out quite alone. Many of my men informants were still active at even older ages, engaging in activities such as traveling over the tundra to fishing sites or pulling in heavy loads of fish in nets for a packing plant.

In previous publications I have acknowledged the aid of many persons, agencies, libraries, and museums in my archival, bibliographic, and field research. Those listed below have provided help that I have been unable to acknowledge before or have been of repeated assistance. I am again indebted to my long-time friends, Ruth Towner and Carrie M. McLain, for their hospitality and support in Nome. In 1964 Rev. and Mrs. Maynard Londborg in Unalakleet and Bertha Stedje in Teller provided accommodations, as did Mr. and Mrs. William E. Dodd in Shaktoolik and Mr. and Mrs. Charles Christensen in Wales in 1968. Friends like Mabel Johnson of Kotzebue have taken me places where a visitor without private transportation finds it difficult to go.

I have been grateful during the course of my research and writing for the helpful efforts of many other persons. In Alaska, special recognition goes to Robert A. Arnold, Federal Field Committee for Development Planning in Alaska; Howard W. Pollock, former congressman from Alaska; Robert and Rachel S. Simmet; Martha Wilson, M.D., Alaska Native Medical Center; Arthur Nagozruk, Jr.; Caroline M. Reader of the Bureau of Indian Affairs; Maurice Kelliher, district judge of the Second Judicial District; Gladys Musgrove, University of Alaska Extension Service; David M. Hopkins, U.S. Geological Survey; John and Lucy Poling, Jim Richardson, and Otto and Kathie Schulz.

In Washington, D.C., Donald J. Orth, U.S. Geological Survey, provided me with various supplementary materials; and Jack Marquardt of the Smithsonian Libraries facilitated my work in the then uncatalogued book collection and papers of William H. Dall. Richard C. Berner, University of Washington Libraries, and Ted C. Hinckley, San Jose State University, provided manuscript materials. I am grateful to Ernest S. Burch, Jr., Raymond H. Fisher, Richard A. Pierce, and Verne F. Ray, who read the manuscript and gave considerable helpful criticism. I am also indebted to Rhea Josephson for her aid in translating Russian sources.

D. J. R.
May 1973

Contents

Illustrations

Introduction

THE object of this study is the description and analysis of changes that took place in the Bering Strait area of Alaska during the historical period, 1650–1898, chronologically and topically. It is a history of both Eskimo and white man as recorded principally in explorers' and travelers' accounts, government reports, teachers' and missionaries' writings, miners' stories, and Eskimo recollections—an accumulation of events and activities that created the characteristic Bering Strait culture found at the end of the nineteenth century.

Bering Strait Eskimos have had a longer and more involved relationship with Europeans than almost any other Alaskan Eskimos, yet less is known about the aboriginal peoples of this area than of almost any other part of the state. For example, few persons are aware that the early inhabitants were divided into many tribes, each with its own name and territory, and that in the 1970s Nome, the urban center of the area, comprises an amalgamation of these tribes.

Therefore, as an important part of this history, it has been essential to reconstruct tribal organization and political organization of traditional Eskimo culture. Early observers often reported that the Eskimos had no political organization or government, but this was an oversight resulting from language barriers and a tendency to gauge all aspects of the culture—even complex ones like religion and social organization—by the external simplicity of Eskimo life. Yet data about political organization and land tenure are scattered throughout eighteenth- and nineteenth-century reports, which together with my field notes present a composite picture of the tribes probably not too far from reality at any one point during the nineteenth century. Although the printed chronicles offer only a tiny sample of the totality of culture, and are sometimes glossed with explorers' value judgments or personal reactions to disagreeable practices, it is all we have to work with. The majority of men who penned those early accounts apparently did try to be as objective as possible—no mean accomplishment in the days when every explorer seemed to carry with him the uncompromising standards of Christian civilization.

Northern ethnic studies have concentrated for the most part on archeological or contemporary problems with little emphasis on the in-between historical studies of indigenous inhabitants. For example, the gold rush spawned dozens of books about mining and travel adventures, but few about Eskimos. Teachers and government officials, however, wrote many reports and sometimes popular books over the years, ranging from first-rate firsthand observations like Edward W. Nelson's *The Eskimo about Bering Strait* and Harrison Thornton's *Among the Eskimos of Wales, Alaska*, to crude and biased accounts like Arthur H. Eide's *Drums of Diomede*.

Few anthropologists have worked in the Bering Strait area, and little has been published specifically about Eskimo history. Most of the published studies have concentrated on special areas of ethnography or contemporary culture. Albert C. Heinrich's papers and doctoral dissertation on kinship and related subjects are of special excellence, and since 1966 anthropologists have increased their interest in the area. Sergei Bogojavlensky undertook a two-year study of King Island people between 1966 and 1968, which culminated in a doctoral dissertation, and in 1968 Thomas Correll began a study of the structure of two Eskimo populations (northern Alaskan Eskimos and central Canadian Eskimos) at Unalakleet. During 1969–70 the director of the project, Ernest S. Burch, Jr., extended it to Kotzebue. (Although Kotzebue is outside the tribal scope of this study, it will necessarily enter into various historical interpretations.)

Archeological investigations have likewise been comparatively few, mostly in the nature of preliminary surveys (like those of Henry B. Collins and Diamond Jenness); but the work of J. Louis Giddings at Cape Denbigh, Helge Larsen at Deering, and, recently, that of John Bockstoce near Nome and Bruce Lutz at Unalakleet are slowly adding perspective to Bering Strait prehistory.[1]

Anthropological neglect—especially ethnological—of the Bering Strait area is almost self-explanatory. The jumbled tribal relations that resulted from Eskimos being transplanted to "white" villages like Nome, Saint Michael, and Teller presented little challenge to the recovery of early ethnographic data, and anthropologists working with native peoples in the whole of Alaska had their hands full trying to salvage ethnographic data from tribes and villages in less acculturated areas. The effects of events that reach back to time beyond memory still linger, however, and though tangible changes at any one time were small compared to the cataclysm of the 1898–1900 gold rush near Nome, each was important for its part in the development of Bering Strait Eskimo culture.

1. This study does not attempt to correlate archeological antecedents with the historical aspects of change. However, the reader is referred to the following recent résumés of northern archeology, in which further exhaustive references can also be found: Dumond 1969; Campbell, ed. 1962, especially the papers on western Alaska; Giddings 1967; Giddings et al. 1960; and Irving 1971.

The Eskimos of Bering Strait, 1650–1898

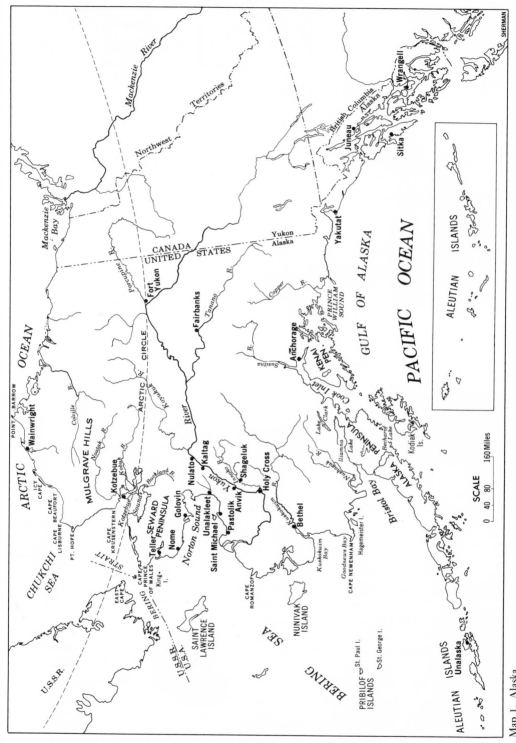

Map 1. Alaska

CHAPTER 1

The Bering Strait Region

In the heart of the Bering Strait region, Cape Nome rises precipitously from the sea between the weather-beaten town of Nome and the cabins of Nuk, a sprawling aggregate of summer fishing camps where hundreds of house depressions in the earth remind one of villages long dead. The gravel road that parallels the beach from Nome to Nuk cuts into the profile of Cape Nome above the old site of Ayasayuk, a once-prosperous village on the edge of a bountiful sea where Eskimos used to hunt white whales, walrus, and seals, and where their descendants now camp in wooden cottages with glass windows.[1]

In the twentieth century the feeling from the cape is not so much isolation as loneliness, not so much desolation as desertion, for people have come and gone, forming an unbroken chain of human occupancy as rediscovery followed upon discovery in a great wilderness. From the top of the cape, Norton Sound is a plate of blue that fuses with a soaring sky along its outer edge, a spatial immensity that technology of the 1970s cannot seem to dent. This famous cape, only ten miles from Nome, has never been more lonely. Sometimes not a ship is in the sea, or an airplane in the sky; and of course, no umiaks or kayaks—the Eskimo's own boats—now break the surface of the ocean. From certain positions high on the cape, the town of Nome is lost from view; the cabins built on the site of Ayasayuk on the lower slopes are obscured by thick copses of alders and willows; and the road is swallowed beneath its own embankment. There is not a sign to show that man has ever been there before.

Now in the 1970s the greater part of the Bering Strait region has this same look of forever. Before the gold rush of 1898–1900 foreign visitors left few mementos—a building or two here and there, some telegraph poles, or a derelict ship—all quickly appropriated by the Eskimos or the elements. After

---

1. A storm on 12 November 1974, after this manuscript was finished, destroyed all of the fishing camps at Nuk and at other places along the coast.

the gold rush, tons and tons of indestructible metal from castaway machinery at every mining site up and down the coast and back in the valleys swiftly acquired the timeless look of the tundra as they slowly rusted into commemorative monuments to the twentieth century. Except for villages of European-styled houses, a few miles of roads, and the tailing piles left by dredges that chewed the gravel for gold, the land is not much different from the time of its first discovery. Only the people have changed.

The discovery of the land mass now called Alaska can be traced to Siberia at two different points in history. First, during the Pleistocene period when the two were connected by a vast plain known as the Bering "land bridge," men were able to move slowly eastward on the land or along the shores; then, during the seventeenth century A.D., the Russian Cossacks learned about land and its inhabitants across the body of water now called Bering Strait.[2] For millennia, the earliest men had moved eastward and southward and become permanent residents on land now beneath the sea. Many years later the water rose to separate the continents and to give the coasts of Siberia and Alaska their present shape. When the Cossacks came to eastern Siberia from the west, the Eskimo and Indian tribes of Alaska had already occupied their territories from time immemorial, undisturbed by explorers; but the Chukchi and Eskimo tribes of Siberia knew about them and considered them to be numerous and rich. The first step in the second discovery of Alaska was getting information from the Siberian tribes about the "great land" (*bolshaia zemlia*) known to lie across the ocean.

Bering Strait in its narrowest geographical definition includes only the Diomede Islands and the closest tips of the continents of Asia and America, that is, East Cape (Cape Dezhnev) in Siberia and Cape Prince of Wales in Alaska, only fifty-five miles apart.[3] In the past, the term "Bering Strait" on the Alaskan side has also included a large area extending as far north as the Chukchi Sea and as far south as the Yukon delta. For example, E. W. Nelson in *The Eskimo about Bering Strait* included people all the way from Saint Michael to the region north of Kotzebue Sound, and the provenience of an ivory carving in the British Museum is listed in the catalog as being "from Point Hope Behring Strait." Today Bering Strait usually refers only to the Seward Peninsula and adjacent islands, but the Bering Strait of Alaska in this study also includes the coastal area of Norton Sound as far south as Saint Michael.

The total area of Seward Peninsula and the coast of Norton Sound occupied by Eskimos is more than three times the size of Massachusetts, or about 26,000 square miles. Seward Peninsula alone is larger than either Denmark or Switzerland. This area is 5 percent of the land surface of Alaska,

2. For an understanding of Pleistocene conditions in the North see Hopkins, ed. 1967.
3. The present spelling, Bering Strait, was established by the United States Board of Geographic Names, and any other spelling is considered incorrect, although in the past the name has been spelled Bering Straits, Behring's Straits, Behring's Strait, and Beering's Strait.

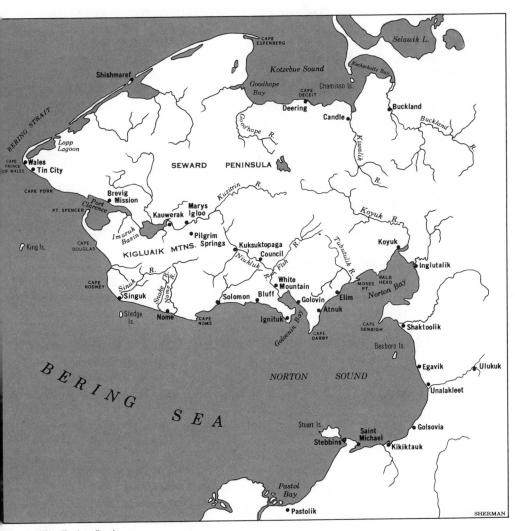

Map 2. The Bering Strait area

but its 5,500 inhabitants of 1973—more than 4,300 of whom live on Seward Peninsula—constitute only about 2 percent of its population.

Except for about forty square miles near Cape Espenberg, this area lies south of the Arctic Circle and is characteristically subarctic. The popular notion of "Eskimo country" as being a flat, treeless monotony of ice and snow or tundra (that useful Russian word for an arctic land area covered with lichens, moss, and grass) fits the Bering Strait area only in part. Generally, the terrain is gently rolling, but a number of extensive mountain ranges raise their lofty spires—steep and craggy with pockets of snow—in splendid isolation, and geologic secrets abound in out-of-the-way places: miles upon miles of pitted lava beds on the upper Kuzitrin River; conelike hills that rise abruptly from the northern plains; and thousands of lakes, ponds, and pondlets thrown down like pieces of a gigantic jigsaw puzzle along the lonely *tapkak* ("sandy strand") between Shishmaref and Cape Espenberg and on the flats east of Nome.

Large expanses of tundra cover the flatlands and hillsides, but marshes, tangled brushland, and forests also claim huge areas. Though rivers like the Baituk and the Mint in the Wales area have scarcely a twig on their under-nourished subarctic banks, the Pilgrim (or Kruzgamepa), eighty miles eastward, has noble stands of cottonwoods and alders stretching back from its deep, clear water; and southward, in a sweeping arc from the upper Fish River, past Golovin, and along all the rivers down the coast to Unalakleet are forests of spruce and birch, or what the Siberian Russians call taiga. One explorer to the Koyuk countryside likened the rolling tundra and copses of spruce to his native English "parkland."

Temperature, precipitation, and winds of the different seasons vary from year to year, although the summers are cooler and the winters are warmer than in the interior of Alaska around Fairbanks. The weather also varies considerably from place to place in the Bering Strait area, and Nome's weather can be called typical only insofar as the Nome records contain the only official data of depth for comparative purposes. Nome's figures can be greatly misleading, however, because when Nome is under drizzling skies, Unalakleet, on the Norton coast, might be basking in a lazy warm haze; Wales, northwest of Nome, might be almost freezing with a stiff wind; and Pilgrim Springs, about forty-five miles north of Nome at the edge of the Kigluaik Mountains, will be swarming with mosquitoes at 80°F.

Nome's official figures, nevertheless, reassure one that it is located in the subarctic. The average July temperature is 54.6°F. It has been as low as 44.4° in July, and as high as 84°, but once I saw the mercury stand at 86° for several hours one rare July day in 1968, after the temperature tables used here were published.[4] Relative·humidity will be between 82 and 90 percent. In a normal July, 2.2 inches of rain will fall, accounting for a fair percentage of the year's total precipitation of 17.88 inches. The prevailing wind from the

4. Weather data are taken from Searby 1968, p. 15.

WSW blows at a mean hourly speed of 10.2 miles. Only three days will be clear; six, partly cloudy; and the rest, cloudy.

In January the average daily maximum and minimum temperatures are 11.5° and −2.7°. In 1963 it reached 43° above, but in January 1919 it plunged to 47° below. Nome old-timers claim that the all-time low was 51° below zero in November 1918, during the influenza epidemic. Unofficial temperatures of 50° and 60° below zero have been recorded inland on the Pilgrim River and at Marys Igloo, where summers, at the other extreme, can be uncomfortably hot. In January at Nome, the relative humidity is about 77 percent, and the almost constant winds increase the discomfort of a cold day.

Shore ice usually forms toward the end of October and merges with the northern pack ice sometime in November. Autumn is the stormy season, and wind from the southwest in September or October is sure to bring a tempestuous sea that batters coastal villages. But winter soon sets in, and the ice locks to the land and becomes immovable except in the Bering Strait itself, where it churns and shifts all winter long. The sun does not disappear completely from sight as in the higher latitudes; during the darkest months of winter, the sun rises and sets each day, and the inhabitants live by daylight for a few hours. In March the days begin to creep out from their winter dimness, and by April, though snow may still cover the ground, one day meets the next in twilight, and a sunset may last the whole night through. In the spring, millions of geese and ducks rush back to the arctic swamps, and flowers suddenly spring up from the edge of a snowdrift. Except in hidden wintry spots, the snow quickly sinks away, and by June and July the sea's current has transported the ice pack north.

During the nineteenth century, there were twenty-two tribes, or political units, in the Bering Strait region (as described in Chapter 9). Three tribes, Buckland, Candle, and Deering, lived on northern Seward Peninsula, but were related culturally and linguistically to the Kotzebue Sound area. Their common boundaries with Bering Strait tribes to the south led to friction, which in turn affected tribes even farther south.[5] Two distinct Eskimo languages, Inupiak and Yupik, came together in the Golovnin Bay area.[6] There,

5. For discussions of tribal relations, see Chapter 9.

6. Linguistic classifications use an unnatural phonetic transcription, Inupik, rather than Inupiaq (or Inupiak). Bringing up this spelling is like beating the poor old horse when he is already dead, but there is no such word as Inupik. For that matter, there is no word Inupiak—it should be pronounced with the back k, or "q"—but I am capitulating to the final k for orthographic conformity. To say "Inupik" is a mispronunciation, and anyone who has heard an Eskimo speaker pronounce the word would never omit the diphthong "ia."

The singular, Inupiak, and plural, Inupiat, are used extensively in Alaskan news items today as well as in the names of various Eskimo organizations, for example, "Inupiak Development Corporation, Inc., Unalakleet" and "Inupiat Arts and Crafts Association." The masthead of the *Tundra Times* reads, "Inupiat Paitot, People's Heritage." Robert Mayokok, Eskimo artist and writer, wrote in one of his booklets, "The name the Eskimos use for their own race is 'Inupiak' which means 'ordinary man'" (1951, p. 2).

D. E. Dumond recognized the conflict between Eskimo pronunciation and linguists' fiction in a paper, "On Eskaleutian Linguistics, Archaeology, and Prehistory," but explained that he used

the Fish River and Cape Nome dialects of Inupiak met the Unaluk dialect of Yupik. The Buckland, Candle, and Deering tribes spoke the so-called Malemiut dialect of Inupiak, and all others to the north and the west of Golovin spoke what could be called the Bering Strait dialects (also Inupiak), although Wales and Little Diomede diverge slightly. Those who speak a Bering Strait dialect consider their speech to be similar to all other Bering Strait dialects, but different from Malemiut.

Bering Strait dialects can also be called "Kauwerak-related dialects" because of their similarity to the speech of Kauwerak village, which once lent its name as a linguistic designation to most of Seward Peninsula. The tribes speaking these dialects could form a compact group of "Bering Strait tribes" on this basis as well as on geographical contiguity were it not for differences in subsistence quests and settlement patterns.

Bering Strait history can be divided into six broad time periods based on the character and scope of European activities that began in Russian Siberia and continued in Russian America (which later became American Alaska). Changes were gradual and sometimes imperceptible until the gold rush at the end of the nineteenth century when Eskimo culture, already considerably changed from its aboriginal state of mid-seventeenth century, was altered even more swiftly. The periods are based on significant landmarks of change among the Eskimos as well as on events of political importance to the nations that ultimately acquired use of Eskimo lands.

The first period, which is a prehistoric one that ends in 1650 with Cossack arrival in eastern Siberia, only slightly concerns us here because it preceded all written records, all direct European contacts, and acquisition of nonnative goods and ideas. The prehistoric period was a time of purely aboriginal Eskimo culture of internal development and external interaction with neighboring indigenous Asiatic and Alaskan tribes.

The other periods and their inclusive dates are: Russian inquiry about the Great Land, 1650–1778; European exploration, 1778–1833; coastal commerce, 1833–67; Americans at Bering Strait, 1867–98; and contemporary life, 1898–1970s. The phrase that characterizes each period indicates the most conspicuous activities during the period and does not exclude other important activities; nor is an activity mutually exclusive to one period. For example, European exploration continued into the last half of the nineteenth century.

The second period began when Cossacks arrived in eastern Siberia and ended in 1778 when Captain James Cook charted the coast of northwest Alaska. This period could be called prehistoric for the Alaskan side of the

---

the spelling Inupik because of its orthographic parallel to Yupik, "realizing that most of our designations of peoples and of languages are nonsensical to the people concerned" (1965, p. 1253). Although Yupik is more nearly Yukpik or Yu'pik, depending on the speaker, I am conforming also to linguistic usage here with Yupik. While an Eskimo might consider Yupik to be a phonetic lapse, he would think Inupik a pretty bad mistake.

I shall generally use Unaluk as a linguistic designation, and Unalit as a tribal reference.

strait; but the inauguration of European trade, and considerable diffusion of nonnative traits across the strait during these 130 years, made it prehistoric only in a figurative sense. The events of this period took place for the most part in Siberia, but they must be given consideration for a thorough under-standing of subsequent activities on the Alaskan side of the strait.

The third period dates from Captain Cook's visit in 1778 until the mid-1800s, or more precisely, 1833, when Saint Michael was established in the southern part of the area. The major features of the coastline were recorded by Cook, Joseph Billings, Otto von Kotzebue, Mikhail N. Vasiliev, Gleb S. Shishmarev, Vasilii S. Khromchenko, Adolf Etolin, and Frederick W. Beechey.

After 1833 commercial trade in the area was of prime importance. This was especially so after 1848, when hundreds of commercial whaling and trading ships, most of them from the east coast at first, and then from the young city of San Francisco, brought some of the worst aspects of western civilization to the Arctic—intoxicating liquor, guns, and an undisciplined exploitation of natural resources.

After 1890, schools, missions, and reindeer herds became firmly estab-lished at Bering Strait, and the teachers and missionaries contributed to the discovery of gold in 1898. The subsequent rush of 1899–1900 to the Nome area combined with the measles epidemic of 1900 to affect native culture in a way that no event had done before, and at no other time in the historical period could the ending of one era and the beginning of another be seen so clearly. The sixth and last period, with its emergence of the Eskimo people as a political force in their native land, calls for separate treatment in a further volume of Bering Strait history.

CHAPTER 2

Siberian Information about Alaska,
1650–1732

BEFORE 1732, all information about Alaska came through the Russian Cossacks from Siberian Eskimo and Chukchi tribes.[1] By mid-seventeenth century, the Cossacks had arrived on the Kolyma River in northeastern Siberia, 800 miles from Wales, Alaska, but closer than any other Europeans to Bering Strait. Siberians and Alaskans visited each other across the strait—probably not often and sometimes with war in mind, but they did not live in the isolation often attributed to them. From 2,300-foot Cape Mountain behind Wales, Siberia's coastal hills loom high above the horizon and the Diomede Islands appear to ride like rocky whales in a glassy sea on a calm, sunny day. After the umiak was invented, the strait became an intercontinental highway, its coastal fringes occupied by peoples who had more or less the same way of life.

The beginning of the Siberian chapter of Russian history consists of legendary events and conflicting stories. Especially prominent is the tale of a great Cossack hero, Vasilii Timovievich, better known by the pseudonym Ermak or Yermak, who arrived in the western foothills of the Urals with his fighters after a series of escapades. There three generations of the Stroganov family had carved out an empire based on salt mines and fur trading, but were blocked from further expansion by the territory of Kuchum Khan. Ermak defeated the khan in 1582 and took possession of Sibir, Kuchum's capital and gateway to what would ultimately be called Siberia.[2]

1. George V. Lantzeff, discussing the Cossacks in his *Siberia in the Seventeenth Century* (1943, pp. 67–69), says that "the origin of the word cossack is still in dispute."
2. William Coxe, the eighteenth-century clergyman who wrote about Russian discoveries, said that the name Siberia was not derived from the village name, Sibir, "that fort being by [the Tatars] called Isker. Besides, the Southern part of the province of Tobolsk, to which the name of Siberia was originally applied, was thus denominated by the Russians before the invasion of Yermac" (1787, p. 281n).

From then on, the Cossacks and fur hunters spread swiftly to the east, and in 1644 Mikhail Stadukhin discovered the Kolyma River at about longitude 160° east. A trading post was founded five years later on the Anadyr. The huge, barren Chukchi Peninsula in the far northeast corner of Siberia directly opposite Seward Peninsula was completely unknown to the Cossacks at that time—and for good reason. The courageous and stubborn Chukchi tribes were unwilling to yield to demands that they pay furs as tribute (*iasak*) or tax to the tsar; consequently, for many decades after their arrival on the Kolyma and the Anadyr the Cossacks were kept occupied by the complications of conquering the Chukchi. But in the 1780s the Chukchi and the Cossacks finally came to terms when an accelerated trade in tobacco and furs made a truce expedient.

Although the administrative and trading settlements of Yakutsk, Nizhne-Kolymsk, and Anadyrsk were far from the Bering Strait proper, they were important centers from which information about the land to the east was evaluated and dispensed to the western Russian capitals. Yakutsk, although 1,700 miles from the strait, was Russia's eastern outfitter for expeditions that explored and fought in Chukchi territories long before Vitus Bering's second Kamchatka expedition of 1741, which resulted in the official discovery of Alaska.

Many events important to the history of northwest Alaska originated on the Kolyma River on the bleak northern shores of Siberia. In 1648, when Nizhne-Kolymsk was only four years old, the Cossack Semen Dezhnev set out on a voyage that purportedly resulted in the discovery of the Bering Strait. The record of his deed, which apparently was unknown to his contemporaries, was unearthed from the Yakutsk archives in 1736 by Gerhard Müller, Siberia's first historian, but not published until 1742 and 1758.[3] It was written in the form of a report dictated by Dezhnev in 1655 to counter Stadukhin's claim of having discovered the Anadyr River and its commercially valuable deposits of walrus ivory tusks in 1649. Dezhnev insisted that he was the discoverer, but his obscure language in explaining his arrival and whereabouts on the Anadyr lends itself to various interpretations.

According to Anatole V. Baikaloff, the name Sibir or Siberia was used by many nationalities and was first mentioned in "the Chinese chronicle *Yuan-Chao-Mi-Shi* under the year A.D. 1206," and in Russian chronicles in 1406. He discusses several possible derivations of the word: a mutilation of *sever*, meaning "north" in Russian; the borrowing of the name of a mythical mountain, Subur; and his own explanation, the joining of two Turkic words, "*su* or *sü* 'water' and *berr* or *birr* 'a wild unpopulated land,'" which are found in variant forms in Turkic and Mongolian languages (1950, pp. 287–89).

Siberian events have been summarized from Bancroft 1886, pp. 14–16; Coxe 1787, pp. 275–97; Forster 1786, pp. 476–82; Golder 1914, pp. 17–31; Hulley 1953, pp. 30–39; Lantzeff 1943; Longworth 1970, pp. 47–75; Semenov 1944; Wrangell 1840, pp. xvii–cxxxvii. *Eastward to Empire* by Lantzeff and Pierce, which was published after this manuscript was finished, is the most complete summary of Siberian history to 1750 in English.

3. The first information, published anonymously, was in 1742 in *Primechaniia k Sankt-Peterburgskim vedomostiiam* in an article, "Izvestie o severnom morskom khode Rossiian iz usti nekotorykh rek, vpadaii shchikh v ledianoe more." It has now been attributed to Müller (Raymond Fisher communication).

Müller, who was a historian for Bering's expeditions, concluded that Dezhnev and seven boats had sailed east from Kolyma along the Arctic coast in the summer of 1648 (apparently an unusual, ice-free summer) to a place below the mouth of the Anadyr, where he wandered for ten weeks before discovering the river.[4] This supposed feat of sailing more than two thousand miles in one short arctic summer along the usually ice-choked northern shore of Siberia and south through Bering Strait in their primitive boats was subsequently viewed with suspicion by many, including seafaring men acquainted with northern waters.[5]

Not until 1838 was the improbability of such a voyage presented in a professional critique when Petr A. Slovtsov, a Russian historian, refuted Müller's interpretation.[6] Since then, writers of Siberian history have found themselves in opposite camps, and numerous papers and books have been written to try to prove whether Dezhnev did or did not sail through the strait. According to the Soviet writers, Dezhnev's place in Siberian history is akin to that of Christopher Columbus in American history, as a great explorer and discoverer.[7]

The only detailed critical analyses in English have been written by the American historians Frank A. Golder and Raymond H. Fisher in 1914, 1956, and 1973. After examining the original documents, Golder supported Slovtsov's conclusions that Dezhnev had not sailed the strait or seen the Diomede Islands. Fisher refutes Golder, and in his paper of 1973 adds information that Soviet historians have recently unearthed, including the original petitions, which had been incorrectly copied for Müller's use in several places.[8]

To some persons, the fact that Dezhnev's contemporaries had never heard of this voyage is proof that he did not sail through the strait, because if he had, so the argument goes, his achievement would have been a landmark in Russia's constant pursuit of new geographic and cartographic information as

4. Samoilov 1945, p. 93; Müller 1761, pp. v–viii.

5. Gavriil Sarychev, in 1787; James Burney, who accompanied James Cook on his northern expedition of 1778, in 1819; and Ferdinand von Wrangell, who explored the coast of northern Siberia between 1821 and 1824, were not convinced that this journey had taken place (Sarychev 1806, pt. 1, p. 36; Burney 1819, pp. 60–76; Wrangell 1840, pp. xxvi–xxxiii).

6. Slovtsov 1886, pp. 56–59. Slovtsov said that when he checked the documents in the Yakutsk archives, he found them uncatalogued and "thrown around."

7. Two authors have presented arguments for both sides: N. N. Ogloblin, an archivist who unearthed petitions made by Dezhnev concerning the river and the tusks, and Viacheslav A. Samoilov (Ogloblin 1890, pp. 54–60; Samoilov 1945, pp. 93–106. Ogloblin published the text of Dezhnev's first four petitions for payment of accrued pay, the first in 1662.

8. Golder 1914, pp. 67–95; Fisher 1956, 1973. Golder reprinted Müller's account of Dezhnev's voyage in both the original German and in English translation (pp. 268–88), and extracts of Dezhnev's report in Cyrillic orthography and in English translation (pp. 282, 287–88). The facsimile extracts were taken from "Dopolnenia k aktam istoricheskim, volume 4, document 7"; and from "Zhurnal Ministerstva Naradnavo Prosveschenia [*sic*], December 1890, 303." The latter is Ogloblin's original article, an offprint of which is deposited in the Slavic Room, the Library of Congress.

the Siberian frontier expanded eastward. One of Russia's principal goals was to find and to develop a water route from icebound Kolyma on the northern Siberian coast to the southern port of Okhotsk, but navigational problems were so monumental that few vessels—even large ones—successfully sailed more than a few miles along the northern coast of Siberia until A. E. Nordenskiöld's journey in 1878–79.

Dezhnev's report contained the first ethnographic information about Little Diomede Island people, who belonged culturally, and later politically, to western Alaska. He said that men of the "islands" wore pieces of bone in their chins. These ornaments, or labrets, were not used by Siberians. The ambiguous language of the report suggests that this news could have been learned without going to Bering Strait, because Alaskan Eskimos were sometimes prisoners of the Chukchi, and Dezhnev would have had an opportunity to see or hear about them during his long residence on the Kolyma River before writing his petition.[9]

But the importance of Dezhnev's report to the history of Seward Peninsula is yet to come in this chronicle. Through a misunderstanding more than a century later, in 1779, it was thought that a Russian fort called Kheuveren on the American side of the strait was inhabited by bearded Russians descended from survivors of a Dezhnev boat that had drifted to Alaska. We shall leave this mysterious village to its chronological place in the 1760s, when imagination and rumors transformed it from a real Eskimo village to a nonexistent Russian fort that would be treated as a historical fact for decades thereafter.

During the seventeenth century, the tsarist government constantly sought information about the geography of both Siberia and the "great land" known to lie across the sea to the east, and requested many maps to be made. The first map to show land beyond the shores of Siberia (which might be either Alaska or Saint Lawrence Island) was one of Kamchatka dated 1700 in S. U. Remezov's atlas compiled in the early eighteenth century.[10] A long peninsula lies near and parallel to the Chukchi Peninsula in a north-south direction. On it is written the information, "Small land newly reported. Many settlements," and a name, "Kynyntsy," which may have referred to the Alaskan Eskimo village of Kingigan, or Wales.

Data about Alaska were not known—or at least not preserved—until 1711, when Petr I. Popov, a Cossack, was sent by the Yakutsk government to the northeastern Siberian tribes to collect tribute and to obtain information about the land to the east. Cossacks as a group had learned little about the geography of eastern Siberia or North America across the strait during their first sixty years in Chukchi territory. The Chukchi not only resisted the Cossacks

9. The "cape" to which he referred might have been Cape Shelagskii, about 350 miles west of Bering Strait, because Gleb Shishmarev said in 1821 that people of Shelagskii also wore such pieces (Shishmarev 1852).

10. Efimov 1949, map, p. 34; Efimov, ed. 1964, map 48.

but were enemies of the Alaskan Eskimos, a situation that would have prohibited the exchange of much information.

In 1711 Popov gave his report to Matthew Skrebykin of Anadyrsk, and though he failed to get tribute from the Chukchi, he learned something about the country opposite Siberia, thirty years before Vitus Bering would "discover" it. In 1758 Gerhard Müller reported Popov's journey, as well as other information about America, in German and Russian. In 1761 it was translated into English. The English version differs in several places from the German and the Russian, and in the following quotations omissions in the English are italicized and placed within brackets while corrected or clearer translations appear as unitalicized bracketed interpolations.[11]

Popov's report apparently had combined information about Saint Lawrence Island and the continent of America, but the reference intended was to the "large country" of Alaska. There, said Popov, lived people who had a different language and way of life. They wore labrets and waged war against the Chukchi, using bows and arrows. Popov saw ten of the foreigners held as prisoners among the Chukchi. In one day's time (that is, twenty-four hours) the Chukchi could row across to the land of the foreigners, which had a variety of animals, vegetables, and trees. Popov estimated the Chukchi population to be two thousand or more, but said there were three times that number across the sea, "which is confirmed, not only by the Prisoners, but by one of the *Tschuktschi*, who has often been there."

Müller published another account about the continent of America, which had been obtained in 1718 from Chukchi who had gone to Anadyrsk "to

11. Popov's report is found on pages 56–60 of Müller's German edition, 1758, and on pages xxiv–xxv of the English edition, 1761. A large part of Müller's German edition is in Russian in volumes 1 and 2 of *Ezhemiesiachnia sochineniia i izvestiia o uchenykh delakh* (Müller 1758a). Bogoras (vol. 2, pp. 689–90) also published a translation of Popov's original report from the Russian.

The following is the verbatim report by Popov, summarized in the text. (Omissions in the English version are supplied, italicized, in brackets, and a corrected or clearer translation is bracketed, unitalicized.)

Opposite Anadyr Cape on both sides, said Popov, "an Island is said to be seen at a great Distance, which the *Tschuktschi* call a large Country, and say, that People dwell there who have large [teeth set in, which project through the cheeks]. These People are different in their Language, and Manner of Living, from the *Tschuktschi*, who have waged War against them Time out of Mind. Their Weapons are, like those of the latter, Bows and Arrows. *Popow* found ten Men of these People disfigured with their projecting Teeth; these were Prisoners of War among the *Tschuktschi*; and he observed [that the inset teeth were cut from walrus teeth]. In Summer Time they sail [i.e., *"fähret"* in German; the Russian version says, "can row across with oars"] in one Day, to the Land in Baidares . . . and in Winter Time, going swift with Rein Deer [*over the ice*] [they can also go in one day]. As on the [cape] there are no other Animals but Foxes and Wolves, and even these are scarce for Want of Wood, so on the other Land are found all Sorts of Beasts, as Sables, [*ermine, Arctic foxes*], Wolves, [*wolverines*], white Bears, [*and*] Sea Otters. The Inhabitants keep large Herds of tame Rein Deer: they live by catching of Sea Animals, [eat also] Berries, Roots, and [greens, and live like the Chukchi without any government. For cutting wood they find there cedar, pine, fir, larch, which kinds of wood Popov] observed in the Baidares and Huts of the *Tschuktschi*."

Bancroft summarized Popov's journey (1886, p. 27n) but inferred that the Chukchi traded for wood from America, and did not gather it as driftwood: "the Chukchi sometimes obtain [wood] for their bidars [*sic*], weapons, and huts."

acknowledge the Dominion of the *Russians*."[12] The report contains informa-
tion similar to that of Popov's, but also says that "the Inhabitants have
Dwellings and fortified Places of Abode, [surrounded by] Ramparts of
Earth. . . . The Number of Men in that Country may be twice or three
Times as many as that of the *Tschuktschi*, who are often at war with them.
[*Their weapons are bow and arrows.*]"

Müller was able to believe that information, "but now," he continued,
"*follows something fabulous.* There are likewise said to be People in this Country who have Tails like Dogs; speak their own Language; are often at War
among themselves, and are without Religion: They wear Cloaths like the
former, and live upon wild Rein Deer and Sea Animals. Another nation
there, is said to have Feet like Ravens, covered with the same Kind of Skin as
theirs. They never wear Shoes or Stockings."

About 1710 Ivan Lvov made a map showing what is undoubtedly Alaska.
This map of northeastern Siberia included the Anadyr area, Chukchi Peninsula, Bering Strait, and a land mass placed in the position of Alaska. Müller
discussed the map in his history, but did not publish it.[13] Aleksei V. Efimov,
however, recently printed it in a Russian geography and deciphered the
descriptions written on various geographical features.[14] In this map, south is
at the top, so that America and Siberia are reversed east and west from
present-day maps. Müller published all of the inscriptions written on the
map, but because the secondhand translation (into English from German
from the original Russian) is not accurate, I have translated the original
Russian handwritten script as transcribed by Efimov. For example, in the
English and German editions the name Kigin Eliat, meaning "inhabitants of
the large land," appears as Kitschen Eljat. However, the original, Kigin
Eliat, approximates the name of Kingigan (or Wales) even more than the
Kynyntsy on the Remezov map of 1700. At any rate, it is apparent that an
Alaskan place name appeared in print for the first time either in 1700 or 1710.

Lvov's map shows a large islandlike land mass lying in the Alaskan area.
On it is written: "The land is big [or the Big Land?], and people live there
who in Chukchi are called Kigin Eliat. [If spoken fast, this sounds like
Kingikmiut, or 'people of Kingigan.'] Their language is individual [i.e., their
own], and they wear parkas from sable and fox; and foxes and deer, and all
kinds of animals, sable, and fox, and deer are there. Their yurts are in the
ground; they fight with bows; the forest there is pine, and larch [deciduous
trees?], fir groves, and they have a walled settlement [*ostrog*]."[15]

Lvov placed two sausage-shaped islands of almost equal size between this
land and the Chukchi Peninsula. At first glance it appears that the two

12. This account is found in Müller 1761, pp. xxvi–xxvii; 1758a, 1:202–4; 1758b, pp. 60–62.
The date 1718 is omitted in the English edition.
13. Müller 1761, pp. xxii–xxiii.
14. Efimov 1948, between pp. 98–99; Efimov 1950, p. 111; and Efimov, ed. 1964, map 55.
Efimov is the source for the statement that Lvov got his information from Popov (1950, p. 113).
15. Efimov 1950, p. 114.

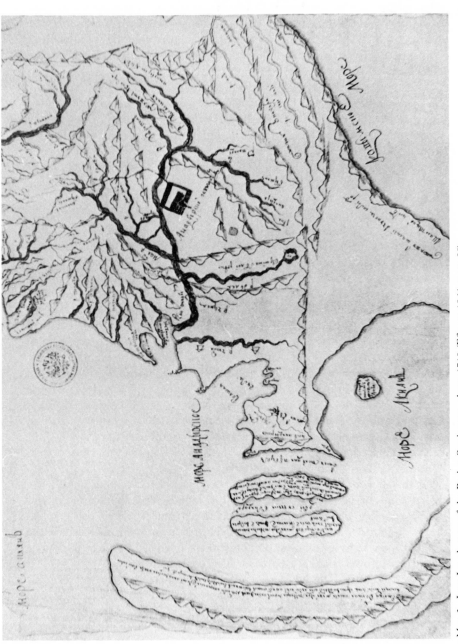

Map 3. Ivan Lvov's map of the Bering Strait area, about 1710 (Efimov 1964, map 55)

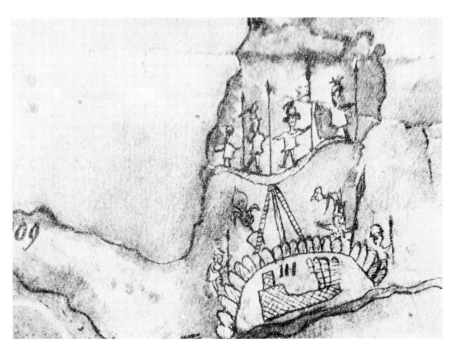

A "fort," reported to be on the "Kheuveren River," is the first known illustration of northwest Alaska, drawn in Siberia from hearsay by Nikolai Daurkin in 1765. (From Fedorova 1964, p. 98)

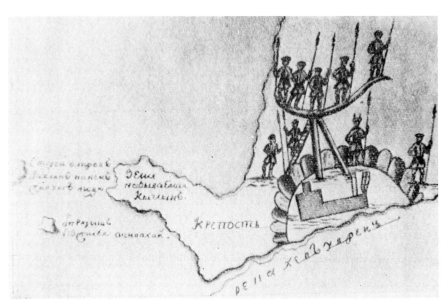

Another drawing of Daurkin's fort (about 1770) makes the clothing and dwelling look European. (From Fedorova 1964, p. 101)

The first known published illustration of northwest Alaskan Eskimos: "Inhabitants of Norton Sound, and their Habitations," drawn in 1778 by John Webber. (From James Cook's *Voyages*)

"Inhabitants of Norton Sound," drawn by I. G. Vosnesenskii in 1843. (From Blomqvist 1951, p. 270)

Diomede Islands were mapped seventeen years before Bering had discovered only the larger one, but Lvov's inscriptions clearly reveal that only one is a Diomede and the other is Saint Lawrence Island. The inscription on the island nearest Alaska reads: "On this island live people who in Chukchi are called peekel toothy [with large teeth, or labrets]. Clothing is of duck[skin], and they have ostrogs." [16] On the island nearest Siberia is inscribed: "On this island live people who in Chukchi are called Akhiukhaliat [the name used for Saint Lawrence Islanders]. The language is their own, they wear clothes of duck and loon, and eat walrus and whale. And it is treeless, and instead of wood they use bone and cook with fat [seal-oil lamps]." [17] Between the two islands is the phrase, "two days [forty-eight hours, or two complete days] in baidars." No such notation would have been needed if the two islands were Big and Little Diomede, only two and a half miles apart.

Whenever additional information about northeastern Siberia was gathered, corrected maps were made by cartographers in Tobolsk and Saint Petersburg. A map of Kamchatka was printed in Johann Baptist Homann's atlas of 1725, which, according to Efimov, was based on Lvov's map of the Bering Strait area, including the islands, with the addition of a huge land mass farther south, which appears to be Saint Lawrence Island. A notation on Big Diomede says, "uninhabited island" (which it was not), and on Little Diomede, "island on which people live." [18]

Still other reports came from Siberia with "new" information about the land to the east. In 1730 Afanasii Melnikov, who had been sent from Yakutsk in 1725 in a further attempt to subdue the Chukchi, submitted a report that was mentioned in the instructions that Vitus Bering took with him when he set out to discover the "great land" in 1741. Melnikov's report added little to what was already known—or at least to what we now know had been previously reported—but he said that two men with "walrus teeth fastened to their own" had come "from an island in the sea" on a peaceful visit while he was at Cape Chukchi in April 1730.[19]

Bering's voyage of 1728 along the coast of northeastern Siberia and through the strait that now bears his name was the first expedition organized directly under imperial auspices. It was the biggest and most costly venture up to that time in the Russian search for new geographical information. Peter

16. The meaning of the word "peekel" is unknown. According to Bogoras (1904, pt. 1, p. 20), East Cape people were called "Pe'ekit," apparently in derision. Collins thought that Lvov's "Peekeli" referred to East Cape (1937, p. 18). Several other places, however, were named from the root of this word.

17. In Müller's English version (1761, p. xxii) the translation for fat was "train oil," which referred specifically to whale oil in writings of the eighteenth and nineteenth centuries. The original Russian word is *zhir*, or fat.

18. Efimov 1950, p. 113*n*; Homann 1759–[84], map 67. Homann's map is also printed in Efimov 1948, p. 100; Efimov 1949, between pp. 42–43; Efimov 1950, p. 112; and Efimov, ed. 1964, map 58. According to Raymond Fisher (personal communication), the land mass I call Saint Lawrence Island might be the mythical Juan de Gama Land.

19. Golder 1922, p. 30.

the Great, whose lifetime passion was sailing, originated plans that eventually led to the several discoveries of Alaska. Bering's principal goal in 1728 was to find a way to America.[20] After leaving Saint Petersburg on 5 February 1725 (Peter the Great had died several days before), Bering's expedition of men, horses, wagons, tools, books, food, and scientific instruments took three years to get to Kamchatka, where a boat was finally built. They set sail on 13 July 1728; but Bering hugged the Siberian coast and though he discovered and named Saint Lawrence Island on his way north, he saw no other land because a wall of mist and fog closed off the entire ocean. He knew that the North American continent lay to the east, but with more than six weeks of sailing weather remaining at those latitudes, he inexplicably turned southward north of East Cape on 16 August.[21] On his way south he discovered and named Saint Diomede (now Big Diomede Island), but did not see the smaller island nor the continent of North America, barely thirty miles away.

The importance of the Siberian reports about Alaskan Eskimos before Europeans had seen any part of Alaska is in the reporting of a few generalities such as tribal and international animosities that could not be learned from archeological sites and the recording of certain cultural traits that had persisted into the nineteenth century: the use of bows and arrows and a wide variety of foods, especially vegetal products, and the wearing of wolf tails, labrets, and raven ceremonial regalia. The homely details that Müller found difficult to believe were valuable pieces of ethnographic information. As long ago as 1711, Bering Strait Eskimos wore wolf and foxtails on their belts, a custom that prevailed until the late nineteenth century, partly as decoration, partly to enable the wearer to acquire the swift characteristics of these animals. (The Polar Eskimos of northwest Greenland had used tails on their clothing to provide extra warmth at the junction of jackets and trousers.) The Eskimos also performed raven dances that continued to be popular more than two centuries later. Likewise, the barefooted Eskimo was not a fiction: Billings and Kotzebue subsequently observed Eskimos without footgear on Seward Peninsula.

The use of the terms "fortified places" and "ostrogs," however, is puzzling because the Bering Strait Eskimos did not build permanent defenses or live in fortified or palisaded villages.[22] Perhaps the terms referred to the semisubterranean houses that resembled mounds or ramparts, to villages on the steep

20. Communication from Raymond Fisher.

21. The sailing season often extended into fall. When I lived in Nome and freighters still brought cargo, the "last boat" usually arrived sometime in October. When Eskimos were still permitted to travel between Alaska and Siberia, they often went in their umiaks as late as 17 October (*The Eskimo Bulletin* 4 [July 1898]).

22. "A station was known either as zimovie, ostrojok, or ostrog. A zimovie was a log cabin or underground hut for winter use, and was not unlike the present day 'barrabaras' of the natives and white hunters of Alaska. Two or more zimovies with some means of defense were known as ostrojok. An ostrog was an enlarged ostrojok surrounded by a wall" (Golder 1914, p. 26).

rocky slopes of the islands, or to temporary defenses of skins and stakes known to have been erected north of Bering Strait and possibly at Kauwerak village itself.

A significant contribution of these reports is the observation that Eskimos *rowed* across the strait. This statement, made before Bering's journey in 1728, suggests that umiak sails seen by late eighteeth-century explorers were possibly not aboriginal. It also implies that Dezhnev did not sail through the strait, for had he done so the Chukchi and Siberian Eskimos, who have always been skillful adapters, would immediately have borrowed such a labor-saving device.

In the controversy over the Dezhnev voyage, the Eskimo side of the journey has been overlooked. The old boats of the Dezhnev party had square sails of skin, which became almost useless when wet and, like the Eskimo and Chukchi sails, could sail only with the wind. (Fisher, in his 1973 paper, says that according to new data presented by Soviet writers, the pre-Soviet description of the boats as shoddy and poorly built no longer holds; they were instead substantial vessels often sixty feet long and fifteen feet wide with canvas sails—yet they still could sail only with the wind.) When the Eskimos used sails on their umiaks, they never failed to take along their paddles; and if they lost the wind on a coastwise journey, or if it was blowing in the wrong direction, they would pull the umiak along the shore with a rope, often with the help of dogs. In 1816 Kotzebue said that the Chukchi were amazed that the *Rurik* could sail so close to the wind, "and every time when we put in with contrary wind, they collected on the shore in groups, to admire this phenomenon. . . . They are not able to sail but with a very good wind."[23] The square sails used by the Dezhnev boats, then, would have been of dubious practical use on a two-thousand-mile trip going both southeast and southwest in one summer's time, especially in water that was known for continual ice barriers.

Another fact often overlooked in the Dezhnev controversy is that the wooden vessels of many subsequent explorers and travelers in Arctic waters were unable to stand up under the pounding of the surf on landing. The Arctic is a graveyard of broken boats. The Eskimo umiak has proved its superiority over all other boats time and again, and it seems unlikely that one of the old Dezhnev boats could repeatedly land on shore—as they surely must have done in their long journey in completely foreign waters—without damage or destruction. The experienced coastal Eskimos knew their ocean well, and always followed the coastline except when they struck out from shore to go to one of the nearby islands or to cross the strait to Siberia, where the sheltering Diomedes awaited them halfway.

23. Fisher 1973, p. 15; Kotzebue 1821b, 1:261. John Bockstoce thinks that sails on umiaks were pre-European on the basis of some heretofore "unidentified objects," which he has associated with rigging on sailing umiaks (personal communication).

Finally, as will be discussed in later chapters, native information about specific events that transpired years before cannot be trusted. Native traditions about European activities were scarce and inaccurate, and early information was often garbled because of the ever-present language barrier. It is therefore unlikely that in 1710 Cossack Lvov was told at East Cape that the Russians had come sixty-three years, or two generations, before to exact tribute, and had been refused.

CHAPTER 3

Information about the Alaskan Side of Bering Strait, 1732–79

INFORMATION about northwest Alaska continued to be scarce during the eighteenth century. The Cossacks avoided the Chukchi Peninsula not only because of Chukchi resistance but because sable hunting, a major Cossack activity, was better in southern Siberia. A remarkable event, however, transpired during the early part of the century, namely, the first sighting of the northern Alaskan mainland, a shore that would not be seen again for almost fifty years when Captain James Cook sailed along the coast in 1778. On 21 August 1732, Mikhail Gvozdev and Ivan Fedorov discovered Alaska near the present village of Wales in their little ship *Gabriel*. Although this event was acknowledged on a few early maps, it has been relegated to comparative obscurity both by the interest and publicity attending Bering's official discovery of Alaska in 1741 (which had been preceded by immense preparations) and by the decidedly informal circumstances under which Gvozdev's discovery took place.

The chances are small that Gvozdev's discovery will supersede Bering's, but perhaps one day the credit will be shared. A map of 1769 placed both discoveries in perspective: "1730 [sic] Coast discovered" (printing placed near Wales) and "Part of America that the Russian Sea Captains Bering and Chirikov had discovered in 1741" (placed on the map on the southern coast of Alaska).[1]

In 1732 the campaign against the stubborn Chukchi continued full blast under the able command of Dmitrii Pavlutskii, a dedicated Chukchi fighter and successor to the equally devoted Afanasii Shestakov, who had succumbed to a Chukchi arrow in 1730. In accordance with his orders to extend his conquests to the islands and land that existed without doubt beyond Siberia, Pavlutskii ordered Gvozdev, who was a trained surveyor, and Jacob

1. Homann 1759–[84], map 45.

21

Hens, a skilled pilot, "to sail around Kamchatka Cape [in May 1732] to the mouth of the Anaduir and opposite Anadirski Cape to what is known as the Large Country, examine and count the islands there, and gather tribute from the Inhabitants." Hens, who became ill at the time of sailing, was replaced by Fedorov, who also became sick and spent most of the voyage in bed. Even when he was well enough to be on watch he was so melancholy that he could not write in the logbook. The burden of the journey then fell solely on Gvozdev.[2]

The *Gabriel* reached Cape Anadyr on 3 August, and "from there went to the islands [Saint Lawrence?] to collect tribute."[3] They sailed close to the Siberian shore searching for Big Diomede, discovered four years earlier by Bering; and although one of Bering's men, named Moshkov, accompanied them, they did not see it until 17 August. A headwind forced them to stay near Chukotski Cape on the Siberian shore where they saw "many Chukchi with whom we tried to enter into conversation but without much success." With an improved wind on the nineteenth they set sail, but "our attempt to land [on Big Diomede Island] was resisted by a shower of arrows, to which we replied with muskets. After a great deal of difficulty the natives told us that they were Chukchi [i.e., Eskimos] and that some of their people had fought with the other Chukchi against Pavlutskii. In cruising about the island, which is about two and a half versts long [1½ miles] and a verst wide [⅔ mile] we came across other natives but all refused to pay tribute. We made a landing and examined their homes, and from the island we saw the Large Country [Alaska]." After a successful landing on Big Diomede, they attempted to land on the smaller Diomede, "but meeting with an unfriendly reception," returned to the ship and sailed to the "Large Country," where they anchored about two and a half miles from shore on 21 August.

"It was now Fedorov's watch," said Govzdev, "and he, without consulting any one, gave orders to haul up the anchor and approach the southern point of the shore. From there we could see huts [probably the village of Wales]." They did not land, however, because of a rising north-northwesterly wind, which forced them out to sea.

Leaving his anchorage off the Alaskan coast, Gvozdev proceeded "on a

2. Information about this discovery of America is taken primarily from Gvozdev's 1743 report as translated by Golder (1914, pp. 160–62); but I also consulted the original Russian accounts by Polonskii and in *Zapiski Gidrograficheskago Departamenta*, vol. 9 (1851, pp. 78–107). Polonskii's article is mainly about Gvozdev's 1741 report and the other is about the report of 1743. Further comments by Golder are found in his pages 158–59. Wickersham said that Gvozdev's "preliminary report . . . of 1741 [is in the Archives of the Marine Ministry], Papers of Count Chernishev, 1762–68, No. 367, pp. 46–49, MS. Publ. in Golder, F. A.: Bering's Voyages, vol. 1, pp. 22–24; and in Russian Expansion on the Pacific 1641–1850, pp. 160–162" (Wickersham 1927, p. 322). Golder's reference, however, was to Gvozdev's 1743 report to Spanberg.

Discussions of the Gvozdev-Fedorov voyage by recent Russian writers can be read in Belov 1956, pp. 260–63; Efimov 1948, pp. 160–75, with verbatim documents on pp. 236–43; Efimov 1950, pp. 170–85; and Grekov 1960, pp. 49–54.

3. In the eighteenth century, Saint Lawrence Island was thought to be composed of several islands.

southwest course and by doing so came to the fourth island." King Island, as well as the Alaska mainland, was thus discovered by Europeans for the first time in 1732. One of the island inhabitants came to the *Gabriel* in "a leather boat which had room for but one man. He was dressed in a shirt of whale intestines which was fastened about the opening of the boat in such a manner that no water could enter even if a big wave should strike it. He told us that Chukchi [Eskimos] lived in the Large Country, where there were forests, streams, and animals. We had no opportunity of going shore, and from the distance we could not tell whether all that he told us of the Large Country was true or not." On 22 August the *Gabriel* sailed from King Island, and on the twenty-eighth entered the mouth of the Kamchatka River.

In 1886 Hubert Howe Bancroft concluded that the expedition sailed as far south as Norton Sound since Fedorov, who was supposed to have kept a journal for his "personal remembrance," said that "there was also timber on this land, spruce and larch," and that they sailed along the shore for five days without seeing an end to the land, turning back when the water became too shallow for safety.[4] Sailing to Norton Sound does not agree with Gvozdev's reports, which said that they went along the coast only as far as King Island before returning to the Kamchatka River.

In November 1732 Gvozdev asked Fedorov to help make a land map of the country they had seen and to add information to the logbook, which he had failed to record during his watches; but Fedorov declined to cooperate, answering that he had been trained in affairs of the sea, not of the land. Gvozdev then abandoned his project for the time being.[5]

Soon after Fedorov's death in February 1733, Gvozdev sent a report of their journey and the incomplete logbook to Okhotsk, but the Admiralty College in Saint Petersburg learned of the event only five years later by accident from a seaman returning from Siberia. No one ever explained why government officials in Okhotsk and Yakutsk were negligent in reporting to Saint Petersburg what surely would have been exciting news to Russia's scientific men and fur traders.

About the time of Bering's second voyage, officials in Okhotsk asked Gvozdev and another member of his expedition to write further reports clarifying their discoveries. This they did. Martin Spanberg, who had been one of Bering's assistants, saw extracts of these reports and requested even more complete information, which Gvozdev supplied in 1743. On the basis

4. Bancroft 1886, p. 41*n*. Neither the time nor the chronology, according to Gvozdev's information, permitted an additional five-day journey to Norton Sound. Golder did not mention the existence of Fedorov's private journal or any such discrepancies, and the article in *Morskoi sbornik*, referred to by Bancroft in his "sources," mentions only a joint Gvozdev-Fedorov logbook. Possibly Ivan Petroff, Bancroft's Russian collaborator, got his notes confused, because it does not seem likely that Fedorov would have kept a private journal when he was unable to keep the official logbook up to date.

5. *Zapiski Gidrograficheskago Departamenta*, 1851, 9:102–3. In a recent publication by V. A. Divin, a map illustrates Gvozdev's round-trip journey. The return track bears directly south from Cape Prince of Wales, and veers west to the western end of Saint Lawrence Island (1971, p. 81).

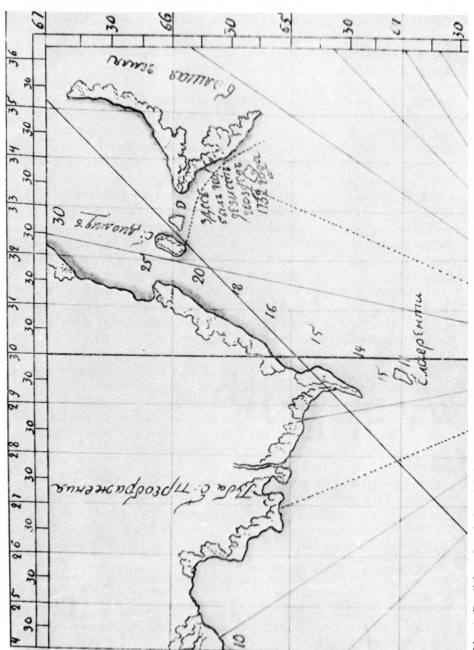

Map 4. Detail from Gvozdev's and Fedorov's map, corroborating their visit to the Bering Strait in 1732 (Efimov 1964, map 70)

of Gvozdev's reports of 1741 and 1743, they collaborated on making a map of the Bering Strait area. This map, with the distinctive shape of Cape Prince of Wales and four islands in the strait, leaves no doubt that Gvozdev was there (see Map 4).[6]

Gvozdev's journey was overshadowed by Bering's expedition, especially as related in the writings of Gerhard Müller, who lived in Yakutsk from 1735 until 1737. Although in 1758 Müller wrote a short paragraph concerning the Gvozdev discovery, it seems strange that he did not give it more attention since, as a leading historian, he presumably had access to the logbook of the *Gabriel*, Fedorov's journal (if there was one), and the Gvozdev-Spanberg maps.

Müller placed the words, "Coast Discover'd by Surveyor Gwosdew in 1730" on his map of 1758, but his short paragraph about the discovery in his text is cryptic and puzzling:

Schestakow sent orders to Tauiskoi Ostrog that the Cossack, Tryphon Krupis-chew, should go to Bolscheretzkoi Ostrog, in a vessel adapted for the sea, from thence double the southern headland of Kamtschatka, make the harbour of Nischnei Kamtschatzkoi Ostrog [lower Kamchatka fort], and proceed farther with the same vessel to the river Anadir, and invite the inhabitants of the large country opposite to it, to pay tribute to Russia. If Gwosdew, the navigator, chose to go in this expedition, he should take him on board the vessel, and shew him respect. There are no intelligences of what were the consequences of these orders; we only know that, in the year 1730, Gwosdew, the navigator, was actually between 65 and 66 degrees of north latitude, on a strange coast situate [*sic*] opposite, at a small distance from the country of the Tschuktschi, and that he found people there, but could not speak with them, for want of an interpreter.[7]

Golder concluded that Gvozdev thought he had discovered a large island—and not the continent of America—because he mentioned four islands, which Golder interpreted as the two Diomedes, the mainland of Alaska, and King Island, or "the fourth island" of Gvozdev's report. I am convinced, however, that Gvozdev knew he had discovered a continent, because the Gvozdev-Spanberg map, which Golder apparently did not see, clearly shows a mainland *and* four islands, the fourth island being Fairway Rock.[8] The four islands drawn on the Gvozdev-Spanberg map were copied

6. Bancroft 1886, p. 41*n*; Efimov 1949, between pp. 70–71. In the 1880s Bancroft said that only copies of the original map were in existence, but he did not publish any. Efimov apparently was the first to discover and publish this map. Some of the copies are listed in footnote 8.

7. Müller 1761, p. 11. In the original English translation, all proper names and place names are in italics, but for readability I have eliminated the italics.

. Müller's error in dating apparently resulted from careless writing. Hens, Fedorov, and Gvozdev had taken the ship to the Anadyr River and back to Kamchatka, but not to the coast of Alaska in 1730. They returned to the lower Kamchatka for the winter of 1731–32, and then sailed to Alaska after further orders from Pavlutskii (Golder 1914, p. 158).

8. "Karta Fedorova-Gvozdeva-Shpanberga," in Efimov 1949, between pp. 70–71. Other maps with four islands in the Strait area based on this information are in Efimov 1948, between pp. 168–69 and pp. 174–75; Efimov 1949, between pp. 68–69; Efimov 1950, pp. 183, 191, and between pp. 192–93; Efimov, ed. 1964, maps 69, 70, 110; and Belov 1956, between pp. 260–61.

on other maps at that time, and later explorers often called Fairway Rock the "third Diomede Island."[9]

Apparently Bering knew of this first discovery and the existence of Alaska when he sailed for America in 1741 because Georg Wilhelm Steller, the expedition's naturalist, said that Bering "had originally planned to leave Kamchatka early in May and *after discovering America* to spend the winter there and return to Asia the following year" (my emphasis).[10]

Neither Gvozdev's nor Fedorov's name has been commemorated on a map of Alaska in the English language, despite the fact they were the first discoverers of Alaska as well as of Little Diomede Island and King Island. They were also the first Europeans to see a mainland Alaskan village and to land on Big Diomede Island.

THE "KHEUVEREN" LEGEND

Shortly after the discovery of southern Alaska in 1741, Russian fur traders began to sail to the Aleutian Islands and the Gulf of Alaska, where sea otters and fur seals abounded. The concentrated attention paid to fur hunting in this part of Alaska effectively postponed European intrusion into the unexplored and unknown Arctic. Printed and manuscript accounts about Russian America between 1741 and 1778 were almost exclusively devoted to the Aleutian Islands. Peter Simon Pallas, a German historian who led a scientific expedition for the Saint Petersburg Academy of Sciences to Siberia between 1768 and 1774, has preserved a small amount of information about northern Alaska obtained during those years.[11] Pallas' writings and Müller's before him contain almost all that was known about northwest Alaska until the end of the eighteenth century.

Pallas recorded two especially valuable accounts about northern Alaska. He summarized Nikolai Daurkin's report and map of the Chukchi Peninsula

Another map of slightly different shape with four islands was prepared in 1742 from the expedition's material by Jacob Lindenau (Belov 1956, p. 262).

Nikolai Daurkin's original map of 1765 (see Chap. 4) also has four islands with a dotted line connecting them to both continents. The line goes to the American continent from both Fairway Rock and King Island (Grekov 1960, p. 209; Efimov, ed. 1964, map 128). Other Daurkin maps with four islands are found in Efimov 1950, p. 151, and Efimov, ed. 1964, maps 129, 130, 131. Ivan Kobelev's map, printed in German in 1783 and in Russian in 1784 (see Chap. 4), also has four islands, but in more realistic locations (Masterson and Brower 1948, opposite p. 92; Chernenko 1957, p. 125; Efimov, ed. 1964, map 174). Kobelev's map in German was originally published in Pallas 1783 as plate 1, and will be discussed in detail later on.

9. For example, Ivan Kobelev in 1779, Martin Sauer in 1802, and Frederick Beechey in 1831 called Fairway Rock the "third Diomede island." Kobelev called it Usken on his map. Sauer said, "Okivaki [but Okevachi on his map] is the third and smallest [island], 10 miles distant, south by east"; and Beechey said that Eskimos camping on Choris Peninsula in Kotzebue Sound called the Diomede islands, "Noo-nar-boak, Ig-narlook, and Oo-ghe-eyak [Fairway Rock]," and King Island, "Oo-ghe-aboak."

10. Golder 1914, p. 181.

11. Masterson and Brower 1948, p. 11; *Bering's Successors, 1745–1780*, is an English translation of Pallas' writings. The annotations and footnotes contain valuable explanatory and bibliographical information.

and opposite land (Alaska) made in 1765, and Ivan Kobelev's report of 1779, which included the first census of the Diomede Islands and a remarkable map of Seward Peninsula villages.[12] Daurkin, a Chukchi man who became a Cossack, and Kobelev, a Cossack *sotnik* ("leader of a hundred men"), were primarily responsible for the transformation of the Eskimo village, Kauwerak, on the Kuzitrin River into a Russian fort rumored to be inhabited by descendants of a Dezhnev boat crew lost in 1648. (Kauwerak is pronounced *kaue'rak*, and sometimes *kavi'rak* in other dialects. As reported in early Russian sources, *kheuveren*—probably pronounced *kave'ran*—had the Chukchi ending, *-en*.) A number of explorers actively searched for this mythical Russian settlement well into the nineteenth century without success, but Soviet historians and geographers still believe that it existed somewhere. One writer has unequivocally stated that the first Russian settlements in Alaska—"Kheuveren" among them—date from the middle of the seventeenth century, or eighty years before Gvozdev discovered Seward Peninsula and one hundred years before Bering discovered southern Alaska.[13]

Despite repeated unsuccessful attempts to locate this fort, the legend refuses to die. The first expedition to inquire into the matter of a Russian fort was that of Joseph Billings, under Russian auspices, in June and July 1791 near Cape Rodney. Martin Sauer, the expedition's secretary, wrote that there was no European fort to his knowledge (only a settlement "built largely of driftwood," according to Lieutenant Gavriil Sarychev) and "not withstanding all my endeavours, I could not find any body that knew aught of this matter, or had ever heard of any such place existing."[14]

The second expedition to seek the Russian fort left Kodiak Island in 1818 under the leadership of Petr Korsakovskii, who was sent by the Russian-American Company to explore both the Nushagak River and the Kheuveren, ·despite Sauer's and Sarychev's maps clearly showing the Kheuveren flowing into the Bering Strait more than five hundred miles away from the Nushagak. Korsakovskii was unable to get to the Kheuveren River.

The third expedition was that of Vasiliev and Shishmarev in 1821. Lieutenant Aleksandr Avinov of the expedition asked about the existence of Russian villages when they were in the vicinity of Cape Newenham and Goodnews Bay. Vasilii Berkh, the historian, said that he "collected reliable information from local inhabitants that northward along the whole American shore, so far as is known to them, lived one nation. *The report by those who were in these places with the land expedition of 1818 and 1819* [Korsakovskii] under-

---

12. Daurkin's report in Pallas 1781, pp. 245–48, is quoted and discussed in Masterson and Brower 1948, pp. 27*n* and 64–67. Kobelev's report, as summarized by Pallas in 1783 (4:105–11), is translated in Masterson and Brower, pp. 93–96. The report is slightly different in Efimov 1948, pp. 228–33, and Efimov 1950, pp. 264–68. Daurkin's map is discussed by Fedorova (1964, pp. 97–105), and information about Kobelev's report and map is given in Chernenko 1957, pp. 121–26.

13. Efimov, as quoted by the Russian editors of Zagoskin 1967, p. 27.

14. Sarychev 1952, p. 244; Sauer 1802, p. 258.

taken by the American Company in Kadiak that some European people lived on the mainland coast north of the Kuskokvin [*sic*] River proved to be incorrect."[15]

Finally, in 1861, Petr Tikhmenev, reviewing the activities of the Russian-American Company and Korsakovskii's inquiries, said that information "received about the white men from the natives was so conflicting that it was decided to repeat the search. Investigation made in the following years proved that the supposition that there are descendants of the cossacks in America is groundless."[16]

Yet, in 1944 the legend reappeared more vigorously than ever as "a lost colony of Novgorod" in a reputable journal. The colony this time was supposedly situated on the Kenai Peninsula, four hundred miles south of Seward Peninsula, because a site of thirty-one "well-preserved European houses" was reportedly found during a "United States government survey" in 1937. Such a European village is unknown today, but on the basis of an unconfirmed archeological site and on a letter from a Russian priest, Father Herman, in 1794, the author decided that the houses were "nothing else than those of the long lost colony founded by the subjects of Ivan the Terrible [i.e., Dezhnev's men]." This is pure fiction.

In 1948, Aleksei V. Efimov, a Soviet historical geographer, concluded from the unsupported evidence contained in this article that "it can be considered as proven that a Russian settlement appeared in Alaska about 300 years ago in the seventeenth century," and that "Alaska had not only one but several, and possibly numerous, Russian settlements" similar to this, dating back even before the first discovery of Alaska in 1732.[17]

In 1967 Richard A. Pierce, while participating in an Alaskan history conference, urged that this "item of Alaskan history [be] laid to rest."[18] I hope that the discussion presented here and in later pages will clarify the circumstances that contributed to the growth of this mythical fort and will bury the folk tale of a seventeenth-century Russian settlement in Alaska for the last time.

THE CONTRIBUTIONS OF NIKOLAI DAURKIN

The reports of Daurkin and Kobelev contain information about the Bering Strait area found nowhere else prior to Captain Cook's voyage, and are especially valuable when analyzed with data from field research. Daurkin and Kobelev were well acquainted by the time of their employment in 1785 as interpreters and guides in Siberia for the Billings expedition and in true

---

15. Berkh 1823b, pp. 15, 20–24. Berkh spells Korsakovskii's name "Korsanovskii."
16. Tikhmenev 1939–40, pt. 1, p. 302.
17. Farrelly 1944, p. 34; Efimov 1948, p. 152. To complicate matters, Efimov also concluded that the Kheuveren was the Yukon River (see fn. 31). On 9 August 1970 Father Herman was canonized, the first Alaskan Russian Orthodox monk to be so honored. Saint Herman lived in Alaska between 1794 and 1837 (Black 1970, pp. 14–15, 55).
18. Pierce 1968, p. 71.

Siberian fashion did not get along with each other.[19] Kobelev was born in Anadyrsk in 1739 and held a high rank as a *sotnik*, serving as the first official Cossack interpreter of the Chukchi language. Vladimir Bogoras said that he lived to be over one hundred years old, and was mentioned as late as 1849.[20] Daurkin was older than Kobelev and was probably in his late fifties during the Billings expedition. He had been captured when a boy by Major Pavlutskii during the Chukchi campaigns of the 1730s, was reared by Pavlutskii's wife and trained as a Cossack.

In 1761, Daurkin had been sent back to Chukchi territory by the government ostensibly to visit his relatives but secretly to investigate fur trading possibilities and to persuade his former countrymen to submit to Russian sovereignty and to pay tribute. His "official report" of this trip was couched, for the most part, in the typical general phraseologies of the period and at first glance seems to be merely a stylistic parroting of scholarly papers. However, it actually is a plagiarism of five consecutive pages of Gerhard Müller's volume three of *Sammlung Russischer Geschichte*, which included discussions of Popov's narrative account of 1711, Ivan Lvov's map of 1710, and an "anonymous Chukchi communication." Why Daurkin should have resorted to even the slightest plagiarism—which has gone undetected all these years—is not clear, because he possessed new and provocative information about both Saint Lawrence Island and Alaska. He added new data about Saint Lawrence Island to his official report, but put his information about Alaska only in his diary and in notations on his map. Perhaps friends in Yakutsk, aware of the rewards for well-turned official phrases, aided Daurkin in following Müller's successful format. Müller had voiced his distrust of strange-sounding (but, as we now know, ethnologically valid) data, and Daurkin's conformity to generalized but believable information—lifted from the pages of the master himself—suggests that Daurkin probably thought that his new material would not be taken seriously. Perhaps he was right, because Colonel Friedrich Plenisner, his commanding officer, elevated him to the Siberian nobility for his efforts.

Even Pallas viewed Daurkin's map and notations with considerable skepticism, saying, "I will not guarantee its trustworthiness in all respects," and relegated discussion of it to a footnote.[21] Yet Daurkin's map was only the second one to show a degree of accuracy for the Alaskan coast north of the Aleutian Islands. Daurkin drew a more extensive coastline than that of the Gvozdev-Spanberg map of 1743 and recorded three northwest Alaska place names for the first time: "Tikegan," or *tikera* (Point Hope); "Okibian," or *ukivuk* (King Island); and "Kheuveren" (Kauwerak). He also added another

19. The men of Bering's expeditions quarreled; Fedorov and Gvozdev quarreled; and the governor of Irkutsk wrote to Captain Krenitsin in 1765, "It seems to me that there is something in the air of Okhotsk that causes all officers stationed there to quarrel" (Bancroft 1886, p. 161*n*).

20. Fedorova 1971a, p. 157; Bogoras 1907, p. 699. John D. Cochrane, the British naval officer who hitchhiked across Siberia in the 1820s, said that Kobelev's son was an interpreter at the Anyui market in 1821 (Cochrane 1824, p. 268).

21. Masterson and Brower 1948, pp. 27*n*, 67; Pallas 1781, pp. 248, 284*n*.

version of Wales, "Kyng-Myn."[22] Thus, at least four villages of northwest Alaska were known to the people of Siberia before Captain Cook sailed along the coast of Bering Strait.

In discussing another Daurkin map dated 1765, Pallas said that Daurkin reported the country to be inhabited by "people whom the Chukchis call Khrakhai, who speak the same language, possess reindeer, and have much copper, as well as arrowheads, knives, kettles, etc., of that metal. He says that much timber of various kinds grows opposite the Chukchi Peninsula, and that the fortified settlement of a ruler, Inulam [Inalun, in the original German], is situated on the River Chevuren."[23] The map as drawn by Daurkin included the Chukchi Peninsula and the Siberian coast from Cape Dezhnev to the mouth of the Kolyma River, as well as a long stretch of the northwest Alaska coastline, including Seward Peninsula and four islands, three of them placed in the strait and "Okibian," or King Island, situated opposite the mouth of a wide "Kheuveren River."[24]

The map apparently created more excitement among geographers and historians than Pallas' account suggests, because shortly thereafter numerous copies were made, including one by Colonel Plenisner. One of the principal features of Daurkin's original map is a drawing of a typical Eskimo dwelling on the banks of the Kheuveren River. The building is surrounded by what appears to be a fence made of oval objects. Inside the "fence" are men dressed in Eskimo clothing. The notations on the map read: "The fort near the Kheuveren River has been constructed; the structure is a wooden one; and they have an elder [or chief] called by the name Inakh Lun [Inalun] who is not tall, and is not only fat but also is strong; who [i.e., the people] came from their far lands not many years ago; according to my inquiry is said that he arrived in 1761 and built the fort."[25]

Subsequent copies of the map slowly transformed this Eskimo "fort" into a Russian military garrison, the building and its "defenders" becoming so Russified that there is no doubt that a Russian post is intended. Eskimo clothing was replaced by caftans, pants, boots, and tricornered hats; and the original crudely drawn building, which had been filled in with cross-hatchings (an artistic device often used on ivory engravings by nineteenth-century

22. Daurkin's names, which all end in "n," are from Masterson and Brower 1948, p. 27*n*, and Fedorova 1964, p. 97. The *n* ending was a common Chukchi one for comparable Eskimo names that ended in *ak* or *uk*. Daurkin, who spoke the Chukchi language, apparently preferred the Chukchi version. In Siberia, the Chukchi villages of Uwelen and Nuukan are also known today by their Eskimo names, Ulak and Niwogak (Rudenko 1961, pp. 23, 41).

In speaking of the "first" and "second" maps of northern Alaska, I am referring to those with coastlines that conform somewhat to reality. There were many earlier maps made by armchair geographers, but these were imaginary representations of land *thought* to lie east of Siberia.

23. Masterson and Brower 1948, p. 27*n*; Pallas 1781, p. 245*n*.

24. Copies of Daurkin's map are illustrated by Efimov in the *Atlas* (1964), maps 128, 129, 130, 131; and in Grekov 1960, p. 209. Fedorova, who discusses the map in detail, illustrates a small portion in the vicinity of Port Clarence and the copies made by Sergeant Andeev and Colonel Plenisner (Fedorova 1964, pp. 98–101).

25. Fedorova 1964, p. 98*n*.

Eskimos), became a trim, squared-up edifice of solid color.[26] It cannot very well be resolved at this late date which was responsible for the creation of a mythical Russian settlement in Alaska—the metamorphosis of this fort through the medium of illustrations or Müller's publication about the foundering boats of the Dezhnev expedition. In any event, the two probably went hand in hand in the transformation.

Daurkin's original building, on the right bank of a deep river said to be forested with birch, pine, cedar, and silver fir trees, was drawn in a distinctive Siberian style of the eighteenth century with its peculiar lack of perspective.[27] The fence around the structure, which probably represented a ceremonial house, appears to lie on the ground, and devices resembling a pole and two ladders rise above the fence to support, at their apex, a curved "platform" on which stand four men wearing parkas and unusual headdresses, each man holding a spear. This looks like a watch tower, and is considered to be such by Svetlana Fedorova, a Soviet ethnologist. Outside the fence are three men in similar garb also holding spears.

This drawing is the first known illustration of war or raid (myth or reality) in the Bering Strait area, and specifically in the Port Clarence–Kuzitrin River (that is, the "Kheuveren River") area, where every old folk tale expert knows "the last Siberian invasion," a story proudly related as a resounding victory for the Alaskans. The many versions of this story seem to be related to a single event that stood out either because of its magnitude compared to other "invasions," or because it was the only time that Siberians fought on the Alaskan coast; but now is the time to look at this specific folk tale relative to Daurkin's drawing of a fort.

Several elements of the drawing correspond to those in the various versions of the "last Siberian invasion." For example, all versions place the "battle" near Kauwerak (not far from Marys Igloo), which was a village of seven or eight houses, a large ceremonial house, and about fifty persons in the 1850s. The village was located on a slight rise on the left bank of the treeless lower Kuzitrin River, and received its Eskimo name, Kauwerak ("gravel bar"), from the only gravel bar in this generally muddy part of the river.

The drawing of the "fortress" appears to illustrate defensive measures that I have recorded in two versions of the folk tale, two hundred years after Daurkin drew his map. Both John E. Kakaruk and William Oquilluk, of Kauwerak parentage, said that skihs from umiaks were used to barricade the rear of the village against attacks by Siberians. Young men with spears went outside the barricade, and the old men and women stayed within. The "fence posts" in Daurkin's drawing, therefore, probably represent umiak skins.

Other portions of the drawing also correspond to supposed "fortifications" around the village mentioned in the folk tales. Because of the flat perspective, the towerlike structure may represent pathways, ditches, or bulwarks on the

---

26. Fedorova discusses and illustrates changes in the drawings on pp. 97–101.
27. For example, see drawings of Okhotsk and Petropavlovsk in Golder 1914, pp. 167, 179.

ground beyond the fence rather than in the air above it. The four men on the curved surface might be an advance guard of defenders at the rear of the village, which was most vulnerable to attack, being located across the tundra from a downstream bend of the river where invaders could leave their boats and sneak into the back of the village. Uneven terrain behind the old house mounds might have been old ditches dug as defenses, although Henry B. Collins, the archeologist who made a reconnaissance examination of the old site long after it was abandoned, thinks they are probably natural phenomena resulting from ground ice.[28]

A Kauwerak folk tale attempts to explain these topographical irregularities as a consequence of village construction. According to Kauwerak tradition, the settlement was founded by a legendary man named Tudlik (or Tuulik, but not Inakh Lun of Daurkin's tale) who

invited people [after a time of famine] from the upper end of Tuksuk clean up to Nokthapaga [Noxapaga] to make a village, and so they chose the place where that little sandy bar, that's all the sandy bar between the upper end of the river and below. . . . That place was all flat, there was no hill, no knoll, no place close to river, but he told them to make village, and they dig in the back, this ground from here, there, and not close by, and a little further in order to build up the houses. The front houses is facing to the river, and the back of the houses faced to the west. So, in the middle of this town, on the riverside, they built a great big dance hall they call *kazgi*. . . . They bring all the driftwood from the coast in order to build the houses. So, that means he takes quite a while to prepare to make the village there which is called Kauwerak.[29]

The Siberian wars ended during the time of the great Tudlik, founder of Kauwerak, at which time only "two men of the whole army of Siberia" were left. They were sent back to Siberia to carry the message that they had better not attack Kauwerak again, or else all would be killed.

In recent years, the identification of the Kheuveren River as the Kuzitrin has been arrived at independently by M. B. Chernenko, a Soviet historian, and myself; but Chernenko, lacking field data, did not associate Kheuveren with the Eskimo village, Kauwerak.[30] Fedorova took exception to Chernenko's identification of the river as the Kuzitrin and concluded that it was the Koyuk River. She based her assertion partly on Pallas' placement of this river flowing into Norton Sound (she did not realize Pallas was in error), and partly on the supposition that the Kheuveren River was unforested (the "fort" was supposedly on a forested stream). The upper courses of the Kuzitrin and the nearby Pilgrim River, however, sustain large stands of willows, alders, and cottonwoods, individual trees often growing larger than spruce on the Koyuk.[31]

28. Personal communication, 16 December 1963.
29. Story as related by William Oquilluk, summer 1964.
30. Chernenko 1957. When I wrote "Kauwerak, Lost Village of Alaska" (1964a), I was unaware of Chernenko's paper.
31. Chernenko attributes Efimov's error in identifying the Kheuveren as the Yukon to the lack of archival data. My conclusions were based on both field data and printed sources. Sauer

IVAN KOBELEV TRANSFORMS A VILLAGE

Daurkin's "Kheuveren" was an Eskimo village, but according to Ivan Kobelev, the same village on the "Chevren River" was a Russian fort called "Kyngovei." Kobelev apparently was the first to suggest that the village had been established by Dezhnev's men 130 years before. According to Sauer's report on the Billings expedition of 1791, "Kobeleff, speaking of a river in the vicinity of this place, relates, that on its border is a small town containing a church and ostrog, built and inhabited by Russians. *He supposes them* to be the remains of the shipwrecked companions of Deshneff, a Russian adventurer who left the river Lena with seven vessels in 1648" (my emphasis).[32] Kobelev never visited the village, and his information about it apparently stemmed from his misinterpretation of sign language made by Kauwerak people visiting on King Island in 1791 (see Chapter 4). It should be mentioned here that no Eskimos living between Saint Michael and Kotzebue Sound and northward had folk tales about white men coming from Siberia.

Earlier, in 1779, Kobelev, like Daurkin in 1765, had been sent by the government "to scout among the Chukchi nation" and to visit the Diomede Islands.[33] He left Penzhinsk Bay for the Anadyr River on 22 March 1779, and reached the Diomedes on 27 July. He spent four days on "Imaglin" (Big Diomede Island), where he counted a total of 203 men and 195 women, including children, in two villages. Despite his comparatively long visit, he had little to say about the island. It had no timber and no animals except "bluish-tan" Arctic foxes. The "food of the inhabitants [consisted] of whales, sea dogs [seals], and walruses." The people spoke the same language as the "wandering Chukchi," which, according to Pallas' German account, would refer to the people known as the Reindeer Chukchi, who moved from place to

---

and Sarychev both mentioned that the Kheuveren was in the vicinity of the Seward Peninsula (Sarychev 1952, p. 244; Sauer 1802, p. 258).

Chernenko discussed the erroneous identification of the Kheuveren as the Yukon in his 1957 publication. It is also discussed in the footnotes to the life of Zagoskin (Zagoskin 1967, p. 30*n*).

Many printed sources provide information that the Yukon and nearby rivers flow through forests, but information about the upper Kuzitrin is hard to get, except by visiting the river. Sauer, however, had mentioned that the "Ka-ooveren" was "well-wooded" near its source (1802, p. 258). Apparently the Kuzitrin, which means "the new river," was once called Kauwerak or Kheuveren, and a version of the name still remains as the "Kaviruk River," in use on maps less than three miles from the old village site. Up to 1900, maps used several variations of the word Kauwerak for the Kuzitrin: Cov-vee arak (Hydrographic map 68, 1890–92); Kaviavaxak (Dall map, 1869); and Kaviavazak and Covearak rivers (Coast and Geodetic Survey map, April 1898), for example.

32. Sauer 1802, p. 258.

33. Daurkin was not instructed specifically to go to the Diomedes; in 1763, however, a Senate instruction from F. G. Soimonov had directed N. Shalaurov to inspect the islands, but the voyage did not take place (Chernenko 1957, p. 122).

All quoted and paraphrased material about Kobelev is from Pallas' summary in his *Neue nordische Beyträge* (1783), 4:106–11, but especially from the English translation by Masterson and Brower (1948), pp. 93–96. The Russian account is in *Sobranie sochinenii . . .* (1790), 5:369–76 (the Library of Congress has a copy). Efimov 1950, pp. 264–68, is essentially the same, and Chernenko 1957 quotes portions of Kobelev's 1779 journal.

place. But the term *peshim Chukcham* in the Russian account published by Chernenko means something altogether different, that is, it refers to the Sedentary Chukchi, who lived like Eskimos. Kobelev obviously meant Eskimo in this context because Eskimos were called Chukchi at that time in Siberian history. (The word Eskimo did not come into the literature of the Bering Strait area until Frederick W. Beechey, the English explorer, used it consistently in 1831.)

On 31 July Kobelev went to the island Igelyin (Little Diomede), where he counted eighty-five men and seventy-nine women, including children. These islanders cooked their food over "sea-dog oil, which they pour from containers made of whalebone." Like the Saint Lawrence Bay Chukchi, they remembered Cook's ships, which had sailed past the islands three times, anchoring for four days "on the south side [of Big Diomede] near the village of Uneglekhlen where the commander stayed ashore and was presented with martens"; however, neither Cook nor Captain King, who took command after Cook's death, mentioned anchoring near the islands or receiving gifts.[34]

According to Pallas, Kobelev heard here a story that seemed to verify rumors of a Russian fort on the opposite shore, lending credence to an "old tradition" in Anadyrsk that the fort's inhabitants were descendants of Cossacks who had "sailed from the mouth of the Lena along the coasts of the Icy Sea round the Chukchi Peninsula [and were] lost on the return voyage to the Kovyma [Kolyma]." (The "old tradition," we recall, was well known only after 1736 when Müller had discovered Dezhnev's 1655 report in the archives.) Pallas said that Kobelev heard the story from the

chief of the inhabitants of this island, Kaiguny, son of Momakhun, [who] called himself a native of America and declared that he had first come to the island in his later years. According to his story there is supposed to be on the American mainland a village called Kyngovei on a creek called Chevren [apparently a composite of Kingigan at Cape Prince of Wales and Kauwerak, two villages ninety miles apart[35]], that is inhabited by Russians. It is said that they still retain their Russian speech, pray from books, write, worship before holy images, and are distinguished by their large and heavy beards from the other Americans, who grow only scattered hair on their faces and assiduously pull it out. Kobelev asked the islanders to take him across to the

34. Masterson and Brower 1948, p. 95; Pallas 1783, p. 111. In August 1778 Captain Cook sailed north past the Diomedes, which "could afford us little shelter. Instead of anchoring, therefore, we continued to stretch to the westward"—that is, toward the Siberian coast. He then sailed along the coast of Alaska as far north as Icy Cape; on his return south he discovered Sledge Island. After Cook's death in the Hawaiian Islands, Captain King in 1779 (the same year as Kobelev's visit) sailed north and back south through the strait. He did not anchor near the Diomedes (Cook and King 1784, vol. 2, p. 445; vol. 3). Perhaps Pallas confused Cook's stay of "four days" with Kobelev's four-day visit on Big Diomede.

35. Kobelev's confusion about two villages ninety miles apart was not surprising when nothing was known about the geography of northern Alaska. These two villages were on exceedingly friendly terms and were alternate hosts for the messenger feast, an intervillage trading festival that specialized in the exchange of sea and land products.

The Russian version of Kobelev's account spells the village Kymgovei and the river, Khevrene.

mainland to this supposed Russian colony; but they would not consent to do so, because the tribute-paying Chukchis who had conducted the sotnik to the islands had strictly charged the islanders not to take their Russian guest across to the land of America, lest he be exposed to danger for which they would later be held accountable. The chief of the island, however, promised to deliver a letter in Russian that Kobelev gave him to the Russians alleged to live in America. . . .

Kobelev takes this occasion to report further that in the Chukchi village of Kangun Tsvunmin he knew a Chukchi, Ekhilka, who formerly, for trade and war, had gone as often as five times to the American mainland and had become very friendly with an inhabitant of the island of Ukipan [King Island]. This friend was said to have come to the aforesaid Ekhilka on Imaglin Island [Big Diomede], bringing him a board 3 spans long and 5 verchoks wide, which was carved on one side with red characters and on the other with black. The islander had reported that this board had been given to him by bearded people, to be delivered to the Russians who at that time still had a garrison in Anadyrsk. The name of the river and dwelling-place of these bearded people was given by him exactly the same as by the afore-mentioned Kangunei. The Chukchi was told that the writing was directed to the same Russians who traded iron [Chernenko's version reads: "The Russians needed iron and asked to deliver their letter to the Anadyr fortress"[36]], which is exchanged chiefly with the bearded people. He was told also how these people pray together in a large yurt, make the sign of the cross, and set up little boards out of doors with written characters, before which they hold common prayer. . . .

All this might very well be Chukchi fables, for Kobelev had let himself be told, and entered in his journal, that in America, no great distance away, there were people with two faces, one in the back of the head and both provided with speaking mouths, though only one was adapted to taking nourishment. He was told that these people lived in a village called Tapshan [in the Russian account it is written "Tapkhan," clearly the equivalent of Tapkak, the Eskimo name for the coast between Wales and Cape Espenberg]. He also heard of cannibals, who were supposed to live, however, in a hot, southern region of the American mainland.

Reality was often not far removed from fiction at any time in Eskimo mythology, and the line that separated the two was often completely erased by the time it had crossed a few tribal boundaries, not to mention an ocean. Therefore, the not uncommon folk theme of two-headed creatures had entered Kobelev's notebook as a biological fact. Yet, a large amount of information passed from one tribe to another along all of the western Alaskan coast; and if the Eskimos of the North had learned about a "hot, southern region of the American mainland [southern Alaska]," it is possible that the rumors of a northern Russian settlement were based indirectly on activities of Russian fur hunters who had been in the Aleutian Islands and southern Alaska for over thirty years. By 1779, thousands of fur hunters had spent summer after summer pursuing fur seals and sea otters in their ships, and winter after winter waiting in their land quarters for a new season to begin. As early as 1743, ships were built especially for Alaskan voyages at the ports of Kamchatka and Okhotsk, and the sixty or so voyages undertaken before 1779 were well known to Siberian military officers, especially Colonel Plenisner,

36. Chernenko 1957, p. 124.

Daurkin's superior officer, who, as commander of the Kamchatka garrison from 1761 to 1766 and at Okhotsk thereafter, apparently was aware of all activities directed toward America.[37]

The concentrated activity in both Siberia and southern Alaska was bound to reap facts that could be transformed into fiction. Before 1750, Emilian Basov, on his second voyage, visited Copper Island, or Mednyi Ostrov, now one of Russia's possessions at the very end of the Aleutian chain, where he found copper.[38] This island doubtless was the source in Daurkin's report of "much copper, as well as arrowheads, knives, kettles, etc., of that metal," because copper deposits were unknown in northern Alaska at that time. In 1755 Petr Yakovlev was sent to Copper Island to examine the deposits, which became widely known thereafter; and in 1757 Russians were mining enough copper to permit Andrei Tolstykh, a famous navigator, to give Tunulgasan, the chief of Attu, "a copper kettle and a full suit of clothes of Russian pattern."[39]

Copper Island was apparently well known in maritime circles. In 1787 or 1788, a ship captained by William Peters, an English trader from the Orient, with a crew of seventy English, Indian, Arabian, and Chinese sailors, was wrecked on nearby Bering Island, where Peters had wanted to load up copper, having been "misled by the exaggerated accounts of the quantities of copper found upon those islands."[40] The island may also have been the source for the "holy images" or "boards out of doors" mentioned in Kobelev's report for "at Vsevidov's Harbor are standing crosses, indicating by their inscriptions that . . . a Kamchadal of Bakhov's [Basov's?] crew was killed by an avalanche of snow, April 7, 1750."[41] Yet, certain Eskimo practices of using carved objects on burials and in outdoor ceremonies could also have been interpreted as religious images. For example, at Kauwerak (Kheuveren) itself, divination boards with masklike carvings were consulted out of doors by the medicine man every morning during the winter caribou hunting season.[42]

By the 1790s, Europeans had not yet been on the Alaskan mainland north of the Aleutians, but the Aleuts on Unalaska had already "suffered greatly by

37. Gibson 1968–69, p. 210. Berkh 1938, pp. 1–80; Tompkins 1955, pp. 11–26; Bancroft 1886, p. 153. Berkh lists the voyages at the end of the Russian edition of his history of the discovery of the Aleutian Islands (1823a), but they were omitted in the English translation.

38. Bancroft 1886, p. 101; Berkh 1938, p. 6.

39. Bancroft 1886, p. 118. Georg Wilhelm Steller, the naturalist of Bering's expedition of 1741, said that the people of America might have "possessed cutting tools of copper" when he observed a whetstone streaked with copper (Golder 1925, p. 53).

40. Sauer 1802, p. 281.

41. Masterson and Brower 1948, p. 63. Bancroft also said: "A cross which was preserved on the island for many years, bore an inscription to the effect that Yefim' Kuznetzof, a new convert (probably a Kamchatka native), was added to Bassof's [*sic*] command on the 7th of April 1750. It is probable that the baptism of this convert took place on the island, and that the name of the man was added to Bassof's list only when he became a Christian" (1886, p. 101*n*). Bancroft apparently took this information from "Sibirsky Viestnik," 1822, nos. 2 to 6.

42. Field notes, 1961.

their disputes with the Russians, and by a famine in the year 1762; but most of all from a change in their way of life. No longer contented with their original simplicity, they long for Russian luxuries. . . ."[43] By 1770, "the pioneering age in the history of the Russian expansion across the Aleutian Chain was ended";[44] so by 1779, when Kobelev visited the Diomede Islands, there had been ample opportunity during more than a quarter of a century for the fact and reality of Russians in America to transform a real Eskimo village into a fictitious Russian fort in the face of the vast ignorance of the geography of a huge and distant North.

Tikhmenev's conclusions supposedly buried this myth forever, but in the event that it should show further signs of regeneration, two questions should be kept in mind: by what genetic magic had the Cossacks been able to maintain a purely Russian physical identity after seven generations of Eskimo mothers dating from 1648? And through what clairvoyance did these great-great-great-great grandchildren of 1779 (all Eskimos by then) know about a Siberian trading post at Anadyrsk, which had not yet been built at the time of the alleged shipwreck 130 years before?

The period from 1648 to 1779 was a pre-European, prehistoric one for the Alaskan side of the Bering Strait; but for the Siberian side, European settlements were established wherever possible. Undoubtedly much more information was obtained about Alaskan Eskimos than that preserved in the printed sources, but what we do have corroborates native traditional stories that the area of the Bering Strait was indeed "one world," despite the fact that fifty-five miles of water separated the continents. The same information, however, reveals that the communication was far from unrestricted; people of the two sides did not live on a friendly basis, raids were expected, and prisoners were taken.

Daurkin's and Kobelev's detailed information obtained in the 1760s and 1770s reflects not only greater industry on the part of Cossacks, but better relationships between Russians and Siberians and between native peoples on both sides of the strait. In 1732 Gvozdev was not permitted by the Eskimos to land on Little Diomede; but in 1779 Kobelev not only landed but obtained the information discussed above, and was able to draw his remarkable map, which will be discussed in the following chapter in conjunction with Cook's voyage. The details of this map could only have come from persons acquainted at first hand with the Seward Peninsula area, since the sixty-nine settlements (sixty-one with names) were recorded in their proper sequence and with a close approximation of their actual names. Since only four Alaskan place names (for Wales, Point Hope, Kauwerak, and King Island) had been obtained in Siberia during the previous century of Cossack inquiry, it seems fairly certain that the inhabitants of Little Diomede were allied at that time with the American side of the strait rather than with the Siberian. It

43. From the diary of Krenitsin and Levashev in Masterson and Brower 1948, p. 58.
44. Hulley 1953, p. 64.

suggests that the Siberians themselves were less apt to make trips to Alaska for trade than to utilize the Little Diomede people as middlemen. Yet this same evidence, and the Diomeders' reluctance to take Kobelev to the Alaska mainland, further suggests that an intercontinental trade of the magnitude observed during the nineteenth century was not yet underway.

Kobelev's mission was the last of the individual efforts by Siberian Russians to seek information about the "big land." With Captain Cook's journey a year before, the north had entered an era when knowledge of the land and of the people at the Bering Strait was to be obtained, for the most part, by expeditions planned in the great capitals of the world.

CHAPTER 4

Explorations of the Late Eighteenth Century: James Cook, Ivan Kobelev, and Joseph Billings

Cook's Observations

WITH the voyage of Captain James Cook, we enter the second period of Bering Strait history. Cook and his men were the first Europeans to walk on the mainland of Alaska north of the Aleutian Islands. Although, like other explorers of this period, they spent comparatively little time in the Bering Strait area, the sum of their occasional observations recorded alterations in Eskimo life between 1778 and the 1850s, when voyages to the strait became commonplace. Changes accruing from the Russian fur trade in Siberia were especially noticeable during the latter part of the eighteenth century, when the northern Alaskan Eskimos added a considerable number of foreign objects to their material culture and became traders themselves.

The only available firsthand ethnographic information for the Alaskan side of the strait between 1778 and 1833 is recorded in these expedition accounts. Despite their meagerness in comparison to the totality of culture observed at any point of time, the observations are valuable for our purposes because archeological data are scarce for the early historical period of northern Alaska and "facts" about Eskimo history as given by informants are invariably inaccurate and mythical in character.

At the risk of promoting antiquarianism (from a historian's viewpoint), I am including verbatim and paraphrased excerpts from these early sources for two reasons: (1) to form a chronological "ethnographic reader" from reports that are often hard to find; and (2) to present the material as raw data for interpretation within a total context of culture change. The ethnographic summaries appear in Chapters 4 through 7, with interpretations and concluding remarks in Chapter 8.

The explorers' observations have to be weighed carefully. Many of their statements about religion, kinship, and social and political organization were often a result of misinterpretation because there was little, or no, language communication. Even the interpreters taken along usually proved to be useless.

Explorers differed in their objectivity and appreciation of the new lifeways before them. Many wrote without judging too harshly; but the filth, the lice, the overpowering stenches, and various disagreeable personal habits of the Eskimos sometimes proved too much for the well-educated, sophisticated representatives of European aristocracy. They then wavered toward ethnocentric evaluation; yet to their credit, they usually excused the distasteful aspects as the inevitable result of human struggles in a harsh environment.

Captain Cook was already a well-known explorer when he and Captain Charles Clerke set out from England on Cook's third voyage in 1776 in the *Resolution* and the *Discovery* for the northwest coast of America to search for a water route from the Pacific Ocean to the Atlantic and to take possession of lands not claimed by other countries. After his first American stop at Vancouver Island, where he stayed about six weeks, Cook sailed in April 1778 to explore (and name) Prince William Sound and Bristol Bay en route to the Bering Strait. He planned to hug the shore on his way north, but by 2 July shoal waters in the Bristol Bay area sent him out to sea, whereby he failed to see the Yukon and the Kuskokwim, two of Alaska's largest rivers. On 5 August Cook anchored for the first time north of the Aleutians near an island, which he named after a sledge that he found lying on a path. The sled was "ten feet long, 20 inches broad [with] a kind of rail-work on each side, and was shod with bone. The construction of it was admirable, and all the parts neatly put together; some with wooden pins, but mostly with thongs or lashings of whale-bone, which made me think it was entirely the workmanship of natives."[1]

They had landed on the only level shore of Sledge Island, visible from the present city of Nome, where they "met with some decayed huts that were partly built below ground. People had lately been on the island; and it is pretty clear, that they frequently visit it for some purpose or other, as there was a beaten path from the one end to the other." (During the nineteenth century, this was the winter home of the people called Ayakmiut.) With the sled as evidence, they assumed that there was winter communication with the opposite shore, on which they "saw some posts & what we suppos'd some indian Villages."[2]

Cook named an opposite cape, Point Rodney, and gave the name King Island to Daurkin's "Okibian," after James King, a lieutenant who succeeded him as expedition commander after his death. On 9 August Cook named Cape Prince of Wales, where he encountered more shoal water. Going far out

1. Cook and King 1784, 2:442–43.
2. Ibid., p. 442; King, in Beaglehole, ed. 1967, p. 1431.

to sea, he said, "We thought we saw some people upon the coast; and probably we were not mistaken, as some elevations, like stages, and others like huts, were seen at the same place. We saw the same things on the continent within Sledge Island [i.e., near Cape Rodney], and on some other parts of the Coast."[3]

After sailing to Siberia and finding Jakob Stählin's map (which accompanied his account in 1774 of the post-Bering discoveries) either "exceedingly erroneous" or "mere fiction,"[4] he returned to the American coast and sailed as far north as a headland, which he called merely Icy Cape despite his supply of aristocratic English names, and then turned southward.

He did not tarry long on the coast he had already observed on his way north because he was eager to find waterways that might lead to the Atlantic Ocean. But he had already missed the Kuskokwim and the Yukon rivers, and was to leave the Arctic without finding the huge water masses now called Port Clarence, Grantley Harbor, and Kotzebue Sound. Until he arrived in Norton Sound (which he named after Sir Fletcher Norton, speaker of the House of Commons and a relative of Lieutenant King's), he made only one observation about the people: on 7 September, about "eight or nine leagues distant" from Sledge Island (or about thirty miles away, at Cape Nome) he saw a light on shore, and two "canoes [umiaks], filled with people, coming off toward us. I brought to, that they might have time to come up. But it was to no purpose; for, resisting all the signs of friendship we could exhibit, they kept at the distance of a quarter of a mile."

At this same place, David Samwell, surgeon of the *Discovery*, said that they saw many fires on shore, and three boats came off "to the Ships, the Indians kept shouting as they approached us, they went alongside the Resolution but did not stay any time."[5]

Cook carefully explored Norton Sound, and named Cape Darby and Bald Head, on the west side of which "the shore forms a bay, in the bottom of which is a low beach, where we saw a number of huts or habitations of the natives"; this was probably at the mouth of the Kwik River.[6] Needing wood and water, Cook and King went up on a bluff, their first time on the mainland. Berries were abundant, and small spruce trees grew on a level plain beyond. On the beach below were caribou and fox tracks, driftwood, and abundant fresh water.[7]

When the wind changed, Cook sailed to the opposite shore, which he named Cape Denbigh, and on 11 September he wrote that

several people were seen upon the peninsula; and one man came off in a small canoe [kayak]. I gave him a knife, and a few beads, with which he seemed well pleased.

3. Cook and King 1784, 2:444–45.
4. Ibid., p. 452. James R. Masterson calls this map a "cartoon" (Masterson and Brower 1948, p. 6).
5. Ibid., p. 476; Samwell, in Beaglehole, ed. 1967, p. 1135.
6. Cook and King 1784, 2:467, 477; Ray, field notes.
7. Cook and King 1784, 2:478.

Having made signs to him to bring us something to eat, he immediately left us, and paddled toward the shore. But, meeting another man coming off, who happened to have two dried Salmon, he got them from him; and on returning to the ship, would give them to no body but me. Some of our people thought that he asked for me under the name of *Capitane*; but in this they were probably mistaken. He knew who had given him the knife and beads, but I do not see how he could know that I was the Captain. Others of the natives, soon after, came off, and exchanged a few dry fish, for such trifles as they could get. . . . They were most desirous of knives; and they had no dislike to tobacco.[8]

On the twelfth they anchored a mile and a half off the coast in the vicinity of Elim (i.e., Bald Head was northeast nine leagues, or twenty-seven miles, and Besboro Island, which Cook named, was southeast fifteen leagues, or about forty-five miles), where they went ashore for driftwood. Said King, "I believe there never was such a quantity [of wood] taken into any ship in such a space of time."

On 13 September Cook said that

a family of the natives came near to the place where we were taking off wood. I know not how many there were at first; but I saw only the husband, the wife, and their child; and a fourth person who bore the human shape, and that was all; for he was the most deformed cripple I had ever seen or heard of. The other man was almost blind; and neither he, nor his wife, were such good-looking people as we had sometimes seen amongst the natives of this [the North American] coast. The underlips of both [man and woman] were bored; and they had in their possession some such glass beads as I had met with before amongst their neighbours. But iron was their beloved article. . . .

For only four knives made from an old iron hoop, Captain Cook was able to purchase almost four hundred pounds of fresh fish.[9]

Lieutenant King, in a separate party, had met the same family when

a canoe [umiak] full of natives approached us; and, beckoning them to land, an elderly man and woman came on shore. I gave the woman a small knife, making her understand, that I would give her a much larger one for some fish. She made signs to me to follow her. I had proceeded with them about a mile, when the man, in crossing a stony beach, fell down, and cut his foot very much [he was barefooted]. This made me stop; upon which the woman pointed to the man's eyes, which, I observed, were covered with a thick, white film. . . . The woman had a little child on her back, covered with the hood of her jacket: and which I took for a bundle, till I heard it cry. At about two miles distance we came to their open skin boat, which was turned on its side, the convex part toward the wind, and served for their house. I was now made to perform a singular operation on the man's eyes. First, I was directed to hold my breath; afterward, to breathe on the diseased eyes; and next, to spit on them. The woman then took both my hands, and pressing them to his stomach, held them there for some time, while she related some calamitous history of her family; pointing sometimes to her husband, sometimes to a frightful cripple belonging to the family, and sometimes to

---

8. Ibid., pp. 478–79. In the log of the *Discovery*, Captain Cook had written that in return for the knife and beads, the man "gave me two or three red fox skins that were sewed together, so as to make a kind of dress" (Beaglehole, ed. 1967, p. 437*n*).

9. Cook and King 1784, 2:480–81; King's journal, in Beaglehole, ed. 1967, p. 1433.

her child. I purchased all the fish they had, consisting of very fine salmon, salmon-trout, and mullet; which were delivered most faithfully to the man I sent for them.

"The frightful cripple" was described by King in his journal as a young lad who "had a disorder in his face which had already destroy'd one eye, & the sides were much Swell'd, & one half of his mouth & Nose in a sad condition," and "his Legs were so contract'd that he was oblig'd to crawl about on his Knees & hands."[10]

King's description of the Eskimos' physical characteristics is the first that we have for the Bering Strait. "The man," he said, "was about five feet two inches high, and well made; his colour, of a light copper; his hair black and short, and with little beard. He had two holes in his under-lip, but no ornaments in them. The woman was short and squat, with a plump round face; wore a deer-skin jacket with a large hood; and had on wide boots. The teeth of both were black, and seemed as if they had been filed down level with the gums. The woman was punctured from the tip [of what?] to the chin." In his manuscript journal, King said that the woman had "little sore eyes," and "some of their jackets were made with a good deal of Taste, & instead of resembling a close shirt or farmers frock, as amongst the other Indians, those had an opening at the hips & hung down before & behind in a circular flap; they wore leather breeches, or rather trowsers, that came half way down the leg, & some had boots. All their Jackets had hoods to them, & we did not observe that they had any other covering to the head."

"Deer," or caribou, apparently were plentiful along the coast during the summer, because the woman said that two men had gone into the woods to hunt some which they could buy.

On the fourteenth, a party of men went ashore to cut spruce branches for brewing beer, and on the fifteenth the ships sailed to the southeast side of Cape Denbigh to a bay called "Chaktoole" by the natives. From Cook's chart, he apparently anchored near the mouth of the Sineak River where "a few of the natives came off in their small canoes, and bartered some dried salmon for such trifles as our people had to give them." At daybreak the next day, nine men, "each in his canoe, paid us a visit. They approached the ship with some caution; and evidently came with no other view than to gratify their curiosity. They drew up abreast of each other, under our stern, and gave us a song; while one of their number beat upon a kind of drum, and another made a thousand antic motions with his hands and body. There was, however, nothing savage, either in the song, or in the gestures that accompanied it."[11]

Surgeon David Samwell said that the Norton Sound area was "thinly inhabited, the Houses are built together in small Villages on the Sea Shore

10. These quotations and the following information on the natives' appearance are from pages 481–82*n* in Cook and King 1784, vol. 2, and King's journal in Beaglehole, ed. 1967, pp. 1439, 1440.

11. Cook and King 1784, 2:483, 484. Chaktoole is spelled "Chachtoole" in Cook's original journal, and Chachtoolai in King's journal (Beaglehole, ed. 1967, p. 1438).

but we saw a lonely hut here & there on the flat Land at a great distance from any others," and Lieutenant King said, "I do not suppose we saw a hundred Souls in all the Sound."

From the combined notes of Cook, King, and Samwell, the dwellings were described as being built aboveground; of different shapes, though mostly square; and constructed with logs either laid horizontally or slanted vertically. Logs formed the floor and the roofs, which were chinked with moss, sod, and stones. Houses were six feet high at the middle and were from eight to eighteen feet long and wide (King and Samwell do not agree on size); a fireplace was built at the entrance, with a smoke hole above. Small logs placed on the other three sides were covered with mats for sleeping. They also had temporary huts of logs erected in a conical shape. In these caribou and bird bones were found.

The Eskimos seemed to subsist mainly on dried fish and berries, of which they had "great quantities" in birchbark pails. They had dogs, and many skins of wolves, foxes, ground squirrels, and caribou hanging up. They used bows and arrows, a double paddle for their kayaks, and sleds.[12]

On the fifteenth, Captain Cook sent Lieutenant King to climb the heights of Bald Head to ascertain whether Bald Head was on the island of "Alatska," or whether it was connected to the "Continent of America." From his vantage he saw many rivers, including a large one to the northward (the Koyuk), and concluded that all of the land he could see was part of the mainland.

Therefore, on 16 September Cook decided that "it was high time to think of leaving these northern regions." He continued south from Norton Sound, discovered and named Cape Stephens and Stuart Island, and saw Eskimos of the Saint Michael–Stebbins area for the first time. "Before we reached Stuart's Island, we saw two small islands [Beulah and Whale], lying between us and the main; and as we ranged along the coast, several people appeared upon the shore, and, by signs, seemed to invite us to approach them"; but the ships continued on.

Cook left the Arctic without having discovered a passage to the Atlantic Ocean, but he had charted the northwest coast of Alaska for the first time. King said in his journal that because of Cook's ascertaining "the true distance between the Continent of Asia & America . . . Philosophers will no longer find any difficulty in accounting for the Population of America."[13]

Cook's map had at last laid down the general outlines of a coast reported from Siberia for many years, but in the more than five-hundred-mile coastline between Kotzebue Sound and Saint Michael Cook recorded only

12. King's journal in Beaglehole, ed. 1967, pp. 1432, 1440; Cook and King 1784, 2:484; Samwell in Beaglehole, ed. 1967, pp. 1136, 1137. It is uncertain, even from an examination of Cook's chart of anchorages, whether these dwellings were situated near the mouth of the Sineak River at an old camping site, near the mouth of the Shaktoolik River, or on the southeast beach of Cape Denbigh below the old site of Nukleet. Giddings thought the dwellings referred to this place (1964, p. 11).

13. Cook and King 1784, 2:489–90; King's journal in Beaglehole, ed. 1967, p.1436.

one native place name, "Chaktoole," which was placed on the first edition of his map in 1784. The second edition, in 1794, however, had acquired thirty more settlements and numerous rivers, bays, and islands, which undoubtedly came for the most part from Ivan Kobelev's map, drawn one year after Cook charted the coast, but five years before the first publication of Cook's map. The second edition of Cook's map gave credit for the information as "lately procured from St. Petersburg and other places."

KOBELEV'S MAP

Kobelev's map is unique not only for the fact of its being made without benefit of a base map or a personal survey of the Alaskan mainland, but because it includes bays, rivers, and islands "discovered" much later by Europeans, and sixty-one settlements that have stood the test of twentieth-century inquiries.[14]

The settlements appear to be located in two groups 200 miles apart, one on the Seward Peninsula and the other on the coastal delta of the Yukon and Kuskokwim rivers. These geographical locations had never been questioned before I began mapping settlements at Bering Strait, whereupon I found that all were situated on the peninsula and the shores of Kotzebue Sound. Furthermore, Kobelev had recorded his settlements in the same geographic sequence as mine, rendering most of the names with a degree of phonetic fidelity despite the differences in time, language, and field methods. After I had ascertained that all of the settlements were in the Seward Peninsula area with none south of Norton Sound, there remained the puzzle of why Kobelev's surprisingly accurate map contained the blunder of separating consecutive settlements into two groups so many miles apart.

The answer is simply that the fault lies not with Kobelev but with Pallas, who redrew Kobelev's map for his history. Pallas said that since the Eskimos "did not indicate the distance of [the villages] they are put down on the accompanying chart only by guess, *though the coast is laid down* from the observations of the English" (my emphasis).[15] This guesswork and a misinterpretation of Cook's chart distorted the entire map. Despite Pallas' implications of using "English" information, he actually borrowed very little of Cook's coastline, and what he did borrow—Norton Sound and the coast to the south—was to cause no end of trouble, especially in the identification of the Kheuveren River as the Kuzitrin, which both Daurkin and Kobelev had drawn correctly as emptying into a bay in the position of the extensive waterways leading to Port Clarence (see Chap. 3). Pallas arbitrarily called this body of water Norton Sound.

14. Kobelev's map was published originally by Pallas in vol. 4 of *Neue nordische Beyträge* (1783) and reprinted in Masterson and Brower 1948. The same map with names in Russian was published in 1784 and reproduced by M. V. Chernenko in his article of 1957, on p. 125, and in Efimov, ed. 1964, map 174.

15. Masterson and Brower 1948, p. 95. The comparison of Kobelev's and my villages is in Ray 1971a, pp. 4–7.

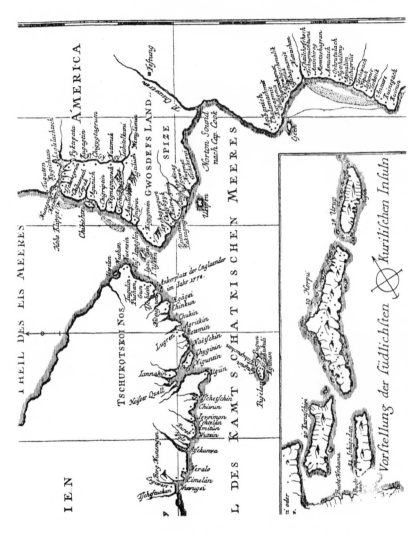

Map 5. Ivan Kobelev's map of the Bering Strait, 1779 (Pallas 1783, pl. 1)

Another puzzling question about Pallas' German map was Kobelev's omission of the large and important village of Kauwerak but the inclusion of many smaller settlements. Kobelev most certainly had not omitted the village, for the Russian map has both a Kheuveren River and a Kheuveren village; Pallas merely called the village "Festung" or fort.

Kobelev was the first person to record the Eskimo name for Sledge Island, which is Ayak (Eyekh in Kobelev's Russian and Ejech in the German), and to map the Goodhope River. On the German map, the name of this river appears to be Gygy, but on the Russian map it is Kvik, or "river," in Eskimo. It is definitely the Goodhope, however, for at its mouth Kobelev placed a settlement, Pyktepata, which means "mouth of the Pittuk," the Eskimo name for this river. A nineteenth-century village at this site was called Pittukpaga. He located six other settlements on the river, but disregarded other streams (including the Kuzitrin) that also had occupied villages and camps at that time. As early as 1779 Ivan Kobelev was faced with one of the problems of ethnological inquiry, the possible skewing of information by the choice of informants, because those persons who answered his questions on Little Diomede Island apparently were acquainted with a limited interior area of Seward Peninsula.

OBSERVATIONS MADE BY THE BILLINGS EXPEDITION

In southern Alaska lucrative fur-hunting projects were underway between the years 1778 and 1791, when the northern seas were again left to the Eskimos. In 1783 Grigorii Shelikov and Ivan Golikov established their first permanent settlement at Three Saints Bay, Kodiak Island, after one of their ships had returned to Siberia with an incredibly rich cargo of furs in 1778. Within a short time, Shelikov's organization began to supplant the independent fur hunters who had been taking sea otters and fur seals from every nook of the southern coast.

Russia was not the only country searching for furs. England, France, and Spain sent ships to the Alexander Archipelago and Prince William Sound as early as 1779. The United States of America, a republic only thirteen years old, entered the competition in 1791 after Captain Robert Gray had returned home in the *Columbia Rediviva* from China, where he had sold sea otter skins obtained in trade north of Portland Canal near Juneau. From then on, the Yankee traders in their "Boston" ships and the English in their "King George" ships sailed and traded everywhere in Russian territory south of the Aleutians.

Although the Russians in America did not extend their explorations north of the Aleutians until 1818, the imperial Russian government had looked with great interest on northern Alaska, but more as an eastward expansion of its Siberian territory than a northern extension of its American colonies. Catherine II, prompted by the successes of Russian fur hunters as well as by Captain Cook's explorations for England, hired Joseph Billings—one of

Cook's assistants—to explore northern Siberia and Alaska, to investigate the fur trade, and to try to establish a firmer claim for the Russians, since the English fur traders were approaching the Russian possessions by sea from the south and by land through Canada.

Billings left Saint Petersburg for Okhotsk to build ships for the expedition in 1785, but he did not go to the northern part of Alaska in the *Glory of Russia* (*Slava Rossii*) until 1791. Having explored Prince William Sound in 1790, Billings planned to explore Cook Inlet the next year. As soon as he had arrived there, however, he precipitously left for the coast of Siberia. Gavriil Sarychev and Martin Sauer, the expedition's lieutenant and secretary, respectively, ascribed this action to egotism; yet his departure may have been influenced by the independent fur hunters who looked upon his explorations as governmental interference in their rich territory.[16]

His sudden decision to sail to Siberia and thence to Cape Rodney did result, however, in the most complete ethnographic information about an Eskimo tribe north of the Aleutians up to that time. Perhaps he decided to go to Cape Rodney, where he anchored for four days, to track down rumors of the Kheuveren "Russian fort," because in Siberia he had learned that Kobelev had crossed the strait in a fleet of skin boats early in the summer to try to find it.

The combined observations of Sauer, Sarychev, and Karl H. Merck, naturalist of the expedition, give us a description of a nearly aboriginal way of life only forty miles northwest of Nome. Not until twenty-five years later, in 1816, would Otto von Kotzebue visit several other tribes in the Bering Strait area. Many of the details are from Merck's account in German, which has never been translated into English. Merck kept a number of journals, but only one—about the Yakuts of Siberia—was published at the end of the expedition. His journal about the Tlingits, Aleuts, and Eskimos was later discovered in Leipzig and published in *Baessler-Archiv* in 1937.[17] Billings did not write a report, but Sauer and Sarychev both published their manuscripts shortly after returning home, Sauer's in English and Sarychev's in Russian, which was translated almost immediately into English.

On 28 July 1791, the *Glory of Russia* cast anchor eight miles from shore in "latitude 64° 20′, longitude 164°, Sledge Island, 78° West, distant 9 miles, Cape Rodney, NW 75°, 9 miles," and Billings, Merck, Afanassi Bakov (the ship's master), and Mr. Voronin, artist of the expedition, went ashore with a

16. Bancroft 1886, pp. 291, 301. Bancroft discusses Billings' journey on pp. 282–303. Billings probably was also considerably frustrated by the behavior of his incompetent seamen. Sarychev said that most of them had never been to sea and were constantly seasick (1806–7, 1:57).

17. Another Merck journal is a 64-page manuscript about the Chukchi deposited in the Leningrad public library (Bronshtein and Shnakenburg 1941, p. 80). The authors say that nine sheets of twenty-six designs drawn by the artist Voronin accompanied the Chukchi manuscript, "Beschreibung der Tschutschi, von ihren Gebräuchen und Lebensart." A. Jacobi edited the ethnological notes about Alaska in *Baessler-Archiv* (see Jacobi 1937).

Information about the Cape Rodney Eskimos is combined from Merck's notes (Jacobi 1937); Sarychev 1806–7, 2:44–46; and Sauer 1802, pp. 242–48.

"Redoubt Saint Michael (in Norton Sound)," drawn by I. G. Vosnesenskii in 1843. (From Blomqvist 1951, fig. 22)

Saint Michael in 1866. (From French edition of Whymper 1871)

Saint Michael Eskimos posing near their houses and drying racks. (Photograph by Miles, 1902–3)

number of guards and sailors in two boats. One of the boats returned shortly to the ship with news that they had found "inhabitants [near the mouth of a small river, probably the Sinuk], and having met with a kind reception from them, they should pass the night on land."[18] The officers walked on a narrow path where they met two Eskimo men who blocked their way, making a stand "with the points [of their lances] toward us." The Europeans threw some beads on the ground as a friendly sign, whereupon the Eskimos "turned the points of their lances behind them, and approached without hesitation." The men wore no trousers, thus exposing the genitals, and were barefooted. Billings gave each of them a copper medal and a few beads.

The officers were invited to the Eskimos' home about two and a half miles away, where skins were spread out for them before a driftwood fire. Their hostess gave each a thin piece of marten skin, apparently a ceremonial gesture, and fish and venison to eat, "but the intolerable stench of the hut took away all appetite on our part." They thought that they were in a village, but next morning they learned that it was only a camp consisting of a single-family skin tent erected for fishing and for hunting caribou, which were abundant nearby.

The *Glory of Russia* remained in the area for four days, and the Eskimos traded so eagerly that Sauer said "they [did not] scruple to part with their arms, and even stripped themselves giving their clothes for beads, knives, &c." They exchanged skins of black and red foxes, river otters, martens, lynxes, and wolverines, "vests" of young caribou and Alpine hare, wooden bowls, "trifles" made of "walrus teeth," adzes of jade or green jasper, bows and arrows, and spears for the Europeans' iron, metal buttons, knives, blue glass beads, "coral," and "pearl-enamel," but apparently no tobacco. Merck implied that the Eskimos were clever traders, their policy being to give only half value for what they got, "proof that one can make out better by receiving than by giving." This, however, may have been written in jest, because Billings purchased a kayak (that is, a "single-seated baidar") for only "one row" of glass beads, and Bakov procured an umiak for "pearl-enamel."

Meanwhile, a skin boat went out to trade with those remaining aboard ship. The umiak had "at its stern an extended bladder hung on a pole, and at the poop two red foxes on another pole, which we, of course, regarded as friendly signals. They continued, however, some time in their position without offering to approach, and with their hands raised aloft." Sarychev "commanded the sailors who were on the deck to do the same, as a token that we were unprovided with any offensive weapons."

Finally taking courage, the Eskimos boarded the ship, leaving their arms in the umiak. They could not make themselves understood, although interpreters from Unalaska, Kodiak Island, and Anadyrsk were on board. Sauer said that the natives "regarded every thing . . . with admiration, but did not

18. Sarychev 1806–7, 2:44.

appear to be of a pilfering disposition." One of the Eskimos accidentally broke a small pane of glass, "which threw them all into a state of dismay. He immediately offered his lance by way of indemnification; but we made him understand that it was no loss, by putting in another, and laughing at his concern, which pleased them all very much."

As soon as the Eskimos prepared to leave the ship, the sailors began to sing a Russian song, whereupon they returned on board, listened, and then reciprocated with a song and a dance. "This dance [by two men] consisted of many vehement gesticulations of the whole body, particularly of the hands and head, which they twisted round on all sides with great dexterity, at the same time springing from place to place, in conformity with the singing and beating of the drum."

At another time, the women danced with the men, keeping their feet in one place while moving their arms and hands—palms flat—slowly from one side to the other in front of their faces. Their bodies swayed up and down very slightly as they flexed their knees. They were accompanied by singing and drumming on a tambourine with a wooden stick.

The people, Sauer said, were "well limbed, rather tall, had fine open and agreeable countenances, and were handsome and healthy." Their dress was very neat and clean. Men wore trousers of soft caribou with the hair turned in and of sealskin, with the hair outside, reaching to various lengths—to the thigh, the knee, or the ankle. The pants of red- or yellow-dyed leather were tight, well made, and held up by a drawstring. Lightweight boots, which had thin soles of sealskin, reached to the calf or to the knee, and were tied around the ankles with a narrow red thong. The shorter boots were made of beautiful white leather and embroidered with colored hair and sinews. The Eskimos also had a one-piece sealskin outfit of trousers and boots, and a complete suit of "tanned" sealskin—hood, gloves, and boots—which was entered through the top and laced up around the neck.

Their parkas were decorated with muskrat and marten fur, and sometimes with a narrow fringe of caribou fawn around the bottom. The hood was pointed, and a small ribbon of caribou fur or a small fur tassel was sewn at the peak. The front was trimmed with wolverine, wolf, rabbit, or caribou fur. The waistband was a narrow leather thong from which a number of wolf or fox tails hung at the sides and a caribou snout in front. In bad weather, a long rain shirt of gutskin with a hood was worn over the clothing and fastened in front with a sinew cord from which dangled the red feet of the sea swallow. The front edge of most hoods was trimmed with little tufts of animal hair.

Their hair "was almost as short as if shaven," and although most men had no head covering, a few wore a crownlike band of sealskin thongs, and one man had a little wooden hat similar to those worn by Aleuts. The hat was unpainted, but had three vertical rows of carved ivory walrus heads on the front and an ivory fish on each side. The men had mittens of tanned caribou skin and wore labrets of ivory, "green jasper," "dark jasper," or blue glass.

Women's clothing consisted of a hooded skin garment reaching almost to the knees and cut up the sides to form a rounded extension front and back. A strip of wolverine fur was usually sewed around the bottom below a welted seam of caribou fur. Several of the women wore straps around their chests and back. Their leather waistbands were decorated with the incisor teeth of caribou and fastened in front with pieces of ivory. Children frequently wore bells made in Russia.

Both women and men had hanging from their ears glass beads alternating with curved pieces of iron and bone strung on long leather strips. Some boys wore strings of beads interwoven in hair that fell over the forehead. Women braided their hair around the ears, and some had a two-strand plait shaped into a circle. One woman had her hair braided with small pieces of otter skin, the ends peeping out from the hair. Feminine tattooing consisted of one vertical or two broad diagonal stripes running from the lower lip to the chin. The women had various designs tattooed on their forearms and wrists, and wore copper or iron bracelets on their forearms.

The women, though bashful, were attracted to the blue glass beads and coral, and "when we kissed them they blushed." Merck said that they appeared to get along well with their husbands, who did not trade them off (as they apparently had seen in Siberia).

Merck described their tent as conical, of pole-frame construction, and covered with untanned sealskin held in place with taut thongs. On one side a piece of gutskin served as a window. Halfway up the interior frame was a circular support. A plank frame, decorated with ivory chains and carvings of sea animals and fish, was placed around the smoke hole to ward off rain. The floor of the tent and the sleeping planks around the side were covered with mats. Caribou skins were used as bedding outdoors.

The winter homes had a stone-lined sunken fireplace. The people cooked in round clay pots, which were narrow at the top and decorated with a border of short incisions. They used wooden buckets, bowls, and spoons, and rendered sea mammal fat in whole sealskins with a bone opening. They dipped up the liquid oil from a wooden bowl with pieces of meat and fish, which they ate with a great deal of noise. Women chewed "larch resin" (spruce gum?) for enjoyment.

Fish nets, to which bladder floats were attached, were made of knotted sinew. Fish and sea mammal meat were dried on outdoor racks. Dogs pulled sleds. The two-man drill was used to make fires, one person twirling a stick in a cavity on the floor to make sparks that were caught in dry grass placed nearby.

The Eskimos had armor made of both wood and bone, and used bows and arrows, spears, and harpoons. On the forearm, an archer wore an oval, arched wristguard of bone or iron, and on a thong round his neck, a small, broad knife and a whetstone of green jasper. On the left side was carried a partitioned quiver of sealskin, the bow placed in one-half of the quiver and the arrows in the other. The bows were strengthened by caribou sinew, and the arrows had points of "green jade, calcedoni, and ivory." The ivory head of the harpoon was one and a half feet long, into which was inserted an iron point shaped and sharpened by the Eskimos. Ready-made points were also obtained from Izhiga (Gizhiga) through Chukchi traders.

On 31 July, after anchoring between Sledge Island and Cape Rodney, two miles from the mainland, "on which we found several summer jurts [tents] erected in different places," the *Glory of Russia* sailed again for Siberia. Despite inquiries, they failed to learn anything about the mythical Russian fort on the banks of the "Kheuveren," only fifty miles from where they were anchored. Sauer rightly concluded that no one had ever heard of such a place.[19]

At Saint Lawrence Bay, Siberia, the expedition met a number of Chukchi who "introduced our people to the women when they had no other articles of trade. These, however, were not their wives, but prisoners taken from their American neighbours, with whom they are frequently at war. The cause of the last affair between them was this: both parties meeting, on the chace [*sic*] of sea animals, quarrelled; an engagement commenced, in which the Americans took one baidar and made the crew prisoners; the other, returning, procured a reinforcement, made a descent on the American coast, carried off a few women, and then peace was restored."[20]

KOBELEV'S TRIP TO ALASKA

Billings learned in Siberia that Ivan Kobelev (the mapmaker of 1779), accompanied by Nikolai Daurkin, had crossed the Bering Strait to Alaska in a fleet of umiaks before the *Glory of Russia* arrived at Cape Rodney in 1791, and prompted by this information, especially because of interest in the search for the "Russian" fort, Kheuveren, Billings sailed directly to Cape Rodney. Neither Sauer nor Sarychev mentions Kobelev's trip in his account, since neither had any firsthand knowledge of it; but Kobelev's journal is proof of his interesting adventures and his obsession of trying to locate the "Russian" fort. Kobelev furthermore was the first European to go ashore at Wales and King Island, and he again visited both the Diomedes.

In March 1791 Kobelev had negotiated with an East Cape man, Opreia, to take him to the Alaskan side of the strait. Although Opreia was on friendly terms with the Americans, it was only with great difficulty that Kobelev persuaded him to take him across in his skin boat.[21]

19. Sauer 1802, p. 258.
20. Ibid., pp. 250–51, 252.
21. Chernenko 1957, p. 131. The information about Big and Little Diomede islands and King Island is taken from Kobelev's journal, published in Chernenko's article, pp. 131–35. The entire

Kobelev said that on 4 June 1791 ten umiaks (there were seventeen in all, seven of them belonging to Daurkin's contingent) rowed to Imaglin Island.[22] On Imaglin, or Big Diomede Island, he counted 103 males and adolescents, and approximately 115 females and young children. The inhabitants ate the meat of sea animals and wore clothes made of bird skins. The males had pierced lower lips into which were inserted walrus ivory or stone labrets. They were friendly and treated him very kindly because of his previous visit in 1779. He characterized the inhabitants as daring and cheerful. On good days, men and women often gathered together outdoors, but in inclement weather they congregated in their dwellings (or "yurts"). At such gatherings the women customarily sang songs, and men and women danced in couples for a long time, finally dispersing to their homes.

They lived in wooden dwellings covered with stone and sod. The entrance-exit was made underground, about four sazhens (twenty-eight feet) long, but some had a hole cut in the floor, which also served as the entrance. In the ceiling there was a small window covered with skin peeled from the whale's liver. The wood in their houses was fir and cottonwood that had drifted from America. They burned oil for cooking in the winter.

After a six-day stay on Big Diomede Island, Kobelev sailed on 10 June to "Igellin Island," or Little Diomede. Kobelev said that the people were similar to those on Big Diomede and had the same language. They lived in the same kind of dwellings, had the same customs, wore the same bird-skin clothing, and ate the same sea-mammal food. The population consisted of forty-five males and adolescents and fifty-five females and young children. They also treated him exceedingly pleasantly.

On 11 June his dreams of going to the American continent materialized when he visited a settlement called Kigigmen (Wales). He said that the village had about fifty dwellings similar to those on Big and Little Diomede islands. He found no inhabitants and surmised that they had left because of famine, dispersing along the coast north and south. He had also learned the previous winter on the Chukchi Peninsula that Siberians had attacked the village and had taken women and children prisoners. It therefore appeared, he said, that they had left mostly out of fear, expecting another attack. And Kobelev did observe that twenty skin boats and approximately 150 men had gathered for a "campaign" to a northern area called "Tapkhan" (*tapkak*, the name for the coast between Wales and Cape Espenberg).

Kobelev said there was no timber at all near the sea, but many kinds grew in the mountains, a day's trip with dogs. Kobelev and his party rowed

report is printed in *Sobranie sochinenii* . . ., vol. 5, 1790, a copy of which is in the Library of Congress. Page references are given here to Chernenko's article for the convenience of the reader who might like to read the journal in the more easily obtainable *Letopis severa*.

22. Kobelev's and Daurkin's rivalry was never more obvious than on this trip. Kobelev failed to mention Daurkin's presence in the flotilla of skin boats, and Daurkin erased Kobelev's name from a "letter" written on a slab of ivory in 1791. In this letter, Daurkin referred to himself as "Nobleman Daurkin" (Fedorova 1964, p. 109).

southward from Wales hoping to find the "Kheuveren" River. They saw many small, but deserted, settlements. They could not enter the mouth of the river (or what they thought was the river), however, because of a great deal of ice. Since all of "Kheuveren Bay" (Port Clarence) was still covered with ice, as in winter, Kobelev decided to go to "Ukipin Island" (King Island).

At sunrise on 12 June they rowed to King Island. When they saw that the islanders had spotted them in the sea, the Chukchi of Kobelev's party stopped their skin boats, donned "kuiaks" (Chukchi armor), and took spears and bows and arrows in hand, as in battle readiness.[23] Kobelev asked them why they were preparing for war when they were not coming for war, and they explained that that was the custom of the King Islanders, who would meet them in just such a manner. As they approached the island, the inhabitants came down to the shore dressed in armor, with lances and bows in hand, and arrows on the strings; but after they landed they invited everyone to their dwellings.

Kobelev said that King Island was a very small but lofty island, and the village was built on large knolls on the hillside. The dwellings were the same as on Big Diomede. There were about 70 males and adolescents, and 100 females and young children. The males had their lower lips cut in Big Diomede islander fashion. The men had six or eight wives. The language was the same as on Big Diomede and among the "pedestrian Chukchi" (i.e., Eskimos) who lived near East Cape. They had no chiefs over them. The people ate sea animals, whale, walrus, and seals, and wore clothing made of "deer" skin, which they got from the mainland.

Kobelev was treated with great friendliness and was told, through an interpreter, to walk through the settlement and look at everything. They began to trade the same day. The King Islanders bartered marten parkas, foxes, wolves, wolverines, otters, lynxes, and deer (caribou) bedding, which were obtained from the American mainland. The Russians bartered spears, knives, hatchets, palmas (long knives with a wide, one-sided blade attached to a long handle), iron pots, various trade beads, and glass beads.

On the island he found ten Americans who lived on the Kheuveren River (that is, in the village of Kauwerak on the Kuzitrin River). They had come the year before in three skin boats to trade. The Americans treated him amicably and with kindness. Through an interpreter, they said they had heard his name long ago when he had first visited the Diomedes (in 1779). The Americans talked a lot, but Kobelev could not persuade the interpreters to translate a single statement other than that they had heard his name long ago. Finally, the interpreters no longer stood near Kobelev and the Kauwerak people in order to avoid translating.

To show "a big and lasting friendship," the Americans stroked their faces

23. The following is the explanation of "kuiaks" in one of Chernenko's footnotes: "Chukotkski armor of thick leather, bone, wood, and later, metal disks" (1957, p. 133).

and chests, and then Kobelev's face and chest. They pointed to their land and pulled on his clothes, apparently inviting him to visit them. When he spoke Russian, they pointed to their tongue with their finger and to their land. They crossed themselves surreptitiously, Kobelev said, when his companions joined him, and waved toward their land. He concluded that these actions indicated that Russian-speaking people lived across the strait, although we know that they must have been attempting to tell him something quite different because there was no Russian settlement there. Kobelev decided that the Chukchi who had brought him did not translate his conversations with the Americans for fear their commerce across the strait would suffer if the Russians became friendly with the Americans. (But if the men with Kobelev were actually Chukchi, and not Eskimo—as the name Chukchi often meant at that time—it would partly explain why there was little translating of the American Eskimo conversations.) Kobelev wrote that a mainland Eskimo, who had heard on Little Diomede Island that he was to be on the Chukchi Peninsula for a year, had gone to East Cape to see him the summer before (in 1790) but was killed by the Siberians. (According to Chernenko, the Chukchi were protecting their trade monopoly.)

On 14 June Kobelev left King Island, and the departure was similar to the "welcoming"; both sides were armed.[24]

24. Ibid., pp. 133–35.

CHAPTER 5

Kotzebue at Shishmaref Inlet and Goodhope Bay, 1816

AT THE turn of the nineteenth century, furs went from Alaska to Russia by two routes—through the independent Eskimo traders of northern Alaska, and via the Russian-American Company and its hired hunters and traders in southern Alaska. The company's northernmost trading post was more than six hundred miles from the narrowest part of Bering Strait. In 1791 Alexander A. Baranov had become manager of Shelikov's company, which in 1799 was granted a twenty-year charter under the name, Russian-American Company. It became a powerful trading monopoly with traders based eventually as far north as Unalakleet. The Russian government's decision to grant a monopoly was based partly on reports of the Billings expedition about the abusive conduct of fur hunters toward natives. To some observers, the change seemed a turn for the better; but to others the company's treatment of the Aleuts and Tlingits was no less cruel, only better organized and more official.

Under the company, the skillful and courageous Aleuts continued as sea otter hunters, traveling in fleets of hundreds of kayaks, sometimes hundreds of miles away as otters grew scarce. By the 1790s the sea otters had been exterminated in the Aleutians and were decreasing in Prince William Sound and Cook Inlet. The Russians pushed on farther east to Yakutat, and then south to a large Island, where Baranov finally made his permanent headquarters, successively called Fort Saint Michael (Mikhailovskii), New Archangel (Novo-Arkhangelsk), and Sitka, the administrative seat for a territory one-fifth the size of the continental United States.

Under its first charter, the Russian-American Company was granted not only complete monopoly of fur trading and hunting in the Russian colonies but the privilege of exploring and occupying lands to the north and to the south not already possessed by another nation. The company had to wait to exercise its privilege northward, as it was occupied in the south by several events, not the least of which was the unexpected resistance of the Tlingit Indians, whose ancestral grounds they had appropriated by establishing the town of Sitka.

Before the first northward expedition (which got no farther than the Nushagak and Kuskokwim rivers) left Sitka in 1818, an expedition financed by Count Nikolai P. Rumiantsev and commanded by Otto von Kotzebue left Russia to search the Arctic for an all-water passage from the Pacific to the Atlantic. Kotzebue saw the Alaskan coast first near Cape Prince of Wales in July 1816. From three miles away he could see "many jurtes [dwellings] and frames built with whalebones, to dry fish on" and several groups of people admiring the ship "without making the least preparation for coming on board."[1] Sailing north from Cape Prince of Wales, he observed "Many habitations, which cover the coast, [indicating] a numerous population."[2] On 4 July Kotzebue and a number of sailors landed near a village (later named Shishmaref) on the coast north of Wales. All of the dwellings, which were built in a straight row, were deserted, the occupants having fled on sight of the ship; but a lot of fawning, friendly dogs greeted them.

Kotzebue's party entered many of the semisubterranean iglus, which were all built on the same plan, except for one that had two extra side rooms. Each had an earthen-walled entranceway three feet high and two rooms. The first, a storeroom, was ten feet long, seven feet wide, and seven feet high and contained long-handled sieves and pieces of black blubber. The other, a living room, which was entered through a hole only a foot and a half in diameter, was ten feet square and six feet high with ceiling, walls, and floor made of smoothly finished drift logs. Sleeping benches of wide boards had been installed a foot and a half above the floor opposite the entry; small shelves had been placed on the side walls; and a piece of translucent gutskin served as a window at the highest point of the ceiling.

Soon after leaving the village, Kotzebue discovered he was on an island (named after Gavriil Sarychev, by then the vice-admiral of Russia), and his hopes of sailing to the Atlantic were raised by seeing an inlet (named Shishmaref after Gleb Shishmarev, his lieutenant) stretching eastward to the horizon, especially when an umiak with black sails entered from the southwest and disappeared in the east.

The Shishmaref Eskimos had their first, and not entirely auspicious, encounter with Europeans shortly after Kotzebue began exploring the inlet. As the two foreign boats drew up at the north end of the island for lunch, two Eskimo men clad in gutskin parkas swiftly paddled their kayaks from the opposite shore to "within fifty paces," stopped, and began to count them. They could not be persuaded to come ashore, but did not keep out of range of gunshot. After they had observed them for some time "they threw two darts

1. Kotzebue 1821b, 1:198.
2. Ibid., p. 199.

towards their habitations, probably a signal agreed upon; but we continued our course to the east."[3]

Kotzebue returned to the ship after a brief exploration, followed by twenty Eskimos in two umiaks rowing "with all their might" to overtake them. Kotzebue said that the men were dressed in short shirts of caribou and dog skins, but some were half naked. All wore labrets and had their hair cut short. They were well armed, and the men in one of the umiaks tried to seize Kotzebue's boat, and with "piercing cries, and hideous grimaces, they threatened us with their lances." Kotzebue threatened to fire his gun, pointing first at one, and then another, but they laughed, being unacquainted with firearms. Only when the Russians drew their sabers did they draw back. They then followed them to the *Rurik*, "behaving submissively and amicably," but would not go aboard.[4]

The notes made by Ludovik Choris, artist of the expedition, described their material possessions in more detail than did Kotzebue's: arrows with flint and ivory points; Russian lances with iron tips; large Chinese blue and white beads. They had the same kinds of furs to trade as at Billings' time. They were reluctant to sell their weapons, but took off their clothing for tobacco because "it was what they liked best."[5]

Northward from Cape Prince of Wales the coast appeared to be very much inhabited, and when Kotzebue went ashore—apparently near the east end of Cape Espenberg—to investigate the direction of the coast, he saw five umiaks with fifty men coming from the east.[6] "At the head of each boat was a fox-skin, on a high pole, with which they beckoned to us, uttering, at the same time, the loudest cries." Soon the men, armed with lances and bows and arrows, landed and sat down on the ground in a large circle, "two chiefs [seating] themselves apart from the rest." Kotzebue and his men were armed with guns and swords, but the Eskimos had left their weapons in the boats. They had, however, concealed knives in their sleeves, and "they spoke very much, but, unfortunately, we did not understand a word."

To demonstrate his friendship, Kotzebue distributed tobacco (although Choris said that they specifically asked for it),[7] and "the chiefs received a double portion," which they smoked in small wooden pipes with stone bowls. Kotzebue also gave the two chiefs knives and scissors, a new and curious tool, every man snipping his locks as it went round the circle. They were dressed like the Shishmaref Inlet men, and some were barefooted.

More umiaks approached from the west, making "forty of their boats, each

3. Ibid., p. 203.

4. Ibid., pp. 204–5.

5. VanStone 1960, pp. 147–48. James W. VanStone has translated from the original French the parts of the Choris account concerning the North.

6. Kotzebue 1821b, 1:206. Information concerning Cape Espenberg (except that quoted from VanStone's translation of Choris) is taken from ibid., pp. 208–11.

7. VanStone 1960, p. 148.

of which contained about a dozen or twenty of their men, rowing from all sides toward us." They would not board the ship, but wanted to trade black fox skins, which Kotzebue was unable to buy because he could not meet the price of a two-foot long knife made especially for the Siberian trade. They would not sell their skins for less, yet traded "many trifles of their workmanship" for "knives, looking-glasses, tobacco, &c" with such glee and joking that Kotzebue could not believe that these men and women were "the serious inhabitants of the north." Choris, however, interpreting their trade a little differently, said that they showed no inclination to trade: "They took willingly the objects we offered them, but wished to give nothing in return." Kotzebue, becoming annoyed by their "ambiguous attitude," fired a cannon. They fell to the bottom of the boats, and when they got up, invited them to the beach, "promising us some women."[8]

Kotzebue said that the "Americans" or "Indians," as he called them, were "infinitely happy when they fancy they have cheated any body," and because they never laid aside their "lances, bows, arrows, and a knife, two feet long in a sheath [it] proves that they are in constant wars with other nations." He had learned in Siberia that

the Tschukutskoi live in eternal enmity with the Americans; and my venerable guest [a Chukchi] without hesitation, declared them all to be bad men. As a proof of his assertion, he said, that they behaved friendly as long as they considered themselves weaker, but robbed and murdered strangers without hesitation, if they were strong enough, and were able to do it without danger; and, for this reason, he thought they wore knives in their sleeves, and use their wives to entice them. They immediately recognized several portraits, which M. Choris had taken on the American coast, by the bones [labrets] below the under lip; and one of my guests cried with vivacity, drawing his knife, "If I meet such a fellow with two bones, I shall pierce him through."

Yet Choris said that they "learned that often the inhabitants of the American coast, on Bering Strait, go to trade as far as the Kolyma."[9]

Kotzebue sailed toward the east to what he hoped was a passage to the Atlantic Ocean, but in the early part of August concluded that there were no openings in that direction.

Kotzebue resigned himself to the disappointment that he had not, after all, found the northern water route, and turned his attention to exploring the northern coast of Seward Peninsula. On 10 August he sailed out of Eschscholtz Bay and anchored about ten miles northeast of the present town of Deering where eight Eskimos in an umiak (" among whom was one whom we thought we had seen before") visited the ship, but they were apprehensive and would not go aboard, being "constantly prepared for flight." Kotzebue said that in trading the Eskimos treated them contemptuously, "offering us little rags of rats' and dogs' skin in exchange." When the Russians laughed at

8. Ibid.
9. Kotzebue 1821b, 1:262; VanStone 1960, p. 148.

such goods, the Eskimos finally advised them "to put the rags in our noses and ears."[10]

Kotzebue sailed toward the southwest, and came to a headland that looked like an entrance to a bay, but upon learning that it was only an irregularity in the coastline he called it Cape Deceit, a name that acquired a double meaning when more Eskimos arrived in umiaks to trade with "readiness . . . in cheating." This time the Eskimos were accompanied by two young girls who wore glass beads in their ears and thick rings of iron and copper on their arms. The occupants of one of the boats, which had a black eagle skin hung on a pole, sang to the accompaniment of a tambourine. The people wanted only to trade large beads for cutlasses, which Kotzebue did not have. "Perceiving that we did not have much to their liking, and that we eagerly desired their clothing, their ornaments, and their weapons, they would not sell us furs, and brought us all sorts of objects sculptured from walrus teeth, and pieces of these teeth on which they had drawn designs." Choris illustrated these pieces of engraved ivory, which are the first known ethnological examples of this kind of art.[11]

On 12 August Kotzebue and his men landed on a point near the broad estuary of a river flowing from the west (probably the Nugnugaluktuk River) where they met two Eskimos, an "elderly man" of about forty and a boy of sixteen, armed with spears and bows and arrows.[12] Though well dressed in lightweight skin clothing, they were barefooted. When they saw that Kotzebue's men were armed, they walked to a hill, drew their bows, and the man "called out something to us in a roaring voice." Kotzebue put down his arms and walked alone to meet them, whereupon the Eskimos immediately did likewise. Kotzebue and the man embraced, rubbing "our noses frequently together"; but when Kotzebue asked several of his men to approach, the man again took his stand with bow and arrow, and "roared as before."

Shishmarev, unarmed, had joined Kotzebue, and they were invited into the conical walrus-skin tent. There were skins piled on the ground, weapons, baleen fishing lines, a boat, clothes, and earthen pots.[13] The young boy eagerly provided Eskimo names for objects when he saw Kotzebue taking notes, but the woman was interested only in Kotzebue's buttons and tried secretly to twist them off. Not succeeding, she sent her two young children to try to bite them off. "To save my buttons, I gave her a looking-glass."[14]

The father presented a "martin's skin" to both Kotzebue and Shishmarev, who reciprocated with gifts, including tobacco. Kotzebue's immediate con-

10. Kotzebue 1821b, 1:222.
11. VanStone 1960, pp. 149, 150; Choris 1822, pl. 4. So far as is known, Cook and Billings did not collect engraved pieces in 1778 and 1791. The history and development of Alaskan Eskimo graphic art, including ivory engraving, is discussed in Ray 1969.
12. Unless otherwise indicated, information about the Eskimos encountered at the Nugnugaluktuk River and Cape Espenberg on 12 and 13 August is from Kotzebue 1821b, 1:225–36.
13. VanStone 1960, p. 149.
14. Kotzebue 1821b, 1:226.

cern was to find out how long the river was and if it connected with water to the south. In answer, the man seated himself on the ground and "rowed eagerly with his arms; this business he interrupted nine times, closing his eyes as many times, and resting his head on his hand. I learnt by this, that it would take nine days to get to the open sea through this branch." This information, of course, was false.

Father and son walked arm-in-arm with Kotzebue to the boats, "laughing and joking [which] appeared to me to be rather forced, on the part of the savages." When Kotzebue asked where they got their European goods, the man pointed to the entrance of the sound "where people came to them in boats, who gave them the beads, tobacco, and also wood for making their bows and arrows, in exchange for furs and ready-made articles of dress." The Eskimo then proceeded to show in pantomime how they conducted their trading:

He knew very well how to instruct me in their manner of dealing: the stranger first comes, and lays some goods on the shore, and then retires; the American comes, looks at the things, puts as many skins near them as he thinks proper to give, and then also goes away. Upon this the stranger approaches, and examines what is offered him; if he is satisfied with it, he takes the skins, and leaves his goods instead; but, if not, then he lets all the things lie, retires a second time, and expects an addition from the buyer. In this manner the dealing seems to me to continue without speaking, and there is no doubt but the Tschukutskoi obtain here the skins for the Russian trade.

On their way to the boats they saw a large squirrel called "Tschikschi" (*siksik*) which the man caught on the run. He brought it "triumphantly to us, and laughed heartily at our unskilfulness." Kotzebue took advantage of the man's exuberance to see what effect the shooting of a gun would have. The reactions to the killing of a snipe were all that he had anticipated: astonishment, fright, and discomposure. As soon as the older man had regained his wits and decided not to flee, he promptly divested himself of a musket he had been carrying for one of the sailors and would not touch the dead snipe, which, Kotzebue said, "had inspired him with the greatest respect for the terrible instrument."

Back at the boats, Choris was sketching portraits, and when Kotzebue and the Eskimos returned, he quickly drew one of the father, causing his son to hold "his sides with laughter when he saw his father's face drawn in the book." At lunch, the Eskimos admired everything, particularly the plates, knives, and forks, but saved their meat and biscuits to take home. As soon as Kotzebue and his men left to explore the wide estuary, the "Americans, who remained on shore, staid a long time in the place where we had dined, and we saw them busily looking about, in the hope of finding something that we might have left that could be of any value to them."

Kotzebue tried for several hours to enter the river, but "in vain, as we every moment ran upon shoals." He landed once again near the Eskimos' tent to give his tired sailors a rest, but the Eskimos, repenting too intimate an association with the strangers, hastily packed their tent and belongings into their skin boat and moved to the opposite shore. Toward evening, Kotzebue's "agreeable repose" was broken by a sentinel announcing that eight umiaks, each with twelve men, were coming from Cape Deceit. The umiaks drew up on shore, and the men built several driftwood fires, letting their dogs ("of which they had many") run loose on shore. Kotzebue decided to return to the *Rurik*, anchored about six miles south of Cape Espenberg, since he felt he was outnumbered with his fourteen men. As soon as the sailors had had a few hours' rest, they returned to the ship under cover of darkness as the "savages sat round their fire crying out and beating their drum."

They were at the ship only a short time, however, when two umiaks arrived, and the occupants tried "to cheat us every way in the sale of some of their small works, and laughed heartily when they could not succeed. They have probably learnt the common rule in trade, to show the worst goods first, from the Tschukutskoi, as the latter from the Russian merchants." When Kotzebue would not buy their trinkets, they brought out black fox skins from the umiak but, as before, would not trade for anything less than the long large knives that Kotzebue could not provide. In their umiak Kotzebue recognized an iron lance as the kind manufactured in Siberia for trade only with the Chukchi. For the first and only time during the voyage in the North, a man climbed aboard the *Rurik*. He was "a robust young man, whom I took to be the chief, as all his commands were punctually obeyed."

At Kotzebue's request this man drew the nearby cape on a slate, which he "represented as a bending point of land. Upon this he drew a number of habitations, which he called Kegi [at Cape Espenberg, possibly a variant of *kikiktuk*, or island] whither he, in a friendly manner, invited us." Upon returning to his skin boat, the man and his companions had dinner of a freshly killed seal. After cutting "open its belly, . . . one after the other put in his head and sucked out the blood. After they had sufficiently drunk in this manner, each cut himself off a piece of flesh, which they devoured with the greatest appetite, and it may easily be imagined how their naturally frightful countenance looked after such a repast."

Kotzebue named the bay "Good Hope, as I might really hope to make a very remarkable discovery here" during the following year's explorations, and on 13 August 1816 he gave the large sound his own name in "compliance with the general wish of my companions. . . . Inconsiderable as the discovery of this sound may be, it is an acquisition to geography, and may serve the world as a proof of my zeal; for, in truth, even Cook has treated this coast rather negligently."[15]

Kotzebue planned to return north the following year after spending the

---

15. Ibid., p. 238. Choris said, "The Captain gave his name to the gulf that we had just traversed" (VanStone 1960, p. 149). Kotzebue named Cape Espenberg after a friend who had cruised round the world with Captain Krusenstern, whose name he gave to the northern cape of the sound.

winter in San Francisco, but ice blocked his way into Bering Strait as far as the eye could see as late as 10 July 1817. In addition, he was suffering from a lung disorder, and he therefore decided to abandon his search for a water route from the Pacific to the Atlantic.

His sponsors were convinced that the journey had been a near failure: he not only had curtailed his first year's explorations but had abandoned those of the second. Yet he had made valuable observations of the fur trade on Seward Peninsula and he suggested that the Russian government establish a series of trading stations north of Bering Strait, for he predicted that the Hudson's Bay Company would soon branch out from Canada to the Bering Strait.

CHAPTER 6

Russian Explorations, 1820–22

RUSSIAN explorations between 1820 and 1850 were prompted to some extent by English traders and overland explorers coming from the east, about whom Kotzebue had warned as early as 1816. Competition with British ships on the seas of southeast Alaska had long been formidable for the Russians, but the successful inland enterprises of the Hudson's Bay Company and the North West Company by the end of the eighteenth century also posed increasing problems as they moved west across Canada.

Shortly after 1790 the North West Company established posts on the Mackenzie River, which Alexander Mackenzie had discovered in 1789 while searching for a water route to the northwest Pacific Ocean and Cook Inlet. In 1805 and 1806 the company established trading posts in the vicinity of Peace River on McLeod, Stuart, and Fraser lakes.[1] In 1821 the North West Company and the Hudson's Bay Company united under the latter's name, and established Fort Stikeen in southeast Alaska in 1840 and a post at Lapierre House on the Rat River in 1847. Lapierre House was only a few miles from the headwaters of the Porcupine River, a tributary of the Yukon, but this relationship was not discovered until 1851, eighteen years after the founding of Saint Michael in Alaska near the mouth of the Yukon.

Trading by foreigners in Alaskan waters was a constant worry to the Russians who were distressed both by the tremendous volume of barter between foreigners and natives—an average of fifteen foreign ships a year took from ten thousand to fifteen thousand sea otter skins before 1821[2]—and by the unfair advantage that the superior English and American trade goods had over the Russian. Vasilii M. Golovnin, who was sent to Alaska in 1818 to investigate the condition of the Russian-American Company, reported that English and American trade was considerably detrimental to the company's finances.[3]

1. Innis 1956, p. 204.
2. Okun 1951, pp. 74–75.
3. Ibid., p. 78.

Golovnin's report of 1819 about foreign trading in Alaska was widely read, and in 1820 resulted in the company's prohibiting its American agents from trading with British and American ships.[4] In 1821 it was stipulated that foreign ships cruising within 100 Italian miles (115 English miles) off the shores of Russian America north of 50° north latitude (which also included Siberia) would be confiscated by a Russian warship. With this ukase Russia affirmed its claim to Russian America in terms of exclusive occupancy of both land and sea. Great Britain and the United States protested the ukase and were unwilling to recognize Russia's claim to territory that was becoming increasingly important to both. One of the principal purposes of the edict was to keep out those foreigners who were poaching on Russian domain. Even before official protestations were brought by England and the United States, however, Alaskan agents of the Russian-American Company had decided that the restrictions were ridiculous and unfavorable to the company because the foreigners not only were trading extensively with the Indians on the sly but were unable to bring goods that were sorely needed by the Russians for their own use and as Indian trade goods.

In 1824 a treaty between Russia and the United States set the southern boundary of Russian territory at 54° 40′ north latitude and provided a ten-year period of unrestricted freedom for each to fish and to trade—except liquor and firearms—with natives in the other's territorial waters. Pessimists in the Russian government predicted that the granting of unrestricted movements to the United States in all parts of Russian America would toll the end to Russia's power.

In the early 1820s the Russian-American Company in Alaska and the imperial government of Russia made plans to increase their knowledge of resources and geography north of the Aleutians both by land and by sea. The company wanted to enlarge its trading territory in order to gain renewal of its charter, which expired in 1819. By 1818, when Petr Korsakovskii (or Korsanovskii) was sent by the Russian-American Company to establish a redoubt on the Nushagak River and to look for the Russians on the "Kheuveren" River, northern geography was still largely unknown except for Captain Cook's diagrammatic outline of the coast, Kobelev's map of Seward Peninsula, and Kotzebue's discovery of a few bays and inlets.[5] Europeans had not yet seen the Kobuk, the Kuskokwim, the Noatak, or the Yukon rivers, so it is not surprising that Korsakovskii was unable to learn anything about the Kheuveren (Kuzitrin), 500 miles from the Nushagak.

In 1819 the Imperial Navy, independently of the Russian-American Company, undertook further northern explorations primarily to search for the northwest passage. Four ships left Kronstadt on the Gulf of Finland to participate in one of Russia's most ambitious exploring expeditions. Two of

4. Ibid., p. 82.
5. Information about Korsakovskii's expedition is found in Tikhmenev 1939–40, 1:306, and Berkh 1823b, pp. 20–24.

the ships, the *East* and the *Peaceful*, went to the Antarctic; the *Discovery* (*Otkrytie*), under command of Mikhail N. Vasiliev, and the *Good Intent* (*Blagonamerennyi*), under Gleb S. Shishmarev, headed for the north Pacific and the Arctic Ocean, where they explored during the summers of 1820 and 1821.

Also in 1821 the Russian-American Company sent two ships from Sitka, the *Golovin* under command of Vasilii S. Khromchenko and the *Baranov* under Adolf Etolin, to investigate the Bering Sea and coast northward to ascertain native trade routes across the strait. In addition, a fifth vessel, a small boat that had been built for Vasiliev in Sitka the previous winter, joined the four other ships. In 1821 the sailings of the five kept them in almost constant view of western Alaskan Eskimos as they ranged from Siberia to the far north of Alaska beyond Icy Cape; discovered Cape Romanzof, Golovnin Bay, and Nunivak Island, and definitely learned of the existence of the Yukon River; completed the surveying of Saint Lawrence Island begun by Kotzebue; discovered Point Hope; and recorded the first use of firearms in northern Alaska. All of these accomplishments—with the exception of the discovery of Golovnin Bay—belonged to Vasiliev and Shishmarev, yet their expedition has scarcely been noticed in Alaskan histories.

One of the principal objectives of the expedition was to find a passage from the Pacific to the Atlantic, but in this endeavor, like Kotzebue in 1816, they failed. Because little has been published in English about this expedition, I have summarized their itinerary from Vasilii Berkh's history and the journals of Midshipman Karl K. Hillsen and Lieutenant Aleksei P. Lazarev of the *Good Intent*. From these sources I have chosen information of importance for the general Bering Strait area, although a large part of their activities occurred on the southern coast of Kotzebue Sound. One of their observations enables us to settle the question of whether the Eskimos of northern Alaska had acquired firearms before the usually accepted date of mid-nineteenth century, when whalers first sailed through Bering Strait. In 1820 the Russians accused the Americans of selling guns to Eskimos, but this charge has been considered a fabrication by American writers. One, geographer Don Charles Foote, has said that there "is no evidence to support this claim." Here, in Hillsen's journal, is the evidence.[6]

6. Berkh 1823b, pp. 4–20. The meeting of the Eskimos near Elephant Point and activities nearby are from Hillsen 1849, 66:226–31, paraphrased from the Russian translation by Josephson and Ray 1971, and from Lazarev 1950, pp. 199–216. See also Ray 1975 for a verbatim account of the encounters near Elephant Point.

In 1886 Bancroft said that "no report of the expedition is extant, but the voyage was continued at least as far as East Cape" (Bancroft 1886, p. 526); yet by that date a number of summaries and the long narrative account of the voyage of the *Good Intent* by Hillsen had been published. No official account ever appeared, possibly because the consensus was that the voyage was a failure, or because the captains were too busy to write anything.

Neither C. L. Andrews nor Clarence Hulley mentions this expedition, and William H. Dall devotes only sixty-two words to it in a chronological listing of events in his history (1870, pp. 331,

SHISHMAREV AT KOTZEBUE SOUND, 1820

The *Good Intent* and the *Discovery* sailed together from Kronstadt until they reached the south Pacific, where they undertook separate courses northward. Arriving at Unalaska on 30 May 1820 (Old Style; twelve days later, New Style), Shishmarev procured four umiaks and six Aleuts from the Russian-American Company, but was unable to get an interpreter acquainted with the northern language. On the nineteenth of June he sailed north to Saint Lawrence Island, and on the thirtieth proceeded to Kotzebue Sound. Near the eastern cape of Saint Lawrence Island, Hillsen said that they saw "hundreds of thousands of walrus" on the edge of the seemingly endless ice floes.

For more than a week the *Good Intent* encountered almost constant fog and ice blocking the entrance to the sound. Finally, said Lazarev, on the evening of 9 July they were able to come close to Cape Espenberg, where forty-eight persons in five umiaks neared the ship to trade furs, but were not brave enough to venture aboard. They were clothed in ground squirrel and muskrat parkas. The men wore labrets, the chiefs having large ones. The Russians tried to buy their weapons, but without success because the Eskimos wanted only to trade fox skins for axes and big knives. Their prices were high, and they tried surreptitiously to substitute an inferior object for one already offered in trade. Not needing furs, the Russians gave them tobacco, to which the Eskimos paid almost no attention.[7]

The ice suddenly moved out of the sound on the tenth, said Hillsen, and they sailed east. By evening, having got only halfway into the sound, they had just dropped anchor when three large skin boats arrived. Their occupants stepped "fearlessly on deck, and traded marten and otter skins for axes, cast iron pots, knives, and needles, but immediately went back without having traded even one tenth of their cargo. They took almost no tobacco and wanted only big knives, guns, powder, and lead, but as it was forbidden to sell them these articles, they stopped trading and returned to shore."[8]

The next day the *Good Intent* anchored on the east side of Chamisso Island. The *Discovery* had not yet arrived; the weather was bleak; they could not undertake astronomical observations; they were terribly bored. Shishmarev proposed that they examine the northeast bay where he had seen "mountains

---

332). A summary of this journey was published in *Zapiski Gidrograficheskago Departamenta* in an account of northern explorations by Ivashintsov (1849, 7:106–16). Shishmarev's observations of the Chukchi during the year 1821 were published in the same journal for 1852. In 1851, Hillsen's account was summarized in *Archiv für Wissenschaftliche Kunde von Russland* (vol. 9, pp. 272–94), and several other short summaries and progress reports were published. According to Golder (1917, p. 125), the journals or logs of both the *Good Intent* and the *Discovery* were located at one time in the Saint Petersburg archives.

The entire expedition, which left Kronstadt together, consisted of Faddeia F. Bellingshausen in the *East* (*Vostok*) and Mikhail P. Lazarev in the *Peaceful* (*Mirny*), which explored the Antarctic when Vasiliev and Shishmarev were in the Arctic.

Foote 1964, p. 17.

7. This trading episode is not mentioned by Hillsen.

8. This trading episode is not mentioned by Lazarev.

of ice" in 1816 (near Elephant Point). Twenty persons left on the morning of 14 July in the sailing tender with provisions for three days, four swivel guns, and a skin boat. Shishmarev had told them that the shore was uninhabited, but to their surprise they saw—near the end of a long sandspit—a large settlement consisting of 101 conical skin tents and, opposite each, an overturned umiak. They were met by about 150 persons who came down to the shore armed from head to foot with bows and arrows, spears, and "even with long rifles." (Lazarev does not mention the guns.) Hillsen said that Shishmarev was undecided whether to go ashore or to return to the *Good Intent*, but the Eskimos, seeing their indecision, began to wave skins and to shout, "toki, toki," which the Russians later learned meant "trade, trade."

Hillsen said that the Eskimos appeared to be overjoyed with their arrival and constantly yelled, "toki! toki!" Trading started immediately. They did not want tobacco or other small things that were valued elsewhere (i.e., in southern Alaska and Siberia), but knives, hatchets, needles, scissors, cooking pots, and especially gunpowder and lead were asked for. Seeing that they could not get the latter, they stopped asking and were satisfied with the regular trade goods, for which they exchanged their weapons, clothing, otter, marten, bear, and fox furs. Generally, their asking prices were very high. (Lazarev does not mention gunpowder or lead. He said that the captain gave tobacco to all. The women shouted "titita, titita" incessantly, and the men tried to buy beads.)

The tribe called itself "Tatui," a word probably related to *tutu*, or caribou, and lived "to the southeast" (i.e., on the Buckland River). Lazarev said there were 200 in the village; Hillsen, 300. As was customary, Shishmarev gave the chief a medal and invited him to eat with him. The Eskimos danced and threw a child up on a skin to the accompaniment of singing.

After dinner, Shishmarev's party prepared to leave but, said Hillsen, they noticed that the Eskimos, who had been armed only with knives after their initial encounter, now had many weapons. They became obstreperous because they did not get powder and lead, and gathered in groups, provoking the sailors. The Russians left, but were forced to return to shore after running into rough weather that broke both masts. The Eskimos, shouting, came down to the shore, apparently to stop them from landing. The Russians ignored them and waved kerchiefs, calling out "toki! toki!" after which the Eskimos quieted down and let them go ashore and put up their tents. Shishmarev ordered the men to give gifts to "the chief and the principal warriors who were easily distinguishable because of the respect paid to them by the rest of the crowd." In vain they asked the Eskimos to return to their own settlement and leave them alone, but they continued to crowd around the tent and to shout, "toki! toki!" and even began pilfering things like the cover of a copper kettle and a long kitchen knife.

After several unpleasant altercations with the Eskimos during the night, the Russians left again, and were not far from shore when the Eskimos reappeared and shot a whole cloud of arrows at them, which did not cause any harm because they covered themselves with walrus skins. The Russians did not return the fire; they wanted only to get away from the arrows. "But," said Hillsen, "when they started to shoot guns, and the bullets began piercing the skins, the captain ordered us to fire a falconet ball over their heads. Hearing the whistle of the ball, they quieted down for an instant, but soon, raising a horrible cry, shot arrows and bullets at us again, and dashed toward their baidars, pushing them into the water in order to pursue us. Then the captain ordered us to aim the falconet at the largest of them. The cannon fired, and the ball ripped out the entire side of the baidar wounding one man." With that, the Eskimos abandoned further attempts to attack and returned to their settlement.

On 16 July the Russians saw the *Discovery*, which had been at Petropavlovsk until 21 June, near the outer edge of Kotzebue Sound. On 27 June the *Discovery* had met an American brig, the *Pedler*, near Saint Lawrence Island.[9] As if following the *Discovery*, the *Pedler* anchored in Kotzebue Sound on the sixteenth, and the captain, "Pigot" (William J. Pigot), went aboard the Russian ship, explaining that he had come from the Hawaiian Islands to trade furs with the natives. Shishmarev told him that he should go to the smaller part of the bay (i.e., to the east) to trade, but warned him not to go ashore and to take precautions when the Eskimos came on the brig, because the people were "crafty and angry." Shishmarev's men told him about their recent unfortunate adventures and "advised him of the principal article [i.e., firearms] they required." Nine months later they met Pigot at Oahu Island and learned that his trading had been successful.

Lazarev said that the brig with thirty men had come to trade "furs, leather, sables, rifles, and so on" with the inhabitants and, with reluctant admiration, admitted that the Americans materialized on the scene with trade goods almost immediately after a new geographical discovery had been made.

On 18 July the *Discovery* and the *Good Intent* sailed past Cape Krusenstern as far north as Icy Cape, where they were turned back by ice. On 2 August they surveyed 90 miles around a cape that Vasiliev named Golovnin after the famous navigator, Vasilii M. Golovnin, but which Beechey afterward changed to Point Hope. Both ships headed south to spend the winter in California and Hawaii. Shishmarev surveyed Saint Lawrence Island, and Vasiliev left a precut boat in Sitka to be assembled under the direction of Lieutenant Ivan Ignatiev the next year.

VOYAGES OF AVINOV, ETOLIN, KHROMCHENKO,
SHISHMAREV, AND VASILIEV IN 1821

The *Good Intent* and the *Discovery* returned to Sitka from the south in the spring of 1821 and on 30 May, with the newly built boat in tow behind the *Discovery*, went to Unalaska. The *Good Intent* then sailed to the Siberian coast,

9. Lazarev 1950, p. 214.

and the *Discovery* towed the new boat to Cape Newenham, where Vasiliev placed Lieutenant Aleksandr Avinov in charge. He directed Avinov to explore the coast as far north as Cape Darby and to rendezvous with the *Discovery* by 20 July at Stuart Island; but circumstances compelled Avinov to go instead to Petropavlovsk.

Shishmarev's explorations in 1821 in the *Good Intent* were almost entirely confined to the coast of Asia and Saint Lawrence Island, although on 4 July, on his way northward along the American coast, he discovered, but did not name, Cape Romanzof. This point of land was sighted and named thirty-eight days later by Etolin.[10] After leaving Cape Romanzof, he touched at only one other place on the American coast, at about 67° 34' north latitude (near Cape Mulgrave) to get wood and water. On 21 September he ended his Arctic voyage at Petropavlovsk.

Vasiliev had in the meantime discovered Nunivak Island on 11 July, naming it "Discovery Island" after his ship. Not finding Avinov at Cape Darby, he sailed north to Cape Lisburne, across the ocean to Asia, back to Lisburne, and south through Bering Strait, where he met Shishmarev near the Diomede Islands on 11 August.[11]

After this meeting, Vasiliev sailed again to Cape Darby and still not finding Avinov (who had sailed to Kamchatka because of troubles with the boat and crew), proceeded to Stuart Island, where he sent Lieutenant Roman Boil ashore for information. This represented the first personal encounter with people who were from the Stebbins area. The Eskimos said they had seen no foreign ships, but told him about a large river called the Kuiukht-pak (the Yukon) located south of the cape.[12] On 8 September Vasiliev returned to Petropavlovsk via Saint Lawrence Island. In 1822 both the *Discovery* and *Good Intent* sailed home to Kronstadt via the Hawaiian Islands.

Meanwhile, the Russian-American Company expeditions were carrying out their orders. Etolin preceded Khromchenko to Hagemeister Island by about a month, having surveyed the vicinity and the mouth of the Nushagak River.[13] After 1 July both Khromchenko and Etolin sailed to Stuart Island, where Khromchenko found himself in dangerously shallow water caused by the discharge of a large river,[14] and for the second time in two months Russian navigators became aware of the Yukon.

Khromchenko sailed north and on 22 July discovered a bay west of Cape Darby called "Tachik" by the natives. On this first visit of Europeans to this body of water, now called Golovnin Bay, five umiaks approached the ship soon after it had cast anchor.[15] "With them in a baidar were Americans who,

10. Berkh 1823b, pp. 16, 48.
11. Ibid., pp. 12–14; Hillsen 1849, 67:232.
12. Berkh 1823b, p. 14.
13. Ibid., p. 45.
14. Ibid., pp. 51–52.
15. Khromchenko intended to name the bay after M. I. Muraviev, manager of the Russian-American Company; but Muraviev himself later requested it be named for Golovnin.

although they resembled them in features and clothing, had a different language." The inhabitants living on the bay told the Russian interpreters that these people had come from the west for purposes of trade and were returning home the next day. These "Asiagmutes," or Sledge Islanders, departed with skins hung up around the sides of their skinboats "probably against drafts." Khromchenko sailed to Norton Bay, where he cast anchor two miles from land. Vasilii Berkh, who has given us the only account of this voyage, said that Khromchenko went ashore and was given "detailed information concerning the position of the shores," but he does not tell us what it was. Khromchenko then inspected the coast from Shaktoolik Bay to Cape Stephens, but not meeting any inhabitants, sailed back to Golovnin Bay.[16]

Taking advantage of pleasant weather at that time (around 27 July), he explored the part now called Golovnin Lagoon and discovered a large river with five outlets, or what is now called the Fish River. According to Berkh, the inhabitants said that Tachik was connected with Shishmaref Inlet by a continuous waterway, which took five days to navigate. In 1821 Khromchenko probably recorded this erroneous information—which was subsequently placed on many maps—but he clearly explained in his account of his next year's explorations, published in 1824, that it was necessary to portage between two rivers: "The Kveigat Tuksmuk [Niukluk River? Tuksuk?] approaches at its source to another river that flows into the sea and they called this river Kaviiaiak [Kauwerak]. The crossing from one river to the other, [the Eskimos] said, is rather difficult since at this place there is a mountain, Kinkhtyriuk, but it is not that steep, so travelers always carry baidars and baidarkas over it."[17]

On 10 August 1821 Khromchenko left Golovnin Bay for Sitka via Cape Romanzov, Nunivak Island, and Unalaska.[18]

KHROMCHENKO AT STUART ISLAND AND GOLOVNIN BAY, 1822

The next year, 1822, Khromchenko and Etolin sailed north together from Sitka in the *Golovnin* (or the *Golovin*) to continue the work of 1821.[19] They visited the Nushagak River and Hagemeister Island, and then proceeded north to Norton Sound and Stuart Island, where they anchored near a small river in the vicinity of its northeast cape.[20] Etolin and Khromchenko went ashore in umiaks and landed at a settlement not far away. Kayaks soon appeared from the east (probably from Cape Stephens). They approached

---

16. Berkh 1823b, p. 53.

17. Khromchenko 1824, pt. 11, p. 247.

18. Information about Etolin and Khromchenko in 1821 is taken from Berkh 1823b, pp. 45, 46, 47, 49, 52–57.

19. Berkh (1823b, p. 45) and Bancroft (1886, p. 546) spell the name of the vessel *Golovnin*; Hillsen (67:225–26) and Khromchenko (pt. 10, p. 265) spell it *Golovin*.

20. The material that follows is paraphrased from my translation of Khromchenko's narrative, pt. 10, pp. 177–85, 240–42. This has been translated by VanStone, ed. (1973).

slowly and cautiously and, though reassured by the Russians' greeting, looked at them in complete silence for a long time and would not answer their questions after they neared the shore. Finally a man asked them where they had come from, and why? The answers given by the Russians satisfied them and they began trading furs, but asked very high prices.

One of the old men gave Khromchenko information about Stuart Island or "Kikh-takh-pak" (i.e., "big island") and in the sand drew a map of the mainland shore that extended from this island to a little south of the "Kuikhpag" ("big river," or the Yukon). He also told the Russians he had received a kitchen knife from a three-masted ship, probably the *Discovery*, the summer before, when the captain made inquiries about a one-masted ship.

After the Russians had returned to the brig, they were visited by thirty-five kayaks. Over their squirrel parkas these Eskimos wore two whale gutskin parkas, which also served as hatch covers for the kayaks in bad weather. The Russians had met some of the men in the kayaks the year before. One made a long speech, and the others stroked their heads, faces, and chests with their hands, then turned their palms up and extended their arms toward them, "showing by that that they were as peaceful as we."

Most of the people were from "Tauk" (Atuik, near present-day Stebbins), southeast of the ship. They began to trade beaver, fox, and otter furs for iron knives, kettles, pewter pipes, and Cherkassy tobacco, "often reproaching us that we were paying them less for the furs than the Aziagmuts."

About midnight the trading stopped and the "Kikh-takh-pagtzis" went to their settlement and built a number of fires along the shore at the water's edge, which Khromchenko thought were for fishing. The mainlanders went into the strait (probably Stephens Pass), saying that they would return the next day at dawn.

At five in the morning the Russians were again surrounded by "a few Americans" who asked them to go ashore. Khromchenko sent some sailors with his clerk Karsanovskii, and went himself in the afternoon. His old acquaintances came down to meet him, but others sat in scattered groups, sorting their trade goods and paying no attention to him. Through sign language the Eskimos complained that they were unable to get tobacco for their pipes, and Khromchenko distributed a few tobacco leaves to get rid of them. Instead of leaving, however, they sat down nearby on the ground for a smoke. Every woman had tinder and flint, which he learned was procured from the Sledge Islanders.

Because Khromchenko could not see any differences in the dress, physical characteristics, or language of the inhabitants of Stuart Island and of those living on the opposite shore, he concluded that all were from the same area on the mainland and used Stuart Island only seasonally. On the island at that time there were about two hundred persons, equally divided between men and women.

These people appeared generally to have a weak constitution and a dried-up look, which he attributed either to a lack of food or to excessive smoking of tobacco. Khromchenko reported syphilis for the first time on the shores of northern Alaska (unless the crippled youth seen by Cook's expedition had also been a victim) and said that it had developed to such an extent that many persons were disfigured and had deep ulcers covering their faces and bodies. He concluded that women were more severely infected than men because more of them had their noses eaten away. Khromchenko thought that the people took advice from shamans, who treated their various ailments, because he did not see a single chief.

Their parkas were made of ground squirrel and caribou fawn skin, and men's breeches were of sealskin, the women's, of bird skins. Footwear consisted mostly of Chukchi reindeer skin boots, which they bought from Sledge Islanders. Young men and women wore beads of various colors and blue trade beads around their necks, and women wore several iron and copper bracelets. The men cut their hair short, and the women had two pigtails, rubbed well with fat, over their temples. Men wore labrets of blue beads or polished stones, and both women and men had pierced ears, the men wearing bones, beads, and leather bands instead of earrings.

In the summer the people dried large quantities of fish, and in the fall they killed deer (caribou), trading the skins to the Sledge Islanders. There were many indications that caribou lived on Stuart Island itself. The people had pewter pipes for smoking, knives, some tobacco, and glass labrets. Khromchenko said that "women are complete slaves of men; they attend to the most difficult jobs, prepare food for winter, during travels carry heavy burdens or serve as oarsmen in baidarkas; build dwellings, and so on."

As soon as the bad weather moderated, Karsanovskii took a census of Tauk, finding many dogs, tents, and sleds on the beach. There were forty "yurts" (dwellings) of various sizes, and about two hundred persons, probably the same ones they had seen on Stuart Island, since Khromchenko said that all of the people had left the island shortly before Karsanovskii went to the village.

On 5 August Khromchenko sailed to Golovnin Bay, casting anchor six miles from "Chinik settlement" (now the village of Golovin). The next day, two kayaks with two old acquaintances from the year before, Chikun and Taipa, came from "Uzhigalit settlement" (a name unrecognized by Eskimos today, but possibly a camp called Igluchauik). The two men climbed aboard immediately and were overjoyed to learn they could get tobacco and pipes. They came up to each sailor, repeating "Kuianna—Kuianna," which Khromchenko erroneously interpreted as meaning "our friends, our friends"; it means "thank you, thank you."[21]

Soon after, Chief Chavysmiak arrived in a skin boat with seven men and two women. "The Americans who were with us told their countrymen all

21. Information about Golovnin Bay is taken from Khromchenko 1824, pt. 10, pp. 242–47, 297–311.

that they could learn from us, and hugged each other for joy, shouting every minute, Kuianna!" The silver medal that Khromchenko had given Chavys-miak the year before was now the property of his son, but he showed Khromchenko a bronze one that he had received from the commander of a three-masted vessel (probably the *Discovery*) in 1821 at Cape Darby four days after Khromchenko had left.

The Eskimos remained aboard until sunset. The following day at sunrise, two large and twelve single-hatched "baidars," carrying a total of thirty-two men and women, again surrounded the ship. "Americans acquainted with us came aboard; they were subsequently agents of their countrymen in trade." As soon as trading began, Khromchenko went to Uzhigalit to buy fresh and dried fish for needles and tobacco, and found that the wood they had chopped the year before lay there untouched.

On a second trip to Uzhigalit with Karsanovskii, Khromchenko "stopped near rocks located across from Uzhigalit. It is impossible to express the joy with which the Americans met us. The words, 'Kashat Kuianna,' were repeated many times by the crowd of this savage people; many pushing each other, ran toward our baidarkas and with all possible care carried them out of the water." Finally, the Eskimos quieted down and dispersed into groups. The women, who were preparing supper, did not participate in the conversations. Karsanovskii began to trade, and Khromchenko went with Eskimos to nearby lakes to hunt waterfowl. But after Khromchenko had shot a snipe, the natives, unacquainted with firearms, would not approach him, and they remained silent even after he called out to reassure them.

Meanwhile, Karsanovskii had received information about two Russians, "Vasiliev and Vorobiev," from a man named Tungan, and though it was growing late, Khromchenko wanted to remain ashore to learn more about them. Tungan was reluctant to repeat his stories, pleading a very bad pain in his eyes; but finally he was persuaded to explain how he had met the men. During a trip from "Nikhta" (Kingigan) at Cape Prince of Wales to Golovnin Bay, he was carried out to the open sea in his kayak during a sudden storm. Three nights later he arrived in an unknown land called "Chuakak" (Saint Lawrence Island). The inhabitants received him hospitably, and he lived there for a very long time—for how many years, he did not know. The inhabitants were poor and ate the meat of whales and walrus and traded their skins to a neighboring land called "Kuslit" (Siberia), situated a night's ride from the western end of the island.

Tungan located all of the places on a map in the sand. First, he drew the American shores from Golovnin Bay to Bering Strait; then, the islands "Aziiak" (Ayak, or Sledge Island) and "Ukivok" (King Island), where the people lived "on completely steep rocks and mostly occupied by trading furs with people who live on Kuslit land." He drew the islands in the strait and the opposite cape and northward. Opposite Ukivok he drew the "Kavsiak" (Kuzitrin) River, which, he said, the King Islanders often visited. In the fall they traveled occasionally to Golovnin Bay. He then drew the coast of Siberia (Kuslit land), where he had met Vasiliev and Vorobiev; as proof, he repeated words that he had often heard them speak, including "some swear words, which are used by our [Russian] common people." Returning from Siberia with King Islanders, Tungan proceeded homeward through a pass that separated the headwaters of the Kuzitrin and the Niukluk, over which two other men, Nuksiuk and Abysk, had recently traveled.[22]

On the next day, Tungan went to Khromchenko's ship and drew his sand map on paper. Khromchenko gave him a silver medal. Tungan asked for traps, explaining that he would teach his people how to use them, because he had seen them used many times by Vasiliev and Vorobiev and knew how to set them with care. Khromchenko did not say whether or not he complied with his request.[23]

Tungan was very curious about Russia. He asked whether "many people were left there, and who governs there?" He wanted a drawing of each new foreign land that he was told about, and Khromchenko said that he "asked me for a piece of paper and he drew on it all those distant lands according to what I told him, and he kept asking, is this right? He then spoke at length to his people, and finally said, 'See how many people, besides us, live in this land!'"

After the Eskimos had left the ship, Etolin and Khromchenko set out for Rocky Cape, passing many platforms covered with drying fish. After meeting Karsanovskii and the Aleuts, they stopped at a small settlement where Chavysmiak lived in a dwelling situated about 350 feet from the water. The Russians were treated to whale meat and cooked fish, "but due to the awful smell, none of us would try it except the Aleuts who considered it a great delicacy." Then the Eskimos presented a dance, which Chavysmiak said was usually performed only on ceremonial occasions. The Russians thought the dancing monotonous and the singing rough, repetitive, and unpleasant to the ear. The dance began with the following pantomine: "First, men formed a circle, then one of them beat a tambourine and started to sing in a mournful voice. Another stepped into the middle, leaning forward somewhat; with every gesture he stamped his foot and looked in all directions as if apprehensive, and stealthily drew a bow and shot an arrow. All this was repeated in the same sequence four or more times, always accompanied by a few words pronounced in a frightened voice." After the dancing, the Eskimos showed them how they turned over in their kayaks, a skill they had practiced from early childhood.

22. This route was probably over Mosquito Pass (Eskimo name, Ukinaruk) between the headwaters of the Niukluk River and Belt Creek, a tributary of the Kuzitrin. I think that the river "Tuksmuk" refers to the Niukluk—it can be no other—but Khromchenko attached the wrong name to it, for I have never heard of any other name but Niukluk for this river. He may have got the name confused in his notes with Tuksuk, a well-known river between Imuruk Basin and Grantley Harbor. In Russian script, the "t" looks like an "m."

23. Khromchenko 1824, pt. 11, pp. 55, 56, 57.

Here Khromchenko saw a young girl, not ten years old, who already had a husband, twenty. "When I asked why such a young girl was already married, her mother answered that if she had no husband at her age, everyone would laugh at her, and she would later be scorned by all."

At this point Khromchenko ended his narrative, but Berkh wrote that he left Golovnin Bay on 10 August, went to Saint George Island via Cape Romanzof and Nunivak Island, and reached Sitka on 7 September.[24]

24. Berkh 1823b, pp. 55–57.

CHAPTER 7

Beechey's Expedition of 1826 and 1827

AT SHISHMAREF INLET AND KOTZEBUE SOUND, 1826

THE failure of the Vasiliev-Shishmarev expedition to find a northwest passage spurred the Russians to further plans for reaching the Atlantic Ocean by sea from the Pacific. In 1824 Count Rumiantsev, who had financed Kotzebue's expedition in the *Rurik*, proposed a new plan of exploration for M. I. Muraviev, manager of the Russian-American Company in Sitka, in which Rumiantsev and the Russian-American Company would share expenses to send an expedition north to finish Kotzebue's and Shishmarev's explorations. The expedition would originate in Sitka and be commanded by Khromchenko, assisted by Etolin, and would sail to Icy Cape and proceed by land to the mouth of the Mackenzie River on the Arctic Ocean. Almost simultaneously, Sir John Franklin was preparing for a second Arctic expedition, down the Mackenzie River and hopefully west to the Pacific Ocean. Rumiantsev said: "If it will happen that both expeditions will meet, then the glory of this undertaking will belong both to Russia and England. On the other hand if Russia will do nothing and the English will reach Bering Strait, Europe will be right in criticising us for letting other nations do the exploration work in our seas and on our coast when our Asiatic and American possessions are in such close proximity."[1]

The money was allocated, but the voyage never took place. Rumiantsev died and his heir disapproved of spending money for explorations, especially since the pending voyage of Frederick William Beechey of the English navy to Bering Strait was looked upon as a duplication of efforts. The principal purpose of Beechey's expedition was to give material aid to John Franklin (and to William Edward Parry, whose expedition was also a part of the English plans) if they got to Bering Strait; and though this mission was never fulfilled, the results of Beechey's voyage overshadowed all expeditions before

---

1. Tikhmenev 1939–40, 1:335.

it—Russian or English—both in geographical discoveries and ethnological observations.

Beechey was twenty-nine years old when he was appointed to the command of the little schooner *Blossom* in January 1825, having served under Franklin in the north Atlantic in 1818. Beechey reached Petropavlovsk in June 1826 and sailed northward in July through Bering Strait, hoping to meet Franklin at Chamisso Island between 10 July and the end of October. (Beechey's orders read that he was to return to the strait in 1827 if Franklin had not arrived in 1826.) As Beechey passed through the strait, "for the sake of convenience, I named [three] islands. The eastern one I called Fairway Rock, as it is an excellent guide to the eastern channel . . . the centre one I named after the Russian Admiral Krusenstern [now Little Diomede]; and to the north-western island [Big Diomede] I transferred the name of Ratmanoff, which had been bestowed upon the supposed discovery of Kotzebue."[2]

He came to the American side of the strait a few miles north of Cape Prince of Wales and, sailing north, came to "a considerable village of yourts [Shishmaref village]" on Sarichef Island, and a number of "noisy and energetic, but good-natured" visitors came out to the ship in several umiaks.[3]

"They willingly sold every thing they had, except their bows and arrows, which they implied were required for the chase on shore; but they could not resist 'tawac' (tobacco) and iron knives, and ultimately parted with them." Their bows were reinforced with whalebone (baleen), and their arrows and spears had tips of bone, flint, or iron. Beechey said that clothing was typical of the area—short parkas and well-oiled gutskin shirts—but that they also had "a jacket made of eider drakes' skins sewed together, which put on underneath their other dress is a tolerable protection against a distant arrow, and is worn in times of hostility." They wore caribou skin breeches and sealskin boots, both held up by drawstrings. At the ends of the drawstrings on the pants were attached "a tuft of hair, the wing of a bird, or sometimes a fox's tail, which, dangling behind as they walk, gives them a ridiculous appearance. . . ."

Many of the people were afflicted with eye diseases. Men wore labrets made of granite, jade, and "a few of large blue glass beads let into a piece of ivory which formed a white ring round them," usually an inch in diameter. He later bought a huge one of finely polished jade, three by one and half inches.

Staying only a brief time at Shishmaref Inlet, Beechey entered Kotzebue Sound on 22 July, dispatched a barge to explore an inlet he named Hotham, and sailed to Chamisso Island. While at Hotham Inlet, the *Blossom* was visited by several skin boats with ten to thirteen men in each, who came out specifically to trade "skins, fish, fishing implements, and nic-nacs," requesting in exchange mainly "blue beads, cutlery, tobacco, and buttons." Although

2. Beechey 1831, 1:246–47.
3. Information about Shishmaref people is from ibid., pp. 247–49.

Hotham Inlet is outside the boundaries of this study, these "nic-nacs" may have been made by Wales people who were visiting, fishing, and trading in the area at that time. On a "walrus tooth shaped something like a shoehorn [that is, a shaped walrus tusk used for taking blood from dying animals]" were engraved

a variety of figures of men, beasts, and birds, &c. with a truth and character which showed the art to be common among them. The reindeer [caribou] were generally in herds: in one picture they were pursued by a man in a stooping posture in snowshoes; in another he had approached nearer to his game, and was in the act of drawing his bow. A third represented the manner of taking seals with an inflated skin of the same animal as a decoy; it was placed upon the ice, and not far from it was a man lying upon his belly with a harpoon ready to strike the animal when it should make its appearance. Another was dragging a seal home upon a small sledge; and several baidars were employed harpooning whales which had been previously shot with arrows. . . .[4]

Between 30 July and 28 August, the *Blossom* sailed as far north as Cape Beaufort and back to Chamisso. Beechey suspected that the Eskimos who were camping on Choris Peninsula had molested flour that he had buried in a barrel for Franklin. It was strewn on the ground and the iron hoops taken away. His suspicions increased when the Eskimos came out in an umiak the next morning, dancing and drumming in what Beechey interpreted as a conciliatory manner, betraying knowledge of the flour as they "put their fingers to their tongues, and spit into the sea with disgust."[5]

The next morning Beechey learned that these people were from a village called "King-a-ghe" (Wales), and his observations are the first ethnographic notes about the largest village of northern Alaska in the vicinity of the first discovery of Alaska. They were "on their travels towards home with cargoes of dried salmon, oil, blubber, and skins, which they had collected in their summer excursion along the coast." The Eskimos greeted them enthusiastically, the men meeting them "with their arms drawn in from their sleeves, and tucked up inside their frocks. They were also very particular that every one should salute us, which they did by licking their hands, and drawing them first over their own faces and bodies, and then over ours. This was considered the most friendly manner in which they could receive us," but they would not permit them to come near their tents, and "seemed determined to resist, even with their weapons, which were carefully laid out upon a low piece of ground near them."[6]

The Eskimos gave them a meal, however, and traded with enthusiasm and not a little guile: "they tried to impose upon us with fish-skins, ingeniously put together to represent a whole fish, though entirely deprived of their

4. Ibid., pp. 251, 257. Beechey's collection of Eskimo utensils and art objects is now in the Pitt Rivers Museum, Oxford University, and will be the subject of a monograph by John Bockstoce in the museum's monograph series.
5. Ibid., pp. 283–84.
6. Ibid., pp. 284–85.

original contents; but this artifice succeeded only once: the natives, when detected in other attempts, laughed heartily, and treated the affair as a fair practical joke." But Beechey said that they were generally honest, and often sought the advice of old women when "in doubt about a bargain."[7]

Beechey wished to visit another group on Chamisso Island because they "differed in several particulars from those upon the peninsula"; but when they came to say they were leaving, he visited them instead, and the people on Chamisso later slipped away unobserved. Some of the sailors, however, had visited their camp of four tents and several skin boats and reported:

> Like the party on the peninsula, they were on their return to winter-quarters, with large heaps of dried fish, seals' flesh, oil, skins, and all the necessary appurtenances to an Esquimaux residence. They had four tents and several baidars, which were turned over upon their nets and fishing-tackle for protection. In one of their tool-chests was found a part of an elephant's tooth [mammoth or mastodon], of the same species as those which were afterwards collected in Escholtz [*sic*] Bay. . . .
>
> The women of this party differed from the females we had hitherto seen, having the septum of the nose pierced, and a large blue bead strung upon a strip of whalebone passed through the orifice, the bead hanging as low as the opening of the mouth. One of them, on receiving a large stocking-needle, thrust it into the orifice, or, as some of the seamen said, "spritsail-yarded her nose." A youth of the party who had not yet had his lips perforated wore his hair in bunches on each side of the head after the fashion of the women, which I notice as being the only instance of the kind we met with. . . .
>
> Red and blue beads, buttons, knives, and hatchets were as usual the medium through which every thing they would part with was purchased. The men were more excited than usual by a looking-glass. . . .[8]

Meanwhile, Beechey was visiting the people from "King-a-ghe" at their camp on the peninsula. There were twenty-five persons, seven skin boats, and five tents made of sea-mammal skins stretched on poles, the floors made of broad planks. Several dogs were tied to driftwood logs, and dried salmon and whale intestines on stretchers were suspended from driftwood frames. Beechey estimated that besides "a great many skins of oil, blubber, and blood, they had about three thousand pounds of dried fish."[9]

Beechey and his men were led to the tents where they were offered dried fish and berries in rancid oil, which they declined, and were treated to a dance by all of the Eskimos, who were now dressed in their best clothes, some having tippets of ermine over their shoulders, and others wearing a headband adorned with seal claws attached by strips of skin every two inches. "A double ring was formed in front of us by men seated upon the grass, and by women and children in the back ground, who composed the orchestra," and a number of men danced energetic and exhausting dances. Then, a little girl about eight years of age

7. Ibid., p. 285.
8. Ibid., pp. 286–87.
9. Remarks about Wales people on Choris Peninsula are from ibid., pp. 287–93.

"St. Michael Man Casting a Bird Spear," about 1880. (From Nelson 1899, pl. 58)

"Malemut Family with Dog Sled," about 1880. (From Nelson 1899, pl. 75)

The village of "Kegiktowruk" (popularly known as Klikitaruk) in 1866, now an archeological site between Unalakleet and Saint Michael. (Dall 1870, p. 128)

"Eskimo Igloos, Corwin Lagoon, Alaska [near Golovnin Bay]," at the turn of the twentieth century. (Photograph by F. H. Nowell)

joined the jumpers, but did not imitate their actions. Her part consisted in waving her arms and inclining her body from side to side. . . .

A grown-up female now [joined] the party, and appeared to be the prize of contention among several young men, who repeatedly endeavoured to ingratiate themselves with her, but she as often rejected their offers and waved them away. At last an old man, all but naked, jumped into the ring, and was beginning some indecent gesticulations, when his appearance not meeting with our approbation, he withdrew, and the performance having been wrought to its highest pitch of noise and animation, ceased.

After the dance they engaged in a brisk barter during which the Eskimos never raised or lowered their prices, though they pilfered some of the goods put out for their selection.

They understood making a good bargain quite as well as ourselves, and were very wary how they received our knives and hatchets, putting their metal to the test by hacking at them with their own. If they stood the blow they were accepted; but if, on the contrary, they were notched, they were refused. A singular method of deciding a bargain was resorted to by one of their party, almost equivalent to that of tossing up a coin. We had offered an adze for a bundle of skins; but the owner, who at first seemed satisfied with the bargain, upon reflection became doubtful whether he would not be the loser by it; and to decide the doubtful point, he caught a small beetle, and set it at liberty upon the palm of his hand, anxiously watching which direction the insect should take. Finding it run towards him, he concluded the bargain to be disadvantageous to him, and took back his goods.

These people would not permit writing in notebooks, and refused to talk when they were open. This annoyed Beechey because he could see numerous differences between them and the people farther north.

On his first visit in July Beechey said that the Eskimos drew a chart of the coast on the sand, "of which I took very little notice at the time." But they again drew him the coastline on the sand and depicted the hills and mountain ranges with sand mounds; the islands with pebbles; villages and fishing stations with sticks; so that finally, Beechey said, "we had a complete topographical plan of the coast from Point Darby to Cape Krusenstern." In this way Beechey learned of a previously unknown body of water called "Imaurook" (now Imuruk Basin) connected by a river to a harbor. Through pantomime, he learned that the entrance was so narrow that "two baidars could not paddle abreast of each other." The river described was the Tuksuk Channel, which is swift and narrow, but with room for many boats placed side by side; thus the pantomime meant only that the stream was narrow and swift compared to other meandering streams of the area.

They also told Beechey about a river called "Youp-nut" between Wales and a bay called "I-art-so-rook" (Ayasayuk, or Cape Nome). Beyond this was the entrance to Norton Sound, which was the extent of their knowledge. They placed a village called "Iden-noo" at Cape Prince of Wales, "and a little way inland another, named King-a-ghe, which was their own winter residence." The word Iden-noo is unknown to Eskimos now, but may have been a pronunciation of the part of Wales called Agianamiut, or a name referring to an abandoned village nearby. Beechey also learned the Eskimo names for islands in the Bering Strait: Noo-nar-boak (Big Diomede), Ig-narlook (Little Diomede), Oo-ghe-eyak (Fairway Rock), Oo-ghe-a-boak (King Island), and Ayak (Sledge Island).[10] They had no name for East Cape, Siberia, nor could they tell him about any other part of the Asiatic coast.

The English were given an affectionate farewell, and the chief rec-ommended that they leave soon, indicating in pantomime that it would be very cold in about twenty days. Sighting two small boats with sails through the fog on 6 September, Beechey thought that Franklin had arrived; but they turned out to be Eskimo umiaks, which landed nearby. The people, who Beechey thought were from Wales but "of much lower station" than the others he had met, unloaded their boats, erected tents, and were settled in their camp within an hour, everything

in as complete order as if they had been established there a month. . . . No better idea could have been conveyed to us of the truly independent manner in which this tribe wander about from place to place, transporting their houses, and every thing necessary to their comfort, than that which was afforded on this occasion. Nor were we less struck with the number of articles which their ingenuity finds the means of disposing in their boats, and which, had we not seen them disembarked, we should have doubted the possibility of their having been crammed into them. From two of these they landed fourteen persons, eight tent poles, forty deer skins, two kyacks, many hundred weight of fish, numerous skins of oil, earthen jars for cooking, two living foxes, ten large dogs, bundles of lances, harpoons, bows and arrows, a quantity of whalebone, skins full of clothing, some immense nets made of hide for taking small whales and porpoises, eight broad planks, masts, sails, paddles, &c., besides sea-horse [walrus] hides and teeth, and a variety of nameless articles always to be found among the Esquimaux.[11]

Beechey and his men were greeted warmly by the two families, "each of which had its distinct property, tents, baidar, &c." When two of the girls moved, "several bells were set ringing," which Beechey thought had been suspended under their clothing as charms, because one larger than the rest (of three or four) was placed in such a way that it "must have materially in-commoded the ladies in their walking." The thirteen-year-old girl had a single blue line on her chin, but the other, about ten, had none. Their mother, who was "extremely good-natured, lively, and loquacious," an-swered their questions and provided many Eskimo words. As Beechey sketched the older girl, the mother impatiently snatched the paper away several times; and the father, "observing what I was about, called to his son to bring him a piece of board that was lying outside the tent, and to scrape it

10. Beechey said, "It is singular that this island, which was named Sledge Island by Captain Cook, from the circumstance of one of these implements being found upon it, should be called by a word signifying the same thing in the Esquimaux language." In this Beechey was wrong. Ayak, the Eskimo name for the island, means "broken off and left the shore," referring to a de-tached cliff, or a brace, or a pole. This word has an etymological relationship to Ayasayuk, or the name for Cape Nome, which in profile looks very much like the face of Sledge Island.

11. This information is taken from Beechey 1831, 1:294–300.

clean, which was very necessary indeed," and promptly drew a sketch of Beechey, aping his manner, but was "extremely puzzled to know how to place [a hat] upon the head he had drawn."

The inevitable trading took place. The sailors bought a boatload of dried salmon as well as "skins, ornamental parts of the dress of her tribe, and small ivory dolls" for "blue beads, brooches, and cutlery, which . . . were transferred to a stone vessel half filled with train-oil."

The next day the Eskimos visited the ship, going reluctantly aboard and "leaving with their comrades in the boat every valuable article they had about their persons." As they went about the ship, Beechey could understand why the chain cable and a sailmaker sewing a bag interested them more than the many unfamiliar foreign objects. The iron chain, Beechey supposed, represented to them "the result of prodigious labour" because their chains were cut, without a break, from one solid piece of ivory. The animals illustrated in *Rees's Cyclopaedia* were given names in Eskimo, and the Eskimos' immediate recognition of the animals from pictures impressed Beechey, for they were "far more intelligent than might have been expected from the difficulty that naturally occurs to uncivilized people in divesting their minds of the comparative size of the living animal and its picture."

Having finished their duty as informants, the Eskimos became impatient to leave. Presents were exchanged, and they "pushed off their baidars, rested on their paddles for a minute, and made off as fast as they could, to give us an idea of the swiftness of their boat, which seems to be a favourite practice."

On visiting them again the next day, Beechey learned "that the price of every article had been raised several hundred per cent., and that nothing of reasonable value would induce them to part with either bows or arrows; so that our generosity of the preceding day had not left any durable impressions."

On this visit Beechey observed a smoking party—men, women, and children. They used a small pipe, which "would contain no more tobacco than could be consumed at a whiff. To these instruments there were attached a pricker and a strip of dog's skin, from the last of which they tore off a few hairs, and placed them at the bottom of the bowl of the pipe to prevent the tobacco, which was chopped up very fine, being drawn into the mouth with the smoke." A pinch of tobacco mixed with pieces of wood was placed in the pipe, and "the senior person present took his whiff and passed the empty pipe to the next, who replenished it and passed it on, each person in his turn inflating himself to the fullest extent, and gradually dissipating the fumes through the nostrils. The pungency of the smoke, and the time necessary to hold the breath, occasioned considerable coughing with some of the party, but they nevertheless appeared greatly to enjoy the feast."

Beechey thoroughly explored the sound between Spafarief Bay and Cape Espenberg, and discovered the Buckland River, where the Eskimos were found to be hostile. On 13 October the *Blossom* left to spend the winter in San Francisco and the Hawaiian Islands.

AT CAPE RODNEY AND PORT CLARENCE, 1827

In August 1827 Beechey came to the American shore near Cape Rodney and landed near "several yourts, and a number of posts driven into the ground, and in the lake we found several artificial ducks, which had been left as decoys; but we saw no natives." They noted a huge accumulation of driftwood on the beach, and several herds of caribou on the tundra between the beach and the hills.[12] Beechey, in the *Blossom*, sailed almost immediately to Chamisso Island, where he hoped to find Franklin; but Master Thomas Elson, in the barge, was ordered to examine the coast between Cape Rodney and Kotzebue Sound for the opening, "of which the Esquimaux had apprised us the preceding year by their chart upon the sand," and to further investigate Shishmaref Inlet.

On 11 August Elson returned with the news that he had discovered the bay and was visited by natives, who drew him a chart similar to that of the preceding year. Beechey decided to examine the bay, which he later named Port Clarence, when he returned from accompanying the barge for further examination of Icy Cape, Point Hope, and areas to the north.

On the way south, Beechey spent the night of 30 August off Cape York, named "in honour of his late Royal Highness."[13] On 31 August they entered "a spacious harbour [Port Clarence] capable of holding a great many ships of the line," and then a second body of water, which Beechey named Grantley Harbor.[14] He was unable to explore Imuruk Basin, which he called an inland lake, or the Tuksuk Channel, which he learned the Eskimos called "Tokshook."

At the entrance of [Tuksuk] there is an Esquimaux village, and upon the northern and eastern shores of the harbour there are two others: the population of the whole amounted to about four hundred persons. They closely resembled the natives we had seen before, except that they were better provided with clothing, and their implements were neater and more ingeniously made. Among their peltry we noticed several gray fox and land-otter skins, but they would not part with them for less than a hatchet apiece. In addition to the usual weapons of bows and arrows, these people had short iron spears neatly inlaid with brass, upon all which implements they set great value, and kept them wrapped in skins. Among the inhabitants of the village on the northern shore, named Choonowuck [Singloak], there were several girls with massive iron bracelets. One had a curb chain for a necklace, and another a bell suspended in front, in the manner described the preceding year at Choris Peninsula.

There are very few natives in the outer harbour. On the northern side there is a village of yourts [Sinramiut or Apalrurik], to which the inhabitants apparently resort only in the winter. At the time of our visit it was in charge of an old man, his wife, and daughter, who received us civilly, and gave us some fish.

Some of the dwellings were half filled with water, filthy, and "in a very ruinous condition," but would be occupied again upon the return of the

12. Ibid., 2:531.
13. Ibid., p. 541.
14. Information about the Port Clarence area is from ibid., pp. 541–45.

inhabitants after the freeze-up. One of the dwellings was very large and intended to be used as an assembly room. Near the village was a burial plot, the bodies wrapped in skins and placed on driftwood with kayaks, sled frames, and other articles placed near them.

The daughter had the hammer of a musket hanging from her neck, and "held it so sacred that she would scarcely submit it to examination, and afterwards carefully concealed it within her dress. She was apparently very modest and bashful, and behaved with so much propriety that it was a pleasure to find such sentiments existing beneath so uncouth an exterior."

At "Nooke" at the entrance to the inner harbor, they saw some "Esquimaux fishermen, who reminded us of a former acquaintance at Chamisso Island, and saluted us so warmly that we felt sorry their recollection had not entirely failed them." The Wales people whom they had seen last year at Kotzebue Sound were now fishing on the southern shore of Grantley Harbor. Beechey decided that Wales "must be of importance among the Esquimaux villages upon this coast . . . judging from the respectability of parties from that place."

Beechey did not visit the village of Kauwerak, but it was important because, in estimating the population between Point Barrow and Cape Rodney, he said that "the whole population, I should think, including Kow-ee-rock, would not amount to more than 2500 persons. I do not pretend to say that this estimate is accurate, as from the manner in which the people are dispersed along the coast in the summer time, it is quite impossible that it should be so; but it may serve to show that the tribe is not very numerous"; yet, during the summer, he added, "almost every point of land and the mouths of all the rivers are taken possession of by the tribe."[15]

Beechey reached Chamisso Island on 10 September and found the barge wrecked and three seamen drowned. (The body of one was buried on the island "by the side of our shipmate who had been buried there the preceding year.") The Eskimos in the vicinity were apparently from the Buckland River, a tribe that belongs culturally to the Kotzebue Sound area; but the hostility and insolent behavior of the twenty-four men who fought the English on Chamisso Island were in considerable contrast to other Eskimos on Seward Peninsula and Norton Sound. An Eskimo was killed in a fight, for which the Eskimos had prepared by scooping out five man-sized pits in a ravine and dressing in battle garments of a layer each of eider duck skins and caribou skins.

Beechey was the first to recognize definitely that the people he saw were "Esquimaux," but who had hitherto been called natives, Americans, Indians, or savages. (Captain Cook thought they "resembled" Eskimos.) He furthermore called them "western Esquimaux" in his comparative account of eastern and western Eskimos—the first on record—"in order to distinguish

15. Ibid., pp. 568, 569.

them from the tribes inhabiting Hudson's Bay, Greenland, Igloolik, and indeed from all the places eastward of Point Barrow. This line ought properly to be drawn at M'Kenzie River, in consequence of certain peculiarities connecting the people seen near that spot with the tribe to the westward, but it will be more convenient to confine it within the above-mentioned limits." [16]

Beechey's remarks about the western Eskimo in a section devoted to general subjects—dwellings, burials, clothing and personal fashions, weapons, implements, language, population, and arts and crafts, including the making of ivory chains—brought the Alaskans, whose culture differed considerably from the already well-known Canadian and Greenland Eskimos, to world attention. Beechey said that their winter pursuits, which he was unable to observe, "must consist in the constructing of implements for the forthcoming season of activity, in making clothes, and carving and ornamenting their property, for almost every article made of bone is covered with devices." [17] Yet despite their summer visits, they could not learn much about activities of that season, either, because the Eskimos "relinquished all occupation on our appearance to obtain some of the riches that were on board the ship." [18]

16. Ibid., pp. 567–68.
17. Ibid., pp. 569–70.
18. Ibid., p. 573.

CHAPTER 8

Bering Strait Culture, 1778–1833

Summary of Cultural Characteristics

The observations made of the Bering Strait Eskimos during the years 1778 and 1827, six years before the establishment of the first European settlement north of the Nushagak River, give glimpses of the character of Bering Strait culture and provide data for discussions of territorial occupancy, tribal relations, aboriginal and European trade, and the use of tobacco.

Much of the information collected by the Cossacks at second hand in the early eighteenth century had proved to be true: the Big Land was a land of many people, rich in furs and food; the men even wore tails of wolves, went barefoot, and were warlike.

The firsthand observations showed that the Eskimos had adapted themselves technically and psychologically to the limitations of man and the universe. They were not experimenting with means to exist in the Arctic—that day apparently was long past—but were living in a well-developed culture where life was far above a mere existence level and was filled with the luxury of the arts, songs, and dancing. That does not mean they were unreceptive to new objects for making life easier or more enjoyable, but they were conservative, and content enough with their ways so that many of their customs continued unchanged until the latter part of the nineteenth century.

Their way of life appeared to be stable during the whole of this period, with the exception of a gradual acquisition of European trade goods and a resultant development of trading techniques. At no time during this period were trade goods unknown, but the use and acceptance of European commodities had increased markedly by 1827.

Intertribal Relations

No Eskimo tribe lived as an isolated unit. Any one tribe was acquainted with an exceptionally large area, and interaction was extensive with numerous other groups. This can be deduced from native maps of the time, which included the territory of several tribes as we now know them. A map drawn at Stuart Island in 1822 extended from the island to a point south of the Yukon; another drawn at Golovnin Bay included the mainland and islands from the bay to Bering Strait; a map of 1826 showed features from Cape Krusenstern to Cape Darby. The Eskimos of Bering Strait were acquainted also with Siberians on both a warlike and a peaceful trading footing. There was no information as yet about Indian-Eskimo relationships.

The explorers were usually treated well and were universally offered venison, fish, and a slip of "marten's skin" (apparently as a recognition of special esteem). This behavior contrasted with such evidence of conflict as the Eskimos' possession of offensive and defensive weapons, their meeting explorers with bows drawn or spears at hand, the continual demand for European weapons, and the holding of Alaskan prisoners in Siberia. For the most part, the Eskimos showed considerable reluctance to board foreign ships, but had almost overcome their timidity by 1827. From Billings' time, the ships were met by insignia—fox or eagle skins—indicating they were friendly traders, and with physical gestures—arms extended, or various arm and hand movements—to show they were unarmed.

Tales collected by Kobelev and Kotzebue indicated that defenses for war were of more concern to the people living in the immediate vicinity of the strait, where Siberians were most likely to come, than among other tribes. Neither armor nor the presenting of weapons was mentioned in the Norton Sound area. Only the "Tauk" people made peaceful motions upon meeting the Europeans.

Apparently there were actual raids and unfortunate encounters with Siberians (and this goes back to Cossack information) during this period. For example, the Billings people were offered Alaskan Eskimo women, who had been taken prisoners in a retaliatory raid after a quarrel while sea mammal hunting, probably over an infringement of hunting rights on the sea ice. An American, wanting to see Kobelev at East Cape, was reported to have been killed because the Chukchi thought that he was encroaching on their trading rights.

Eskimos had also become traders, and early writers' recording of Eskimos' presence in foreign territory is an indication that tribal alliances were then in effect as families went to neighboring territory and traders went to far places. Explorers' accounts have given us the following information: the Sledge Islanders were absent from their village in 1778; Kauwerak people visited and traded on King Island in 1791; King Islanders, according to Khromchenko, often visited Kauwerak; the Shishmaref people were away from their village in 1816; the King and Sledge islanders were both spoken of as being traders in Siberia in 1821 and 1822; Wales people were away from their village in 1779, and later, in 1826 and 1827, Beechey met families from Wales at Kotzebue Sound and Port Clarence. It was probably during such jaunts that jade (from the Kobuk River) and spruce gum (from either the Kobuk or Fish River) were obtained. There were also indications that well-traveled overland trails connected some tribal territories.

By 1816, despite their "eternal enmity," the Alaskan Eskimos and Siberian Chukchi (or Eskimos) visited each other's land. Choris said that the Alaskans often traveled as far as the Kolyma River to trade, and in 1821 John D. Cochrane, an adventurous Englishman, indeed did meet two of them at the Anyui Fair (an intertribal trading market) in the Kolyma region.[1] The Siberians took goods from Siberia to Kotzebue Sound, where they carried on a mute trade. But the general attitude during this period was vigilant, suspicious, distrustful, and hostile, apparently rooted in a long-standing tradition between the peoples of both continents. It obviously did not extend (in its traditional form, at least) to foreigners with large ships, except for the example at Eschscholtz Bay in 1820, and even then the show of arms when embarking and disembarking was toward men in an umiak with native interpreters. This was also true of the formalized battle readiness on King Island as reported by Kobelev in 1791.

Cook's and Khromchenko's remarks from the Norton Sound area give us clues to the dating of the migration of the so-called Malemiut of the Kotzebue Sound area to Unalit territory south and east of Golovin. This migration, which will be discussed at greater length in Chapter 10, had apparently not begun by 1778, or even by 1822. Khromchenko mentions only "Aziagmiut" (Sledge Island) traders, and not Malemiut, who were constantly mentioned after the 1840s. The evidence in King's and Cook's reports of 1778 is even more positive. In the Cape Denbigh–Shaktoolik area, which later was occupied by Malemiut-speaking persons, Cook obtained the Unaluk pronunciation, "Chaktoole," for the Malemiut "Shaktoolik," and King obtained a list of words from "Norton Sound" (apparently at Cape Denbigh) which has been identified by several Unaluk speakers as being entirely Unaluk.[2] Furthermore, Cook describes the summer dwellings as being of turf and wood, not the round or conical skin tents used by the inhabitants north of Golovnin Bay, especially the Inupiak when traveling. Neither did he see the large umiaks characteristically used by the Malemiut, even when they moved into the southern territory.

Khromchenko's remarks about the Sledge Islanders' speaking a language different from those at Golovnin Bay also helps to locate the western boundary of the Unaluk speakers between Golovnin Bay and Cape Nome, a division that has, until recently, been erroneously placed much farther east and south, at Shaktoolik.[3]

1. Cochrane 1824, p. 268.
2. Cook and King 1784, 3;554–55. Identification of words in King's list was made by four Unalakleet residents. Four of the twenty-three words are cognates of Malemiut and Kauwerak dialects.
3. See also Ray 1967b, pp. 389–90.

Settlements and Subsistence

The Eskimos occupied the land intensively, that is, as intensively as possible within a hunting-gathering economy where a large territory is necessary for optimum utilization. In summer, the explorers saw settlements and occupied campsites everywhere on the coast (inland waters and streams were not investigated during this period); and though nothing was learned at first hand about winter life, settlements that were occupied during winter at the end of the nineteenth century had been observed by 1827: Stebbins, Shaktoolik, Elim, Golovnin Bay, Cape Nome, Sledge Island, King Island, Cape Rodney, Little Diomede Island, Grantley Harbor, Wales, Shishmaref, Cape Espenberg, and Goodhope Bay. Kobelev's map filled in the blank spaces of the explorers' map with dramatic testimony to the intensive use of the land.

Wales, the largest village of all ("50 yurts" in 1791), was visited only briefly by Kobelev, who did not describe it; but Beechey, upon meeting inhabitants of that village at Kotzebue Sound and Port Clarence in 1826 and 1827, rightly concluded that it was of considerable importance. Kauwerak was not yet visited, but there was no lack of information concerning it.

Though the Eskimos were greatly tempted to quit their regular routines to visit the ships, their activities—the catching and drying of innumerable salmon and hunting caribou—presented an atmosphere of considerable industry.

Caribou lived along the coast everywhere during the summer, and apparently on Stuart Island. Some of the summer camps were used for caribou hunting as well as for fishing and gathering berries. Observations of caribou everywhere along the coast go a long way to explain the presence of caribou bones in coastal sites, when it was once thought that caribou only roamed inland. In the 1820s the Stebbins people sold their caribou skins to Sledge Islanders.

Although drying racks loaded with salmon and other meat were often mentioned, the literature is quite silent about the actual techniques of procuring fish and game. Nets of knotted sinew were used in conjunction with bladder floats to catch fish, and Cape Rodney people used decoys for ducks. Bows, arrows, and spears were probably used to hunt caribou.

The winter home was a semisubterranean structure of wood and turf everywhere in the area, even on the islands, where rock was also utilized in construction. The houses of 1816 at Shishmaref Inlet were fairly roomy, with floors and benches of wooden planks. In the Cape Denbigh area the summer dwellings were of wood and turf, but farther north, conical tents of tanned seal or caribou skin were used. Merck's description of a Cape Rodney tent—with the luxurious addition of a gutskin window—gave us the first information about carved images hanging indoors from a wooden frame.

Clothing and Art

Throughout all of the area, clothing was made of the same materials—mainly sealskin, caribou, and ground squirrel—and on the same pattern. The women's coats (later called parkas) were cut up on each side leaving a rounded front and back flap. Bird skins were also used at Stebbins, and muskrat at Kotzebue Sound. Parkas were made in several lengths. Both men and women wore trousers, though the men sometimes dispensed with them and, furthermore, went barefoot. Clothing ornamentation was not elaborate, but great care was given to trimming parkas with ornamental furs and to sewing sinew decorations on footwear. (The name mukluk was later adopted as a generic name for this footwear from the Unaluk word for bearded seal, or *maklak*, which is used for the soles.) The Eskimos of Cape Rodney used leather that was dyed red and yellow, and made both parkas and mukluks for dress-up occasions. Gutskin coats were worn to protect fur clothing from dampness, especially in the kayaks, and whole slip-on suits were used for very wet work. Clothing styles appeared to remain conservatively the same throughout the entire period.

Both men and women took pains with their hair, the men universally wearing it short with bangs to the eyes, sometimes with a sealskin crown of thongs round their head. The women neatly braided their hair and wound it around the ears, and often intertwined it with beads or strips of fur. Men of the entire area wore labrets, and it is interesting that many wore extremely large ones made of trade beads or jade, probably as a status symbol, since these huge things must have been very uncomfortable. Women tattooed their chins, with vertical lines and, at Cape Rodney, put intricate designs on their arms. Women wore copper or iron bracelets as well as a variety of appealing European objects: musket parts, bells, uniform buttons, and medals, some apparently used as amulets. Both men and women wore beads in their ears, and at Wales women wore them in the septum.

Their attention to detail in the manufacturing of clothes, utensils, implements, and weapons did not stop with utilitarian objects. They carved ivory chains, figurines in the form of animals for tents and on wooden hats, and engraved realistic scenes on ivory. The drill bow illustrated by Choris shows a control of line and design that suggests long practice. Subsequent to this information, however, it has been learned that the Eskimo man was an excellent mimic, and the ability to copy drawings at a first attempt and to draw maps from memory was especially marked among Bering Strait people. The first mention of graphic art in 1816 does not necessarily mean that this form was new, but the absence of previous observations and the fact that there are no drill bows in archeological sites and few satisfactorily dated pieces of any graphic art from prehistoric times in western Alaska leads me to think that this art developed during historical times. The availability of metal engraving tools, probably not used in quantity until the end of the eighteenth century, was also a factor. Cook's remarks suggest that there was a limited use of iron, which is corroborated by Dall's statement that it was unknown to the Unalakleet Eskimos until two generations before 1867.[4]

Household Utensils, Weapons, and Transportation

European trade goods fell into two main classifications during this period: weapons and luxury items. They consisted of spears and knives made by Russians especially for the Siberian trade, iron points, beads, bracelets, and tobacco. After 1822 European pipes were commonly traded. No explorer observed iron kettles among the possessions of the Eskimos, though Kobelev in 1791 and Khromchenko in 1822 said that they used iron pots as Eskimo trade goods. The Eskimos at this time universally used wooden dishes and clay containers, incised at the top with simple ornamentation,[5] and in which food was presumably cooked. They dipped fish and meat into a communal bowl of oil, etiquette apparently stipulating that it be eaten with a great deal of noise.

Mats, supposedly of grass, were mentioned, but no baskets. Fat was obtained by placing chunks of blubber into sealskin pokes until they had turned to oil, a practice that extended well into the twentieth century. In 1791 the two-man drill was used for fire-making, but by 1822 the people at Golovnin Bay were using steel and flint obtained from the Sledge Islanders. King Islanders had slat armor by 1791, as did the people at Cape Rodney. At Kotzebue Sound, eider duck and caribou skins were also wrapped around the body for protection against arrows. Spears, harpoons, and bows and arrows, which were carried in quivers, were used. Bows were reinforced with sinew at Cape Rodney, and with baleen at Wales. Wristguards were made of bone or iron.

The Eskimos of Kotzebue Sound were unacquainted with firearms in 1816, when Kotzebue showed off his gun; those of Golovnin Bay had no knowledge of them in 1822. Firearms were contraband trade goods among the Russians, and the guns found at Kotzebue Sound in 1820 were not only traded illegally but were apparently the only arms obtained by the Eskimos until mid-nineteenth century. It appears certain that Eskimos both shot at Shishmarev's party and obtained more guns and ammunition in 1820, but where had the Eskimos received the guns they used?

Before 1820 several ships could have sold guns both in Siberia and Kotzebue Sound. Cochrane, describing the final day of the Anyui market in 1821, said that the best furs were held back by the Chukchi traders, who wished "to make the Russians believe that they had no want of tobacco, as they could get it much cheaper in the bay of St. Lawrence, from the ships which casually call there."[6] Many of these vessels, which were based in the

---

4. See Ray 1969; Dall 1870, p. 143.
5. Oswalt (1953) discusses Seward Peninsula pottery and ornamentation.
6. Cochrane 1824, p. 264.

Hawaiian Islands, were owned by John Jacob Astor, who had hoped to acquire a trading foothold in Kamchatka and the Arctic through his Kamchatkan agent, Peter Dobell, and others who had charge of his ships. Three of these could have been in the Arctic even earlier than 1820, or between 1815 and 1820: the *Forester*, the *Pedler*, and the *Sylph*.[7] Americans had been on the coast of Kamchatka even before 1815, because Baranov had agreed to at least seven contracts with American captains for sea otter hunting and for trading between 1808 and 1812, and at least two of them had disposed of the skins at Kamchatka or Okhotsk.[8]

The *Pedler* was the same vessel that had evacuated the colonists from Astor's Astoria in Oregon in 1814. This brig traded during 1814 and 1815 in California and Hawaii, and was held by the Russians from July to October 1815 at Sitka for selling ammunition to the Indians.[9] The *Pedler* then sailed to New York for trade goods and on to Hawaii, where William Pigot took command;[10] thence to Sitka, where 2,620 sealskins were purchased, and to Kotzebue Sound, where she met the *Good Intent* in June 1820.[11]

The year before, Pigot had prevailed upon Count Rumiantsev, who had financed Kotzebue's expedition, to send an American captain named Gray (not Captain Robert Gray) on an unnamed ship, "also [belonging] to Pigot [i.e., to Astor]," to verify the geographical accuracy of Kotzebue's map in connection with the continuing search for the northwest passage.[12] But, according to Lazarev (from information given him by Vasiliev, who had learned it from P. I. Rikord at Kamchatka in 1820), Rumiantsev did not realize that the American proposal actually meant Russian sponsorship for a voyage to investigate fur trading possibilities north of the Bering Strait.

Gray sailed through the strait in 1819 to Shishmaref Inlet and then along the coast to Kotzebue Sound in the ship's longboat, testing the depth of water. When Gray returned to Kamchatka, he told Governor Rikord that Kotzebue's map was wrong and that he would make corrections. He said, furthermore, that he or another brig would return to Alaska in 1820 for further explorations. Therefore, when Shishmarev saw the *Pedler*, and knowing the circumstances of Gray's journey, he was curious to see if the brig were really exploring and whether Gray had corrected Kotzebue's map. The *Pedler*, of course, was trading and not exploring, and a so-called corrected

7. Golder 1917, p. 130; Howay references.
8. Bancroft 1886, pp. 479–81.
9. The *Pedler* was held by the Spanish at San Luis Obispo between August and October 1814 for illegal trading on the California coast. Between this time and July 1815 her movements are unknown, but Kenneth Porter said that a visit to the Hawaiian Islands "would, however, have been a logical procedure, as would trade along the coast, both of California and farther north (Porter 1931, 2:644; Porter 1932).
10. Bancroft 1885, pp. 271–72; Howay 1933, p. 127; Porter 1930b, p. 504; Porter 1931, 2: 644.
11. Howay 1934, p. 20. Kenneth Porter, who accumulated a vast amount of information about the *Pedler*, did not mention its voyage to the Arctic in 1820.
12. Information about Gray is from Lazarev 1950, pp. 214–16.

map that they had with them appeared to be merely a rough copy of Kotzebue's original map on very thin transparent paper with a few minor
changes, the "Americans not having had time to transpose it onto good
paper."

Thus, the presence of Gray's vessel—the only American ship known to
have been off the northwest Alaska coast before 1820—is almost conclusive
evidence for the origin of the firearms encountered by the Shishmarev contingent at Elephant Point.[13]

Kayaks and umiaks were used for summertime travel by the Eskimo, the
latter at the Bering Strait proper holding ten or more persons. The large ones
reported by Beechey from Wales held an incredible amount of goods as the
Eskimos traveled to and from their summer trading and fishing grounds.
During the early nineteenth century, fleets of kayaks seemed to greet explorers in Norton Sound, whereas fleets of umiaks met them farther north.
Cook's use of the word "canoe" for both umiak and kayak is confusing, but
his remarks suggest that the kayak was used more than the umiak, which he
rarely mentioned in all of his sailing along the coast—only three times between Cape Prince of Wales and Saint Michael, with the exception of the
"canoes" at Cape Denbigh.

The scarcity of skin boats in the strait area at Cook's time is not readily
accounted for. Perhaps the inhabitants stayed out of sight because of fear or
because they did not see the ship. The latter was extremely unlikely, however, because Eskimo curiosity and vigilance over the sea from high places
formed an almost continuous surveillance along the coast.[14] Farther south, in
the Cape Denbigh area, umiaks were probably not common. Giddings found
only two fragments considered to be umiak parts (dated around A.D. 1400)
and two pieces of cottonwood bark that might have been umiak models or
toys in the whole of Nukleet culture.[15]

Paddles were used for both kayaks and umiaks, and sails were apparently
little used until Kotzebue's time. He was the first to report their use at

---

13. For a detailed discussion of the introduction of firearms, see Ray 1975, from which portions of this discussion are taken. Lazarev did not mention any of the many incidents involving
firearms, probably for official reasons, since he very much wanted to get his manuscript published at the end of the expedition. He did mention that he had seen two muskets in 1820 at Saint
Lawrence Bay, Siberia. Foote said that the "Russians admitted the firearms might have originated at the Kolyma fair just as well as from Captain Meek," quoting Lazarev as his source
(Lazarev 1950, p. 303; Foote 1965, p. 162). This is a mistranslation, however. What Lazarev actually said was that the two English muskets were probably traded from Americans since "it is
not permitted to sell firearms to savages at Kolyma."

14. Large areas of the coast can be seen from various vantages on high hills. From a hill south
of Kotzebue one can easily see Cape Blossom, Cape Krusenstern, and, on extremely clear days,
Cape Espenberg. From Shaktoolik one can see the Golovin hills in one direction and beyond
Unalakleet in the other. From the high hills back of Unalakleet, Cape Nome can be seen faintly
on a clear day and beyond Saint Michael in the other direction. From the town of Unalakleet one
can see Stuart Island and Cape Denbigh. From the Koyuk airfield, both Cape Denbigh to the
south and Cape Darby to the southwest loom large.

15. Giddings 1964, p. 89.

Shishmaref Inlet in 1816. The maneuver of turning over in a kayak was a source of much pride as early as 1822, and the umiak was reported to be used as a temporary shelter, turned over on its side, while traveling during the summer.

Well-built sleds were seen and dogs were always mentioned toward the later part of the period. The subject of dogs can exemplify the danger of inferring that certain peoples lacked an object or trait from negative evidence. Neither Cook nor King mentioned seeing dogs, though they supposed the Eskimos had them because of the sled on Sledge Island. One can scarcely overlook the presence of dogs. Later explorers never failed to mention the numerous dogs and their howling, which can be heard for many miles over water and tundra. In later years, too, dogs were left to fend for themselves on islands when the inhabitants were on the mainland. The omission of this information, therefore, pointed to few or no dogs on the Alaskan coast in 1778. But in Samwell's journal we find a notation that at Shaktoolik "they have Dogs about their Houses." Yet, Cook's and King's inattention to the dogs may have been more or less consistent with the facts, for Giddings found few dog bones in his excavations at Nukleet, dating from A.D. 1100 to 1700 (and possibly as late as Cook's time), and interpreted his findings as an absence of dog traction on a large scale until about 1710.[16]

Pathology

The observations about illness abolish the popular romantic idealization of a pre-European utopian life without sickness. Years before a permanent European settlement was made in this area, eye diseases were common, and there were blindness, crippling, and syphilis. To diagnose pathology from descriptions made by untrained observers two centuries before is admittedly a shaky venture, but I asked Dr. Martha Wilson, service unit director, Alaska Medical Center, Anchorage, for her assistance in identifying the probable causes for the examples of blindness and crippling observed by Captain Cook in the Elim area. The conclusions, however, are mine alone. Both illnesses probably were the result of injuries, but they also could have originated from tuberculosis, which has always been thought to have been introduced by the white man.[17] The description of the blind man's eyes suggests corneal scarring, probably from trauma but possibly from an acute inflammatory condition of the cornea and 'conjunctiva called phlyctenular keratoconjunctivitis (PKC), which is believed to originate from air-borne tuberculosis organisms coming into direct contact with the conjunctiva. The widespread occurrence of PKC among Alaskan Eskimos could be accounted for if the woman's cure of spitting directly into the man's eyes had been a common practice.

16. Ibid., pp. 82, 83, 84, 186. Samwell, in Beaglehole, ed. 1967, p. 1137.
17. I am entirely responsible for the statements about tuberculosis and its possibilities of aboriginal occurrence. Dr. Wilson would be reluctant to make a commitment on such slim evidence.

Another cause for both the deformity and the blindness could have been rheumatoid arthritis, a hereditary condition that can result in an eye condition called uveitis. The severity of the crippled man's deformity also suggests Pott's disease, an illness causing extreme dwarfing and a hunchback from tuberculosis destroying the anterior parts of the vertebrae. If the eating away of this man's face was due to syphilis, Cook had ample reason to say that "he was the most deformed cripple I had ever seen or heard of." The presence of these abnormal men furthermore does not fit the popular notion that the old and the maimed were disposed of. Subsistence conditions in Norton Sound apparently were so favorable that comparatively unproductive members of a group lived normal lives along with their compatriots.

Khromchenko's diagnoses of syphilis near Stebbins suggests that syphilis was either aboriginal or had been transmitted from the south from tribe to tribe. It is usually thought that syphilis was introduced by non-natives. Khromchenko's observations were made at least five hundred miles from the nearest permanent trading post, which had been established by the Russians on the Nushagak River only three years before. The Aleuts of the Aleutians had probably contracted syphilis by 1792. The disease apparently reached a peak in 1798, and could have spread northward through native tribes, but Wendell Oswalt concludes that it was uncommon north of the Alaska Peninsula.[18] Khromchenko's observations are thought-provoking especially in the light of the possibly afflicted youth farther north around Elim in 1778. It is unfortunate that so little information was recorded about the health of the peoples of the vast western Eskimo area at the time of the earliest explorations, or of the physical contacts of the sailors; but it is obvious from these examples of only a small sampling of the entire area that physical disorders were of no small magnitude before the era of white settlement.

The Eskimo and the White Man

We gain many other insights into Eskimo life from these accounts. Besides showing the Europeans great hospitality, and delighting in dancing, singing, and artistic pursuits like sewing and fine ivory work, the Eskimos were wily traders. Honesty reared its fair head quite often, but deception and guile were consistently tried throughout the period, especially northward from Cape Rodney. The Eskimos would not trade unless they received exactly what they wanted, or unless an object met with their approval. A row of enamel (buttons) in exchange for a kayak may seem to be a decidedly lopsided bargain, but the enamel was a luxury item probably unobtainable through the regular Siberian sources while a kayak could easily be replaced. On the other hand, their refusal to sell furs for anything less than a Siberian saber suggests that the furs were hard to get and could bring a much greater price without any trouble from a Siberian trader. During this period, the Eskimo

18. Oswalt 1967, p. 75.

trader was in control of the trading sessions and had established the value basis for his goods.

There is little said in the accounts about relations between European men and Eskimo women. At Cape Rodney, Merck's remarks suggest that the men wanted women but that the husbands would not accede to their request. At Kotzebue Sound, Choris penned the hopeful note that the Eskimos would return to shore for some women for the officers. On the Siberian side, the favors of the female Americans were traded when there was nothing else to offer. In the Golovnin Bay area, girls were married as early as ten years of age, and the Stebbins women, according to Khromchenko, were the "slaves" of men. King Islanders apparently practiced polygyny—as most of the tribes did, we later learn.

The presence of shamans was acknowledged but not discussed by any explorer. Only one instance of a possible transvestite was mentioned from Wales in 1826.

The accounts contain a number of remarks concerning the subject of chieftainship and its considerable responsibilities, despite the lack of communication between the explorers and the Eskimos; yet all information not derived empirically is unfortunately suspect, as is shown by Kotzebue's mistake of believing (through pantomime) that a waterway extended from Kotzebue Sound to the south through the Nugnugaluktuk River, and by Kobelev's conclusion that the King Islanders' gestures meant that Christian Russians lived in a fort on Seward Peninsula.

THE ANYUI FAIR, TRADE, AND TOBACCO

Trade was the only subject that was consistently discussed in enough detail by all explorers to gauge a definite change throughout the period. The scanty amount of European trade goods possessed by the Cape Denbigh people in 1778 and the comparative wealth of goods by those of Kotzebue Sound in 1827 are indicative of the steady increase in goods across the strait.

The observations made by explorers from Cook to Beechey have demonstrated not only the gradual growth of intercontinental trade but the change in wares traded: from almost no knowledge of tobacco to a great passion for it; from small bits of iron to spears and knives made in Siberia especially for trade. Archeological sites show little evidence of a large native trade before European goods became available, although a large part of such a trade would probably have consisted of soft goods—reindeer skins, oil, and wooden wares—which would have left comparatively few traces. In aboriginal times, however, the Bering Strait Eskimo would have had little need to trade over long distances for goods, especially to another continent, because he had several alternative methods of obtaining native goods: through utilization of his own tribal resources; through tribal alliances; and by participation in the formalized intertribal trading ceremony called the messenger feast.

The development of an intercontinental trade cannot be accounted for by either the passage of time or an exchange solely of traditional Eskimo goods. By all evidence, it was dependent on a number of factors: (1) the cessation of Chukchi-Cossack hostilities in the 1780s, which allowed Chukchi traders to serve as middlemen between Russians and Alaskan Eskimos; (2) a sufficient quantity of trade goods, which would not be absorbed by the Russians and Siberians on the long journey across Siberia; (3) a commodity in Alaska that would be of great enough value to the Russians and the Chukchi to make the long and difficult journey from Russia to northeastern Siberia worth the effort; and (4) traders to carry the goods in Alaska.

All of these requirements were satisfied with the establishment of a large trading market on the Anyui tributary of the Kolyma River in 1789. Although eight hundred miles from the strait, it was to have far-reaching effects in Alaska. The market was first organized for the exchange of tobacco and American furs that had already begun to be of importance to Chukchi rovers who developed into specialized traders with the inauguration of the Anyui market. The demand for fox and marten furs created the first change in the economy of the historical Eskimos, because these furs, destined for European consumption, were not traditionally used by Alaskan Eskimos except in ornamentation of fur clothing. Alaskans not only began trading as links in a chain of traders that originated in Indian territory to the east and ended at Anyui, but began trapping the animals themselves.

Local Eskimo markets apparently developed into large international markets after the trade in European goods began. Otto von Kotzebue reported a mute trading session between a Chukchi or Siberian Eskimo man (as described to him by an Eskimo), but neither he nor Beechey mentioned the Kotzebue trade market, which grew very large and important during the latter part of the nineteenth century, when native Siberian and Alaskan goods, including furs, and European products were brought together. This omission may be due to the explorers' not visiting Sheshalik, its earliest location on the north shore of Kotzebue Sound,[19] but more probably because it was only a very small local gathering at that time. Such a local market—for courtship, social intercourse, and sometimes fishing as well as trading—also existed at Point Spencer, which in aboriginal times was larger than the Kotzebue market, according to my informants. Within the large definition of Bering Strait, local markets were located at Sheshalik, Point Spencer, Stebbins, and Pastolik for the exchange of local Alaskan Eskimo products; but from the available data already given, it appears that there was little intercontinental trade until after the introduction of European goods.

Doubtless some native trade goods crossed the strait in aboriginal times, but even observers in Siberia like Bogoras were really speaking about a trade in European goods when discussing "aboriginal trade"; as a matter of fact, in his "ancient trading tales" the principal theme is tobacco, which was not

19. Ernest S. Burch, Jr., personal communication.

traded at the strait until the eighteenth century. In another statement he said, "Even before the arrival of the Russians [in Siberia], a lively traffic was carried on . . . between Asia and America across Bering Strait," the Reindeer Chukchi and Eskimos of East Cape exchanging "reindeer-skins and ready-made garments" for "blubber, thongs, and seal-skins."[20] The authenticity of this information is questionable. Bogoras had no archeological support, and he received this information roughly two hundred fifty years after the first Cossacks had come to Chukchi territory, which analogously would mean that the Aleutian Islanders of 1973 could recall what happened in 1723, eighteen years before Bering discovered Alaska. If pre-European trade had been as large as thought, then the Chukchi would have had considerably more information to give the Cossacks about Alaska than they did, because the intercontinental trade during the nineteenth century was often carried on by personal representatives of both continents.

The trade in domesticated Siberian reindeer skins, which formed a large part of nineteenth-century exports to Alaska, was also only just developing during historical times because reindeer herds did not attain their size and importance for trade until the Chukchi made peace with the Russians, and after fairs like the Anyui market were established. Only after the beginning of peace did the Chukchi spread west and southwest and expand their reindeer breeding, thus developing a new product—reindeer skins—for trading to Alaska during the nineteenth century.[21] Bogoras himself said that shortly after the founding of the Anyui market, "the products of reindeer-breeding were . . . of very slight importance, while at present [around 1895] they amount to about three fifths of the total Anui purchases."[22] I think it is also of considerable importance that none of the explorers before the mid-nineteenth century described clothing made from the distinctive mottled skin of the domesticated reindeer.

The establishment of the Anyui market was made possible by a truce of peace between the Chukchi and the Russians of Siberia. The Cossacks had not carried on an active military campaign against the Chukchi since Pavlutskii's time of the 1730s and 1740s, but the Chukchi had continued to resist Russian domination and had refused to pay the *iasak* or tax. In 1784, however, peace became possible when "[Major Shmaileff] completely settled all disputes, and reconciled the [Chukchi and Koryak] nations with the Russians."[23] In 1788 Banner, the governor, made peace with the western Reindeer Chukchi near the Kolyma River, and the effect of the end of hostilities between the Cossacks and the Chukchi reached everywhere into Chukchi country.

Almost simultaneously with the founding of the Anyui market, fairs at

20. Bogoras 1904–9, pt. 1, p. 53.
21. Antropova and Kuznetsova 1964, p. 804.
22. Bogoras 1904–9, pt. 1, p. 57.
23. Sauer 1802, p. 69.

Gizhiga and Kamenskoye on the Okhotsk Sea were patronized by the Chuk-chi around Anadyrsk.[24] But these markets, located far from the trading sphere of the northern Chukchi and the Bering Strait, contributed only a small percentage of the goods for the Alaskan trade.

The market on the Anyui was the most important factor in the tremendous growth of the Bering Strait trade around the turn of the nineteenth century. In conjunction with American whalers and traders during the second half of the century, it contributed to the growth of the market at Kotzebue. From the very beginning of Cossack settlement, a few independent Russian traders had traded with local tribes on the Lena and Kolyma rivers, and by 1787— just before the founding of the Anyui market—enough goods had reached the Chukchi tribes, whose territory lay at the edge of the Kolyma district, to cross the strait. In that year the Billings expedition saw Alaskan products at Saint Lawrence Bay, Siberia: fox, marten, and rabbit furs, muskrat skins, umiaks, and "arms," which the Chukchi were planning to trade for Russian goods at Gizhiga on the Okhotsk Sea and with "the wandering peddling traders about the estuary of the [Kolyma]." At Saint Lawrence Bay, the Chukchi also traded "with their female prisoners [from Alaska], receiving in return rein-deer, copper and iron kettles, knives, beads, and such articles [but tobacco was not mentioned] as the rovers obtain from the Russian traders."[25]

The Anyui market was first described in English translation in the 1820s by Midshipman Matiuschkin of Ferdinand von Wrangell's expedition and by John Cochrane, of the English navy.[26] At that time, Fort Anyui had twenty houses, a large wooden building, and about two hundred inhabitants. The fair was located in Yukagir territory, but was attended by Lamuts, Tungus, Koryaks, Tshuwantzi, Chukchi, and Russians, and in 1821 by two "Kar-goules," or Eskimos, from Alaska.[27] Yet the market existed especially for the benefit of the Chukchi, who sometimes traveled for six months with their families and reindeer sleds from the Chukchi Peninsula with their Alaskan furs. Cochrane said that the Chukchi who came to the market in 1821 lived on the Chaun River and transferred their goods to the East Cape and Saint Lawrence Bay Chukchi (which probably included Eskimos, too, since the term Chukchi also meant Eskimos at that time), who in turn sent them to Alaska. A chief from East Cape was present in 1821, however. In all, there

24. Bogoras 1904–9, pt. 1, p. 58. Ferdinand von Wrangell said, however, that annual fairs were held prior to this at Anadyr and "Kammenoje," but that the Anyui fair was of greater advantage to the Russians (Wrangell 1840, p. 115*n*).

25. Sauer 1802, pp. 251, 253.

26. There may be a number of earlier accounts in Russian archives. Bogoras drew heavily on material in the Kolyma archives for his account. Information about the Anyui market is taken from Bogoras 1904–9, pt. 3, pp. 700–5; Cochrane 1824, pp. 251–56, 261–73; and Wrangell 1840, pp. 89–92, 114–18.

27. Cochrane said that "descendants of the Yukagiri inhabit the banks of the two rivers Aniuy, and serve as a sort of neutral nation between the Russians and Tchuktchi." According to him, the Yukagir had considerable Russian admixture (p. 252).

were 68 Chukchi men, 60 women, and 56 children, 250 sleds, and 500 reindeer, each of which could pull 150 pounds. Most of the Russian merchants came from Yakutsk, almost a thousand miles away.

The Chukchi brought Alaskan furs, bear skins, walrus thongs, and walrus tusks, and by 1821 there was a brisk trade in kettles, hatchets, knives, wooden and metal pipes, scissors, needles, beads, and a little cloth, besides the usual tobacco. The market generally lasted three or four days during the first week of March, although Cochrane said that in 1821 it lasted seven days, three more than usual.

From Matiuschkin's account we are able to get an idea of prices the Bering Strait Eskimos got for their furs. In 1821 the trading commissioners decided that the Russian traders at Anyui would give 2 poods (72 pounds) of tobacco for 16 fox and 20 marten skins (and "other articles in proportion") for which the Chukchi had paid ½ pood (18 pounds) of tobacco to a native middleman. Tobacco was selling then at 3½ rubles a pound.[28] According to Matiuschkin's rates, the middleman (East Cape Chukchi or Eskimo man) would have received about 1¾ rubles a skin, and if there had been another middleman or two the amount finally accruing to the Alaskan trapper would have been very small, less than a ruble, or 20 cents a pelt *in trade goods*.

Both Cochrane and Matiuschkin described the frenzy and noise of the excited Russian merchants as they raced to get the choicest furs from the self-possessed Chukchi standing calmly near their loaded sleds. Although the market of 1821 was considered to be a good one, the Chukchi sold less than a third of their most valuable furs in return for only half of the tobacco on hand because apparently their sleds did not have the capacity to hold any more besides other wares.

Tobacco, an indigenous American plant that had to travel round the globe eastward from the New World to Alaska, was eagerly sought by Alaskan Eskimos. The tobacco was used as an intoxicant, and only a tiny portion was mixed with wood shavings at one time, the Eskimos retaining all of the smoke in their lungs until they became unconscious.

It has often been assumed that tobacco came to the Bering Strait and then to Alaska either with Dezhnev on his alleged voyage, or with the Cossacks who had founded Nizhne-Kolymsk and Anadyrsk in the 1640s; but tobacco probably did not arrive in Alaska until around the 1750s, at the earliest. In the 1580s the first Cossacks who crossed the Urals did not have tobacco with them because both its cultivation and smoking had barely started in Europe. Once tobacco reached Russia, it was swiftly adopted; but its use and sale were temporarily banned under penalty of death by Tsar Michael in 1634, and this ban was not repealed until 1697 by Peter the Great.[29] This fact alone

28. Wrangell 1840, pp. 89, 117; elsewhere in Wrangell's account, prices given were 8 to 10 rubles for a red fox; 2½ to 3 for white stone fox; 7 to 10 rubles for blue fox; and 50 to 150 for black fox. Ermine was not included (p. 89).
29. Price 1961, p. 19.

meant that there was little chance that tobacco was present in Siberia until the early 1700s. Punishment for disobeying the edict of 1634 was harsh and swift, ranging from exile in Siberia to death; but as time went on, enforcement became less strict, and Peter (who, along with many other Russians, had been secretly smoking) removed the ban and actively sought a tobacco trade. Tobacco had entered Russia from Circassia, Poland, and Sweden for a long time without duty, and the income that would be derived from taxing this popular commodity was attractive enough for Peter to go against the wishes of the church, which had been instrumental in issuing the original ban.[30]

The Russian Tobacco Company, which won a monopoly for importing tobacco into Russia at the time of Peter the Great, was not permitted to sell tobacco in Siberia.[31] Even before this, the Stroganovs had resisted all attempts to sell tobacco in their territory, and the small amount of tobacco that got to western Siberia—so far from eastern Siberia and Alaska—was consumed there. The remote parts of that vast country had to await a regular supply of tobacco in large enough quantity that could be considered surplus over the supplies needed to satisfy first the regions nearest Russia. By the time of the Anyui market in 1789, this had been accomplished.

If tobacco did not arrive in Alaska before the 1750s, it would explain why it was not a regular trade item, apparently unknown to the Eskimos according to Cook's, Kobelev's, and the Billings expedition's remarks. Only in 1816 did an explorer, Kotzebue, finally observe Eskimos actually using tobacco. The entry of tobacco into Canadian territory did not occur until the late eighteenth century, and possibly later. According to Alexander Mackenzie, the Dogrib and Slave Indians in the interior of Canada were not used to tobacco in 1789, and Vilhjalmur Stefansson said that people at the mouth of the Mackenzie River did not receive tobacco until 1821.[32]

Only after the founding of the Anyui market was a stable, regular supply of tobacco available for northeastern Siberia and the whole of Alaska, but the four thousand pounds traded annually at that time seem very small for the demands of more than sixty thousand persons in these two areas, and was probably one of the reasons it was smoked only a pinch at a time. By the 1820s tobacco was a primary article of trade, having supplanted the sabers and long knives so eagerly sought from Billings and Kotzebue only a few years before.

The tobacco trade easily made one world of two important continents, and was to make striking changes of peace and territory among the Alaskan Eskimos.

30. Ibid., pp. 22–29.
31. Ibid., pp. 62–77.
32. Stefansson 1921, p. 40. Stefansson's estimate of the time period of the eastward travels of tobacco appears to be even later than those presented herein.

CHAPTER 9

The Tribes of Bering Strait

THE explorers have given us bits and pieces about settlement patterns, subsistence economy, and territorial distribution of the Eskimos; but before proceeding beyond the first permanent European settlement in the Bering Strait area, this chapter will explain the actual tribal distribution, summarize political organization, and discuss the utilization of land. These interpretations are based on a number of printed and archival sources, the major ones of which are mentioned in the references for the subsistence summaries, and on data obtained from about sixty selected Eskimo informants. Much of the information is necessarily taken from accounts published toward the end of the nineteenth century; but the settlement and subsistence patterns were quite stable throughout the century, with the exceptions noted. Therefore, the summaries also pertain to the period 1778–1827, at which time the Malemiut had not yet begun their southward move.[1]

TRIBAL DISTRIBUTION

Early writers used various linguistic names to mean "tribe," but the linguistic spread rarely coincided with any tribal unit. Within the Bering Strait area it is usually agreed that there were more than twenty tribes during the early nineteenth century. Any uncertainty about the exact number is due to lack of information about the autonomy of a particular group or village at that

1. The subjects of political organization and settlement and subsistence patterns for Seward Peninsula alone have been discussed in greater detail in Ray 1964b and 1967b. I have done further field work in the Unalakleet and Saint Michael areas on settlement and subsistence patterns since both papers were published. A complete discussion of place names, including settlements, is found in Ray 1971a.

There is no consensus among those working with social and political organization of Eskimos what the aggregate of persons I call "tribe" should be known as: "tribe," "group," "regional group," or "deme." All of these terms have been applied to essentially the same groupings of people. Use of "tribe" here is partly to strengthen the description of Eskimo political organization, and to help correct the long-standing popular notion that all Eskimos were nomads with chaotic political and social systems.

time. Although all of the tribes appeared to be similar from the vantage of the greatly differing tribes in Canada or Greenland, there were many basic variations among the Bering Strait groups. One of the most important was the food quest, which fell into three patterns during the nineteenth century: whaling-walrus (whale, walrus, seal, and fishing); caribou hunting (caribou, seal, beluga, and fishing); and small sea mammal hunting (seal, beluga, fishing, and caribou). It is sometimes difficult to place tribes specifically into the latter two categories, but I have made caribou hunting a separate pattern because several tribes clearly depended on caribou for the larger part of their food and clothing.

Included in the whaling-walrus pattern were the tribes of Little Diomede and King islands, Wales, and to a lesser extent, Sledge Island and Cape Nome, although the latter two would more rightly belong in small sea mammal hunting. It is of interest that these three islands contain few streams, and that Wales and Cape Nome on the mainland are not located on large rivers. During most of the nineteenth century, however, Sledge Island and Cape Nome were not whaling peoples, and probably did not get many walrus either, though informants said that their grandparents had told them that large herds of walrus came fairly close to Sledge Island and Cape Nome as well as to Besboro and Stuart islands farther south.[2]

Tribes that lived almost exclusively on caribou in the winter, and actively hunted them in organized drives toward corrals, were Kauwerak, Koyuk, Goodhope, and, so far as we know, Inglutalik, Egavik, and Shaktoolik. All of these tribes also ate large quantities of fish and, in various degrees, small sea mammals. All of the other tribes fell into the small sea mammal hunting category, but hunted caribou whenever possible, and of course caught fish and other products of the rivers and the sea. These tribes were the Cape Espenberg, Shishmaref, Port Clarence, Ignituk, Fish River, Atnuk, Unalakleet, Kikiktauk, Saint Michael, Stebbins, and Pastolik.[3]

Other places, like Cape Douglas, Moses Point, and the Nome, Snake, Sinuk, and Tubuktulik rivers, which became well known later on for various reasons, were actually campsites within a larger tribal territory, and their inhabitants were not considered to be autonomous tribes during the

2. Not much is known about whaling and walrus hunting around Cape Nome and Sledge Island, but informants told me that walrus and whales could be seen with the naked eye long ago, and Zagoskin heard the deafening sound of many walruses on the ice pack that stretched from Cape Rodney to Cape Romanof, after leaving Sledge Island (Zagoskin 1967, p. 89). William B. Van Valin found a collection of ceremonial whaling objects on Sledge Island, among them ivory chains for umiaks, whaling charms, and large wooden models of men and women, all used in whaling festivities. Van Valin said that the oldest living Eskimo told him that these objects had belonged to a very old man who had inherited the collection (1944, pp. 47–48).

3. Since the publication of my paper, "Land Tenure and Polity of the Bering Strait Eskimos," I have separated the tribes originally put under the name Tapkak into Goodhope, Cape Espenberg, and Shishmaref. In identifying the tribal names I am using an English place name in conjunction with the original native site name for their principal village, but in most cases, it is a geographical, not a linguistic, equivalent. For some tribes, like Shaktoolik and Koyuk, there are no English equivalents.

nineteenth century. Other problematical tribal occupancies are the mouth of the Fish River and the upper Unalakleet River. During the early part of the nineteenth century it is uncertain whether the lower Fish River was occupied by the Unaluk-speaking people of Golovin or by the Fish River people, who spoke a Kauwerak-related dialect. According to the traditional occupancy pattern of a small river, one of the groups would have claimed its entire length at one time. If it were the Fish River people, they would have been located as a wedge between Unalit tribes, because both the east and the west coasts of Golovnin Bay were occupied by Unaluk speakers.

From the 1840s on, Indians lived on the upper Unalakleet River in what had been Eskimo territory. The principal village inhabited by the Ingalik Indians was "Ulukuk," which is derived from the Eskimo for slate, *uluksruk*, used in making ulus, or women's knives. Eskimo tradition says that the entire length of the Unalakleet River was once occupied by the Eskimos; therefore, Ingalik residency was probably coterminous with the changes caused by the beginning of European trading in Siberia and the readjustment of Alaskan Eskimo population groupings.

According to folk tales from all Eskimo tribes adjacent to Indians, inter-tribal relations were strained and often tragic. In Eskimo tales from Fish River, Golovin, Atnuk, Koyuk, Unalakleet, and even Shishmaref, the Indians were always the aggressors. All of the tales have a duplication of traditional elements, especially the complete annihilation of the villagers or the survival of only one or two persons, usually an orphan boy. Although Eskimo-Indian relations were probably no worse than were Eskimo inter-tribal relations, there was nevertheless a real fear, day in and day out, among tribes on Eskimo-Indian boundaries, at least according to all of the stories related by twentieth-century Eskimos. The Eskimos lived with vigilance, which was intensified when they hunted toward Indian country. There, an unexplained death or a missing man was attributed to an Indian. An Eskimo mother sometimes disciplined an unruly child with threats that an Indian would get him if he did not behave. This feeling of distrust and fear between the two races continued until well into the twentieth century (although there always had been occasional marriages and considerable freedom in trading); and one of the triumphs for the natives of Alaska was the formation of the Alaska Federation of Natives in October 1966, when Indians and Eskimos were able to work together for a short time on a common front to fight for a large sum of money and title to their aboriginal lands in the Congress of the United States.

A Bering Strait tribe consisted of people with a common language and culture who lived within well-defined boundaries recognized by themselves and contiguous tribes. The Alaskan Eskimos were not wanderers without a fixed abode or identification with a specific territory; nor did they use land indiscriminately. A tribal territory was usually composed of the drainage area of one large river and its tributaries, as well as smaller rivers in the area;

but sometimes it consisted of only a piece of coastland. Within the boundaries were one large permanent village of semisubterranean dwellings made of driftwood and sod, many seasonal campsites, and often several small villages considered to be year-round residences of one or two families. Summer camps for fishing were usually one-family camps, but in some areas they accommodated as many as ten. Year-round villages of one family were more commonly found on the seacoast than on the rivers. Seasonal dwellings were conical or hemispherical skin tents during the summer north of Cape Nome (walrus-hide houses on King and Diomede islands), and wooden huts for winter caribou hunting; but in Unalit territory, the Eskimos, except for the Malemiut, usually used wood and turf houses in the summer.

The largest village lent its name to the tribe. Thus, Kauweramiut, or "people of Kauwerak," meant essentially "the people who lived in territory presided over by the people of Kauwerak." In the Eskimo language, all living villages were called by the site name plus the suffix "-miut," meaning inhabitants. (The Anglicization of Eskimo names, or the shortened version without "-miut," is actually the site name.) When the Eskimo political system was in effect, a village was rarely called by the site name alone, but always with "-miut," so that it actually referred to a social conglomerate of persons who considered the place to be their principal home but who traveled widely at different times of the year to other homesites within their territory. The name of this village as a living whole, and *not* the village site, was synonymous with the tribe; therefore, to identify a village as the political unit or the tribe is too restrictive because without exception the large, permanent village was only a home base from which jurisdiction was implemented over the territory and other settlements, including year-round villages and campsites.[4]

Almost everyone left the principal village during the summer, but a few old and young persons usually remained behind in large villages like Wales, Sinramiut, and Cape Nome. The principal village always had a community, or men's house, called *kazgi* at Bering Strait, which was supported by all of the village under leadership of the chiefs. The men's house was the center for the men's indoor activities, meetings of political affairs, and was a guest house for visitors. Women entered the building to bring food to the men and to participate in formal ceremonial and social events. There were several men's houses in the largest villages of this area—Wales, King Island, and Little Diomede—all of which belonged to the whaling pattern. Each men's house represented a different faction of the village. In the men's house the

4. The suffix "-miut" could refer to any group of people in any area. Within the larger tribal territory, an area with only one dwelling would have the suffix refer to the "people of" that place. The "-miut" ending of the largest village of tribal territory only coincidentally was the name that the Eskimos themselves used to denote the tribe or group of persons that claimed a specific territory. This "social aggregation" then became a "political aggregation" in terms of its internal government and external relations regarding its territory and boundaries.

leaders decided foreign affairs, received visitors, dispensed justice in matters of defense, theft, and trespass or murder. Here they also prepared for ceremonial occasions, especially the messenger feast, which, among other things, cemented political relations between two tribes, usually one living on the coast and the other, inland.

Every Bering Strait Eskimo village that served as a capital had a *kazgi* building, an edifice that has been described and lauded by many explorers; but by the time trained observers arrived at Bering Strait, the official functions of the men's house had been considerably submerged by the United States government.[5] On the mainland the men's house was abandoned except as a token physical structure after the gold rush of 1898–1900, the measles epidemic of 1900, and especially after the 1918 flu epidemic.

Every men's house had one or more leaders, or chiefs, who worked in conjunction with an informal council of elders in matters of tribal affairs. Ideally, chieftainship was hereditary, usually descending through a prominent family to the eldest son. It was desirable to begin training for this position at a young age, but actually any man who was a good hunter, had good judgment, and was diplomatic in his dealings with other tribes could fill it. The possession of wealth was both a result of and a contributing factor to chieftainship, and was often due to considerable interpersonal and political dealings.[6] My informants told me that women had never been chiefs.

The mechanisms of government and makeup of the men's house in tribes of the caribou hunters and small sea mammal hunters probably differed traditionally from those of the whalers, where the complicated whaling ceremonies and the maneuvers in selecting umiak crews for exploitation of their resources dominated internal politics. All of the tribes in the whaling pattern had several men's houses that represented various village factions, but there was only one in the caribou and the small sea mammal patterns, no matter how large the village. Caribou hunting focused attention on territorial boundaries, which became of the utmost importance when people depended on the land, and not the sea, for their sustenance. The stress between tribes was magnified when people of fixed abode depended on a migratory animal like the caribou, which they hunted only within a specified territory. Fac-

5. An exception to this in the Bering Strait area is on King Island, where a modified men's house system is still in force, at least in regard to the internal social and political structure of umiak hunting crews who, until their recent permanent move to Nome, hunted walrus in somewhat the same way as they did in aboriginal days (Bogojavlensky 1969; Bogojavlensky and Fuller 1973). A study of the men's house system and whaling crews made by Bogojavlensky omits the wider political role of the men's house regarding intertribal relations, as well it might in the 1970s. This is the only study that has so far examined the functional and sociological aspects of the men's house and its related institutions in the Bering Strait area.

6. An example of choosing a chief who was not the eldest son in historical times was in Unalakleet when Nashalook, the youngest son, was chosen to succeed Deliluk, the eldest son, who died after succeeding his father, Alluyianuk. At the time of Deliluk's death there were two brothers older than Nashalook, but an informal council decided that Nashalook should become the chief because he was able to meet people well, was diplomatic, and was a "better talker" than the others.

tions undoubtedly existed in all of the mainland villages, but the leaders were not concerned so much with intratribal political intrigues and jealousies for exploitation of the sea as for demonstrable tribal solidarity to maintain their tribal boundaries, and subsequently the products of their land.

Encroachment on another tribe's territory could mean death on sight, and according to innumerable folk tales, this was not uncommon. The *inyukutuk*, or "hiding man," of Eskimo mythology was a stranger who inexplicably found himself in foreign territory. He skulked beyond sight of human beings for fear of being discovered and killed, and bones of an unidentified man found washed upon the beach or lying far out on the tundra were thought to be those of such a wanderer. The Eskimo tribes maintained their vigilance of boundaries, not only where they abutted on the land of Indians, who were their perennial enemies, but on other Eskimo land. Members of each tribe were aware of their tribal boundaries, and usually of boundaries of other tribes whom they visited. Eskimos traveled without harm to another tribe's territory if they were known personally to its members, usually relatives; no man traveled for the first time to foreign territory without being accompanied by a person known there. As between sovereign nations today, permission was needed to travel between tribes, and names were the important passports that proved relationships and served as entry to another territory. All of this was considerably theoretical, however, because any person from a neighboring tribe was known to most, if not all, of its members from childhood, and this principle of identification never arose unless faced with the drama of an *inyukutuk*, a real stranger, and a threat. Therefore, in actuality travel between tribes was freely undertaken, and it is understandable why some writers thought that Eskimos could go anywhere and use any territory they wished with no restrictions whatsoever.

Besides informal tribal understandings on an individual basis, there also existed tribal alliances. These alliances probably did not differ much from an informal granting of permission to hunt and fish in other territory, but those that we know existed were pointedly in force for widening the range of subsistence pursuits, and for protection in the event of raids by and wars with Indians or Siberians. These alliances, moreover, were undertaken on the level of trading partnerships (probably the same ones that were in force during the messenger feast), but it became a matter of political importance because tribal lands were used and entry into the foreign territory was a political act.

In principle, any two contiguous tribes could be allies, but the most necessary alliances were between island and mainland tribes, which would have celebrated the messenger feast in December had ice conditions made it possible. Only rarely was the ice of Bering Strait crossed in winter to any island except Sledge Island. The alliances between Little Diomede and Wales and between King Island and Kauwerak had dated back before memory, and entire families would spend a season or almost a year in the other tribe's homeland. On King Island in 1791, Ivan Kobelev met inhabitants of the Kheuveren (Kuzitrin) River, who had come the preceding summer for trade; in 1892, eleven Diomede Islanders wintered at Wales.[7] Sledge Island and Cape Nome also had a similar alliance, though little is known about it. Generally, these alliances provided mainland peoples with ocean products that were often unavailable to them, and islanders with land products—greens, berries, and even caribou. King Islanders were permitted to hunt caribou in Kuzitrin Lake in the summertime and to gather greens at certain places, particularly near Pilgrim Springs. The Little Diomede Island people were known to go with Wales people as far inland as Kauwerak to hunt caribou, and all Sledge Islanders often left their island home for berry picking or fishing on the mainland opposite Cape Douglas, or at the Sinuk River or Cape Nome. In return, mainland inhabitants hunted walrus and crabs near Sledge Island, to which it was sometimes possible to travel on the ice in the spring. Furthermore, during times of possible starvation in the spring or during bad weather, all members of friendly tribes were welcome at places like Tuksuk Channel or Atnuk on Cape Darby where small fish like smelts and tomcods could always be procured.

POPULATION

At the beginning of the nineteenth century, there were possibly 2,500 inhabitants in the productive 26,000 square miles of land between Kotzebue and Norton sounds. The first population estimate of northwest Alaska was made in 1826–27 by Frederick Beechey, who said there probably were 2,500 persons living between Point Barrow and Port Clarence, "including Kowee-rock [Kauwerak]" (but he had not included Wales).[8]

In 1854 John Simpson, a surgeon with the Franklin search party, estimated the population in the area from Norton Sound to the Colville River to be about 2,500, but "probably little more than 2000."

William H. Dall, who had been with the Western Union Telegraph Expedition in 1865–67, thought the population between Saint Michael and the northern Arctic coast at that time was about 3,750 (1,500 on Seward Peninsula, 1,000 on the coast of Norton Sound, 150 on the Diomede islands, 100 on Sledge Island, and 1,000 on the Arctic coast). Dall said that his figures were "corrected from Russian estimates, and, if anything, above rather than below the actual number."

In 1881 C. L. Hooper, skipper of the *Thomas A. Corwin*, estimated that 3,000 Eskimos lived in the area from the Bering Strait (at Cape Prince of Wales) to the Colville River.

The 1880 census did not provide enough figures for a useful estimate, but

7. See pp. 113–14; Lopp diary, 25 September 1892–2 July 1893, entry for 17 December.

8. References for this section: Beechey 1831, 2:568; Simpson in Great Britain Sessional Papers 1854–55, vol. 35, no. 1898, encl. 6, p. 919; Dall 1870, p. 537; C. L. Hooper 1884, p. 101; R. Porter 1893, pp. 7, 8.

the 1890 census arrived at a population of 3,361 from Saint Michael to Point Barrow. Of these, 2,305 lived between Saint Michael and the north coast of Seward Peninsula.

All of these estimates are for the period when there were only a few Europeans at any one time in the whole of Alaska (the estimate of 1890 was ten years before the Nome gold rush and the measles epidemic of 1900), and all estimates fall far short of the huge populations attributed to aboriginal villages by writers, especially Sheldon Jackson, who wanted to blame the white man for the decrease so that his remedial programs would be supported. The population had never been large. Abandoned villages and large archeological sites often gave the impression of a decline from a grand era; but villages were abandoned for many reasons, and even occupied settlements often looked larger than they actually were because empty and occupied dwellings stood side by side.[9]

Yet, from population estimates for separate villages during the early and middle nineteenth century, Beechey's figures appear to be low. Before the beginning of the nineteenth century, we have firsthand census figures for only two tribes, Little Diomede and King Island, obtained by Ivan Kobelev in 1779 and 1791. The figures for Little Diomede are higher than those of the nineteenth century, and those of King Island, lower. It is therefore not possible to decide whether the populations of other places had increased or decreased by the time the first censuses were taken much later in the century. Kobelev's population figures are probably more reliable than any others in the Bering Strait area, with the exception of schoolteacher counts in the villages after 1890. All others, including those of the tenth and eleventh censuses, can be considered only approximations of the actual population because of unreliable census takers and procedures.

In 1779 Kobelev counted 164 persons (85 men and 79 women) on Little Diomede Island, but in 1791 he counted only 100 (45 males and adolescents, 55 females and infants). (In 1779 Kobelev gave the population of Big Diomede as 398, and in 1791, 218). The difference of 64 persons might be attributed to visitors on the island in 1779. The extreme mobility of Eskimo families in the summertime for trading and fishing, and in the wintertime for intervillage festivities, has skewed many population figures. In some cases we know that the population figures of a village included visitors, but in others we cannot be sure. Perhaps the decrease of population on both islands in 1791 was due to deaths, or perhaps one set of figures was wrong. In 1791 Kobelev counted 170 persons on King Island, ten of them from Kauwerak. This figure is lower than any subsequent nineteenth-century figures except the 1880 census of 100.

The largest village in the Bering Strait area, and probably in all of Alaska, was Wales with between 500 and 600 inhabitants or possibly more during the

---

9. Unfortunately, writers are still quoting Jackson's dishonest figures as proof of an enormous aboriginal Eskimo population on Alaska's west coast; for example, see Jenness 1962, p. 7.

early nineteenth century. Wales was essentially two villages, *agianamiut*, on the south, and *kiatanamiut*, on the north, with about equal population. The villages of Wales and King and Little Diomede islands were the largest in the area, and all were walrus hunters, sometimes whalers. Sledge Island and Cape Nome, though partly dependent on walrus, supported small populations; Sledge Island had 50 or 60, and Cape Nome, 60 to 100.

Next in size, generally, were villages of the caribou-hunting tribes. Kauwerak had between 50 and 75 inhabitants. Other large villages were those that were able to combine good small sea mammal hunting with caribou hunting. For example, Shishmaref, with good bearded seal hunting nearby, contained possibly 80 persons, and Ignituk had more than 100. All other villages, except for the puzzling Atuik (Stebbins) which was reported to have 200 in 1822, were smaller and varied from only one family to about 50 persons.[10] Near Deering, Safety Sound, and Cape Denbigh, larger villages appear to have existed in prehistoric times, but the character of the sites built on successive populations may make the sizes deceptive.

SUBSISTENCE ACTIVITIES

The Bering Strait was one of the richest areas of the Eskimo world in fish, sea and land mammals, plant foods, fowl, and eggs. The comparatively high density of population reflected this abundance, particularly on the small islands of the strait and at Cape Prince of Wales, which were near the migration routes of the walrus and the whale.

The large bowhead whale was hunted only by the inhabitants of Wales—and sometimes the islands, even Sledge Island, some of the old Eskimos say.[11] Dead whales that were lodged in the ice sometimes drifted to the islands, where the joyful butchers cut off as much as a thousand pounds of the highly regarded whale skin called muktuk. The only record of how many whales the people of Wales got before the twentieth century is from the writings of Harrison R. Thornton and William T. Lopp, the first teachers. In 1888 Wales hunters got only 1 whale; in 1889, 3; in 1890, none; and in 1891, 1. However, they had struck and lost 12 in 1889, 2 in 1890, and 29 in 1891. In 1895 the crews began singing ancient whaling songs on 1 May, preparatory to whaling, which began on the sixth; but they did not capture one whale that year. Fortunately, a "big" walrus catch supplied the village with plenty of food.

10. Since later population figures were substantially lower for Atuik, this high figure of 1822 may have been the combined populations of Saint Michael, Stebbins, Pikmiktalik, and possibly traders from the North, since 200 was the same number counted a few days before by Khromchenko on Stuart Island (see Chap. 6).

11. Information about the hunting of whales at Wales is taken from my field notes; Bernardi 1912; Curtis 1930, pp. 137–42; and Thornton 1931, pp. 165–71. Bernardi and Thornton wrote eyewitness accounts of various whaling ceremonies. Other information used in this summary is taken from the *American Missionary*, October 1891, p. 367; *The Eskimo Bulletin*, 1895, 1902; Lopp diary, 1895; and Report on Education in Alaska for 1901–2 (1903), 2:1255.

Walrus provided ivory for tools and a ton of meat.[12] The females attained a maximum weight of two thousand pounds, and the bulls, four thousand. The thick skins of females or young bulls were split to make umiak and kayak coverings, and on King Island the square summer houses were covered with hide that had been dehaired and dried until translucent. Rope and mukluk soles were also made from the skin of young walruses. The walrus arrived on the ice in the early part of May, but the largest numbers were killed during June as they came past the islands. In the fall, they usually swam in the water of the ice pack and were harder to kill. The condition and movement of the ice pack toward Siberia sometimes caused a poor walrus hunting season.

Walrus skin was of greater importance than the meat because it was the commodity that permitted these people to make umiaks and therefore to live on the islands and to pursue their game. The number of walrus caught, even at the times when the walrus population was supposed to have been at its lowest, apparently was plentiful enough to build and keep in repair an adequate number of umiaks. A large boat between 35 and 40 feet long required from 5 to 6 split skins, or about 3 walruses. It is evident that the annual catch at Cape Prince of Wales and on Saint Lawrence Island—from the only figures available in historic times—was little more than 1 walrus per person. If there were an average of 1 or even 2 umiaks per 10 persons, there would have been 50 to 100 umiaks in a village of over 500 persons, as Wales was in the 1890s; according to Thornton there were 51 umiaks in Wales at that time. To re-cover or build 50 new umiaks in one year (which, however, was never done), about 250 or 300 walruses would have been needed. In 1890, 322 walruses were caught, ample for umiaks and food, yet Thornton said that Wales people had been accustomed to getting an average of 600 or 700 walruses annually before commercial whalers began hunting after mid-nineteenth century.[13] If this was true, the surplus skins apparently were traded to Siberia and to other mainland Alaskan Eskimos, since the population of the village was not much larger in the 1850s than forty years later during Thornton's time.

Sheldon Jackson used the depletion of walrus herds as a principal argument for congressional support of importing domesticated reindeer from

12. Sources used for the summary about walrus are my field notes; Curtis 1930, pp. 143–44; *The Eskimo Bulletin*, 1897, 1902; Lafortune journal, Mayokok 1951, pp. 31–32; Mayokok 1959, p. 16; Report on Education in Alaska for 1899–1900 (1901), vol. 2, p. 1756; and Thornton 1931, pp. 172–78.

13. Letter, Thornton to Secretary of the Treasury, dated 15 January 1892, New York, U.S. National Archives, Record Group 26. The Eskimos of Wales in early times had a catch of 600 or 700 for a population of 500, and Saint Lawrence Island needed a little over 300 for a population of 267 in 1890 (R. Porter 1893, p. 165). Charles C. Hughes said that traditionally Gambell, with a population of 293 in 1940, had needed 200 to 250 walruses a year for themselves and dogs (Hughes 1960, pp. 50, 136). In 1933, when the King Islanders were living for the most part on native foods, 50 walruses were sufficient for the 175 islanders for meat and skins, but not for ivory carving, which had become an important source of income. In December of the same year they got more than 500 seals. The King Islanders were the only Eskimos in northern Alaska who hunted walrus in a kayak.

"Schoolhouse and Pupils (Eskimo), Swedish Evangelical Union Mission, Unalaklik, Alaska." (From Education Report 1901–2, p. 1255)

"Eskimo Fish Caches at the Mouth of Niukluk River, Alaska," early 1900s. (Photograph by Lomen brothers)

"Drying Fish at Grantley Harbor," 1885. (From Healy 1887, following p. 8)

Siberia in the 1890s, a plan he had devised to help the Eskimos, who, he said, were starving. Yet the great consumption of seals by all of the Bering Strait tribes, and an adequate amount of walrus meat by the walrus-hunting tribes even at the lowest numbers of the herd, did not put them any closer to starvation's door than they had been before Jackson's fallacious arguments. In fact, as we shall see, the reindeer finally benefited most those Eskimos who had never been walrus hunters. In later years, the smaller walrus catches probably resulted from poor hunting conditions as well as reduced numbers. The Wales men sometimes had to go twenty to twenty-five miles into the strait for walrus hunting in their large skin boats, which could hold enormous quantities of meat. They also hunted whales in the middle of the strait in smaller umiaks, towing the whales home.[14]

Bearded seals or *ugruk* (*Erignathus barbatus nauticus*) were usually hunted during May.[15] Almost every tribe living on the ocean caught these huge seals (a female could attain a weight of almost six hundred pounds, and a male, seven hundred), but several areas had especially good hunting: the Tapkak stretch near Shishmaref; around Sledge and King islands; the mouth of the Solomon River; and in Port Clarence. The Eskimos of Shishmaref depended to a great extent on bearded seals, which they often caught from twenty-five to thirty miles offshore on the ice, hauling the meat back home with their dog teams hitched to sturdy sleds built for the purpose.

The beluga, or white whale (*Delphinapterus leucas*), usually swam in schools to places where they could feed on herring, and were most easily caught in shallow water near shore where they had been chased to land by men in kayaks and speared. They were occasionally sighted and hunted in the ocean. At Wales they were caught in nets set close to the beach. The best known beluga shallows were in Eschscholtz Bay, at Koyuk, at Inglutalik, in Golovnin Bay, and near Pastolik, where Stebbins people hunted. Cape Nome long ago was supposed to have been a rich beluga area, and an old village there, still occupied during the gold rush days, was called Setuk (*seto'ak*) or "white whale." (Another beluga shallows on the north shore of Kotzebue Sound is called *Sheshalik*, from *sesualik*, meaning "where there are white whales.") The skin of fresh white whale was considered a delicacy, second only to the skin of black whale.

The sea mammal that was most important to all of the Eskimos except the Kauwerak and Fish River tribes was the seal. The diet of all tribes included

14. In 1865, during one of the hunts in the middle of the strait, the Wales people recalled that they saw the *Shenandoah*, the renegade Confederate Civil War vessel, firing on commercial whaling ships. The war had ended several months earlier (*The Eskimo Bulletin*, 1902). The story of the *Shenandoah* is related in Gilbert 1965.

15. Information about seals, beluga, and polar bears is compiled from my field notes; *The American Missionary*, December 1892, p. 390; Curtis 1930, pp. 144–46; *The Eskimo Bulletin*, 1893, 1895, 1897, 1898, 1902; Keithahn 1963, pp. 72–74; Lafortune journal, Lopp diary, 1898; Mayokok 1951, 1959; Report, Commissioner of Education, 1900–1901 (1902), vol. 2, p. 1467; and Thornton 1931, pp. 158–64, 179–92.

seal meat to some extent because seals swam into bays and lagoons and up the rivers. Therefore, the Kauwerak and Fish River people were able to get them in Imuruk Basin and as far inland as the mouths of the Pilgrim River and the Fish River. The beluga and spotted seal that went into Grantley Harbor were captured in nets near the mouth of Tuksuk Channel. Moreover, inland tribes also went to the territory of their alliances for sealing: Kauwerak to Point Spencer; Fish River to Atnuk. The Kauwerak people camped and hunted in their designated places, and returned home in June or in the early part of July with their meat and oil. Stebbins people established seal hunting camps on Stuart Island, and Shaktoolik Eskimos went at all times of the year to Besboro Island for spotted seals.

In the 1890s, the Wales Eskimos annually captured between four and five thousand "common seals," besides a few of other species, between 15 September and 15 June by shooting or netting, usually through the ice. A net was set through three holes chopped into the ice about sixty or seventy feet away from the edge of shore ice when the wind was offshore. When seals were plentiful, the nets needed almost constant attention, for a dark night, when the seals could not see the walrus thong nets, resulted in large catches. At the village of Kikiktauk, seals were also got in nets in open water during July and September.

Seals were indispensable for meat, oil, and skin. In most places the meat was dried or stored in deep holes (they were placed in a large cave on King Island, and under conical piles of driftwood in the Unalakleet area), or dried and combined with blubber in a poke. The oil was used in lamps, as a condiment for food, and for preserving greens and meat. The hide and sinews were used for clothing, rope, nets, and sewing, and a whole sealskin was made into a storage bag. Intestines were used for waterproof coats, and the fur of an unborn pup was a favorite trimming for clothing.

The second principal food resource of the area was fish.[16] Salmon (silver, dog, and humpback) was the mainstay, but there were many other fish: whitefish, grayling, trout, pickerel, herring, smelts, and even tomcods (as at Unalakleet) in the streams, and whitefish, grayling, and trout in lakes. The varieties and abundance varied from area to area and even different parts of a river. The walrus-hunting tribes had few streams that permitted the large-scale salmon fishing of such areas as Fish River, Golovnin Bay, Unalakleet, and Nome, though the Mint River near Wales had a few salmon and whitefish. Wales and the island tribes fished through the ocean ice for tomcods, sculpin, and flounder, and occasionally the King Islanders caught a favorite small blue codfish. The Wales people, moreover, obtained large quantities of salmon through their own efforts in Kotzebue Sound, where they went during the summers for trading and fishing. This practice was reported by Beechey as early as 1826. King Islanders often fished in Kauwerak

---

16. Data about birds and fish are from my field notes; Curtis 1930, p. 143; Lafortune journal, Lopp diary, 1893, 1894, 1895; and Thornton 1931, pp. 194–200, 208–10, 212.

country, and the Sledge Islanders went to the opposite mainland during the summer.

Lingcod were found in a restricted area on the Kuzitrin, and flounders, in special areas like Wales or across from Teller. There were few whitefish in the Unalakleet River. Smelts and whitefish were commonly caught in April, usually a lean month for food. An especially productive smelt area was the two-mile stretch between Kayona Creek and Square Rock, about fifty miles east of Nome. Herring was usually a "fall fish," although it was also caught in nets in the spring around Unalakleet and Teller. It was put into holes in the ground to ripen, and then stored in seal pokes for the winter.

Summer salmon fishing and sometimes berry picking were carried on at campsites claimed by individual families. These were located at the mouths of almost every tributary to the large rivers, on sections of the most productive large streams, and on the various coastal areas and shores of large bodies of water like Imuruk Basin. Some families had two or more sites for different products at different times of the year. The sites were usually inherited patrilineally, and were considered to belong to a family as long as they used it. Caribou hunting on another tribe's territory appeared to be done in most cases on tribal land, although in some parts of this area caribou hunting rights were also claimed as family hunting areas on certain creeks, as were fishing sites. Permission to use sites for fishing, egg gathering, berries and greens were usually given by the women of the family. The sites varied in size, but rarely covered a square mile.

Silver salmon, the principal fish for human consumption, were usually caught in nets everywhere from the end of June through August. There were few salmon in the rivers of the Shishmaref or the Wales areas, as the salmon bypassed them on their way to Kotzebue Sound. In the Golovin area, the salmon schedule was as follows. The first dog salmon went into Golovnin Lagoon about the first week of June, and continued for about a month. About a week later the "humpies" started to come and ran until shortly after the first of August. Silver salmon began about the twentieth of July, the Eskimos fishing for them until about the middle of August. This was the last of the "big" salmon fishing, although a second dog salmon run began the end of July. In the Port Clarence area, the first silver salmon came about 4 July, or when the ice left the bays. The early fish were fat and oily and were not eaten with seal oil.

King salmon, though not as common as other fish, were eagerly sought in most of the large rivers as far north as Teller. No salmon was rejected since there were many dogs to feed. (Long ago, two or three dogs made up an average team, while a rich man might have five.) Even at the end of the fishing season when the "humpies" and silvers were thin, worn out, discolored, and grotesquely shaped, they were caught, dried, and eaten to fulfill a craving for the different flavor.

By the end of July, the drying racks became full of salmon split in half, the meat gashed horizontally across the body in several places to facilitate drying. At this time the Eskimos ate quantities of boiled fresh salmon. A favorite summer meal was "half-dried" salmon (*angimak*) eaten with *suret* (willow leaves in oil). Partly dried salmon eggs were packed into pokes or barrels with seal oil to be used as a dressing for berries, or to be eaten alone. The eggs and oil were beaten until fluffy, and sometimes mixed with pieces of choice fish, like boned lingcod, which had been wrung of water and rubbed until fluffy.

Pickerel and whitefish were sometimes caught in nets. Tomcods and whitefish were jigged for through the ice with a short stick to which was attached a piece of baleen and a well-made hook of ivory or bone. Between December and May little girls at Wales sometimes got two or three pecks of tomcods a day through holes in the ice. Flounders, also attracted by a lure, were speared through the ice of lagoons as they went out to sea to spawn. In the Kauwerak area, fishtraps were used for whitefish, lingcod, grayling, and pickerel. Pickerel and whitefish were also netted from the shore of the sloughs in the lower Agiapuk (the salmon were found in the main stream). Just before freeze-up, many whitefish were found at Shelton. Nets of sealskin or twisted caribou sinew were used to catch whitefish and pickerel under the ice in Imuruk Basin and Little Salt Lake.

King crabs were caught mainly around the islands and a mile out from the mainland from Cape Nome and northward. There were very few crabs around Unalakleet and southward to Saint Michael, although they were found around Egavik. Crabbing usually took place after the first of January when the shore ice was anchored firmly enough so that it was safe to venture out to the crab's habitat. The king crab was caught in dip nets or by lowering a lure and piece of tomcod, which the crab held onto as he was gently pulled up through the water and the ice. At a few places, such as Wales, a species of clam was gathered on shore after a storm or high tide.

Waterfowl and birds also formed a substantial part of the diet at Bering Strait. On the islands, auks, murres, and puffins were captured in nooses of baleen, and men were let down over the edges of cliffs on ropes to gather eggs. On Little Diomede Island, Eskimos caught birds on the wing with scoop nets. The area near Bluff was rich with migratory sea birds, and the sky around Square Rock became black with soaring bodies when the birds were disturbed. Migratory geese, swans, ducks, cranes, and brant were found in all lagoon and lake areas, but in especially large numbers in the flats between Cape Espenberg and Shishmaref, at Cape Rodney, the Nuk area at Nome, at Golovnin Bay, and on the flats south of Saint Michael. The large Pacific eider duck nested near the bay now called Lopp Lagoon. Swans and cranes were very wary and stayed toward the high tundra ground in flocks as large as forty, but quickly flew away into the mountains when pursued. Geese and ducks were caught in nets during the molting season, or with bolas or blunt-headed arrows cast into a flock of flying birds. Shishmaref people went to inland lakes, where boys and women killed ducks chased ashore by men in kayaks. Eskimos refrained from killing adult birds during nesting time, but they did not hesitate to rob the nests of eggs, or even the young birds. All birds were roasted on the open fire or boiled without evisceration. Handsome storage bags were made of swan and loon skins. Long before Wales people had guns, they found shot in the birds, which they kept for medicine charms. Sometimes, especially on the ice of lakes or lagoons, they lured down flocks by decoy birds fashioned of mud and sticks.

The people also ate seagulls, hawks, shore birds, and owls. Ptarmigan were a very important food resource in the brushy areas of the Nome, Kuzitrin, and Fish rivers. Sometimes these birds formed the principal part of the diet for weeks during the winter. Ptarmigan were caught at that time of year in small snares, which were hung, camouflaged, three or four inches above the ground in the same areas year after year by the same families. In the spring, a caribou sinew net was set at the edge of willows or on sandbars with a stuffed ptarmigan (or a white cup or handkerchief) in the middle. A male and female ptarmigan stayed together all year long, and the jealous roosters were easy to catch if lured by such means into the net. Ptarmigan were boiled in kettles or, in earlier days, cooked with hot rocks in clay pots. Their absorbent feathers were used for cleansing purposes.

Eggs were eagerly sought on the tundra as well as on the sea cliffs, and those that were partly incubated were relished along with those that were fresh. When boiled, the whites of the former become hard and rubbery, and the yolk surrounding the tiny baby bones tastes like a strong soft cheese, not at all unpleasant to my taste (being accustomed to limburger and liederkranz).

Except for caribou, land mammals were of much less importance than sea mammals, fish, and birds.[17] The Koyuk, Inglutalik, and Kauwerak people depended mainly on caribou during the winter before these animals were driven away from Seward Peninsula and Norton Sound in the 1870s and 1880s by extensive use of firearms. Other tribes also hunted caribou in winter back in the hills during the yearly migration. In summer, they stalked them in lakes or along the seacoast where some of the animals had gone to escape mosquitoes.

In the winter, caribou-hunting peoples like the Kauwerak drove caribou toward corrals of rock piles or twigs where the animals were killed by shooters stationed nearby; and in the summertime, when the caribou had separated into small groups, they were chased into lakes by men in kayaks, and speared. Like whale and polar bear hunting, caribou hunting was surrounded by many taboos and ceremonies, and special precautions were taken to propitiate the caribou spirit. The sharp edge of cutting utensils was not used, for instance, and medicine men consulted oracles. A Kauwerak shaman customarily asked a wooden face carved out of the top part of a log planted in the corral to prognosticate their hunting luck. If they were to get many caribou, a

17. Caribou hunting is summarized from my field notes and Hobson, in Great Britain Sessional Papers 1854–55. Small land animals, vegetables, and berries are from my field notes.

lot of blood (red alder dye) ran down the sides of the mouth, but if they were destined to get only a few, there would be little blood.

Caribou meat was boiled for immediate use or dried for winter. Three kinds of caribou skins were used, all cured with the hair on: fawn skins, and "summer skins" and "winter skins" of adult animals. The first two were used for parkas, pants, boots, and for trimming; the winter skins were used for bedding. Caribou "legs," both summer and winter weight, were made into boots. The Eskimo man made a variety of tools from antler, and the woman used caribou sinew, which stretches with the fur, for all sewing except in the seams of boats, which required sinews of larger sea mammals.

Fur-bearing animals like land otter, beaver, and muskrat were not hunted extensively until the beginning of the Russian Siberian fur trade. Wolves and foxes, however, were captured for the long neck fur that was used as ruffs around the face and in decorations like fringes on coats, and tails to be hung on belts. Wolverine fur was especially useful around the face because moisture does not freeze on it; but wolverines were difficult to capture, and were often procured through trade with other tribes.

Polar bears were hunted on the ice, mainly by the same tribes that hunted the walrus. The men often had to go a long distance from the mainland, and even from the islands, to hunt bears, though an important hunting place was a projecting spit of land north of Wales on which lodged the southward-bound ice that carried polar bears. The meat was considered a delicacy, and the fur was made into bedding, wall hangings, and sometimes pants. After traders came to the Bering Strait, the animals were hunted for decorative rugs.

The Arctic hare was caught in nets, snares, or was shot with arrows. This large hare ran in packs of from forty to sixty, and sometimes two hundred, in the interior brush country where the ptarmigan lived. One of my informants said that during the early part of the twentieth century they were so thick in the brush that one could scarcely walk without stepping on them. The meat was eaten, but a prolonged diet without other foods could result in starvation because it had little fat. The skins were sometimes made into jackets and bed-clothes, particularly for children; but the fur was the least durable of all fur in Eskimo territory.

Plant products—roots, greens, and berries—were used as fully as the resources provided. A large quantity of vegetal products grew in the area as a whole, and the women were busy all spring picking the young leaves of willows and many ground plants, and in August and September, berries and roots. Greens and berries were eaten at the time of gathering, but were also preserved for winter, the greens in skin pokes with oil and the berries in wooden buckets without oil. Some of the buckets in the Nome area were as large as two and a half feet in diameter and two feet high.

In the Kauwerak area, the willows were in leaf by June, and the Eskimos craved the young leaves in oil. Willow leaves were also kept in a seal poke for winter. Sourdock was often cooked and allowed to ferment with blackberries in a poke. The whole plant of the wild rhubarb, which was found in certain areas along the Kuzitrin and in special profusion on a hillside near Bunker Hill, was put into pokes. Wild celery, a great favorite, was often eaten raw. In the spring, greens that were found in the stomachs of caribou were relished.

Berry picking season in the Kauwerak area usually began about the first of August. The common distribution of berries was blackberries and salmonberries on flats near a river, blueberries on well-drained hill slopes, and cranberries on top. Berry growing grounds varied, however. Near Shaktoolik the best cranberry and blackberry grounds lay adjacent to the ocean; around Saint Michael the blueberries were on the driest ground, the salmonberries, cranberries, and blackberries were on the flats. An especially extensive field of salmonberries was more than two hours' boating and walking back of the campsite called Chauiyak, south of the Unalakleet River, on a high plateau where berries ripened about the first week of August. In this area, blueberries usually followed the salmonberries, which became white, soft, and tasteless by the middle of August. Salmonberries were also found in abundance near Ungalik, around Koyuk, in special areas of Kauwerak country, and in an area on a small peninsula north of Wales. This berry, which has only one fruit to a plant, is especially vulnerable to poor weather, and a late spring freeze will wipe out the entire year's crop. Cranberries and blueberries were not plentiful around Wales, but blackberries grew in profusion between Wales and Tin City. King Island had no blueberries, but blackberries and a few salmonberries grew there.

In October, women looked everywhere for roots, especially *piknik* (*Eriophorum angustifolium Honckeny*), which the Eskimos referred to as nuts, and *musut* (*Hedysarum alpinum* L), a long, thin root. Both of these were taken from caches that had been stored by mice. After the ground froze, women followed mouse tracks to nests near a "mouse village," where the roots were buried, and after feeling with their feet for a soft spot, dug up the caches with a root pick. In the old days, a woman replaced the stolen roots with a few dried tomcods. *Musut* was stored by the mice in a different place from the *piknik*. In summer, the upper stem of *piknik* was also gathered, and the *musut* pulled fresh from the ground. The ridges of Cobblestone River, southeast of Teller, were well known for the large supply of *musut*, and a creek in the Candle area was so named because of the root's abundance in the area.

No root, leaf, or berry that was edible was overlooked by the Eskimos, except mushrooms, which apparently were never eaten. Likewise, an animal was rarely rejected as a source of food, but in this area of abundance wolves, foxes, and other fur-bearing small mammals were not used as food (squirrels and rabbits were the exceptions). The Eskimos of the Bering Strait also ate the meat of dead animals cast up on beaches. In the summertime this practice was extremely dangerous and often led to botulism poisoning. Whole families were known to have died from such poisoning, especially from eat-ing seal flippers, which rapidly grew botulinum spores within their wind- and sun-hardened skins.

The inhabitants of the Bering Strait used their environment intensively. The food range was so wide over the seasons and throughout each tribal territory that there was little danger of starvation; yet, when threatened, they could rely on certain areas where some kind of food could always be ob-tained. The area as a whole had a variety of resources scarcely equaled in other Eskimo areas, and products not obtainable within tribal boundaries could be acquired through reciprocity of marriage, trading partners, use of other tribal territory, or requests made in the messenger feast. Many of the traded commodities or requests were considered to be luxury items, which these comparatively affluent tribes could well afford.

CHAPTER 10

The Russians Move North, and the Malemiut Move South

THE RUSSIANS

AFTER Beechey's trip and the success of the trading post on the Nushagak River, it was only a matter of time before the Russians would establish a permanent settlement to tap the riches of furs near the Bering Strait. By the end of the 1820s native traders of Alaska and Siberia were exchanging wares in sufficient quantities from traveling traders as well as at the Point Spencer and Kotzebue markets to change considerably the household inventory of every Eskimo in the Bering Strait area. At that time the trader who was a specialist in European exchange appears to have emerged—like those Sledge and King islanders mentioned in the accounts of the 1820s—and to have amassed considerable individual wealth.

At the time when Russians were considering a permanent post in the area, the Bering Strait coastal traders took their goods as far south as Golovnin Bay, Stebbins, and Pastolik; and Buckland River traders were apparently crossing the divide at their headwaters to the Yukon to collect furs of the interior. According to Lieutenant Lavrentii Zagoskin, annual "tribal meetings" took place at "Akshadak-Kosh-kunno," [1] which undoubtedly is the Eskimo village of Attenmut on old maps. Presumably traders from the Kotzebue Sound area also passed through there on their way to Athabascan territory. The people who came from the north into foreign Indian and Eskimo territory, first as traders, then in family groups, have become known as "Malemiut." Their identity and history, which has been subject to much speculation, will be discussed in the second part of this chapter, but we must first look at the Russians who were moving north for the same reason the Malemiut were moving south—for trade.

1. Zagoskin 1967, p. 152.

Fedor Kolmakov, manager of Fort Alexander on the Nushagak River, had told the Russian-American Company that untold wealth in furs abounded between the post and Norton Sound. The company sent out an expedition under I. F. Vasiliev from Kodiak Island in 1829 to investigate, and though this expedition carried on its explorations many miles south of the Bering Strait, its observations and results hastened plans to establish a trading post on Norton Sound. Vasiliev's plans to go to the Kuskokwim River were thwarted by hostile natives, but the next year he visited villages on the lower Kuskokwim. He was the first European to do so. His four guides refused, however, to take him upstream.[2]

One of the Eskimos recommended that the Russians build a trading post near Stuart Island, but such an important step was felt to be premature in the face of insufficient geographical knowledge despite the information received from the expeditions of Mikhail N. Vasiliev, Gleb Shishmarev, and Vasilii Khromchenko almost a decade before. Accordingly, in 1830, Petr E. Chistiakov, manager of the Russian-American Company in Sitka, sent A. K. Etolin in the brig *Chichagov* to explore Norton Sound from Stuart Island to the Bering Strait. Etolin stopped first at Golovnin Bay because of foggy weather, and then sailed to "Aiak" or Sledge Island, and to "Ukivak," or King Island. Petr Tikhmenev, historian of the Russian-American Company, who apparently had access to Etolin's report, said that he "describes Ukivak as a barren rock. 'At the first glance on this wild and morose island, one is astonished how people can live there. The immense quantity of walruses close to its shores solves this riddle. Hunting these animals, the natives barter for them all that they need from the natives on the mainland and so make their living.'"[3]

Returning to Sitka, Etolin reported to the general manager "on the fur trade in places visited by him," and strongly recommended that a fort be established near Stuart Island, which was a central location for trade with Golovnin Bay on the one hand, and with the Yukon River on the other. Two years later, Ferdinand P. von Wrangell, who had succeeded Chistiakov as manager, sent Mikhail D. Tebenkov to Norton Sound to search for a suitable site, and in 1833 Fort Saint Michael (Mikhailovskii Redut) was established on Saint Michael Island.

Before sailing to Golovnin Bay and the various islands for trading, Tebenkov stayed at Saint Michael only long enough to enclose an area of 1,225 square feet with a palisade fence, which was built with the help and permission of Eskimos from two nearby villages. On his return to Saint Michael (having traded in the meantime with King Islanders, but having found no one home on Sledge Island) he was pleased to find many buildings finished, and the fort ready for business.[4]

2. Bancroft 1886, p. 547; Tikhmenev 1939–40, pt. 1, pp. 301–2; VanStone 1967, pp. 9–10; Zagoskin 1967, pp. 79–80.
3. Tikhmenev 1939–40, pt. 1, p. 342. The island names are transliterated from the original Russian, according to a modified Library of Congress system.
4. Ibid., pp. 344–45.

The earliest description of Saint Michael has been provided by Lieutenant Zagoskin of the Russian navy during 1842–44. Zagoskin had put himself in the employ of the Russian-American Company, and in 1842 Etolin, by then manager of the company, sent him to the interior of Alaska from Saint Michael (apparently upon Zagoskin's own suggestion) to obtain reliable information about the best locations for additional forts and trading posts; to see what could be done to divert the Bering Strait fur trade to the Russian-American Company; and to locate the best routes and portages between the coast and the posts for the fur trade. Toward these ends, he intended to explore the Buckland River and Eschscholtz Bay, and to travel to the headwaters of the Yukon and Kuskokwim rivers.[5] Zagoskin's account of his travels contains invaluable information about Eskimo life and events in the area between Unalakleet and the Kuskokwim.

Saint Michael, named after Tebenkov's name saint, was situated on a small cape thirty feet high facing the western shore of Saint Michael Bay (originally named Tebenkov Bay in 1832) on an island of only seventy-two square miles. Three sides of the island are surrounded by the sea, and the fourth, by a narrow stream, or "canal." The land is undulating or flat. The highest point is only 370 feet. It is a treeless and mostly swampy tundra land, and many channels connect innumerable lakes. The location of the fort did not prove to be entirely auspicious, because the company often found getting food, fuel, and water for twenty-five Russians a considerable strain on human energy, and the Eskimos themselves considered it a bleak location.

But its proximity to the mouth of the Yukon (about seventy-five miles away) and its possibilities for defense were important considerations for the Russians at the time. It also satisfied the company's requirements that it be located in a central position for easy communication with both Yukon River people and native traders from the North. Zagoskin said that two native villages, "Tachik" (Saint Michael) and "Atkhvik" (Stebbins), were situated on opposite sides of the island with populations of only nineteen and fifty-seven, respectively.[6] Tachik was about a quarter of a mile from the fort, whose palisaded fence about twelve feet high had been provided with two watchtowers to oversee the entire countryside and "six three-pound cannons," which by 1867 had never been fired, according to the young men of the Western Union Telegraph Expedition. Inside the palisade were the superintendent's house, workers' barracks, two warehouses, a storehouse for trade goods, and a bath and kitchen; outside were the forge, a "kazhim" (a Kodiak Island term adopted for men's house) for visiting natives, and a chapel built during the fall of 1842.

After establishing the fort in 1833, the Russians wasted no time getting acquainted with the surrounding country. On 30 December (Old Style Russian

5. Zagoskin 1967, pp. 81–82.
6. The figures for Tachik and Atkhvik are from Zagoskin 1967, p. 306. On page 100 he gives the population of Atkhvik as 45. Zagoskin's account of the history of Saint Michael is on pp. 96–100.

calendar) of that year Andrei Glazunov and four companions left Saint Michael by dog teams to explore the interior and covered 1,379 miles on the Yukon and Kuskokwim in 104 days.[7] From Saint Michael they traveled north to the village of "Kichtauk" (Kikiktauk, or Klikitarik, as it was later known), where the friendly chief gave them fish and three dogs. Here, Glazunov said, the Inkalit Indians of the Yukon came to sell beaver skins to the Ayakmiut (Sledge Islanders) as they stopped en route to the trading center of Pastolik. The next day, Glazunov's party arrived at a small settlement at the mouth of the "Nigwilnuk" (Nygvilnuk in Russian characters), later known as Golsovia, where the inhabitants fished in summer and hunted caribou with nooses in winter.

Glazunov and his assistants crossed over to the Anvik River, at the mouth of which they found the inhabitants of Anvik village nervously awaiting an attack from Unalakleet Eskimos. A conflict had arisen between them over a caribou hunt, and the Indians reportedly had bested the Eskimos.

Going downstream on the Yukon they came to the village of "Aninhlychtychpack," near present-day Holy Cross, where people gathered from the "Anwick, Pschanukschack, Tschagilük [Innoko] and other rivers" to barter their wares for tobacco and iron implements that had been obtained from "Asiakmüten" (Sledge Islanders) through Pastolik people. Here Glazunov was astounded by the sight of 300 persons packed into the ceremonial house, just under half of a total population of 700. Ten years later, Zagoskin said that the population of "Anilukhtakpak" was only 170, and attributed Glazunov's large figures to the presence of out-of-town visitors for a festival.[8]

From here on, Glazunov's journey, which took him as far south as the Kuskokwim and Nushagak rivers, has no direct bearing on the history of the Bering Strait area, but he demonstrated the utility of the Unalakleet portage to the Anvik River by taking two more trips to the Yukon via this route in 1835 and 1837.

By the time Saint Michael came into existence, King Island had had many European visitors, but Wales was visited only for the second time during the search for Sir John Franklin. Both the King Island and Wales people were known to be agents for the intercontinental trade, but the moving in of Russian traders only 240 miles away did not alter the Siberian-Alaskan trade patterns or the trade northward from the strait so far as we know. Siberian trade actually increased until American vessels cut into their business during the last half of the nineteenth century.

7. Glazunov's account has been summarized here from an extract of his journal in Wrangell 1839, pp. 137–60. This German version was translated from a Russian account, which was published in 1836 (VanStone 1959, p. 39). In 1841 a French translation was made by Henri Ternaux-compans, which has been translated into English by James W. VanStone (1959). The Russian calendar was twelve days behind the Gregorian calendar so, according to American time then, their journey began in 1834.
8. Zagoskin 1967, pp. 193, 307.

The traders who most keenly felt the results of the new post were Sledge Islanders, and some King Islanders and Kauwerak people who had established a regular route of exchange to the south as far as Pastolik and the Yukon. They were so disgruntled, according to Zagoskin and Tikhmenev, that they sought revenge in 1836 by trying to wipe out Fort Saint Michael. The circumstances are not entirely clear in either Zagoskin's or Tikhmenev's account, but a fight took place near Cape Stephens during which the Russians got the worst of it, with one dead and seven wounded. Apparently no Eskimos were injured, although they had only bows and arrows, and the Russians had guns and knives. According to the reports, several hundred Eskimos came in ten skin boats and landed "behind the hills," where they waited until they saw nine Russians leave the fort to get wood. They decided to kill them first and then attack Saint Michael. The skirmish took place at Cape Stephens, however, more than eight miles away, where the Eskimos supposedly attacked the boat with its driftwood tow, which had been stopped by head winds in Stephens Pass.

Despite Russian assertions to the contrary, the so-called plan to destroy the fort may have been an exaggeration of an altercation with but one skin boat, for one of the accounts said that the Russians were saved by the actions of a man name Kurepanov who dragged "the enemy's skin boat into the water . . . the only one used to deliver the pick of the Azyagmyut young men while the rest, some two hundred in number, were hiding behind the coastal hills." After the attack, the exceedingly strong Kurepanov paddled the dead and the wounded back to the fort single-handedly in the appropriated skin boat, and thereby the "fort was saved, and from that time on the Azyagmyut have never dared show their faces on the southern shore of Norton Sound."[9]

This skirmish, however, did not stop the northern faces from showing at Saint Michael or on other places around Norton Sound, and Zagoskin himself said that trading continued because the Russian post had been unable to supply Eskimos to the south with certain native goods like caribou skins, which were procured only from the "Malemiut" (including the Sledge Islanders) who carried on their trade as before with the Yukon and Kuskokwim peoples through the villages of Unalakleet, Kikiktauk, and Pastolik.[10]

Before Zagoskin's expedition, the Russian-American Company had done little to increase trade in the direction of Seward Peninsula. A small step had been taken in 1837 when a supply post was established at the mouth of the Unalakleet River with supplies from the vessel *Kvikhpak*. William H. Dall understood in 1868 that Unalakleet was built in 1840 or 1841, but Zagoskin said that after the 1838 smallpox epidemic at old Unalakleet across the river,

9. Ibid., p. 97; Tikhmenev 1939–40, pt. 1, pp. 346–48. Tikhmenev probably took his information from Zagoskin. See also Chapter 13, the section entitled "The Eskimo and the White Man."

10. Zagoskin 1967, pp. 100, 102, 107.

the survivors "settled in two small winter houses, a quarter of a mile from the company's establishment." This statement suggests that the company was founded before the epidemic of 1838, although Zagoskin's reference to the company buildings might have been anachronistic, speaking of the settlement as it was in 1842.[11]

In its earliest years the Unalakleet post consisted of only one native employee who guarded the company's hut and a large cache of dried fish used for feeding sled dogs. Just before Zagoskin's visit to Unalakleet, a poor fishing season on the Yukon had caused the Nulato Indians to steal fish and supplies from the company's warehouse at Nulato, and to forestall such an occurrence at Unalakleet, Zagoskin decided to make it a permanent post with four employees. It also became a central headquarters for sled dogs. Zagoskin was so greatly impressed by Unalakleet's location and its natural resources—excellent fishing, sea and land hunting, driftwood, fresh water, berry grounds, and good garden soil—that he recommended the fort be moved from Saint Michael, whose only advantage over the years had proved to be its proximity to the mouth of the Yukon. A location for defense had been unnecessary, and its strategic position in native trade routing had been miscalculated. Zagoskin estimated that only five men, instead of the twenty necessary at Saint Michael, could undertake the everyday duties of getting wood, fish, and water.[12] The fort was not moved, but Unalakleet continued to be a trading post, the northernmost Russian settlement to be located on the Alaskan coast. A man known only as Ivan, and who had been baptized in Sitka in 1838, was said to be a trader for the company at "Chinig-miut" (Golovin), eighty miles to the northwest.[13]

Smallpox had reached Norton Sound five years after Saint Michael was built. The epidemic of 1838 in this area, which was rivaled only by the measles in 1900 and the influenza in 1918, swept through tribes from the southern Alaskan border in Tlingit Indian country to Norton Sound. The outbreak had appeared among the Tlingit of Sitka in 1836, apparently brought by Indians from British territory. As the disease traveled north, mortality varied but was reported to have claimed at least 50 percent of the population in some areas. By the winter of 1838–39 it had declined, and by 1840, had disappeared.[14] In the Indian village near Sitka, 400, half the population, died. On Kodiak Island, 736 persons were said to have succumbed. The Aleut population was 6,991 on 1 January 1836, but on 1 January 1840 it was 4,007. At Pastolik the population was said to have been 250 before the epidemic, or twice the number at Zagoskin's time. Unalakleet had thirteen survivors from

11. Ibid., pp. 94–95; Dall 1870, p. 24; Whymper 1869, p. 158.
12. Zagoskin 1967, pp. 95–96, 287.
13. Ibid., p. 126.
14. Information about the smallpox epidemic is from Bancroft 1886, pp. 560–62; Blashke 1848; Kashevarov 1879; Sarafian 1970, pp. 194–203; Tikhmenev 1939–40, pt. 1, pp. 366–69; Zagoskin 1967, pp. 95, 100, 146, 188, 193, 248, 281. The figures of the Aleut decline are from Sarafian 1970, p. 203.

possibly twice that many, and Zagoskin observed that the "native summer camps: Mikhat [*mit-thak*, Eider Duck Island], Chyuplyugpak [*chingikpigat*, Wood Point], Kygali [*kugalik*, Fivemile Point], and Kebyakhlyuk [*kepathluk*, or Eightmile Cove]" had been abandoned.[15]

The Russians checked the epidemic through a vaccination program. In 1838 Dr. E. L. Blashke, the medical director for the Russian-American Company, vaccinated people in the Unalaska district, where only 130 died; and other medical personnel went to the Alaska Peninsula, Cook Inlet, and Bristol Bay. In all, 4,000 were said to have been vaccinated north of the Aleutians, and of the 500 who contracted smallpox at Nushagak, Saint Michael, and on the Kuskokwim River, only 200 died.[16] Obviously the vaccinations successfully halted the northward spread, and there is no evidence that it went beyond Koyuk or Golovin. Aleksandr Kashevarov, who traveled by skin boat between Point Barrow and Kotzebue Sound in 1838, did not mention smallpox in that area.[17]

Kashevarov, who was a half Kodiak Eskimo–half Russian man with a European education, was sent on the *Polifem* (the same ship that took Blashke to Unalaska) to chart the shores of the Arctic Ocean between Point Barrow and Return Reef. Kashevarov's party, with the interpreter, "the Chnagmiut Utukuk" from Kikiktauk, parted with the *Polifem* at Cape Lisburne on 5 July in an umiak and five three-holed kayaks, and rejoined the ship again on 5 September near Chamisso Island in Kotzebue Sound.

Apparently no other Russian-American Company ship sailed north of Norton Sound after the *Polifem* until Zagoskin and the *Okhotsk* attempted to enter Kotzebue Sound early in both summers of 1842 and 1843, only to be turned back by ice.[18] There were equally few sailings after Zagoskin's time, if the logbooks of the Russian-American Company ships, now preserved in the U.S. National Archives, can be relied upon. Between 1850 and 1867, only twelve trips were made to Saint Michael from Sitka. Supposedly only

15. Zagoskin 1967, p. 92. In 1968 Benjamin Atchak of Saint Michael gave me both the present English names and the Eskimo counterparts (in italics) for these campsites in the same geographical order recorded by Zagoskin 145 years earlier.

16. Tikhmenev 1939–40, pt. 1, p. 368.

17. Kashevarov 1879. Before this journal was published, accounts of Kashevarov's journey were published in *Syn otechestva* for 1840 and in a newspaper in 1845.

18. I have reached this conclusion from Zagoskin's statement that the accessibility of the northwest coast of Alaska "was proved by the voyages of Cook, Kotzebue, Vasiliev, Beechey, and finally the Company's ship 'Polyphemus' in the year 1838" (Zagoskin 1967, p. 90).

In the Burke Museum of the University of Washington is a wooden marker about six feet high on which is incised the information: "RAK [Russian-American Company] Expedition of 1838." The museum also has a post with the names, "HBMS Herald September 1848," inscribed on one side, and "HBMS Blossom, September 1826," on the other. Both of these posts came, without question, from Chamisso Island since the dates all agree with the respective vessels' visits to the island, as well as a corroborative notation in twenty-one-year-old Joseph Grinnell's *Gold Hunting in Alaska*: "On Chamisso Island we saw records carved on logs in a fair state of preservation of the visit of 'H.B.M.S. Blossom, 1826,' 'H.B.M.S. Herald, 1848,' and some Russian vessel 1837." He apparently wrote this after he had left the island because he omitted the month, and wrote 1837 instead of 1838 (Grinnell 1901, p. 85).

the barks *Menshikov* and *Kodiak* went beyond Saint Michael—in 1851 and 1854[19]—but it seems likely that some of the ships sailed even farther north in other years. For example, the *Kodiak* was met at Port Clarence in 1853 by the men searching for Sir John Franklin (see Chap. 11).

Zagoskin's plan to intercept the Bering Strait trade by establishing a post in Kotzebue Sound failed to materialize after he learned that he would have to organize the expedition himself, getting together all of the food, clothing, and transportation, since no one from the fort could assist him. One man had rheumatism, one was busy working on accounts, another had to go to Nulato, and Utuktak, Aleksandr Kashevarov's interpreter, flatly refused to leave home because since 1838 he had acquired two beautiful wives and "his wants were fulfilled."[20] Moreover, the superintendent of the post was new to the country and could not be considered reliable for local information. Therefore, in 1842 Zagoskin elected to remain in Saint Michael to prepare for exploring the Yukon instead of returning north on the *Okhotsk* as it went about trading in Siberia and the Bering Strait. He had, however, outlined a plan for fifteen persons to make a prolonged stay in the North, which was never carried out.[21]

Trade between the Eskimos of southern Norton Sound and the Yukon River natives consisted almost entirely of native and some European products for furs and a few products made of wood. In exchange for furs, the Norton Sound people traded caribou skins, thongs, and sinew, sea-mammal oil and skins (particularly from Pastolik), umiaks, kayaks, and European products like tobacco and iron and copper goods. Each year a thousand poods (36,000 pounds) of the highly regarded beluga ("white whale") oil went from Pastolik to Unalakleet, Shaktoolik, and "upper Norton Sound," where Indians came from the interior over the various passes, often with their furs. These furs,

19. Alaska History Research Project 1936–38, 3:374–400. The bark *Menshikov*, with skipper Pavlov, visited Unga, Saint George, Saint Paul, and Unalaska islands, Saint Michael, and Plover Bay (Siberia) between 6 June and 17 September 1851, and the bark *Kodiak* left Sitka on 31 June 1854, also under Pavlov's charge, for Saint Michael and Kotzebue Sound, returning on 25 September.

20. Utuktak was "considered [a leader] by birth in [Kikiktauk] and, for his wealth and ability" (Zagoskin 1967, pp. 89, 129). In 1846 the priest Jacob Netsvetov met "Theophan Medalin . . . a chief of the Kigtaguk village" at Unalakleet and tried to persuade him to marry one of his wives in Christian rites and to let the other one go. Theophan had been baptized in 1843, and was learning the rules and sacraments of the church. Theophan, or Utuktak, agreed to marry one of his wives, but refused to give up the other. In the face of such obstinacy, Netsvetov temporarily abandoned his efforts at reform until he had received further advice from Bishop Innokenty (Alaska History Research Project 1936–38, 2:311).

Zagoskin called Utuktak a Malemiut, but in 1838 Kashevarov called him a Chnagmiut, saying that he spoke a dialect "close to Malemiut." According to my informants, Kikiktauk was known as an Unaluk village until mid-nineteenth century. Edward W. Nelson corroborates this: in the 1870s the mountains near "Kigiktauik . . . swarmed with reindeer [caribou], and in addition to the Unalit many Malemiut had congregated there to take advantage of the hunting" (Nelson 1899, p. 24).

21. Zagoskin 1967, pp. 90–91.

which the Norton Sound Eskimos bought, were then traded to the Russian-American Company for European goods, part of which were subsequently used as trade goods for more furs from the Yukon people.

During a year's time, said Zagoskin, the trading post at Saint Michael obtained between 350 and 500 beaver pelts and about 100 otter and 150 fox skins, almost all from the area south of Norton Sound. But this was really only a portion that could have been obtained if the Bering Strait traders had been persuaded to channel their furs to Saint Michael instead of sending them across the strait, destined for the Anyui Fair more than a thousand miles away. Only five or six years before, in 1837, the Anyui market received from the Alaskan traders 100 beavers, 395 martens, 30 lynxes, 290 red foxes, 40 gray foxes, 7 black foxes, 134 white foxes, 4 blue foxes, as well as 31 marten garments, 13 muskrat garments, and 782 walrus tusks.[22] Furthermore, Zagoskin said that at least 1,000 beaver pelts, 3,000 sables (martens), 500 fox, and about "1,000 otter and beaver of the best quality, which were traded to Kolyma through the hands of the Maleygmyut and Chukchis," remained in native hands from September 1842 through August 1843.[23] Yet, beyond the token traders at Golovin and Unalakleet, the Russian-American Company made no further effort to extend active trade toward the North, and Zagoskin himself seemed to turn his back on the Bering Strait although he well knew from native information that quantities of furs went from the Yukon River to the Buckland via the upper Koyukuk. Instead of trying to stem the flow across the strait by establishing a trading post there, he urgently requested that the Russian-American Company employ an "educated man" rather than just a "literate trader" to tap the vast potentialities of the Yukon and the Kuskokwim.

Saint Michael's history, therefore, was related more to the Yukon River than to Seward Peninsula until the American activities and gold rushes in the latter part of the nineteenth century. Most of the trading statistics and information in the church records of the Russian-American Company dealt with matters south of Saint Michael and on the Yukon River and its delta. The phrase "Norton Sound" was used as a geographical term in both Russian and American writing, but to the Russians it meant mainly the Yukon River, where a fairly large population held out great hope for many conversions to the Russian Orthodox faith. Despite Saint Michael's importance as a trading post, its small population did not seem worth the priest's time and he was rarely there, remaining at his headquarters at Ikogmiut (Russian Mission) on the Yukon, even after the first chapel was built in Saint Michael in 1842. The concentration of population on the Yukon is clearly shown on a map of 1843, which was apparently drawn under the name "Norton Sound" for administrative purposes because twenty of the twenty-six villages on the map,

22. Bogoras 1904–9, pt. 1, p. 56.
23. Zagoskin 1967, p. 183.

and 3,460 of the 3,760 inhabitants, were located on the river, and the remainder on Norton Sound itself.[24]

THE MALEMIUT

The name Malemiut was applied to various tribes at different times, but is now specifically attached to those inhabitants of Norton Sound who had emigrated from the Kotzebue Sound area—especially the Buckland and Kobuk rivers—and who spoke a dialect of the Inupiak, or northern, language. The name is a descriptive one, probably originating from the fact of their living in skin tents while on the move, for Zagoskin said they were called "Maleygmyut or Naleygmyut [meaning] 'people who dwell in blanket-yurts.'"[25]

During the 1830s and 1840s the identity of the people whom Zagoskin called Malemiut is not at all certain, and the name apparently referred to any Eskimo trader from the North. The first so-called Malemiut to arrive in Unalit territory were not those considered to the Malemiut today, but were occupants of Seward Peninsula, because Zagoskin said that "on the shores of the large peninsula framed by Norton Sound and Kotzebue Sound, there are many tribes of the Kang-yulit people, called by their southern relatives Maleygmyut," and on his map he placed the Malemiut as sole occupants of Seward Peninsula.[26]

He specifically considered the Kauwerak and Sledge Island people to be Malemiut: "The Maleygmyut encourage hostility towards us because we have intervened in their direct [trade] connections with the Yukon [and] I much regret that I could not myself undertake a detailed survey of the area occupied by this tribe, when one of their elders invited me to visit him in his village of Kavyak [Kauwerak] in 1842, and volunteered himself to guide me thither." He called the Sledge Islanders "Azyagmyut," but said they were more correctly called "Maleygmyut." His terminology becomes even more confusing when he included the people of the Kiwalik River of the Kotzebue Sound culture area under the term "Azyagmyut," saying a man from "Kualyugmyut [on the Kiwalik River] . . . had killed one of [the Russian] elders when the Azyagmyut attempted to destroy Fort St. Michael in 1836."

Later on, Zagoskin's purely descriptive term, Malemiut, was transferred to those people who spoke Inupiak dialects distinct from the Kauwerak-related dialects of Seward Peninsula, and in the twentieth century the word Malemiut is loosely applied by Unaluk speakers to all Eskimos north of Seward Peninsula, including Point Barrow, Canada, and Greenland.[27]

24. Map of Norton Sound, Alaska History Research Project, Box 294, Manuscript Division, Library of Congress.

25. Zagoskin 1967, p. 124.

26. Ibid., map 2.

27. Ibid., pp. 101, 124, 125. Zagoskin also said that "Naleygmyut" was a "nickname" (p. 103). Perhaps the original spelling was with an "n" if it was derived from the Kuskokwim word *nalik* meaning "tent" (Hinz 1944, p. 196), but with an "m" if derived from the word *maliga*, "to

Some writers have maintained that the aboriginal inhabitants of the shores of Norton Sound were the Malemiut, but there is abundant evidence that only the Unalit lived on the coast of the sound before the Malemiut arrived. J. Louis Giddings, whose excavations on Cape Denbigh have considerably enriched our knowledge of prehistoric cultures, thought that the Malemiut might have been indigenous to this area, but even his excavations point otherwise.[28] In order to place the Malemiut and the Unalit in proper geographic and historic perspective, we must first see how they fit into various linguistic and tribal schemes attempted by Europeans during the nineteenth century.

As we have already seen, it was not fully accepted that Eskimos inhabited northern Alaska until Frederick Beechey's two-volume work was published in 1831. He was the first to definitely identify them as "Esquimaux" and to compare them with the eastern Eskimo; but he did not have sufficient information for a linguistic or tribal analysis of the Alaskans, or his "western Esquimaux." The first two attempts at a linguistic summary of Alaskan Eskimos were made by Aleksandr Kashevarov and Ferdinand von Wrangell in the 1830s. Kashevarov was the first man to classify all Eskimo-speaking tribes of Alaska and to record names of villages and tribes north of Kotzebue Sound from his own experience, although Wrangell's material appeared in print first. Both schemes were compiled mainly from incomplete and random notes that had been made by explorers and traders, with the exception of Kashevarov's data obtained between Kotzebue Sound and Point Barrow.

Kashevarov classified the Alaskan Eskimos according to language into the subdivisions of Kadiaksk, Agolegmiutsk (Aglegmiut), Aziusiagmiutsk (Ayakmiut), and Maligmiutsk (Malemiut).

In general, all the savages inhabiting the shores of Northwestern America, beginning with Kadiak Island northward speak a language of the same root, which can be divided into four main dialects: the first and southernmost dialect is spoken by Kadiaks, Chugachs and northern Aliaksintzes; the second, the lower inhabitants of the Nushagak, Kuskokwim, and Kvikhpak [Yukon] rivers, and in part, the inhabitants of Norton Bay; the third, the inhabitants of the western part of the peninsula formed between Norton and Kotzebue Bays; and finally, the fourth, the northernmost dialect, peoples inhabiting the eastern part of Shaktuli and Norton bays, Kotzebue Sound, and farther, as is evident from the words of the savages along the northern shore of America [he had also said, "My fellow traveler, the savage Utuktak understood well the local savages (at Cape Lisburne) talking a dialect close to the Maligmiutsk"]. All these main dialects are subdivided into several subdialects, each having its own name.

The first two dialects, most resembling each other, are called Kadiaksk and Agolegmiutsk in the colonies. The third may be called Aziusiagmiutsk and the fourth, Maligmiutsk, based on the same as were used for the first two, that is, without

---

follow." To many Alaskan Eskimos, the people of Canada and Greenland speak "Malemiut." After Thomas Correll, an Eskimo-speaking linguist from Canada, left Unalakleet, where he had been conducting research in 1968, my hostess, Mrs. Gonangan, asked me, "Has that Malemiut left yet?"

28. Giddings 1964, p. 115.

any etymological research, but only on the basis of the names of the places visited by Russians where they first heard these dialects. However, the Maligmiuts constitute a separate tribe, inhabiting the eastern parts of Shaktuli and Norton bays and Kotzebue Sound.[29]

Wrangell's main classification was more generalized than Kashevarov's, but he divided the peoples of the Bering Strait area in the following way: "The Eskimos of Bering Strait and those inhabiting the entire extent of the northern coast of America to Greenland we call Northern. Eskimos living south of Bering Strait (beginning around Cape Rodney) to the Alaskan Peninsula, on Kadyak Island and in Chugach Bay we call Southern; and the Islanders of the Aleutian chain are Western."[30] In a section entitled, "People who speak a common coastal language similar to that of the Kadyaks," he further discussed five groups within our definition of Bering Strait: the Tachigmyut (which he located at Saint Michael), the Malimyut (at Shaktoolik), the Aklygmyut (in Golovnin Bay), the Chnagmyut (who he said lived north of the Pashtuligmyut [Pastolik] and west of Cape Rodney), and the Kuvikhnagmyut. He merely assumed that the Eskimo language ranged farther north in Alaska on the basis of Beechey's observations, but ignored, or was unaware of, Kashevarov's information.[31] Wrangell placed the "Malimyut" only at Shaktoolik Bay; but Kashevarov, with his more extensive knowledge, considered Malemiut-speaking people to live both on the eastern shores of Norton Sound (including Shaktoolik Bay) and from Kotzebue Sound "farther" northward.

The people included in Wrangell's five groups did not speak a *common* coastal language, but represented the two Alaskan Eskimo languages, Yupik and Inupiak, and five dialects. Yet his scheme was a beginning in linguistic, and even tribal, classification despite the incomplete and misleading subdivisions between Saint Michael and Cape Rodney. His Aklygmyut of Golovnin Bay obviously referred to the Unalit people, or the "Unaligmiut"; the "k" in Aklygmyut was undoubtedly the result of illegible handwriting, because Henrick Holmberg used "Anlygmjuten" for the inhabitants on the southern shore of Seward Peninsula between Cape Nome and the Elim area in his text and map of 1854, which were based on Wrangell's information.[32]

29. Kashevarov 1845, pp. 2–3.
30. Wrangell 1970, p. 16.
31. Ibid., p. 15.
32. Holmberg 1855, pp. 5–6, and map dated 1854, "Karte des Russischen Amerika." This exchange of "k" for "n" from handwritten material is not a lone example in Russian American history. Korsanovskii suffered the same fate. Berkh first reported Korsanovskii's journey in his compilation published in 1823 (1823b, pp. 20–24). Tikhmenev wrote it Korsakovskii either as a misprint or from misreading the original handwritten journals. Bancroft changed it to Korasakonski, using Tikhmenev as his source. The Russian editors of Zagoskin's writings spell it Korsakovskiy.
VanStone's explanation for Wrangell's subdivisions lying between Saint Michael and Cape Rodney are corrected here since he did not have full field data on which to draw for this area. For a discussion of the etymology of words like *chinik* and *nuk* see Ray 1971a, pp. 11–12.

The small amount of territory that Wrangell gave to the Unalit was but a fraction they actually occupied from Golovnin Bay to the Pastolik River, and at Wrangell's time the Malemiut had not yet settled permanently in the Unalit village of Unalakleet.

Wrangell's "Chnagmyut" is neither a linguistic nor a tribal term, but is a descriptive word, correctly pronounced *chinigmiut* in Yupik and *singingmiut* in Inupiak, meaning "coastal people." The stem of this term, *chinik* or *singik*, is used in many words that denote slightly different geographical configurations having to do with a coastal point or piece of land. Such names on recent maps are Cheenik (Golovin), Sinuk River (opposite Sledge Island), and Sineak River (near Cape Denbigh). The word Chnagmyut was also used by Zagoskin in the 1840s to mean "coastal people," and on a manuscript map of the Norton Sound area dated 1843, the entire coast from "Aziakh," or Sledge Island, to the northern mouth of the Yukon River is given to the "Chnagmiut," with only a small area along the Koyuk River labeled "Malemiut."[33] Holmberg placed the "Tschnagmjut" between the "Paschtoligmjuten" (Pastolik) and the "Maleigmjuten," whom he located east of the river "Kuyguk," or the Koyuk, inhabiting "the coast of Norton Sound from the Unalaklik River through the interior to Kotzebue Sound."

Europeans apparently were considerably confused by tribal designations at Saint Michael. Zagoskin said that Utuktak, a headman of Kikiktauk, was a Malemiut; but Kashevarov, who spent an entire summer with him in 1838, said that he was "Chnagmiut," which applied generally to Unaluk-speaking peoples, and that he spoke "a dialect close to the Maligmiutsk."[34] To Kashevarov, who spoke the Kodiak dialect, Unaluk may have seemed similar to Malemiut.

I do not know what Wrangell's Kuvikhnagmyut refers to, but it could pertain to any number of villages that incorporated the general Eskimo word for river—*ku, ko, kuik*—in its name. I think that he meant *kuinhamiut*, an area around present-day Koyuk, or perhaps the original Unaluk name for Koyuk itself, "Kvynkhakmyut," as recorded by Zagoskin.

Zagoskin and others attempted further linguistic or tribal schemes. Zagoskin's native village names were obtained from visitors to Saint Michael, like the King Islanders, and from Utuktak, Kashevarov's interpreter, who had drawn a map of the coast between Kotzebue Sound and Point Barrow in 1838.[35] Zagoskin gave the entire Seward Peninsula to the Malemiut, but in 1875 Dall gave it to the "Kaviak," his misnomer for Kauwerak. Dall's tribal scheme placed the "Mahlemut" from Shaktoolik northward across the eastern neck of the peninsula to Eschscholtz Bay, and the "Unaligmut" from Un-

33. Manuscript map [1843], Alaska History Research Project, Box 294, Manuscript Division, Library of Congress.
34. Kashevarov 1845, p. 2.
35. Zagoskin 1967, p. 124.

alakleet almost to Pastolik. It lumped King Island and the Diomedes together as the "Okee-og-mut," but Sledge Island was "Asiagmut" (Ayakmiut).

By giving the peninsula to only one "tribe," the Kauwerak, Dall launched a serious and seemingly imperishable error.[36] In order to correct this error, I shall explain how the word Kauwerak came to be used so widely for peoples who had no tribal relationship at all with the one and only tribe of Kauwerak. The use of this name to include all inhabitants of Seward Peninsula resulted from a restricted knowledge about the true geographical extent of the real Kauwerak; a meager knowledge about linguistic relations; and ignorance about Eskimo tribal organization. As we already know, people from Kauwerak also came to Unalit territory as traders, probably before the northern Malemiut did, and indeed were Zagoskin's first "Maleygmyut." When members of the Western Union Telegraph Expedition built headquarters on the spit across from present-day Teller in 1866, they often visited Kauwerak village, which supplied food as well as Eskimo guides to take them to Unalakleet and Saint Michael. Dall, an ambitious young member of the expedition at twenty-one years of age seized upon the startling new information, gleaned secondhand from other members of the expedition, that these people were not "Malemiut" after all, but "Kaviagmut" (Kauweramiut), and he gave them the entire peninsula—which, however, he had not visited himself. His new but erroneous "tribal" classification did not reveal the existence of numerous other tribes on the peninsula, all separate, autonomous groups, each with distinct territory, boundaries, leadership, and dialect. The inhabitants of Shishmaref and old Cape Nome, among the many, would have been incensed had they known they were called Kauweramiut instead of their own names of Kikiktamiut and Ayasayamiut.

In 1880 Ivan Petroff, who was in charge of the tenth census for Alaska, revised Dall's scheme into three "tribes" for Seward Peninsula: Kingigumute (Wales), Kaviagmut (Kauwerak), and Mahlemut. He placed a fourth tribe, the Oonaligmute, from Shaktoolik to the northern mouth of the Yukon. His tribes are only linguistic classifications, however, and while they show the distribution of a group of dialects with greater fidelity than preceding ones, this tribal scheme is indefensible, since each name embraces the people of many tribes that could never be subsumed under the name he gave them.[37] Unfortunately, Edward W. Nelson copied this map almost exactly to accompany his ethnography, *The Eskimo about Bering Strait*. Nelson's much-used map in no way gives a correct linguistic or tribal view of the Bering Strait area, as already outlined in Chapter 9.[38] For the following discussion

36. Ibid., p. 104; Dall 1877, map.

37. Petroff 1884, map 2.

38. The first map in a general work that approximates the reality of tribal distribution is in Wendell Oswalt's *Alaskan Eskimos*, but it, too, is primarily a linguistic map since actual political units are omitted, being subsumed under linguistic terms. It is a good linguistic guide, however, and presents a fairly accurate picture of aboriginal Unalit occupancy.

L. L. Hammerich has added considerable confusion to this problem of linguistic distribution.

of the Malemiut movement to the Norton Sound area, we should remember that at the end of the eighteenth century and the beginning of the nineteenth the coastal area from around Solomon to Pastolik was occupied by people who spoke the Unaluk dialect of the Yupik language.[39]

The "Malemiut"—first the Sledge Islanders, then Buckland or Kotzebue Sound traders, carriers of European goods—were in an especially good position to become acquainted with extensive territory and to choose to settle where their business took them. Kashevarov used the name Malemiut for the first time in his journal of 1838 to refer to persons speaking the Inupiak language. Andrei Glazunov did not mention them during his 1834 travels throughout the Kuskowkim and Anvik areas, where the Malemiut traders later went, but in the 1840s Zagoskin often spoke of their living in skin tents at certain times in the vicinity of Unalakleet, Saint Michael, and Pastolik. Zagoskin said, "Three or four umiaks with Maleygmyut arrive every year at Unalaklik for deerskins, but there is rarely any one among them of the 'faraway' people, that is of those living about Bering Strait." The northern Malemiut probably were already living at Shaktoolik, since both Kashevarov and Wrangell mentioned their residency there.

There is little information about the Malemiut in the 1850s, but by the 1860s they ranged freely along the Yukon and the Kuskokwim, and had moved semipermanently into Unalakleet and Saint Michael. In 1870 Dall wrote two contradictory statements about the Malemiut, which Frederick Whymper, his colleague in the telegraph expedition, did little to clarify with his own writing. In the one statement Dall said that the Malemiut were permanent residents of Unalakleet, and in the other that "two assemblages of

---

He said, "Eastern Eskimo [i.e., Inupiak] comprises, as is well known, the vast territory from Greenland and Labrador, along the North coast of Canada and Alaska, along the East coast of Bering Straits [*sic*] and the Bering Sea down to Norton Sound; the Eastern Eskimo subdialects are mutually comprehensible. The last Eastern Eskimo village, at the Southeastern corner of Norton Sound is Unalakleet; the name is significant: *unalaql:t* means 'the Southernmost'! Proceeding along the coast to the Southwest we come to the next village *tačeq*—St. Michael; the language here is Western Eskimo [i.e., Yupik]. The languages of Unalakleet and St. Michael are mutually incomprehensible, but many persons are bilingual" (Hammerich 1958, p. 632).

Before the Malemiut came in the early nineteenth century, as we have seen, the languages of Unalakleet and Saint Michael were *mutually comprehensible*, both speaking a variant of Unaluk. Only the intruders spoke a language mutually incomprehensible with Unaluk. What Hammerich calls "Western Eskimo" was spoken at least as far north as Golovin, and probably farther in aboriginal times. Even in the 1830s the "last Eastern Eskimo village" was at Shaktoolik, which was probably the only Malemiut-speaking village south of the Buckland River at that time. There is no agreement among Eskimos for the meaning of the name *ungalaklik*. It may mean "from where the south wind blows," "the way the [Unalakleet] River flows south to the ocean," or "where the Unalit live." If it means "Southernmost," or "farthest south," as first reported by Knud Rasmussen (1941, p. 8), it does not refer to the Inupiak language being farthest south, but to some other factor.

39. Zagoskin 1967, pp. 117, 155, 197. The following information about the geographical spread of the Malemiut has been compiled from: informant data; Dall 1870, pp. 24, 157, 161–62, 215–16, 407; Jacobsen 1884, pp. 236, 240–41; Nelson 1899, p. 24; Nelson [1877–81], p. 136; Petroff 1884, pp. 126, 135; Whymper 1869, p. 159; Wrangell 1839, p. 122; Wrangell 1970, p. 15; Zagoskin 1967, pp. 124, 125.

houses [were] occupied [by] the Kaviak, Máhlemut, and Unaleet tribes during part of the year, the latter being the only permanent residents."
Whymper said that the "large village of Malemute and Kaveak Indians" was
permanent, yet went on to confuse the issue by saying: "The Malemutes and
Kaveaks intermingle considerably, and have therefore been spoken of here as
one people. Their habits, manners, and customs are identical, but they speak
different dialects, and inhabit different parts of the country. The former
extend from the Island of St. Michael's to Sound Golovnin, while the latter
occupy a still more northern country adjacent to Port Clarence and Behring
Straits." He did not acknowledge the existence of the Unalit in Unalakleet,
though he said they extended from Saint Michael to Golovnin "Sound."[40]

Many of the Malemiut of the 1860s were members of only a few families.
Foremost was that of Alluyianuk and his four sons and a daughter, all of
whom were born on the Kobuk River (and whose descendants constituted a
large percentage of the population of Unalakleet in the 1970s). Others belonged to Koliak's (*kaleak*), or Isaac's family. Isaac was an itinerant trader
before settling down as an agent for the Alaska Commercial Company in the
1880s at Ukvignaguk near Isaacs Point, a settlement of one dwelling in which
were housed twenty-five of Isaac's relatives and adopted children. Three
other Malemiut men mentioned by the telegraph people were Ark-na-pý-ak,
Ark-hánnok, and Myunuk. None of these persons had been mentioned by
the people searching for Sir John Franklin fifteen years before, which is
another indication that the Malemiut settled permanently only during the
1860s.

The Malemiut apparently had not yet moved to Kikiktauk by 1872, because when Nelson visited there in 1881 he learned from the Russians that
"in addition to the Unalit many Malemut had congregated there [in 1872] to
take advantage of the [caribou] hunting." Ivan Petroff, the census agent, said
that the southernmost Malemiut village in the 1880s was Shaktoolik, but that
a few families had winter homes near Unalakleet. By the 1880s the Malemiut
were also on the Nushagak River, where, Petroff reported, they were engaged in walrus hunting. According to Nelson, they had also gone to
Nunivak Island from Norton Bay. They were also living in the former
Unaluk village of Egavik, and in November 1880 Nelson "found a family of
Malemut living in a miserable hut on the upper part of Anvik River."

The Malemiut apparently did not settle west of Koyuk until after the
1880s, and they probably did not reside west of Isaac's "Malemiut village."
Koyuk itself seems to have become Malemiut only in the 1870s and 1880s
when several Buckland and Kobuk families were drawn there by a huge
caribou migration. Zagoskin recorded Koyuk's name in the Unaluk dialect,
and though his discussion of the village is ambiguous, he suggests that the
Malemiut used it only as a stopping place on the route between the Buckland

40. Whymper 1869, pp. 159, 167.

and Kiwalik rivers and Norton Sound: "The southern Maleygmyut have contact with the northern through the convenient portage from the source of the Kvynkhak [Koyuk] . . . to the Kualyug [Kiwalik] which empties into Kotzebue Sound at Spafarief Bay. They can take kayaks fairly far upstream, and erect fences on the banks for the deer hunt."

Evidence that the Malemiut did not live on Norton Sound during the early historical period is also provided by data from Eskimo informants, who unanimously agreed that the Unalit occupied the entire rim of Norton Sound before the white man came. Most of them said that the westernmost boundary of Unalit territory was near Ignituk, a large village west of Golovnin Bay; but a few said that it had extended westward to Cape Nome and even to Cape Rodney.[41] This can be corroborated by looking at the pattern of Eskimo dialects along the coast of western Alaska. Dialects of both the Yupik and the Inupiak languages formed a regular and progressive pattern along the coast from the Alaska Peninsula to Point Barrow, and adjacent tribes could understand one another. This pattern of mutual intelligibility broke only at the boundaries of languages, that is, between Aleut and Yupik at the Alaska Peninsula, and between Yupik and Inupiak west of Golovnin Bay. The only anomaly in this regular progression of dialects within a language is on the east coast of Norton Sound at Shaktoolik and Koyuk, where the Malemiut were flanked by Unaluk speakers. Since Yupik and Inupiak probably diverged as long ago as 1,500 or 2,000 years, it is thus indicative of a recent intrusion.[42]

Evidence for pre-European occupancy by the Unalit is also seen in the recording of names of Norton Sound in Unaluk by Cook, King, and Zagoskin. Today most of the names still used by Eskimos on the Norton Sound coast are Unaluk, and if a place has three names—in Kauwerak, Malemiut, and Unaluk—the Unaluk word is considered to be the oldest, an often-heard phrase being, "That is a real *old* Unaluk word."[43]

The character and distribution of Malemiut villages during the nineteenth century also substantiate Malemiut occupancy of foreign territory. Most of the so-called villages were only one-family settlements, and Shaktoolik and Koyuk, though sizable places today, were small or abandoned when the Malemiut moved in. The usual Malemiut procedure was to occupy un-

41. Historian C. L. Andrews was also interested in Eskimo culture, and gleaned a great deal of information during his years in Alaska. His notes are preserved in small notebooks at Sheldon Jackson College, Sitka. One of his notes from the 1920s states that informants at Deering told him that in "old times" Unaluk speakers lived from "Chenik to Unalaklit," and that the Malemiut were Kotzebue Sound people. The Nome people called the Kotzebue Sound people Malemiut ("Eskimo-English Vocabularies, Deering Area, C. L. Andrews," undated notebook, probably 1924). In another notebook he wrote: "From Philip A[hsaruk]; Unalingameut [were] people about Nome."

42. Dumond 1965, pp. 1233–35; Chard 1967, p. 95.

43. This linguistic information is taken from Cook and King 1784, 3:554–55; Zagoskin 1967, pp. 125–26; and data from fifty informants in 1964 and 1968. The Fish River has always been considered to be in Inupiak-speaking territory. Zagoskin erroneously identified Ikalikhvigmyut (Fish River village) as the village of Golovin, a mistake that Aleš Hrdlička copied (1930, p. 200).

inhabited places, and only when their numbers increased did they move into larger occupied Unaluk settlements like Unalakleet, Saint Michael, and Kikiktauk. The fact that Shaktoolik was their only village on Norton Sound in 1839 suggests they had had neither the time nor the numbers to have spread farther before the arrival of the Russians.

The scarcity of umiak parts and dog bones in the archeological sites of eastern Norton Sound is another indication of aboriginal Unalit population. As we have already seen, Cook mentioned few umiaks or dogs, and Giddings found little evidence of umiaks or dog traction at Cape Denbigh. In historic times the Unalit used umiaks and dog teams less than did the northerners, the large umiak having developed in the whale and walrus hunting areas where whale hunting crews went out to sea and towed back their catch, and walrus hunters piled their umiaks full of meat. Materials for covering these boats also depended to some extent on a good supply of walrus skins, although bearded seal and beluga could be used. The southern Norton Sound people moved about freely in kayaks, however, as noted by Cook, Khromchenko, and Zagoskin; but after the Malemiut came to Norton Sound, the umiak was seen much more often—in the water, on the rivers, and on top of sleds as the Malemiut portaged from land to water with the changing seasons.

Earlier contacts before the eighteenth-century trade began may have been made by people of the Buckland and Koyuk rivers or between Inupiak and Yupik speakers; but contacts between all tribes were mainly coastal, and no matter how intensively tribes exploited their upland territories for hunting, this very exploitation developed boundary concepts that inhibited a completely fluid exchange of ideas and commodities. Possibly the increasing use of dog traction as well as the growing supply of European goods facilitated overland traveling between Kotzebue Sound and Norton Sound; but almost all tribal intercourse prior to dog traction, which was comparatively late at both Kotzebue Sound and Cape Denbigh (and by inference, in all of the Bering Strait area), would have been through maritime travel.[44]

The spread of tool types, clothing designs, and other culture traits throughout the Arctic shows that diffusion, if not actual exchange, took place in almost all periods; but the latitude of time for apparent changes within an identifiable archeological assemblage was very great, and the persistence of various traits was the result of the conservative nature of Eskimo culture, not the isolation of tribes. Therefore, if the aboriginal political system had been

44. Giddings learned from his excavations that dog traction was fairly recent in both the Kotzebue Sound area and Norton Sound. For example, in the Recent period (A.D. 1700 to present) in the Chukchi Sea area, "some new elements are glass beads, metal in quantity, tobacco smoking, extensive dog traction, lunate stone lamps, and pictographic engraving." In the Bering Sea, during the same time period, "beads, metal, tobacco smoking, and dog traction add on to the prehistoric base. There is less engraving than in the Nukleet periods" (Giddings et al. 1960, pp. 126, 128).

similar to that of the nineteenth century, intercourse between contiguous tribes on the coast would have been extensive, and dissemination of ideas uninterrupted. Contiguous tribes in the interior, which were kept apart by more or less rigid boundaries, were less apt to be on friendly terms, but as trade grew and transportation developed, the barriers to geographical movement were resolved, and the northern Malemiut could move to the south.

CHAPTER 11

The Search for Sir John Franklin at Bering Strait

AFTER the establishment of Saint Michael in 1833, the trading of furs and other goods by the Eskimos for European goods took place in four ways: (1) at the traditional native markets along the coast; (2) exchange with an occasional Russian trading ship at Port Clarence and Kotzebue Sound; (3) trading at Saint Michael; and (4) through occasional native traders working for the Russian-American Company.

The presence of Saint Michael did not seem to alter the trading patterns of the Eskimos: goods continued to be traded across the strait and to the various local markets. The Indians of the interior, however, began coming to Saint Michael and to Unalakleet for trade; and the Kotzebue market grew in size and importance by receiving European goods from a number of sources—Siberia, Russian trading boats, and the Malemiut trader who was traveling deep into the Indian territory for furs.

Until the latter part of the 1840s, Eskimos traded exclusively with Russians, and for Russian goods. Apparently there was no further trading by English or American traders in Alaskan waters from 1820 to 1848. In that year occurred two events which, combined with the activities of the Western Union Telegraph Expedition between 1865 and 1867, propelled the Eskimos into a faster pace of change than ever before.

In 1848 the first whaling ship and the first ship searching for Sir John Franklin's expedition sailed through the Bering Strait. After 1848 the whalers often came in direct contact with people of the islands, but not with those of mainland Seward Peninsula because of shoal waters and the scarcity of whales. The native peoples most directly affected by commercial whaling were those who lived in the strait proper or between the far north Alaskan whaling villages of Point Hope and Point Barrow. Not until a shore coaling station was established at Port Clarence in 1884 was the effect of whaling directly felt by Bering Strait mainlanders. This is discussed in Chapter 13 in conjunction with a summary of this period, and in Chapter 14 with the inauguration of the Revenue Marine Service.

The accounts and papers of the men trying to find Franklin, and the diaries and publications of the telegraph men provide us with rich material about Eskimo places and life not reported before, and establish for the Alaskan Eskimos, so different from those in Canada's distant North, a secure place in the world's literature.

Sir John Franklin was searching for the passage between the Atlantic and the Pacific when his two ships, *Erebus* and *Terror*, were last seen in July 1845 in Baffin Bay. The British government, thinking that he might have succeeded in sailing west to the Chukchi Sea, dispatched ships to the Alaskan Arctic, planning to use Kotzebue Sound as a base of operations. We are indebted to the Franklin searchers for the first detailed description of the village of Wales, and for the first and only substantial eyewitness account of the interior of Seward Peninsula when it was still inhabited by caribou hunters.

Between 1848 and 1854 eight ships of the British Royal Navy and a private yacht sailed to the Bering and the Chukchi seas to look for Franklin's ships. This search, the largest ever undertaken in the history of sailing ships, was divided into three parts: (1) in the waters of the Atlantic Ocean and northern Canada; (2) an overland expedition that went to the mouth of the Mackenzie River via Montreal; and (3) along the coast of northwest Alaska.

The *Herald*, under command of Captain Henry Kellett, and the *Plover*, under Commander T. E. L. Moore, arrived in Bering Strait in 1848. The *Enterprise* and the *Investigator* searched the Atlantic under Sir James Ross and Captain Edward Bird in 1848 and 1849, then joined the *Herald* and the *Plover* in 1850 under the new commands of Captain Richard Collinson and Commander Robert McClure. Two additional ships were sent to Bering Strait only after a hot debate between Sir William Edward Parry and Captain George Back, who contended that they were superfluous because traces of Franklin would probably be found near Melville Peninsula, three thousand miles to the east. (Remnants of Franklin's expedition were found by Captain Francis L. McClintock in the *Fox* on King William Island, less than four hundred miles from Melville Peninsula, during a search made between 30 June 1857 and 21 September 1859).[1]

Four supply ships, the *Amphitrite*, the *Daedalus*, the *Rattlesnake*, and the *Trincomalee*, also went to the Bering Strait; and the *Nancy Dawson*, a Royal Thames Yacht Club schooner, searched at the personal expense of the owner, Robert Sheddon.[2]

1. A concise summary of the most important books and voyages involved in the Franklin search can be found in Firth 1963, pp. 19–24.
2. Great Britain Sessional Papers 1850, vol. 35, no. 107, p. 19. Sheddon became ill in the North and died in Mazatlán, Mexico, during the winter of 1849. A set of the sessional papers is in

The *Plover* and the *Herald* were to have met at Panama in 1848 to sail to the Bering Strait via Siberia to prepare a winter harbor for the *Plover*; but Commander Moore, getting no more than four and a half knots from his ship, was unable to reach Alaska, and so remained at Emma Harbor in Siberia during the winter of 1848–49. Although the *Plover* was the slowest vessel of the whole expedition, it became the best known, spending six consecutive winters and six and a half summers in various parts of the Arctic with two different skippers and crews. A surgeon, John Simpson, was aboard the entire time, and used his cumulative knowledge to write the first ethnological account of the Point Barrow Eskimos.[3]

The *Herald*, on its way to Chamisso Island, stopped at Saint Michael for Eskimo skin boats, which the Russians could not furnish, and an interpreter, which they did. The Russians told them that six Americans were trading for furs in their territory, and after the *Herald* arrived at Chamisso Island on 14 September 1848, it was learned from Eskimos that white men were indeed trading inland to the south. Kellett thought that they might be deserters from an American whaling ship, but they undoubtedly belonged to Alexander Murray's party, which had established Fort Yukon in 1847 for the Hudson's Bay Company of England in what is now Alaskan territory.[4]

After waiting in vain for the *Plover* to arrive, Kellett left for Mazatlán, Mexico, via Petropavlovsk, Kamchatka, where he discharged his Norton Bay interpreter instead of taking him home because of "violent westerly winds." The interpreter received a dollar a day and some warm clothing for his services. The *Plover*, meanwhile, went into winter quarters at Emma Harbor, Siberia, where the men spent the winter exploring and visiting the Chukchi.[5]

The next year the *Plover* arrived at Chamisso Island on 14 July, one day before the *Herald*, which brought the news that whalers were expecting at least twenty whaling ships to sail through the strait that summer "in consequence of the success of one of their vessels last season." It was reported that its master, having read Captain Beechey's description of multitudes of whales in the Arctic, had returned home with four thousand barrels of whale oil, representing only six weeks' whaling time. Kellett took the opportunity

the Library of Congress, and in microcard in other repositories, including the University of Washington library.

3. Simpson's account was published in the Great Britain Sessional Papers 1854–1855, vol. 35, no. 1898, and reprinted in 1875 in *Arctic Geography and Ethnology*, Royal Geographical Society, London, pp. 233–75.

4. Murray 1910, p. 20. Murray knew that he had established Fort Yukon "six degrees of longitude across the Russian boundary" (p. 54).

5. Information about the *Herald* and the *Plover* in 1848 and 1849 is taken from Seemann 1853, pp. 8, 70, 99, 100, 118, 119, 120, 128, 129 (Seemann apparently copied verbatim or paraphrased some of his material from official reports); Great Britain Sessional Papers 1847–48, vol. 41, no. 264; 1849, vol. 32, papers numbered 188, III, no. 7, and V; 1850, vol. 35, no. 107. An account of the *Plover*'s stay during the winter in Emma Harbor can be found in W. H. Hooper 1853.

to ask every whaler to look for signs of Franklin, and both Kellett and Moore offered rewards to the Eskimos for information, a step that resulted in a flood of exaggerations and fabrications during the next five years.

After searching the area during the summer, Moore decided to winter in Kotzebue Sound, and the *Herald* sailed south. In September, Moore visited the Buckland people, who had fought with Shishmarev and Beechey in 1820 and 1827 but now appeared friendly and eager to help. Kellett attributed the difference in their conduct to having an interpreter who could explain his objectives, as well as the fact that for sixteen years they had obtained from Saint Michael knives, kettles, shirts, and handkerchiefs "of gaudy colours, cotton printed with walrus, reindeer, and all the other animals that they are in the habit of catching and representing in ivory. . . . They were latterly very anxious to obtain muskets, and evinced no fear in discharging them."

Although men of the ship visited the Buckland and Kiwalik rivers and Hotham Inlet several times, "beyond these points it seemed difficult to penetrate, the chief difficulty being our inability to induce the natives to act as guides to the habitations of the distant tribes."

When the Eskimos told them about a shipwreck on the Arctic coast, Lieutenant Bedford Pim offered to go to Saint Michael to investigate the rumors of white traders in the interior, since it was thought they might be Franklin's men. Accompanied by Paolo Oclagook, a half-breed Eskimo who spoke Spanish, Pim left the ship on 17 March and returned on 29 April 1850. The trip was far more difficult than he had anticipated. He had troubles with his sleds and guides and almost ran out of food. It took him five days to get only to a village at the source of the Kiwalik River (possibly the winter caribou camp called Kangaruk), and if it had not been for the chief's assistance in procuring a guide, he could not have proceeded. Pim's account does not name a single village—not even Unalakleet—but he traveled via the Koyuk River across the ice to Cape Denbigh, Shaktoolik, Egavik, Unalakleet, and Saint Michael, where he was "received in the kindest manner by Andrea Gusef, the commandant" on April 6.[6] This was the first overland trip on Seward Peninsula undertaken by a white man.

The Search, 1850–51

On 15 July 1850 the *Herald* returned to Kotzebue Sound from Mazatlán. The *Investigator* planned to meet the *Enterprise* at Cape Lisburne, but, missing it, sailed past Point Barrow to the east, where it was abandoned as a derelict in 1852. The other three ships sailed everywhere in the Bering Strait that summer. Captain Kellett in the *Herald* visited Saint Michael to discuss

6. Captain Moore's narrative of the wintering of the *Plover* and Pim's overland journey are in the Great Britain Sessional Papers 1851, vol. 33, no. 97, no. 4 (A) and 4 (B); 1856, vol. 41, no. 2124, inclosure 3 in no. 58; and Seemann 1853, pp. 130–48. Pim died in October 1886, a rear admiral. According to the *Evening Star* (Washington, D.C.), "he loved America and Americans" (5 October 1886 issue, Dall scrapbooks, vol. 14, unpaged).

the possibility of using the Russian trading posts in the interior for their searches, but Kellett learned that their geographical knowledge did not extend into Canada. Collinson in the *Enterprise* cruised around the Chukchi Sea, waiting unsuccessfully to rendezvous with the *Herald* at Cape Lisburne and Point Hope. Moore, in the *Plover*, received permission to send two boats north as far as the Seahorse Islands for another try at tracking down the rumors of the white men, and also to investigate possibilities of wintering near Point Barrow.

Collinson hoped to relieve Moore, who had already been in the Arctic two winters, by remaining over the winter at Bering Strait; but the plan was abandoned mainly because the *Enterprise* was unable to maneuver in either Kotzebue Sound or Grantley Harbor, much to the disappointment of her crew. While the *Enterprise* was anchored in Port Clarence several skin boats came a number of times from the village on the north spit, but Collinson was busy with ship's affairs and turned them away. This injured their feelings so much that they stayed away until just before the ship sailed north. This "encampment," said Collinson, "was fixed on the north spit between the two harbours, and we had latterly as many as five or six boats, each containing eight or ten people, who were somewhat under the control of two chiefs; from them we obtained reindeer's meat in small quantities and fish. Herrings were abundant. . . ."[7]

On 14 September the *Enterprise* anchored near Cape York, where it encountered Eskimos from Wales going to Port Clarence. The Eskimos called the cape "Ipnook" and the beach "Channermuck [Singloak]." They had only inferior skins for sale, stayed only a few hours, and went on. On 19 September an umiak fitted out with a walrus intestine sail and with inflated sealskins at the sides came to the *Enterprise* from Cape Prince of Wales. The Eskimos asked for rum, "and, on being given half a pint in exchange for four walrus tusks, the head man pressed the bottle to his breast and stroked it down with every symptom of affection. This was the first instance that spirits had been enquired for, or even liked when offered."[8]

Returning south, the *Enterprise* rescued an Eskimo family that was drifting in an umiak near Besboro Island. The family, uncertain of its whereabouts, had drifted along the coast for five days after breaking loose from a rope with which they were being pulled around Cape Prince of Wales. Their umiak was thirty-six feet long and six feet wide, and it, too, had a sail of "walrus gut with a patch of an old shirt here and there." The family spent the night in the ship's sick bay, and Collinson learned that they were acquainted with Grantley Harbor and Diomede and King islands, but not Sledge Island. Collinson sailed back to "the large village" at Cape Nome and pointed out the direction they should take to go home. He gave them many gifts and put

7. Collinson 1889, pp. 72–73. The voyage of the *Enterprise* is told in Collinson's journal.
8. Ibid., pp. 73, 74.

Nome, Alaska, in July 1900 (Photograph by Lomen brothers)

Sledge Island and Nome, 1961. Photograph by Dorothy Jean Ray

"Native Village on Sledge Island," 1898. (From United States Treasury Department 1899, p. 126)

"Bidarka [skin boat], Port Clarence," 1885. (From Healy 1887, following p. 58)

their umiak into the water. As the visitors neared the shore, two skin boats left the cape, and after a fifteen-minute conference, all three boats went to the village.[9]

The *Enterprise* stopped at Saint Michael, where Lieutenant John J. Barnard, assistant surgeon Edward Adams, and three able-bodied seamen disembarked. They had volunteered to see whether the white men supposed to be in the interior were Franklin's crew, and to communicate any information they learned to the *Plover* by land that winter.

The *Plover*, meanwhile, continued its preparations for wintering in Port Clarence, and crews of the three ships plunged into the building of the first European house north of Unalakleet, on the north side of Grantley Harbor near the *Plover*.[10] Many of the crew longed to return on the *Enterprise* to warmer climates, but Moore did not want his numbers decreased because "the natives here are so numerous, certainly not so trustworthy, and more independent in their manner than the natives of Kotzebue Sound." Their principal establishment was the large village of "Kavyiak," or Kauwerak, a day's journey away.

Many Eskimos visited the ship during its stay, bringing some six thousand pounds of caribou meat, several thousand ptarmigan, and fish, hares, and berries. Toward the end of December, Moore and other officers and crew made trips to various places: to the village located on the north side of Port Clarence (Sinramiut, near present-day Brevig Mission); to another one sixteen miles up the "Emowrook River" (apparently Kauwerak); and to Kogrukpak, sixty miles from the ship, where they were always sure of obtaining a lot of meat when the caribou migrated northward.

That winter Moore had a female interpreter, "Mary," from Unalakleet, though it is not known into what language she interpreted. Perhaps she spoke Russian, but certainly not English. She said that a party of "English" had been killed by Indians near the mouth of the "Ko-puk," which Moore thought was either the Yukon or the Colville. Moore had received similar reports the year before from natives at Point Barrow, Wainwright Inlet, and Kotzebue Sound; and in a letter sent to Moore from Gariska, the Russian fishing station at Unalakleet, via a messenger named "Yaw-ma-gah-ma-gah-chick," Lieutenant Barnard reported that Gregoria Wanoff, the Russian in charge of Gariska, had been told by "O-tuk-tah-rock," a Buckland River man, that an English ship had anchored off Point Barrow in September 1849.[11] The captain and his crew, being busy on the ice, had refused to trade with the Eskimos, who thereupon murdered "every soul of them, afterwards plundering and breaking the ship up." It turned out that Wanoff had considerably

9. Ibid., pp. 83–85.
10. Information about the winter in Port Clarence is from the Great Britain Sessional Papers 1852, vol. 50, no. 1449.
11. "Otuktahrock" was Arqugaroak, the paternal grandfather of a Swedish Covenant missionary, Lily Ekak Savok. Mrs. Savok was born in 1893 at Buckland.

exaggerated or misunderstood what he had learned, however, because Otuktahrock himself later told Barnard that he had not known about such a vessel,
and was acquainted with only three ships—the two that had visited Grantley
Harbor and the *Plover*, on which he had slept in Kotzebue Sound during the
winter of 1849–50.

In January Moore decided to send a party overland to Saint Michael to get
further information about the continuing rumors of white men in the interior, although he was convinced they were Hudson's Bay Company men. On
1 February Lieutenants Edward J. L. Cooper and Thomas Bourchier, Seamen Thomas Brooker and George Croker, and Taleshuk Nakeevar, a
Russian-American Company interpreter assigned to the *Plover*, set out with
Yawmagahmagahchick for Norton Sound. They traveled through villages and
places that were to become well known to members of the expeditions searching for Franklin: Tia-to-a-lukh (Kektoashliuk), Mat-nak, E-cath-la-ik (Fish
River), Ta-chik (Golovnin Bay), Ta-nich-tok (Ignituk), At-nuck, Ung-cu-
shen (Unguktulik), Choc-too-luk (Shaktoolik), and Top-ca-ma-sua (Tapkamisua), as found in Cooper's report.[12]

On 19 February they met "Caimoke" (also spelled Kaimoki, Kaimoky, and
Kamokin in the accounts)—about whom we shall hear more—and on the
twentieth, at Atnuk, they got a lot of fish and ptarmigan "dirt cheap." From
that place Cooper sent Bourchier ahead. At Tapkamisua Bourchier was given
a letter sent by Adams saying that the Koyukon Indians had attacked Fort
Darabin (now Nulato), wounding Lieutenant Barnard and the interpreter
who had gone there for information about Franklin. When Cooper reached
Unalakleet, he learned that both had died.

To take this news to the *Plover*, Bourchier left Unalakleet with Croker,
seven dogs and a sled, but no guide, on 19 March 1851. Cooper could not
find a native willing to carry a letter to Moore even "were I to offer them all
the presents and tobacco in the 'Plover.'" According to Bourchier's report, he
returned to the ship by way of E'a-wik (Egavik), Tapkamisua, Shaktoolik
(where the natives were too anxious to talk about anything but "the late
attack on the Russian post at Darabin to give attention to my wants"), Atnuk,
Golovin, a hut called Natch-wik (Nutsvik or White Mountain), Nu-luk (Niukluk), a deserted hut Kig-lu-ni-ar-puk (Keluniak, near Council), a hut T-a-
shag-aruk, Cox-o-to-pa-ga (Kuksuktopaga, now called Casadepaga), Muk-
nuk (Cooper's Mat-nak), Kektoashliuk, Kauwerak, and Tuksuk Channel,
through which he passed on 6 April. Here many Eskimo parties were fishing,
since the fish were abundant and the ice completely gone from mid-channel.
At Kuksuktopaga they had found people living in two huts, subsisting entirely on ptarmigan and a little oil.

12. In the report Shaktoolik is also spelled Choc-too-tok, and Tapkamisua is spelled Tor-
que-ma-sua.

THE SEARCH, 1851–52

On 3 July 1851 Collinson reached Port Clarence from his winter's stay in the sunny south. Passing Cape Prince of Wales he saw "several *oomiaks* . . . going to and fro, from *King-a-ghee* to the edge of the ice, walrus-fishing. One or two forsook their occupation and visited us, when, much to our gratification, we recognised one of the women we had picked up in Norton Sound [the year before]; she was no less pleased, and soon made herself quite at home."[13] The next day, three whaling ships, the *Lagoda*, the *Nancy*, and the *Sheffield*, commanded by Captain Royce (who in 1848 had been the first whaler to hunt north of the Bering Strait), and a trading schooner from Hobart Town loaded with fresh meats and vegetables followed him into Port Clarence.

Collinson directed Moore to go to Saint Michael to pick up antiscorbutics promised by Governor Tebenkov and to cross to Asia to pick up dispatches that might have been sent by the Admiralty via the whalers from Hawaii; then to sail north again, and to proceed to Hong Kong if a ship had not arrived with provisions.

As the *Enterprise* prepared to leave Port Clarence for the North, Collinson granted permission to Chimuak, a chief of Grantley Harbor, to tie his umiak astern for the journey to Cape Prince of Wales, but refused a second chief, Kaimoki, though offered many fine furs and walrus tusks. At Wales Collinson saw again the couple he had rescued the year before, and the man presented him with "a large walrus tusk, which had evidently been reserved for the occasion, and wanted to give everybody something, even to the clothes off his back."

During the summer of 1851 the *Plover* again sailed up and down the northwest Alaskan coast and returned to Port Clarence in August, where the *Daedalus* had brought provisions and carpenters to prepare the *Plover* for wintering the fourth time in the ice, the second in Port Clarence.

During the winter of 1851–52 the *Plover*'s crew engaged in the same activities as the year before.[14] Crews went inland for venison and ptarmigan. In January large numbers of Eskimos came to the ship, though fewer than before. Between February and the middle of April, Moore and an Eskimo snared twenty caribou. By the end of March, "large quantities of seals . . . captured by the Esquimaux on the sea-coast [were] readily bartered . . . for tobacco." When the caribou left, the waters of the Tuksuk opened and the Eskimos began to fish. During that winter at least two patients were taken to the ship's infirmary. A man had "acute rheumatism" and a ten-year-old girl died of "consumption . . . too far advanced before she came" three weeks earlier.

13. Information about the summer of 1851 is from Collinson 1889, pp. 128–35.
14. Great Britain Sessional Papers 1852–53, no. 82: no. 36.

In the summer of 1852, Commander Rochfort Maguire succeeded Moore as skipper of the *Plover*, which was repaired by men of the *Amphitrite*, and the *Plover* was sent to Point Barrow for the winter.[15] The subsequent three summers of the *Plover*'s stay belong to the history of the Point Barrow Eskimos.

Two trading vessels arrived in Port Clarence during September 1853: the British schooner, *Koh-i-Noor*, from Hong Kong under command of George Levine (or Devine); and the Russian-American Company bark, *Kodiak*, which sailed all the way into Grantley Harbor.[16] The *Koh-i-Noor* was trading for walrus skins and tusks and had "some very fine specimens of tusks—some the pair weighing 20 lbs., while the average is 5 to 10 and 12 lbs." That summer, "whales, walrus, and seal [were] in the utmost abundance," and Levine hoped to make a return trip in 1854 to trade fresh food to whaling ships.

THE SEARCH, 1853–54

To the men of the supply ship *Rattlesnake*, with Captain Henry Trollope in command, we owe the first description of the village of Wales and the first and most complete picture of life in interior Seward Peninsula before the gold rush of 1899. They were the first white men to make an overland trip from Port Clarence to Kotzebue Sound.[17]

In September 1853, a month of good weather, the crew gathered driftwood for a house built on "Grantley North Spit" to replace the *Plover*'s house, which had already fallen apart from its swampy location. On 5 October Grantley Harbor was partially frozen, and on the eleventh the *Rattlesnake* sailed to "the north-east bight of Port Clarence . . . 1,500 yards from the shore" for the winter. On 16 October the first drift ice arrived and on 28 October two caribou were seen drifting by on an ice floe. An Eskimo in his kayak took refuge on the ship because of the ice; he left on the thirty-first. On 6 November the ship's crew buried the body of a shipmate near the grave of the surgeon of a French whaling ship who had died two years before. Pack ice continued to come into Port Clarence (Grantley Harbor had been frozen since 16 October) until 10 November, when it became stable and for the first time Eskimos came to the ship with dogs and sleds.

Wales and Sinramiut

Captain Henry Trollope planned to cross the Bering Strait to East Cape, Siberia, for information about Franklin, so on 9 January 1854 he left by sled for Wales from where he hoped to cross by way of the Diomede Islands.[18] He was accompanied by C. W. Stevenson, master's assistant, and Tootashik,

---

15. Great Britain Sessional Papers 1852–53, no. 82: no. 39.
16. See also Chapter 10, concerning sailings north of Norton Sound.
17. Activities of the crew of the *Rattlesnake* are found in the Great Britain Sessional Papers 1854–55, vol. 35, no. 1898, pp. 861–900.
18. Most of the village names are given here in the version known to Eskimos today.

a resident of Tuksuk, who had never been to Wales before. They were later joined by Henry Gilpin.

From Trollope's and Gilpin's journals we get the first description of Sinramiut, which had a population of fifty or sixty, and Wales, which was estimated to have between three and five hundred inhabitants. On the way to Wales they were permitted to stay in the "Poa-llalley-tupuc" or "dancing house" at Sinramiut, which the Eskimos also used as a sweating room when the floor boards were removed and a fire built in the middle.

On 13 January Trollope left Sinramiut, accompanied by an Eskimo man named Inneraya, his wife, and a little girl six or seven years old. When they had stopped for the night on a lagoon, the woman made "a fire in no time with a little charcoal . . . and their own strike-a-light, a thing we rarely meet now-a-days, lucifers having put them out of vogue . . . ; the child sung and laughed, and as she was a good humoured little thing, she did good in her way by cheering us all up." Trollope helped put up the oval skin tent, which was made of five or six deerskins sewn together and thrown, skin side out, over flexible poles. They also slept in the tent on the fourteenth, but the next night they stayed in a hut called Agoluk, which appeared to have been built for wayfarers "as there appears a constant communication between Sinnaramute and King-a-ghee." (On his way to Wales Gilpin shared this hut with his guide, "Pow-e-anna," for whom he had the highest praise.) They also rested at Kinauguk near Cape York, where, he said, the people of Sinramiut came to get seals and fish.

Before reaching Wales, Trollope climbed a hill and could see that there was no hope of crossing to Asia because the ice was slowly drifting northward, a condition that was not at all unusual.[19]

At some distance from Wales, Trollope said that "the child had been dressed and adorned by its mother in anticipation of our arriving, and I was quite amused by the eagerness with which the woman beckoned and hastened me forward to be the first to show me King-a-ghee, while endeavouring to explain all its glories. The place is a sort of capital in these parts and has four dancing houses, which is a very expressive manner of estimating the extent and population of a place." Before rounding the cape, the ice had been broken and rugged, but afterward it was as

smooth as in Port Clarence, studded with innumerable holes, each surrounded by a snow wall, within which people were fishing; our arrival seemed to attract a good deal of attention, and as we neared the village, the whole population turned out to meet us; men, women, and children, the latter shrieking and shouting, wrestling and tumbling one over the other with great glee; the anglers left their rods and lines, which they

19. Rarely was the strait crossed in the winter, as Captain C. L. Hooper, of the Revenue Marine Service, summarized it in 1881: "Although the passage from Siberia to America and back is made many times each year by the natives in their skin boats . . . I could not learn that it is ever made over the ice during the winter. The natives say the ice is always broken and subjected to great and sudden changes, rendering any attempts to cross it extremely hazardous" (Hooper 1884, p. 15).

very dexterously haul up and wind on a short rod about two feet long, and accompanied us up the steep bank on which the upper village stands; . . . We had a sort of introduction from a man well known to us, who lives on Grantley Harbour—"Kai-mo-ky" [Kamokin]; and our guide, on inquiring for him, found he was away for seal, but his wife, a very nice-looking woman, invited us in; I was quite pleased with the neat, tidy, and even clean aspect of the interior, the floor smooth, clean swept and polished, two cheerful rows of lamps or lights, burning almost with the brilliancy of gas, gave the place a most comfortable and warm feel, most grateful to us cold and wet as we were; still I must say the odour was intolerable, a mingled smell of urine and burning seal blubber. As the master of the house was absent I determined not to take up our abode at present, but to have a look through the village. The crowd around us was great, but they assured us "Petak-tig a-lig" that they did not steal, but that their neighbours in the lower village were "Anghee-roo-rak tig-a-lig," that is, great thieves. . . . I must do them the justice to say that we lost nothing. . . . King-a-ghee consists of two villages, between which there appears to be some little rivalry; the one we took up our abode in is the upper one, situated a hundred feet or so up the hill, while the other is on a low spit, extending to the N. W. and N. N. W. I estimated the number of inhabitants at about 200 or 250 in each [earlier he had said between 150 and 200]; there were from 20 to 30 tupucs in each, and in each tupuc there are at least 6 or 8 people, and in many 8 or 10; but these sort of estimates must be very vague. [We were] treated with equal civility in the lower village, although their neighbours did give them a bad character. The more we saw of the people the more we admired their clothing; the furs were excellent, handsome, and even tasteful in ornament; the children fat, rosy, and happy, continually wrestling with each other.

Toward evening they watched the seal hunters returning with their light sleds (made differently from the draft sleds), each drawn by four dogs. Although their host had not yet returned, they were invited into the home to unpack, "the woman [giving] us every welcome," beginning to repair their shoes and "even a woollen sock was mended, with a piece of fawn skin." Trollope was favorably impressed by the dwelling he was in, especially the long, low, narrow entrance passage that trapped the cold air.

When two men returned an hour after sunset with three seals, Trollope learned he was in the home of two brothers, "Ar-naark-looke and Eemown [also spelled Elmown] each of whom had two wives and two children, one by each wife [who] went out and thanked them most cordially [for the seals]." The entrance passage "was common to both, as was a cooking house, a miserable dirty hole six or seven feet long, and three or four broad, with a hole in the roof for the smoke; but on the right hand of the passage, another branched off leading to Eemown's apartment [about fourteen feet square, nine feet high in the center, with a shelf along one side of it], which appeared in all respects perfectly distinct from his brother's." They had Russian knives, kettles, and mugs.

The women served dinner of chunks of hot seal meat in rich gravy. A three-year-old child sucked on a piece of blubber that had been roasted over the lamp before nursing at his mother's breast. During the meal the little boy called out, "Ark-hun! Ark-hun!" and his mother "put a wooden drum-like tub made of the bark of the birch towards him, which he placed close to his papa at dinner with his seal-hunting friends, sat down, ——, and ran back to his blubber again. The utensil in question was as near his father on one side as the dish of seal soup was on the other; the odour is not surprising after seeing this."

Many visitors came to see them before bedtime at nine o'clock. Each man slept between his wives, and each child with its own mother.

On 10 January Trollope received a "very civil message" from "Ark-roo-ark," one of the chief people in the lower village, who lived at the extreme of the spit, to visit him. His house was similar to their hosts', "but not so tidy and comfortable." He also had two wives and many children or dependents. Seal hunters arrived from the ice. "The sledges coming in and departing formed a very animating scene. They travel fully four miles an hour, and when they brought in three or four seals behind them, the excitement was general." They saw some fine umiaks, thirty-eight or forty feet long and seven feet wide, on storage racks.

Returning home, Trollope found that Henry Gilpin and Edward Hill, the ship's ropemaker, had arrived with additional provisions. About two o'clock, the "town turned out to see [them] as they did to see me." Trollope tried to explain to the Eskimos the reason for his visit, but without success. He found the language barrier a great hindrance, and the Eskimos did not want to believe that they were there for anything but trade, "all their intercourse with European or American ships . . . so entirely possessed them with this idea."

But his opinion of these people was very high:

They are . . . an intelligent race, and though uncleanly, very far removed from being degraded: in fact, the reverse. They are intelligent and ingenious in a very high degree—displayed in their habitations, in their boats, their sledges, and their weapons. I also think they are an amiable people. I never remember hearing any quarrelling or harsh words even between them, although one or two instances of stabbing have been mentioned, which I have reason to believe took place. One arose from jealousy, caused by success in shooting.

The whole town turned out for their departure on 20 January. Their sled broke down on the way, and as they finished repairing it, were overtaken by Arkrooark, the chief from the lower village, and two other men, who had already heard of their misfortune. They had brought another sled for sale, but the price was too high and they continued on to the ship with the mended sled. "Our friends in the upper village had warned us that these people were thieves, and we certainly suffered some losses."

Kauwerak and the Trail to Kotzebue Sound

By February 1854 Trollope knew the inland country so well from Eskimo information that he was able to name the villages that Mate William R.

Hobson would pass through on his way to Kotzebue Sound, where he hoped to find information about Franklin. Hobson left the *Rattlesnake* with provisions for thirty-eight days and orders to keep a journal, which contains the only existing firsthand account of villages in the interior of northern Seward Peninsula and of nineteenth-century caribou hunting. Although the journal, printed in the Great Britain Sessional Papers, did not include a map said to have been made by the men, I have been able to reconstruct Hobson's route from my field research. This route led up the Kuzitrin River and one of its tributaries to the headwaters of the Goodhope, and down this river to the coast, which Hobson followed to Deering and Chamisso Island.

On 9 February Hobson, accompanied by two seamen, Henry Toms and William Lee, traveled ten miles from the ship to Too-cut-atawne (Tapkak, apparently at the mouth of Tuksuk Channel), where his guide, Tudlig, was to meet him. All thirty residents were suffering from coughs. (Eskimos today use the name Singloak to refer to the old sites and camps on both sides of the Tuksuk mouth.)

At 8:00 the next morning Hobson started out with Tudlig and his wife through Tuksuk Channel and arrived at "Tocsuc, a village of three huts" by 11:30. They crossed Imuruk Basin, and after traveling eleven miles spent the night in an Eskimo skin tent, made like the one already described.

They stayed the night of 11 February at "Cove-e-aruk" (Kauwerak), where they saw seven dwellings, all large, but the inhabitants were away hunting. On 12 February they traveled up the Kuzitrin River and arrived at two small and dirty huts called "Shung-i-ow-ret" (Shungiyorut), where there were thirty people, mostly children.

On 13 February Hobson reached "Kek-to-a-luk" (Kektoashliuk), where he found water flowing in the river and dammed for fishing although it was midwinter. Ptarmigan were very plentiful. At 3:30 they arrived at "Noo-kei-row-e-lek," which had two inhabited huts and fifteen people, who would not permit them to cook anything on their fire, although there was a large one in the hut, because of a "superstition against it."

On 14 February the brush thinned along the river and traveling was easier. During the day they passed two separate inhabited huts. At the second, "Tudlig, who had become exceedingly lazy and useless, wanted to remain," but they continued on after dark until they arrived at an umiak and two deserted huts called "Oa-te-ue."

On 15 February, after three hours of traveling, they passed "Ko-gru-puk" and reached "Obell" the next day. A large number of the fifty inhabitants were children. They had a lot of caribou meat, but few dogs, which they refused to sell to Hobson who needed them. Here Hobson witnessed the performance of a shaman healing a man who had a respiratory ailment. The old shaman seated himself before the fire in a crouching position and for an hour and half shook a skin and uttered "strange guttural sounds" over and over without changing his position the whole time. Later, a woman lifted and lowered the patient's head by means of a stick attached to a skin band tied round his head.

On 17 February Tudlig reluctantly left with Hobson, but en route he overturned the sled—on purpose, it was suspected—on a steep hill and refused to help right it. That evening, after traveling fourteen miles, they arrived at "Poe-loe-low-reuc," which had one inhabited hut and several in poor condition. There were about twenty-five people. For eight hands of tobacco and a bunch of small blue beads they bought another sled to replace the one broken the day before.

Continuing on, they went seven more miles to "Show-e-yuk" (Soiyuk), a village of four huts in "two and two, considerably detached, so as almost to form two distinct villages. The inhabitants are well clothed and have a large supply of venison, which they seem ready to barter. . . . The natives here are less civil than we have found them elsewhere, and evince a strong disposition to steal anything they can lay hands upon." He remained there the rest of the day to obtain a supply of dog food since it would be "the last village met with for several days." An informant located this village for me on the upper Kuzitrin River within the boundaries of Kauwerak territory. Here Tudlig deserted Hobson, possibly because they were planning to cross the mountain divide into foreign tribal territory, and Hobson was unable to "prevail upon any man in the village to become my guide, even for the reward of a gun." Finally, his persistence, and the promise of a double-barreled gun, prompted an old man named "Ow-wock" to accompany him. While packing things on still another newly purchased sled, Hobson discovered that two large knives, the ax, and some small gear, tobacco, and thirty pounds of biscuits had been stolen.

On the twentieth, they set out from Soiyuk, and after about seven and a quarter hours came to a stream called "E-nu-lu-muk," a tributary of the "Cug-i-oe-to-uk" (apparently the upper portion of the Noxapaga River), but "before we got into the course of the river our guide stopped and made a small fire, for what purpose he would not tell me."

They stopped for the night of 21 February at a tiny, uninhabited hut called "E-tum-ner-it." Hobson's orders read that he was to descend the Spafarief (Kiwalik) River to Chamisso Island, but instead he mistakenly had crossed the mountains to the Goodhope River, which he called by its Eskimo name, "Pittock"; and the twenty-eight miles that he traveled from Soiyuk to a village, "Kip-lik-tok," on the river is the distance between Soiyuk on the Kuzitrin and an old village called Pittuk on the Goodhope River, according to Eskimos today. At this village of four huts there were only two women and some children who were dirty and ill-clothed. The men were out caribou hunting. Before they were permitted to enter the village, "the women lit a small fire in the track we were to pass over; they hailed the guide to stop until it was done. . . . They would by no means permit us to chop the dogs' food with the edge of an axe, but had no objection to its being broken up with the back; I have noticed the same thing at other villages." Here Hobson bought an Arctic hare, fifteen pounds of caribou meat, and dog food "for a little tobacco and some needles."

On 28 February Hobson started out with only one sled because he was sure that he was not far from Chamisso; but he had miscalculated by not descending the Kiwalik, and it took him more than two days to get to "Kip-pel-lek" (Kipalut) on Cape Deceit, a village of two good huts and two dilapidated ones. On his return to Kipliktok on 13 March, the population was four men, four women, and two children, all living in one house. On 17 March, after ascending a steep hill, he saw the "Kig-li-qui-ak hills" (the Kigluaik Mountains), which seemed "almost like old friends to us."[20]

On the eighteenth they started out early, not wanting to sleep at Soiyuk, if possible, and hoped to reach Poe-loe-low-reuc on the nineteenth. During the day they saw many ptarmigan and two or three hundred hares in one pack. On the nineteenth Hobson was told to make a long detour because the Eskimos were driving caribou on the hill he wanted to cross. Keeping to the river he came to a hunting hut where he bought venison, ptarmigan, and dog food. There were many caribou in the area, and he said that he could have bought 1,500 pounds of meat had he so desired. "The snow is literally cut to pieces by deer's tracks. . . . Show-e-yok, at present, is indeed the land of plenty, their stages are literally loaded with venison, and there is an immense quantity buried about the place. A man brought me a double haunch as a present directly we arrived. The hut that I am in at present is crowded with natives; they have an immense fire in it, and are eating venison as fast as they can cook it, with appetites that seem insatiable. I have been obliged to commence writing in self-defence, as they are literally overwhelming me with pieces, and I prefer waiting for my own dinner; they are too busy to barter with us to-night. When we arrived, all the village came out to meet us."

When Hobson bought another sled, he again ran into trouble because the seller decided he wanted the sled back as Hobson was prepared to leave on 20 March. When Hobson refused to return it, another young man began to unload it and pushed Hobson back several times when he tried to stop him. After Hobson's assistants quickly reloaded the sled, they left immediately. "Had we resented, or not resisted their conduct," said Hobson, "I think a skirmish would have been the consequence, in which, from their numbers, we should probably have been overpowered, although our firearms were at hand. It is worthy of note, that although the Obell and many river natives are congregated here, all but the Show-e-yok men stood aloof, and showed no disposition to interfere."

The village of Poe-loe-low-reuc was deserted in March. On the way to

20. This is the first recording for the native name of these mountains north of Nome. Their official name is still Kigluaik, although they are locally known as the Sawtooth Mountains.

Obell, which he also found deserted because several persons had died recently, he saw two hunting huts, an hour away from the village, which he had not mentioned on his way north. The inhabitants gave him some boiled meat, and he reciprocated with tobacco. On the twenty-fourth Bourchier met him at Kektoashliuk with more provisions, and on 25 March he passed the still-deserted Kauwerak. A herd of caribou browsed near the houses. At Tocsuc the three small houses were so filled with people that some of the occupants slept outdoors so that Hobson's party could sleep inside. On the twenty-seventh they arrived safely at the ship.

SPRING 1854

During the winter, the crew of the *Rattlesnake* was well supplied with at least a thousand ptarmigan, three-quarters of a ton of caribou meat, and some fish in exchange for beads, buttons, tobacco, and shirts.[21] Trollope also lent guns to several men to hunt caribou on shares. During May the Eskimos brought many flounders. On the first day of June open water surrounded the ship, but the ice did not leave until the eighteenth. "Ar-naark-looke" of Wales paid the *Rattlesnake* a visit, and on 25 June the *Trincomalee*, under Commander Houstoun, arrived. The men of the *Rattlesnake* had seen only one other ship that spring, the *Phiel* from Honolulu, trading for walrus tusks, whalebone, and furs during the last part of June at Port Clarence. She had been near Cape Rodney earlier, but the ice had sent her back to Siberia. Her skipper had traded for four thousand pounds of walrus tusks, three thousand pounds of whalebone, and two or three hundred skins of various animals including marten and sable.

Later that summer Commander Houstoun left the Arctic for San Francisco before he received news that Collinson and the *Enterprise* had sailed from the east into the Chukchi Sea on 8 August. By that time almost the entire coast north of Canada and Alaska had been searched without finding any trace of Franklin's expedition. It was therefore decided to terminate the Bering Strait and Alaskan searches and Collinson sailed south. On his way, Collinson saw forty-two umiaks leaving together from Wales, most of them going northward along the coast, only a few detouring to the ship to trade a few walrus tusks and furs in exchange for rum and brandy, their most frequent requests.

Collinson returned to Point Barrow to recall the *Plover*, which had sailed north for its seventh season in the ice. Both ships returned to Port Clarence where Collinson again met Mr. and Mrs. Kaimoki and learned that Omatoke had become a chief upon Chimuak's death. The *Plover*'s sails, which had been stored in the basement of the house, had been stolen and cut up. Kaimoki and Omatoke had tracked them down and returned them.

21. Information about the summer of 1854 is from Collinson 1889, pp. 328–33; Great Britain Sessional Papers 1854–55, Houstoun report.

Collinson gave Kaimoki the house to preserve it and to protect the *Herald*'s pinnace and gear that had been left nearby on the beach for shipwrecked crews. Maguire purchased a kayak for a double-barreled carbine from Omatoke to add to Collinson's collection of Eskimo boats. On 16 September 1854 the *Plover* and the *Enterprise* sailed from Point Spencer for Hawaii and Hong Kong, and the search for Franklin in the North Pacific and Arctic had ended.

CHAPTER 12

The Western Union Telegraph Expedition, 1865–67

IN THE UNALAKLEET AREA

MEMBERS of the Western Union Telegraph Expedition spent two years, from 1865 to the summer of 1867, on the shores of Norton Sound and the Bering Strait. The expedition's plan to connect the capitals of America and Europe by stringing wire across the wild lands of two continents and under the waters of the Bering Strait captured the American imagination as nothing had before in Russian America, although the search for Franklin's third expedition had tugged strongly at both European and American emotions. The plan was originated by Perry McDonough Collins, commercial agent of the United States on the Amur River, who had promoted his idea in Siberia and had obtained cooperation and franchises for territory from both Russia and Great Britain by 1860. In 1864–65 he acquired the help of the Western Union Telegraph Company (since Cyrus Field's Atlantic cable, laid in 1855, was thought to be a failure with its repeated breakdowns), and Charles S. Bulkley was put in charge of the entire project.

The explorations were divided into three parts the first year: one was in British Columbia, where the telegraph line from San Francisco terminated; another embraced the Yukon River and Norton Sound areas with headquarters at Saint Michael; and the third was situated on the Amur River in Siberia. In 1866 a fourth group of about forty men was sent to Port Clarence to build the line that was to cross the Bering Strait to Siberia.

The three hundred men of the expedition were a diversified lot, but all had tremendous optimism. Almost all were young—in their twenties and thirties—with strong legs and wills to explore for the best routes that the line would follow. The expedition personnel was organized into military ranks, and the officers sometimes outnumbered the men six to one, especially in the northern groups. Seven men of the organization—Robert Kennicott and his six assistants, Henry M. Bannister, Ferdinand Bischoff, William H. Dall, Henry W. Elliott, G. W. Maynard, and Charles Pease—collected natural history specimens and meteorological data for the Smithsonian Institution and the Chicago Academy of Sciences. Two members of the Saint Michael and Nulato contingent, Dall and Frederick Whymper, published books shortly after returning home. Other members based in that area also left journals, all of which were published in whole or in part: Bannister, George R. Adams, William H. Ennis, and Fred M. Smith. The only diary known to have been written by a member of the Port Clarence group is that of Daniel B. Libby, unpublished and unavailable to me at the time of my research.[1] The Port Clarence contingent, however, published the first newspaper in any language in Alaska. *The Esquimaux* was written and "published" under the editorship of John L. Harrington at the little settlement of Libbysville, across the water from present-day Teller, and at Plover Bay, Siberia. It was so popular that it was reprinted in book form in San Francisco in the fall of 1867.[2] Despite the number of diaries and books that appeared in print, only Dall wrote any ethnographic summaries (because of his longer stay in Alaska and his special interests); but comments about settlements, subsistence, and various Eskimo practices were made from time to time throughout most of the narratives.

The young American men at Saint Michael and Unalakleet had a rare opportunity of observing life in Russian outposts. During the first year, 1865–66, expedition headquarters were established at Saint Michael where the commandant, Sergei Stepanoff Rusanoff, who had arrived about 1862, gave them his best hospitality. Fort Saint Michael had changed little since Zagoskin's time more than twenty years before. The palisade fence still enclosed storehouses, barracks, a kitchen, a bath, and the commandant's house. Outside the fence were the church, the blacksmith shop, sheds, a sundial, and driftwood stacked on end in conical piles. According to Whymper, the buildings inside the fence were painted yellow with red roofs, giving the fort a "rather gay appearance." There was a garden about ten by

1. The most complete and up-to-date treatment of the Western Union Telegraph Expedition is in Sherwood 1965, pp. 15–56. Other scholarly discussions of various aspects of the expedition are in James 1942, pp. ix–xi, and Vevier 1959. Journals and publications were written by the following members of the expedition: Adams 1865–67, and his diaries in Taggart 1956 (I have used the original journals here, however, because Taggart omits almost all ethnological information); Bulkley journal; Bancroft 1886, pp. 576–78 (including a short recollection of certain activities by Ferdinand Westdahl in 1878); Dall 1870 (outline of the expedition, pp. 355–59, and a chronicle of his observations in pt. 1); *The Esquimaux*; James 1942 (verbatim journals of Robert Kennicott's first expedition, and some events of the expedition, and journal of Henry Bannister, 1865–66); Smith diary; Taggart 1954 (parts of William H. Ennis' journals); Wemple papers; Whymper 1869. For Siberian activities see Bush 1872 and Kennan 1902. The diary of Daniel Libby is said to be in the Wickersham Collection, Juneau, but it was not made available to me during a visit in 1962.

2. Bound copies of *The Esquimaux* can be found in the Alaska State Library, Juneau; the Bancroft Library, University of California, Berkeley; the Library of Congress; and the Smithsonian Libraries. The University of Washington library has a photostatic copy.

three feet in which a few turnips and radishes grew. Drinking water was obtained from springs on the opposite mainland. The village of Tachik was a half mile west of Fort Saint Michael (Zagoskin had said a quarter mile), and had a men's house and a half dozen houses, each about twelve by fifteen feet, built of spruce logs.[3]

Dall divided the inhabitants of the fort into "convicts, creoles [half-breeds], and natives," who were ruled with an iron hand by the commandant; and Whymper said that they "were a very mixed crowd, including pure Russians and Finlanders, Yakutz, from Eastern Siberia, Aleuts, from the islands, and creoles, from all parts . . . [not] a very satisfactory body of men . . . who had been convicted in St. Petersburg, and offered the alternative of going to prison, or into the service of the Russian American Company!" Many of the men took Eskimo wives, and Whymper said that when expedition members first arrived in Unalakleet, some of the enterprising Russian men set their wives to work making clothing, which they sold at an exorbitant price.

Almost as soon as they arrived in Saint Michael in the summer of 1865 the men began to explore for routes and trees to serve as poles, in which endeavors they employed many Eskimos. Two men frequently mentioned by the Unalakleet contingent were Kamokin from Kauwerak and Alluyianuk from Unalakleet. Kamokin, who had been employed as a guide for Lieutenant Pim of the Franklin search parties, was called "the great chief of Kaviar-zakhmute" by *The Esquimaux*, and the expedition members planned to name a schooner after him.[4] Alluyianuk, originally from the Kobuk River, was a Malemiut chief who supplied the men with large quantities of caribou meat from his hunting grounds throughout the winter. Alluyianuk was "a fine-looking old man, erect and soldierly, and wearing a mustache and imperial; his manners would not have disgraced a civilized assembly."[5]

Other helpful persons were a Kauwerak man, Kupola (or Kupalo)), who had sailed to San Francisco and Hawaii on the Honolulu brigantine *Victoria*, whose "captain (Fish) is a great trader with the Eskimos and we had often heard of his vessel at Unalakleet";[6] the Malemiuts Ark-na-pý-ak, Ark-hánnok, Myunuk, and "Isaac"; and numerous others.[7] Dall said that "I' chuk Kóliak [was] a trustworthy Máhlemut, who on many occasions had been extremely useful to our parties. His only fault was a predilection for liquor.

3. Information about Saint Michael is from Dall 1870, pp. 9–11, 13–14, 33; and Whymper 1869, pp. 153–54, 156.

4. *The Esquimaux*, p. 28; Dall 1870, pp. 135, 154, 162, 408; James 1942, p. 193; Whymper 1869, p. 168.

5. Whymper 1869, p. 168; Dall 1870, pp. 135, 152–54.

6. Adams manuscript diary; James 1942, p. 242.

7. Other men who helped were Shurugeluk, whose nickname was Shuggy; Nuch-angea-ik, called MacGoffin for short; Kakh-e-nakh, or Lunchy; and Ichiluk, nicknamed "New-Years" because he was hired by Kennicott on New Years day. The men also got well acquainted with Saxy, a Sledge Island trader, who became well known later for his many murders. There were also several unidentified men who were given the names of Johnny, Alexi, Tommy, and André.

He was honest, straightforward, and very intelligent. He had received the name of Isaac from some of the traders [his father was called Abraham] who had also taught him to write his name legibly, but the Innuit had corrupted Isaac into Ichuk."[8]

The Port Clarence contingent also made many Eskimo friends. Besides Kamokin there were "Illiac, chief among the Kingeghn [Wales] Indians"; Utamanna at Cape Douglas; Aya-pana, chief at Ignituk; Itak-tak, another chief; and Attzik, chief of Erathluikmute, or Fish River village.[9]

One of the first duties for the expedition members was to establish a base at Nulato on the little-known Yukon River. (Some persons still stoutly maintained that this waterway flowed north into the Arctic Ocean and that the "Kuikpak," the Eskimo name for the lower Yukon, was a different river.) But the men did not even get a start up the Yukon because the little river steamer *Lizzie Horner* would not run, and so the overland route from Unalakleet was again utilized. During the two years of explorations in this area the men boated and walked many times over the triangular area of Saint Michael–Nulato–Port Clarence; they traveled between Unalakleet and Nulato at least a dozen times in the winter of 1865–66, and between Saint Michael and Unalakleet so often they lost count. The next year their journeys were just as frequent, especially with the addition of the new Port Clarence route.

In 1865 the men visited the "Ingalik" [i.e., Koyukon] villages of Ulukuk and Iktigalik on the upper Unalakleet River many times. On 22 December George Adams, whose diary is one of the sources of information for these trips, saw seventy-five Malemiuts "visiting the Ingerlicks." The most data about these villages were recorded in the fall of 1866, when Dall and Whymper traveled to the upper Unalakleet River. On the right bank was located Ulukuk (*uluksruk*, "stone for ulus" or slate), an Indian village with an Eskimo name, containing five winter houses and a men's house built in Eskimo style. (In 1842 Zagoskin said that this village had five winter and five

---

8. Dall 1870, p. 157.
9. Other men were Negougin, a Kauwerak man who died in a rockslide on his way home from Unalakleet; Noozark, a medicine man of Kauwerak; Utuano; Illipoktuk; Mayounak, who probably is the same as Myunuk; and a "Kooskooim, the most powerful chief of the tribes in the vicinity of Norton Sound and the arctic Ocean."

The men at Port Clarence also gave nicknames to the Eskimos, two of the most colorful being "The Flying Dutchman" (whose wife's name was Izabrook), and "Hunky Dora," a favorite young woman around Libbysville.

Names for the Port Clarence area are from *The Esquimaux*. The descendants of Alluyianuk today constitute over half the population of Unalakleet. The names of three of his sons are surnames in the Unalakleet area: Delilak, Nashalook, and Peniptchuk. Saxy, whose Eskimo name was Anakasuk, is now the Eskimo surname Soxie. One of Deliluk's daughters, Carrie, married Soxie's son, Harry, who became a missionary. The name Ark-na-pý-ak probably was Anakpaguk, Saxy's brother, but Anakpaguk was considered to be Kauwerak, not Malemiut. Myunuk is now spelled Myomic as an English surname. Other surnames in the Bering Strait now are Kamokin and Ayapana, but I do not know whether these persons of the 1860s were their ancestors. Isaac adopted a number of children whose surname became Isaac.

summer dwellings and many caches.) Eleven miles downstream was Ik-tigalik, which had been built by the "Ulúkuk Indians" just before Dall visited it, and was known as New Ulukuk to the Russians. (Zagoskin also mentioned such a settlement, however.) In Iktigalik the "Indian house [was] built after the Eskimo fashion and very clean and comfortable." On the right bank of the river were two winter houses and several caches, and on the left bank, about eight or ten summer houses, which Dall described as being built of "split spruce logs driven into the ground, and roofed with birch bark. The door is at the end facing the river. . . ."[10]

The men also made many trips from Unalakleet to Koyuk, according to accounts by William Ennis and Otto von Bendeleben, a member of the Port Clarence group.[11] In December 1865 Ennis and Bendeleben left Unalakleet accompanied by "quite a train of Esquimaux in our front and rear—the old *Malemute* chief Alluyanak, his men, wives and children . . . going with us as far as [Inglutalik], the chief village on Norton Sound" en route to Koyuk. At Shaktoolik they were treated to dancing and presents of whale blubber, frozen fish, dried caribou meat, and seal-lines, which they reciprocated with tobacco. Their host was the greatest hunter on the coast and the richest man of the village, and through him and their interpreters they told the crowd of Eskimos that they would be well treated "as long as they behaved themselves towards us. . . . We were of course the first Americans that had ever been in that part of the globe, and were not a little scrutinized, but to do justice to our Esquimaux friends, we had, during our whole journey and stay in the different settlements, not one complaint to make against these inoffensive people, who seemed rather to feel a relief at having us among them as mediators between the different tribes."

Their progress along the coast was slow because of ceremonies and danc-ing everywhere along the way. The inhabitants of Kuik were especially friendly because of "a small amount of ardent spirits, brought from 'Port Clarence' by two [Kauwerak Indians] lately arrived, one of whom spoke a little English."[12] A place said by Bendeleben to be "a very romantic spot, and to my idea the prettiest part of the country I had yet seen" was probably Koyuk, which had been deserted for thirteen years. The following winter Koyuk became camp headquarters for work crews for the Golovnin Bay district (the area north of Koyuk) and for the Norton Bay district (Koyuk to Unalakleet).

10. Information about the upper Unalakleet River is from the Adams manuscript diary; Dall 1870, pp. 26–37; Whymper 1869, p. 175; and Zagoskin 1967, p. 136. These Ingaliks were prob-ably originally Koyukon people who lived on the Yukon River from the mouth of the Tanana to Kaltag (Loyens 1964, p. 133).

11. Bendeleben in *The Esquimaux*, p. 33; and Ennis, in Taggart 1954, pp. 153–57.

12. Later on in his journal, Ennis describes the festival in very general terms as a "ten-year festival." He also said he was able to see the bladder festival at Unalakleet, but he only quotes Zagoskin on this ceremony, saying, "what he observed in the year 1842 I witnessed the same in 1866."

In April 1866 Ennis and several companions left their Unalakleet headquarters for a reconnaissance of Port Clarence, having been appointed by
Kennicott to take charge of explorations of the entire area between Port
Clarence and the middle Yukon River.[13] They more or less followed the
route of the Franklin search parties, along the coast and over the mountain
pass to the Kuzitrin. They were hospitably received at Atnuk, where they
distributed "the usual presents of leaf-tobacco. This is a very old village, and
at one time was densely populated; but some fifteen years ago, a disease
caused great mortality among the natives," although at the time of their visit
Ennis said that "Norton Bay is thickly settled with Indians, and Indian
settlements."

They stopped at Ignituk, and at a village of two huts whose name they did
not learn but whose chief, Itak-tak, was "a very jolly old man." There
Kamokin's son, who had been hired as a guide, "complained of a very great
lameness," and Attzik, chief of Fish River village, agreed to take them to Port
Clarence and back in return for a single-barreled shotgun. Bendeleben said
that "it was indeed well that we had this man, who proved himself one of the
best natives in the country. . . . He was never tired of helping or doing
anything that could in the least contribute to our comfort, and fully deserved
his pay, which was increased on our return by presents of cotton-drilling,
ammunition and tobacco."

Their investigations convinced them that "Nook," where they found many
persons fishing, should be the headquarters for the northern explorations,
and five months later Libbysville was founded on the spit across from
present-day Teller.

The men were very homesick at the end of their first year's work. On the
Fourth of July, 1866, they bridged the chasm between home and the
Eskimo-Russian wilderness by firing "a salute of 35 Guns, one for each state
in the Union. . . . Our guns were only 4 power, and did not make a very
loud report but it was the best we could do."[14]

The actual construction of the lines took place during the second year, and
the two main headquarters on the coast were at Unalakleet and at Port
Clarence, each with thirty-nine men.[15] Dall and Whymper were the principal recorders of activities in the Norton Sound area, although both spent the
greater part of the year at Nulato. Dall had taken over the scientific di-
rectorship after the death of Kennicott, and Whymper was the artist of the
expedition.

Dall's visit to the village of "Kegiktowruk" (or Kikiktauk), where

13. The journey of April 1866 is described by Bendeleben in *The Esquimaux*, pp. 37–38; Ennis
in Taggart 1954, pp. 163–65; and in a letter, Ennis to Bulkley, dated Saint Michael, 30 June
1866, Bulkley journal, pp. 214–19. A cape, twenty-five miles west of Koyuk, probably Moses
Point, was named for Ennis, but the name was never used.
14. Smith manuscript diary, 4 July 1866.
15. *The Esquimaux*, p. 52. Some sources said there were only thirty-five men at Unalakleet.

Kashevarov's interpreter had lived in 1838, provides the only description of this village, now an archeological site. It was "quite a village on the high bank back of the cove." Here the inhabitants had built "a sort of ways . . . of round logs, held in place by large masses of rock. These are necessary, as the cove is very shallow and so full of rocks that the skin boats are very liable to be cut on them at low tide. . . . The village is notable on account of the number of graves scattered over the plain about it, and also for the large size of the dance-house." The seven-year-old men's house, in which men also took sweat baths, was the "largest in the country," and had taken six seasons to build. It was a semisubterranean structure, 25 by 30 feet, 15 feet high at the smoke hole, and was lighted by four saucer-shaped oil lamps. The walls and floor were made of split logs shaped with stone axes, as were the benches, 30 feet long, 44 inches wide, and 4 inches thick. In the cemetery, most of the bodies had been placed in elevated boxes, the sides of which were "often painted with red chalk, in figures of fur animals, birds, and fishes."[16]

When Dall reached Unalakleet, he found the Russian post to be in a dilapidated condition.[17] Two sod houses were built for the telegraph men, but the officers were housed in the two blockhouses, twelve by eight feet in size, at the northeast and southwest corners of the stockade. Within this enclosure were several log buildings: a barracks in which the commander and his family had a room, a store, a cookhouse, a bath house, and a storage shed. Each of the blockhouses had two cannons.

Information about villages varied. Adams said that the Eskimo village near Saint Michael contained twelve houses in September 1865, but in October 1866 there were "some thirty or more houses in it now" and a large dance house. In December 1866 Adams said that the population of Unalakleet was four Russians besides the head man and Eskimo workmen, but in September 1867 Dall said there were only five in all.

The Unalakleet contingent spent the winter digging post holes and erecting poles.[18] This southern territory was divided into three divisions: "Sun Golovene" [Golovnin "Sound"] district, from Golovin to the head of Norton Bay; Norton Bay district from Norton Bay to Unalakleet; and Pera Valley district from Unalakleet to Nulato. Only the first two operated during the winter, and the third for only a brief time in May 1867. The men did not plant the first telegraph poles in Norton Bay district until 21 January 1867.[19]

16. Dall 1870, pp. 16–20 *passim*, 126–28.
17. The description of Unalakleet is combined information from the Adams manuscript diary, 12 December 1866; Dall 1870, pp. 23–24, 131; and Whymper 1869, p. 158–59.
18. Information about the Unalakleet district is from the manuscript diaries of Adams and Fred M. Smith. The Adams diary as edited by Taggart omits all of this information.
19. Said Smith, "After the reading of the Orders we went out and selected two poles which were stripped of their bark and raised on my line. Our last bottle of Whiskey was drank on this memorable ocassion [*sic*]. . . ."
The Port Clarence men, however, had built more than fifteen miles of line to the head of Grantley Harbor by 31 October 1866. Working conditions became so difficult that Libby or-

On 31 January, at −50°F., J. B. Chappel left with his party for the Golovnin Bay district where they were said to have established headquarters at Koyuk, but we know nothing of their activities there.

The Norton Bay district men had a number of camps along the coast, situated at five, nine, twelve, and fifteen miles (Egavik) north of Unalakleet. When they stopped working on 26 April, the line extended in a northerly direction for a total of twenty-eight miles. Near the five-mile camp were two small Eskimo houses, one of which—only ten by twelve feet—once furnished refuge for the telegraph men as well as sixteen Eskimos and eleven dogs during a very bad storm. Adams wrote, "I shall never growl at an Indian house again."

On 14 February four Eskimos were working for the Unalakleet contingent, including Lunchy, the "Boss cook . . . very high toned [who] talks a heap of English to his assistants who do not understand a word he says," and Saxy, the Sledge Island trader. Adams said that the Eskimos thought the telegraph line was "the cause of scarcity of deer [caribou]," but it could also have been because the Eskimos were beginning to use guns, "both flint-lock and percussion-cap."[20]

Although a total of only forty-five miles of poles was erected by the Norton Bay division during the spring of 1867 (apparently seventeen miles extended out from Koyuk), Ennis expected to establish headquarters at Golovnin Bay that summer to connect with the Koyuk lines; but he received news while on a reconnaissance trip in the Golovin area that the work had been suspended because the Atlantic cable had succeeded at last.[21]

AT PORT CLARENCE

Farther north, at Port Clarence, thirty-nine men who had left San Francisco on 11 July landed near Nook on 17 September 1866 and proceeded to build their tiny town despite the success of the Atlantic cable, which they had read about in the first issue of *The Esquimaux* (14 October 1866): "[The] Evelyn Wood . . . brings news of the working of the Atlantic Telegraph Cable. It was completed on the 24th of July [1866] and was in operation up to the date of the bark's departure" (p. 7).

Before they were told officially in 1867 that their efforts had been wasted, the Port Clarence men had erected twenty-three miles of poles and built four buildings at Libbysville (named after their commander, Daniel B. Libby),

dered work to be stopped for the winter in November (Libby to Bulkley, 20 June 1867, Bulkley journal, p. 214). Apparently the Port Clarence men put up lines, but the Norton Sound contingent had no wire and put up poles only (Bancroft 1886, p. 577).

The first pole was erected at Nulato on the upper Yukon on 1 January. Dall said, "After breakfast we went out in a body and raised the first telegraph pole, ornamented with the flags of the United States, the Telegraph Expedition, the Masonic fraternity, and the Scientific Corps. A salute of thirty-six guns was fired,—one for each State . . ." (Dall 1870, p. 59).

20. Whymper 1869, p. 163.
21. Bulkley journal, p. 202.

three of them for the men and their provisions: Main Building (where *The Esquimaux* was published), Smithsonian "Institute," and Tower Cottage. For the "numerous neighborly Esquimaux" they built the West End Hotel. During the year they also established a line camp, "Yankee Jims," fifteen miles from Libbysville at the head of Grantley Harbor, probably near the entrance to Tuksuk Channel.

At the beginning of their stay, Libby established rules of conduct for his men toward the natives. They were not to molest or take away any relic from any grave or graveyard, and were to adhere to one price in trading without haggling and without overbidding each other. They were not to eject the Eskimos roughly from the buildings when they wished them to leave, and were to explain the purpose of the house built especially for their visits.

Because of the difficulty of digging post holes in the frozen ground, one hole sometimes taking two hours, the men stopped working in December and did not begin again until April. They used their free time to make trips to various villages of the area, and often wrote about their experiences for *The Esquimaux*. They visited Tuksuk Channel and Kauwerak many times and the homes of Eskimos en route. Libby and an unidentified writer, probably Mr. Harrington, editor of the newspaper, went to Wales on 26 November 1866, stopping en route at a place called Palazruk.[22]

At Wales they stayed at the "Chief's house" and were entertained in a different men's house during each of the three evenings they stayed there. During the first night they were treated to a "feast" and dancing in a building twenty feet square packed with 150 Eskimos. The dancers were "stripped to the waist, with their fancy knee-breeches and decorated boots, their heads set off with beads and feathers, they pow-wowed in a frantic manner. At one time we counted 14 stalwart men on the floor, twisting their bodies in all conceivable shapes, and deafening ears with their demoniac screeching." In all of the men's houses they were presented with a few pieces of bone and some rope, and at one, a few broken crackers; they gave tobacco in return.

Their estimate of the population, nine hundred Eskimos in ninety houses, is almost four hundred higher than any other made before or after, and appears to be an exaggeration or a misprint. On their first morning they saw an "immense crowd, assembled on raised ground about one-fourth of a mile distant, and who seemed to be attending a mass meeting, or listening to a stump oration. On enquiry we learned that the gathering was on account of bad weather and lack of *cow-cow* [a whaling term for food derived from the Hawaiian *kau kau*], and for the purposes of making offerings and prayers for more food and temperate *selami* [Eskimo for weather]."

During supper of the third night of their stay, one of the chiefs, who was intoxicated, rushed into their house, followed by twenty-five or thirty others. The chief talked excitedly about how bad the Americans were, but,

22. The account of the trip to Wales is from *The Esquimaux*, pp. 15–16.

though they pacified him, they were unable to find out what had caused the outburst.

In January 1867 two men went by dogsled to Amilrok on Point Spencer to buy bearded seals; but being unable to get any because ice had blocked the hunting grounds, they went on to Kalulik at Cape Douglas. Kalulik consisted of two deserted, dilapidated dwellings and an occupied one belonging to Utamanna and his seventeen relatives. There they learned that Singuk, a large village a day's travel to the south, was vacated because the inhabitants were thirty miles away at "Aiyakh" (Sledge Island) hunting bearded seals. "On the 25th we loaded our sledge, and took leave of Utamanna, who said he was sorry we were going, as he liked us very much. He had heard from some source, that the Americans were going to shoot all the Esquimaux, when the ships arrived next summer. This idea we assured him was wrong, and told him we were friends of the Esquimaux, and would always treat them kindly if they would not steal or break our telegraph. . . . He is a model Indian, honest and industrious, and has considerable influence with the natives."[23]

All of the men suffered from hunger during the spring because the company had not provided enough food, and it was difficult to buy it from the natives because they, too, were short.[24] Libby sent the men out to live with the Eskimos, and to hunt and fish for themselves, especially during May. They ate fish mainly, and even seal and walrus, to which they were unaccustomed. A party went to Wales to intercept a whaling ship for supplies. Two men went to Sledge Island, where they expected "to luxuriate, for a time on crabs and other fish, which abound in large quantities about the island." Two others went to Wales twice. A party of three, and another of two, went off in a northerly direction. Three men lived with Utamanna at Cape Douglas and at his other camps. Two men lived with "Darby Gougon," an hospitable Eskimo; and the editor of *The Esquimaux*, in company with Walker and Bendeleben, started out to look for food and for Eskimos to help them, but found neither: "The natives are too much busied with their own pursuits to give heed to our wants, and we have to learn and practice the same means which they employ to keep ourselves in food." Two men of the expedition died and were buried at Port Clarence.[25]

In June, Libby visited King Island, which had about two hundred fifty inhabitants living in walrus-hide houses.[26] Several of the King Islanders became drunk, attacked their boat, and threw everything overboard; but some sober ones prevented further trouble. In July many Eskimos arrived from Kauwerak, and pitched their large, roomy oval deerskin tents near

23. Ibid., pp. 29–30.
24. Report, Charles S. Bulkley, Port Clarence, R.A., 20 June 1867, in Bulkley journal, pp. 214–20.
25. *The Esquimaux*, pp. 34, 38, 44.
26. Ibid., p. 41.

Nook to await the arrival of traders. They had brought many furs and seemed well off, but the telegraph men said that they had become great beggars and were becoming pests around their quarters.[27]

In July the men learned that the Atlantic cable had indeed been a success, and that they no longer lived in Russian America. George Adams wrote in his journal for 26 June 1867, "Clara Bell brought news that the United States bought Russian America for $7,000,000 [$7,200,000] . . . and a torrent of news which left us almost speechless."

The Americans, jubilant about leaving for home, also looked upon their departure realistically.

> The natives around here, will make a good thing by our leaving, numerous things will have to be left which will be of use to them, and the clothes, boots etc., that are thrown away by the party is enough to make a nation rich. At the Yankee Jims station are a couple of coils of wire which, together with what is on the poles will make bracelets enough for all the fair esquimaux damsels in the country. The houses, too, will undoubtedly be appropriated by them, and furnish fine quarters. . . . Old Darby Gougan, whose exertions to supply us with food during the winter are well known to all, just arrived in time to receive a reward for his labors. Captain Libby gave him six dogs and a sled, and the whole party presented him with goods sufficient to make him an *umahlik* among his tribe.[28]

One of the most rewarding aspects of the expedition's activities was the use that Charles Sumner, chairman of the Senate Committee on Foreign Relations, made of Kennicott's and Bannister's information in a speech favoring the ratification of the treaty for buying Russian America. Twice before 1867 Russia had offered Alaska to the United States, the second time just before the Civil War. Both Russia and the United States dropped the discussions about the purchase during the war, but during 1865 members of the Western Union Telegraph Expedition in Russian America were gathering firsthand information about the land Russia wished to sell. Their observations did not affect official policy concerning the purchase, but it did provide Secretary of State William H. Seward and Senator Sumner with positive information for newspaper publicity and answers to questions. The majority of expedition material—mainly narrative accounts—was not published until after the purchase transactions, but descriptions of the territory under consideration were given to American negotiators of the transfer by letters and personal conversations with expedition members who had returned to Washington, D.C. Bannister furthermore gave testimony in person before the committee.[29]

Russian America became Alaska, a name chosen by Sumner, who said that "the name should come from the country itself. It should be indigenous, aboriginal, one of the autochthons of the soil. Happily such a name exists,

27. Ibid., p. 44.
28. Ibid.
29. James 1942, pp. 27–34, 35.

which is as proper in sound as in origin. . . . It only remains that, following these natives, whose places are now ours, we, too, should call this 'great land' Alaska."[30]

The ceremonies of transfer at Sitka were brief and simple, and "without even banqueting or speech-making," said Bancroft, "this vast area of land, belonging by right to neither, was transferred from one European race to the offshoot of another."[31]

POSTSCRIPT, 1867–68, AND ALASKA'S FIRST YEAR UNDER A NEW FLAG

Dall, who was scientific director of the Western Union Telegraph Expedition during its second year, was very much disappointed that the work had been suspended, and though only twenty-two years old, he resolved to continue Kennicott's plans for "scientific research," to "carry them out alone, and at my own expense." As the sails of the *Clara Bell* disappeared in the Bering Sea, he realized that he was the "only person in the whole of that portion of the territory who spoke English."[32]

Life in the Bering Strait area during the first year under the ownership of the United States was no different from the year before. The Russian-American Company continued operations at Saint Michael and on the Yukon until official word of the transfer arrived during the winter; American traders did not begin active competition until the summer of 1868.

Dall's observations during his second year were like those of any natural historian of that time. He wrote of ethnology, geology, ornithology, botany, zoology, and meteorology. His remarks about the Eskimos and Indians often reflect his own biases and are too general to be used profitably in comparative issues, but his writings in *Alaska and Its Resources* are all that we have for this year for the Bering Strait area.

Dall spent most of the winter of 1867–68 at Nulato in Indian territory, but he also penned information about the subjects of Malemiut traders in the Saint Michael and Yukon areas, and the beginnings of the liquor trade. The Malemiut were trading between Kotzebue Sound and Saint Michael. Isaac, for instance, had apparently spent the winter of 1867–68 in Saint Michael and, while snow was still on the ground, had gone to Anvik via Kikiktauk with three umiaks on top of sleds; then, after the ice broke up, he floated down the Yukon, trading. Dall met him and his party of thirty men and women between Shageluk and Anvik. They were trading their own skin clothing, needles, tobacco, guns, and ammunition for furs and Indian-made dishes of wood along the Yukon, and were later going to Saint Michael to meet American trading ships. Dall said that the Malemiut were able to get rid

---

30. Sumner 1867, p. 48. "Alaska" is the name given to the mainland by Aleutian Islanders as land opposed to a small land, or islands.
31. Bancroft 1886, p. 600.
32. Dall 1870, pp. 122, 123. For a summary of Dall's life see Sherwood 1965, pp. 35–56.

of their old guns and surplus ammunition at higher prices to the Indians than they paid for new ones at Grantley Harbor and Kotzebue Sound. The well-armed and bold Malemiut forced the Indians to sell at their price, and were feared when drunk.[33]

Liquor was making its appearance everywhere. During the fall of 1867, Isaac's brother brought two kegs of rum to Saint Michael from Kotzebue Sound. As Dall was preparing to leave for home in 1868, he saw an umiak with two barrels of rum pulling away from an American trading schooner, which was "already the beginning of evils whose future growth none could estimate."[34] This schooner belonged to a company that intended to begin trading at Saint Michael. The ship that Dall was to leave on, the *Frances L. Steele*, was also a trader, commanded by a "Captain Smith" and Mike Lebarge, who had been with the telegraph expedition and would later become a well-known trader on the Yukon.

Dall said that several other American trading companies intended to come into the country. En route to San Francisco via Saint George Island and the Aleutians, Dall said that he had "obtained abundance of evidence that during 1868 great abuses were prevalent in the new territory. One trading company in particular, hoping, by its large capital and connection with the officers of the defunct Russian Company, to crush all smaller concerns, had not hesitated at force, fraud, and corruption, to attain these ends," and he thought that if a territorial government were granted "to the handful of Americans now resident in the territory, it would simply give the stronger companies the power to crush and ruin the weaker ones, and a full opportunity of smuggling and selling liquor would be afforded to the former" and for other tragedies like fur seal exploitation of the Pribilofs to take place.[35]

He was referring to the John Parrott vessels and to the firm of Hutchinson, Kohl and Company, which had bought the stores, ships, and supplies of the Russian-American Company a week before the transfer of Alaska on 17 October 1867. This company's assets were taken over in September 1868 by its owners and placed under the name Alaska Commercial Company, which later became the Northern Commercial Company. Dall went on to become an expert on Alaska affairs, but always critical of the Alaska Commercial Company and its views on the development of Alaska.

33. Dall 1870, pp. 215, 216, 218, 220–22.
34. Ibid., pp. 161–62, 239.
35. Ibid., pp. 240–41.

CHAPTER 13

Bering Strait Culture, 1833–67

DURING this period, attitudes of the Eskimos changed from the watchful, often uneasy, relations with Europeans who had appeared at infrequent intervals over the horizon to a solid person-to-person relationship with new economic dimensions added to the Bering Strait trade. The Eskimos' inventory of European goods changed noticeably during this period, and the consumption of liquor and use of firearms began to modify both behavior and subsistence patterns.

The world became better acquainted with people of a still virtually unknown territory during these thirty-five years. Beechey had identified the Alaskans positively as Eskimos and distinguished them culturally from those living farther east; but the aristocratic Englishmen of the Franklin search parties and the impetuous Americans of the telegraph expedition brought them to life as busy individuals in a thriving culture. For the entire period, the character of white-Eskimo contact was considerably different from before because all of the Europeans remained throughout the winter and the Eskimos visited the white men in their own dwellings. Eskimos were also taken aboard ship as helpers, and a few Eskimos went as far afield as San Francisco and Hawaii. With the exception of the Saint Michael post, there were no white families. A white woman was a rarity, and the first permanent unions between Eskimo women and the non-native men were made in Saint Michael at this time.

INTERTRIBAL RELATIONS

The most important change in tribal relations was the Malemiut's permanent move to Unalit territory. They were drawn to the Norton Sound and Yukon areas first by the furs obtained from interior Indians and southwest coastal Eskimos, and possibly by changing caribou routes; and secondly, by the Saint Michael post. By the 1860s the items they traded for were no longer exclusively Russian tobacco, weapons, and utensils and Siberian reindeer skins, but included American tobacco, guns, and liquor obtained from ships that called at ports on both the Alaskan and Siberian sides of the strait.

Another major tribal move by the 1840s was the crossing from Indian territory to the upper Unalakleet River by a group of Koyukon Indians. (Kaltag, a Koyukon village on the Yukon, is only twenty miles from the headwaters of the Unalakleet River.) By early historical times, interior Alaska Indians had moved down the two large rivers, the Yukon and the Kuskokwim, adopting Eskimo housing, ceremonials, burial practices, and art, but not language. The same kind of change was taking place on the much smaller Unalakleet, where the long-standing trade in European goods (for more than fifty years) between Indians and Eskimos was apparently responsible, in part, for the Indians' entering what my informants told me had always been Eskimo territory. According to Zagoskin, these Ulukuk Indians were the first natives to trade with the Russians at Saint Michael, and the three traders of the village supplied the fort with nine to fifteen hundred beaver pelts a year.[1]

During this period the relationship between Indians and Eskimos was generally friendly, and they traded in the other's territory at specific places. The Anvik Indian traders went to Kikiktauk and the Ulukuk Indians to Unalakleet, apparently without their families; but the Malemiut traders traveled through Indian country with an entire retinue.

During this period there were abundant memories of interracial conflicts as preserved in folk tales, and Eskimo anxiety was periodically reinforced by anticipating raids from an enemy. Although white men never saw Eskimo "wars," Indian and Eskimo guides were reluctant to travel in enemy territory as late as the 1860s. Zagoskin did not reach Kotzebue Sound because his Indian guide refused to take him through Eskimo territory.[2]

Encroachment into enemy territory, especially for killing game, was one of the causes of Indian-Eskimo conflict—just as we saw that arguments over hunting sea mammals on the ice had caused earlier wars between the Siberians and American Eskimos. Conflict appears to have been minimal between Indian and Eskimo groups whose boundaries joined on a large river—as on the Yukon, Kuskokwim, or Unalakleet—and greater between those who had extensive boundaries adjoining in upland territory.

The two races evidently enjoyed a restrained friendship during early historical times, but the high proportion of conflict tales suggests that sometime in the not too distant past Indian-Eskimo relations had been as antagonistic as those between Siberians and American Eskimos. If we accept the stories about Siberian-Eskimo conflicts, we also have to accept those about Indians and Eskimos, because no documented examples of raids or warfare in Alaska by Siberians within historical times exist, except that reported by the Billings expedition (see Chap. 4, "Observations Made by the Billings Expedition").

1. Zagoskin 1967, p. 136.
2. Ibid., p. 153.

All Norton Sound Unalit have numerous stories concerning troublesome Indians, unlike the absence of tales of warfare or raiding between the Eskimos and the Yugelenut Ingalik (Georgetown Ingalik) on the Kuskokwim, for example.[3] Unaluk tales ranged from suspected murder of Eskimos at the hands of the Indians while out hunting to the killing of all Eskimos in a settlement.

The character of Eskimo-Indian contact in the Norton Sound area after the mid-1800s also differed from that on the Kuskokwim, where ethnographic reconstructions have revealed that the population spread in historic times was on an individual basis through Eskimo-Indian marriage.[4] Such marriages rarely occurred at Unalakleet or Saint Michael. I know of no genealogies and only one folk tale, dating back to the mid-1800s, which contain an Indian-Eskimo union. The tale, moreover, has the classic war theme of complete annihilation of the enemy and as such seems highly mythological, especially since the two versions that I got had opposite endings.[5] The story concerns a group of Yukon Indians who forced an Eskimo man married to an Indian woman to guide them in their canoes to attack Golovnin Bay villages. In one version, all of the Eskimos living in Atnuk were killed; but in the other the Indians were either killed or injured when they stumbled on barricades of thong strung along the shore near the settlement, thus permitting the inhabitants to flee.

What may be the only documented example of an Eskimo warfare alliance[6] was the attack by the so-called Azyagmyut against employees of the Russian-American Company at Stephens Pass in 1836. Sledge Island, from which these men (Ayakmiut) supposedly came, never supported a total population of more than forty or fifty, including only about twenty adult males, so their numbers would have been reinforced by men of other tribes. The number of attackers reported by Zagoskin would have been equal to the male population of the entire area from Stebbins to Cape Rodney, a coastal distance of 400 miles. The name "Azyagmyut" could have referred to any tribe of Seward Peninsula because the Sledge Islanders were also called Malemiut by Zagoskin, who even applied the name Azyagmyut to a man from a village on the Kiwalik River (see Chap. 10, "The Malemiut").

On the other hand, since we know of no case in which the alliance for native warfare included more than one other tribe, this entire episode may have been exaggerated, and in the few years between its occurrence and first report may have gotten out of hand like the Kheuveren legend. Nevertheless, this report may have been based on a concerted effort to remonstrate over the loss of trading, and would then have constituted an intertribal alliance against a common foe.

3. Oswalt 1962, p. 11.
4. Ibid.
5. See also Burch's article for a discussion of annihilation as an objective of Eskimo warfare.
6. Ibid.; Ray 1967b, p. 389.

SETTLEMENTS AND SUBSISTENCE

All of the statements made about settlement and subsistence patterns and chieftainship in Chapter 8 hold for this period. In addition, in 1854 the first information was recorded about the interior Seward Peninsula Eskimos, who hunted caribou extensively during the winter, and about the village of Kauwerak. Although many "villages" were only one- or two-dwelling settlements with a population of twenty to fifty, it was confirmed that Wales was a large and important settlement with almost five hundred inhabitants in two separate, but physically proximate villages.

Both the fur trade and the establishment of trading centers began to affect Eskimo settlement patterns. The native village of Unalakleet, which had been re-established by the thirteen survivors of the smallpox epidemic near the fledgling Russian-American Company post, had steadily grown larger. By 1867 the village also included Kauwerak and Malemiut families who lived there part of the year. This place, as well as Kikiktauk to the south, was preferred over Saint Michael by native traders because of portages to the Yukon River. Kikiktauk, which was later abandoned, was a village of twenty-eight persons in four houses during Zagoskin's time, but apparently was larger during the telegraph days. It was as large and important as any settlement in Norton Sound at that time despite its location on a rocky shore, which necessitated the building of ways of rock and drift logs for launching umiaks. The inhabitants relied almost equally on seals and caribou.

From remarks of this time, it is obvious that both houses and "villages" were frequently abandoned for one reason or another, the sum of occupied and unoccupied dwellings making the population seem much larger than it actually was. Other facts brought out in the writings were: the men's house was used as a sweathouse as far north as Sinramiut in 1854; driftwood was still plentiful along all of the coast and was stacked on end in huge pyramids as private property; wooden markers were used to follow winter trails such as that between Wales and Sinramiut. As late as 1867 the Kauwerak people were using oval skin tents while waiting for the trading ships at Port Clarence, but the traveling Malemiut traders often obtained unbleached muslin or cotton tents from the Russians. Caches on stilts were functional architectural components of all villages for storage and protection of goods. It was brought out that houses were often occupied by more than one family. For example, Trollope stayed in Wales with two brothers who occupied separate rooms, each with his two wives and two children. All men who could supported two or more wives.

By the time of Alaska's purchase, four European settlements had been built in the Bering Strait area: the Saint Michael and Unalakleet posts of the Russian-American Company in the 1830s; Libbysville at Port Clarence in 1866; and by stretching a point, the two houses built at Port Clarence by the Franklin searchers, the *Plover*'s house in 1850 and that of the *Rattlesnake* in

1853. The Eskimos continued to live in their warm, stuffy semisubterranean dwellings.

The amount of food provided by the Eskimos for the English crews at Port Clarence in the 1850s seems truly prodigious and contrasts with the telegraph people's experience of hunger a decade and a half later when they had "to live off the country." The forty persons of the telegraph expedition represented a 20 percent increase in population for the Port Clarence–Kauwerak area, which would have taxed the resources of a subsistence economy to the limit during a poor year. Their contingent was larger than an average Eskimo village. At Unalakleet, during this same period, the Russians provided food for the men.

Despite Dall's statement that the caribou had left Seward Peninsula by 1868 because of the introduction of firearms, Kauwerak continued as a living village, and in 1882 had five houses and a men's house. At Zagoskin's time, "innumerable herds of deer feed all along the shore of Norton Sound"; and even during the sixties, despite the introduction of firearms, large herds were still to be found around Unalakleet and on the coast to the south, and were caught in snares and nooses in winter in ravines and valleys. Charles W. Raymond also observed in 1869 that back of the coast between the mouth of the Yukon and Saint Michael the valleys swarmed with caribou, "herds of which are seen feeding on almost every hill."[7]

Because guns were also used in the Unalakleet and Saint Michael area during the 1850s and 1860s (Dall said that guns had supplanted native weapons for land hunting in the Saint Michael area by 1867), there may have been other reasons besides firearms for the depopulating of Seward Peninsula's caribou herds. Perhaps there was a natural shift of the herds to the south, which accords with the statement of one of my Malemiut Koyuk informants who traced her family's advent on Norton Sound from the Buckland area "to the 1870s," when her grandfather followed a huge caribou migration. The date may have been earlier—in the 1860s—however, or at the same time that Alluyianuk and others moved south from the Kobuk.

CLOTHING AND ART

In dress and personal ornamentation the Eskimos were conservative, yet, as in earlier times, they were greatly concerned about their appearance. Zagoskin was received by the Kikiktauk people in their best clothes, and twelve years later Trollope's description of a mother changing her child's clothing for their exciting entry into the metropolis of Kingigan is a classic of its kind.

Clothing styles had changed very little, although perhaps they wore more clothing, because writers no longer reported about the barefooted or half-naked Eskimo. The mottled skins of the dress-up parkas came from Siberia,

7. Dall 1870, p. 147; Jacobsen 1884, p. 275; Raymond 1870, p. 8; Zagoskin 1967, p. 99.

and the women's prize possession was a belt made of caribou teeth, which sometimes represented as many as one hundred fifty animals. Wolf and foxtails were still hung on men's belts, and the rounded style of women's parkas persisted. The Eskimos dressed warmly for out-of-doors, but in the houses they usually wore only breeches. Though it might be −20°F. outdoors and the floor was freezing, it was 80°F. at bench level from the heat of the seal-oil lamps.

A parka made of seal, walrus, or whale intestines was used all along the coast as a protector for fur garments. The Wales people may have made them to sell to other groups, as Trollope was able to buy a number of them on short notice.

"Fancy trim" on parkas and mukluks, or the numerous small geometric pieces of fur sewn together in various designs, seems not to have been the vogue until the twentieth century. Instead, plain strips of fur and dangling tails were the desired trim. These were often very narrow strips of bleached skin, however, sewed in parallel lines with extremely delicate stitches.

The Eskimos used their native clothing for the most part, which had also been adopted by many of the non-natives. Zagoskin made the point that at Saint Michael the Eskimos had retained their native garb, which the Russians also used, whereas at Fort Kolmakov on the Kuskokwim the natives wore European clothes, "even in the winter."[8] Certain articles of European clothing were available in the North, however, and by 1850 the Buckland people on northern Seward Peninsula had obtained printed cotton kerchiefs from Saint Michael, and some Wales men beseeched the telegraph men at Libbysville to sell them their soldiers' overcoats.

Men and women still wore their hair as before, the women's hair braided with pieces of skin and bone, and the men's cut short on top. The women tattooed their chins, and the men wore labrets. A feast was given in the Saint Michael area when a boy was first pierced for these ornaments.

The early explorers were eager collectors, and the Eskimos, in their hunger for European goods, would strip themselves of clothes to satisfy a trade. But nothing is said about the specific manufacture of souvenirs to sell until the Eskimos began to make miniature sleds and snowshoes and to engrave pieces of ivory with various scenes, including foreign vessels at Port Clarence, for the telegraph expedition men.

Information about sculptured and engraved art is disappointingly slight for all of this area and the time span covered so far. This gap may be partially due to the religious emphasis on ornamented and sculptured objects, which meant that the pieces were hidden or not offered for sale. (A drill bow obtained by Mr. Spark of the *Rattlesnake* in 1854, now in the British Museum, is engraved with scenes of the European men's activities, and since the other sides are unfinished, it may have been made as a souvenir.)

During this period various festivals were described for the first time, and

8. Zagoskin 1967, p. 207.

various kinds of art were then described in this context. In 1842 Zagoskin discussed two major festivals, the bladder feast and the memorial service for the dead as well as minor celebrations given by men and women. Mechanical toys were manipulated throughout the bladder feast—an owl with a human head, a seagull, and two ptarmigan. The gull appeared to be catching fish with his iron beak, and the two ptarmigan kissed each other.

An unexplained discrepancy is Zagoskin's assertion that the "coastal Eskimos," unlike the Yukon and Kuskokwim river people, did not use masks in their celebrations. This category included the Saint Michael Eskimos, who used masks extensively in the 1880s and 1890s. Yet north of Saint Michael, and possibly at Saint Michael itself, Berthold Seemann of the Franklin search party said that in 1848 the walls of the men's houses were decorated with tambourines "and sometimes with wooden masks."[9] Even farther north at Point Hope, masks apparently were in constant use during the early part of the nineteenth century. Zagoskin's statement might have been an oversight, because in another place he said that the Ingalik Indians "also do the *coastal* dances at their evening parties, *but without masks*" (my emphasis).[10]

Dall also described various festivals, and claimed that he and two Russians were the first white men to participate in native festivals on Norton Sound.[11] In the dances the men, as before, danced with great vigor and exaggerated actions. The women stood rooted to the spot, described best by Zagoskin as making "gently swimming motions with their arms, but are otherwise as motionless as dolls."[12] The stylistic differences in male and female dancing seemed to crystallize publicly and ceremonially the expected roles of men and women in everyday life, and many of the specific dances performed by the men commemorated specific events or dramatized certain activities like warfare and hunting, which required great strength and courage.

Russian music was introduced with the founding of Saint Michael, and American music, almost thirty-five years later. Zagoskin said that he often heard a young native singing correctly the popular songs of the times, and the telegraph expedition men said that the most frequently played song in 1866 all along the Eskimo coast was "Marching through Georgia," accompanied by the accordion.

HOUSEHOLD UTENSILS, WEAPONS, AND TRANSPORTATION

The sturdy and more useful European kitchen equipment had more or less supplanted traditional pottery at Saint Michael by 1842, and Eskimos were using knives, kettles, pitchers, ladles, and mugs from the local trading post.[13]

9. Seemann 1853, p. 59.
10. Zagoskin 1967, p. 244; Ray 1967a, *passim*.
11. Zagoskin 1967, pp. 119–23, 129; Dall 1870, pp. 149–57.
12. Zagoskin 1967, p. 118.
13. Dall's and Zagoskin's descriptions of Eskimo household and personal belongings are very general, combining all peoples from the Bering Strait with those of the Yukon area in many cases. This material cannot be used satisfactorily for the discussion of just one group.

Boy and girl from Port Clarence, 1899. (From the A. K. Fisher
album of the Harriman Expedition, Smithsonian Institution)

Marys Igloo, 1900. (Photograph by E. A. Hegg. Northwest Collection, University of Washington
library)

Eskimos gathering at Teller, 1900. (Photograph by Miles)

On the first visit to Wales, the people were also using R⟨ ⟩
that had been brought across the strait from Siberia. P⟨ ⟩
ently was the first craft (except possibly basketry) to s⟨ ⟩
superior metal and chinaware. Platters, bowls, and cu⟨ ⟩
preferred for eating purposes, however. The Eskimos⟨ ⟩
pean cutlery since they continued to eat with their ha⟨ ⟩
selves from the common pot, slicing off manageable p⟨...⟩
knife near the mouth before returning it to the pot.

Metal knives, which were in great abundance during the entire period, were no longer the exotic items of trade because iron was easy to get and the Eskimos had already begun their practice of altering tools to suit their own purposes and of making new implements from scraps of metal. Ulu blades at Saint Michael were made of sheet iron;[14] but despite the prevalence of metal, harpoon points were still of ivory, with only a small iron tip added. This was also characteristic of caribou arrowheads, the iron tips replacing slate. As already mentioned, guns were commonplace north of Norton Sound, and were obtained mainly through Malemiut traders from commercial ships that arrived every summer at Kotzebue Sound and Port Clarence. Dall said that the bow and arrow were hardly ever used in 1867, and made the sweeping statement that "it would be impossible at present for [the Eskimos] to obtain sufficient food without guns and ammunition";[15] but this obviously pertained only to land animals, since most aquatic game was still hunted with harpoons and lances, and even the caribou continued to be secured in all areas through the use of snares and various enclosures. Telegraph wire was found useful for a variety of purposes, even though the Eskimos blamed the building of the line for the scarcity of caribou.

Dall is the first to mention the Eskimo woman's needlecase, which at Saint Michael was usually made of the humerus of a swan and decorated with black lines. He also mentioned a notched stick and a string with knots for the keeping of accounts. Zagoskin saw a "wolf-catcher"—a piece of coiled baleen encased in fat which, having been snatched up by the unsuspecting animal, easily slides down its throat in its frozen state and, becoming warm, uncoils from the melting fat and punctures the stomach.

Flint and steel (Trollope's "strike-a-light") and drills were used almost exclusively to start a fire. Matches, which were invented in 1826, had not become trade items in western Alaska by 1867. Soap was not traded either, because it was useless for cutting grease, which of necessity had to be handled by both women and men. Urine was still the most efficient agent for both personal cleansing and the tanning of hides. All of the non-native men complained of the horrible smells in the clothing and on the Eskimo person and in and around the dwellings caused by the use of urine in its various functions, and were sometimes revolted by the accumulated debris of human and ani-

14. Dall 1870, p. 143.
15. Ibid., p. 147.

feces, decayed meat, and rotting skins that had piled up in the entry-
ways, around the dwellings, and sometimes in the houses themselves.

Zagoskin said that the tandem hitching of dogs to sleds was introduced
into Alaska by the Russians, and he was so poorly impressed by Eskimo
management of the dog teams—at least around Norton Sound—that he said,
"The art of travel with dogs is in its infancy."[16] Sled runners of whale's bone
were obtained by Saint Michael people through trade from the North. Trollope reported that the Wales men used small drawing sleds with four dogs for
seal hunting; but when they traveled from place to place, they used a different kind of sled with two or three dogs.

The umiak and the kayak both continued much in evidence, and a
double-holed kayak was observed at Grantley Harbor in 1854. Dall said that
kayaks became smaller in size going northward, and that to launch a kayak at
Sledge Island during heavy seas, two men would hurl the kayak with its
occupant into the water. Though the man might roll under the surface before
righting himself, his gutskin parka kept him dry. Umiaks at Wales were
thirty-eight to forty feet long and seven feet broad, and Zagoskin reported a
Malemiut one, based in Norton Sound, as being fifty-two feet long and
having two masts.

PATHOLOGY

Two important observations can be made during this period about the
well-being and health of the Eskimos. One was that the first-known
epidemic—smallpox—at Norton Sound was severe and apparently trimmed
the population along the eastern shore of Norton Sound by one-third or even
one-half. It did not extend north of Koyuk. The second is that the shaman
was in constant demand for curing their many illnesses. There were respiratory ailments, eye diseases, and skin disorders to rectify. Head lifting,
usually performed by a woman, was also used in the treatment of illnesses.

Very little information is actually recorded during these years about the
Eskimos' health except for the busy shaman, the smallpox epidemic, and a
few other scattered observations. Of exceptional interest, however, was the
prevalence of respiratory disorders and widespread coughing in the
Kauwerak area at the time of first European contact. Two Port Clarence
Eskimos became the first patients of a ship's infirmary (the *Plover*): a ten-
year-old girl, who died of "consumption," and a man who had rheumatism.

Zagoskin mentions a legless woman in the Saint Michael area and the fact
that "so far, venereal disease is unknown on the Yukon or Kuskokwim." If, as
discussed in Chapter 6, the people of the Stebbins area were really afflicted
with syphilis in 1822, where had it originated? Surely not from the Aleutian
Islanders, since the entire Yukon and Kuskokwim territory had been skipped,
according to Zagoskin. Had it then come from one of the expeditions that

16. Zagoskin 1967, pp. 117, 127.

had stopped briefly in places farther north—that of Cook, Billings, Kotzebue, Vasiliev, Khromchenko, or Beechey? Yet, so far in the accounts there have been no observations about suspected venereal disease in the peoples living north of Saint Michael.

The mortality ratio was apparently high. For example, several persons were reported to have died at Obell just before the English arrived in 1854. This would seem to be a large percentage of a village that had a population of only fifty, many of them children. At other places, like Wales, the number of living children per family was small—one or two to a family at most—and infanticide appears to have been one of the principal methods of reducing the population. Putting to death infants of Eskimo-white unions may have been why there were so few adults of mixed blood by the 1860s.

The Eskimo and the White Man

After the Saint Michael post was established in 1833, and the last altercation was behind them in 1836 (the "Azyagmyut"-Russian encounter), the Eskimos nowhere met the white man with lances in hand, nor did the white man post guards while camping. The strangers were no longer strange, and the white man, especially the trader, was a permanent and prominent part of Eskimo life. Though the trading posts of Saint Michael and Unalakleet were far distant from the northern villages, the native traders and families traveling back and forth provided almost constant communication.

Trade was as important as before, and the variety of goods exchanged greater than ever. The Russians introduced both liquor and tea, the latter consumed by the Eskimos in enormous quantities. The Russians were forbidden to sell liquor to Eskimos, although Seemann said around 1850 that the Eskimos had acquired a taste for it from the Russians. The Russians themselves were permitted by officials of the company only a small amount of liquor, but on 1 January 1846 hard liquor was prohibited entirely in Alaska.[17]

The American liquor trade began as soon as the first commercial whaler sailed into Bering Strait in 1848; but the liquor was sold mainly by trading vessels (not whalers), which were often based in Hong Kong or Honolulu. Eskimos consistently asked for liquor from the Franklin people, and Collinson himself said he traded a small amount of rum and brandy to Wales Eskimos in 1850 and 1854. Trollope also gave a bit of grog to his guide. Liquor was obtained by the barrel at Kotzebue Sound by 1867 and also at Saint Michael by 1868, when the Russian-American Company left and the independent American traders took over.

After the 1850s a new trade product, walrus tusks, was sought by whalers and traders. A trade in ivory tusks was not new in the North—it reached back to the mid-seventeenth century with the tusks found and disputed on

17. Ibid., p. 286.

the Anadyr; but the new trade was in ivory from recently slaughtered walrus, not tusks found lying in sand and muck deposits. More will be said about this later.

Besides the changes accruing from acquisition of numerous European objects, even to tribal redistribution, others reflected the new character of white-Eskimo relationships. By 1867 in places where Eskimos and whites were in a continual interchange, the picture had changed somewhat from an Eskimo independence to *seeming* dependence on the non-native. The Eskimos hung around the newly established "towns," entered houses uninvited, and began to beg.

The habit of begging can be traced to certain aspects of white-Eskimo relations. The initial contacts had been principally with Eskimos who had never before seen Europeans or who went out to the ships as traders and, as representatives of a special segment of society, consequently behaved with a guarded formality. Trading had been important from their first meeting with Europeans, though the explorers were not traders. Even into the 1860s the exploring and searching accounts consistently noted that the Eskimos could not understand why they were there if they were not trading. In the native trading operations, there were well-established procedures, routines, and units of exchange through trading partnerships, formalized ceremonial exchanges such as the messenger feast and feasts of the dead, and in independent exchange.[18] Apparently trading techniques and unit price exchange had been familiar for years; but when the white man came in person with unfamiliar objects as well as large quantities of familiar and much-desired items like knives and tobacco, the exchange became skewed. Goods that were to be traded for usual and accustomed objects were sometimes held for such a high price that they were not sold, but others appeared almost to have been given away from the European viewpoint, though obviously satisfying to the Eskimos.

A more important influence on the Eskimo behavior was the trading of knickknacks for foodstuffs (which among the natives was done with equal value in return), and the arbitrary gift-giving and bestowal of goods by the white man when he left the territory. The non-native generosity of giving without expected return was entirely foreign to an Eskimo whose activities were based on a complicated system of reciprocal relationships. The result in the Russian experience was that the Eskimos began to think that the Russians did not value their own trade goods, and so the price of native products rose. The promiscuous giving of gifts caught up with the Franklin party even before they left the country. Five years after the first search ship had anchored in Port Clarence, the Sinramiut Eskimos were very much annoyed that Trollope had not brought presents with him in 1854, having left them instead to be distributed by Gilpin. The telegraph men, by distributing

18. See also Burch 1970, 1972.

many gifts and leaving many unused articles all along the coast, led the Eskimos to believe that they could obtain things merely by asking. Before long, the Eskimos had made a habit of camping in the houses until the men gave them something to get rid of them. The habit of begging had also developed on board ship because the skippers gave gifts ranging from chewing tobacco to sea biscuits to all Eskimos who went out in their umiaks. Without necessity to reciprocate, the Eskimos took for granted they were entitled to receive from those who appeared to have so many material goods.

It is impossible to assess the effect of giving large gifts such as houses and boating equipment to "chiefs"; but Kamokin, who received the *Plover*'s house and other equipment at Port Clarence, later became a successful trader. His position as chief at that time, however, may have been as great a factor in his success, since it provided him with kinship support in a decidedly secure position.

During this period still another unit of exchange had developed: labor. The Russians made little use of native manpower except to buy products of it—foodstuffs and Eskimo garments—since they had a large work force from Russia. The Eskimos furthermore did not appear to want to work around the Saint Michael post until about 1844, and so native employment did not begin substantially until the time of the Franklin search. Russians often needed men as guides or for other help during the founding of Saint Michael, but no volunteers ever came forward and, according to Zagoskin, the superintendent of the fort had to ask the village council of elders to appoint a young man who dared not refuse. Only after 1844 did some of the Saint Michael young men voluntarily hire themselves out to the company.[19] The erroneous stereotype of the Eskimo as a compliant, submissive, and unindividualistic personality would never have originated had the reports of this period been read and evaluated. Throughout these accounts, it is apparent that the Eskimo worked only when he found something to his liking, and then he often quit once he had discovered the nature of labor.

The first jobs were those of interpreter and guide. Until the end of the nineteenth century, the interpreter could just as well have been employed only for local color, because invariably he was unable to understand the people he was hired to talk to. Before 1833 the interpreters were usually employed at Sitka or Unalaska, where languages unintelligible to the northern dialects were spoken. After 1833 interpreters were usually obtained at Saint Michael, where the Eskimos spoke dialects similar to those farther north. The Franklin searchers were the first non-Russians to make use of these men. In Russian-speaking territory and where English was almost unknown and interpreters were said to translate even into Spanish, real communication must have been a rarity, and one is constantly amazed at how effective nonlinguistic communication could be. At the same time it is all the

19. Zagoskin 1967, pp. 106, 124.

more reason to weigh carefully all of the written reports. Trollope in 1853 summarized the interpreters' usefulness: "I have long given up placing reliance on what is told me by people professing to speak and interpret."[20] (One notable exception was Utuktak of Kikiktauk, who had accompanied Kashevarov to the north in 1838.)

Interpreters apparently were satisfied with their jobs. They got to travel and to taste the excitement of life aboard ship. But it was a different story with other kinds of employment. Almost all of the explorers learned that the guides who were "willing" at first eventually became temperamental, uncooperative, and sometimes aggressive. A guide rarely lasted out the proposed trip and usually became rebellious just before entering another tribal territory.

The telegraph men seemed to be more successful in getting the men (mostly Malemiut) to work, perhaps because of the natives' growing familiarity with white man's ways, but also because of their more easygoing American ways and unmilitary behavior (despite their quasi-military organization). The Eskimos generally resisted authoritarian behavior. Even then, it often took a big payment in the form of a gun to induce a man to become a guide.

From the written accounts we cannot always ascertain what specific Eskimo actions resulted from an explorer's personality or attitudes, but the white men apparently tried very hard to maintain amicable relationships, because the success of the expeditions hinged on Eskimo help and cooperation. Especially in the early years, good relations with the "savages" was a basic aim of expeditions. Therefore, the total mass of writings in official reports and accounts presents a fairly consistent front of good relationships, and the authors strove mightily to play down any altercations that might have reflected on an inability to carry out the objectives and orders of the expedition. The hospitality of the Eskimos was always given great prominence in the writings, and indeed the cases of kindnesses in Eskimo dwellings were repeated over and over along the coast. Yet, in cases of trading in or traveling across Eskimo territory, we find many examples of the extremely delicate situations in which the white men found themselves. Besides the almost universal vexatious behavior of the guides, there were many attempts to steal from the white men and to cheat them in trading. As in the experiences of all expeditions before them, the men of the Russian-American Company and of the Franklin search parties found that those most guilty of such conduct were the Inupiak-speakers—the northern Eskimo and the Malemiut. Zagoskin said that although the Eskimos were honest in their dealings with other Eskimos, they sometimes stole from the Russians to be thought a daredevil.[21]

What memories have continued of these days of expeditions and Russian occupation of the territory around the Bering Strait? Scarcely any. Only one

20. Trollope, in Great Britain Sessional Papers 1854–55, p. 876.
21. Zagoskin 1967, p. 107.

Russian surname existed at Unalakleet, and none at Saint Michael, as re-corded in a detailed census of 1967. Little information has been handed down about the white men themselves, and few folk tales contain non-native themes. This is in striking contrast to the repetition of tales concerning Siberian-Alaskan and Indian-Eskimo conflicts, which had taken place long before the white men had arrived. Few Eskimo stories attempt to describe the first white man or the first ship despite an abundance of origin tales in Eskimo mythology: the origin of light, of the world, and of unusual natural features. For example, King Island is explained as a big fish that was caught in the Kuzitrin River and towed out to sea. The few stories of the first foreign man or ship that I know of are told as history and, with one exception, all date from a more recent time than the "first" actually occurred. For example, "the first white man on the Kuzitrin was Davidson" refers to J. M. Davidson (at Davidsons Landing), who mined in the Kougarok area north of Marys Igloo after 1900. Another story of the "first white man" in this area was also about a man of later times, who named the town of Marys Igloo—in 1899.

Only one tale appears to go back to what might be the first man on the Kuzitrin River, for it contains elements that suggest an encounter earlier than the others. A man born in 1896 heard the story from his grandfather, who had met the foreigner when he was a young man. He was tending his ptarmigan snares in the snow when he saw strange footprints on the ground and, looking up, saw a "different-looking man" whom he and his wife named "Kuchsinuek" ("different blue eyes") because his eyes were the color of blueberries when they are not quite ripe. The two approached each other, the Eskimo circling the white man, who extended his hands, palms up. "That white man was thinking how to be friendly." He gave a knife to the Eskimo and needles to his wife and showed her how to thread them. He shot a gun for their benefit.

The man was headed up the Kuzitrin, but they told him to go up the Kougarok River instead in order to avoid the lava beds where he would fall into "bubble holes and never come back." His grandfather's cousin took him up the Kougarok, and the man then went toward the Goodhope River and to Deering.

If this referred to Hobson's trip of 1854, it did not mention his two companions, his sleds, or the guide, Tudlig, who was hired at the mouth of the Tuksuk Channel long before they would have had to decide whether to go up the Kougarok or the Kuzitrin. Moreover, men of the *Plover* had gone to the village of Kauwerak (but no farther) as early as 1850—four years before Hobson's trip—so when Hobson did go to the Goodhope, Eskimos knew about the English ships. The story may be a combination of all of the jaunts that the English sailors took between 1849 and 1854.

The "first ship" stories also appear to be based on much more recent ships than the first. Eskimos smelled the "first ship" before it arrived at Golovnin Bay (possibly whalers trying out whale fat?) and the "first ship" at Sledge

Island had Negro sailors and traded hardtack, flour in cloth sacks, and "Navy plug tobacco," all items sold during the last half of the nineteenth century.

Other information about foreign contacts in Eskimo tradition is scarce. One folk tale has a theme of travel to San Francisco, obviously based on an Eskimo's sojourn on a ship. A Shishmaref shaman had the gift of being able to observe distant events through the broken bottom of a bucket. Once at Kektoashliuk in the Kauwerak area this medicine man "broke another kettle" (i.e., went into a trance) and took his awe-struck audience on a trip as far south as California. He permitted them to peek through the bucket where they could see the snows of winter in the North as they traveled south past open water and a green land to a big bay where many ships were anchored. They returned by the same route to their bleak winter.

Though little remains in Eskimo lore about the white men of this period, the Eskimos at that time were constantly preoccupied with the relationships. Their subconscious thoughts fulfilled their most pessimistic fears and aggressive desires. Zagoskin said that the Indians of Nokkhakat on the Koyukuk River, fearing contamination again by smallpox or some other disease, "purified" his party by setting a fire.[22] This may have been why the Eskimos on the Goodhope River would not permit Hobson to pass until a small fire had burned in their path (see Chap. 11, "Kauwerak and the Trail to Kotzebue Sound").

Rumors were constantly flying concerning the actions of the white men as well as about the Indians, spread especially by Malemiut traders as late as 1867. But the general population, too, seemed to let their imaginations run away, especially when they had been drinking, which was already a common practice in the 1860s. *The Esquimaux* reported that several Eskimos were drunk on King Island when they attacked Libby's boat, and that a Wales Eskimo who had been drinking burst into the room saying that the Americans were no good.

It was a sober Utamanna, however, who told one of the telegraph men at Cape Douglas in March 1867 that he had heard from "some source, that the Americans were going to shoot all the Esquimaux, when the ships arrived next summer"; and later in the year the Eskimos near Shaktoolik told the men that they heard that Russia and the United States were at war. Eskimo rumor was already at work on the affairs of two great countries that had come into their lives, and the west coast of Alaska had become an open window to the world not only during the sailing season of summer but in the winter, when the Russians sent out mail to Nushagak and thence to Sitka in December by dog teams. In the year of Alaska's purchase by the United States there was no turning back to an isolation from the white world and the old Eskimo ways.

22. Ibid., p. 150.

CHAPTER 14

American Jurisdiction
and the Bering Strait Eskimos

Russian America had been divided into five districts: Atka, Unalaska, Kodiak, Sitka, and Northern. The last included the Yukon and Norton Sound areas, but land to the north was almost terra incognita, which the Russians considered to be outside of direct administrative control even in 1867. By that date, Sitka was the most important settlement, with a population of 1,500, including 500 Russians. Kodiak Island was second in importance, with a total of 1,800 persons, including 100 Russians. Unalaska, 1,300 miles from Sitka, with a population of 500, including Russians and creoles, was third in importance. Nulato, 500 miles from the mouth of the Yukon, was the easternmost Russian settlement, and Unalakleet, the farthest north. In 1869 H. H. McIntyre reported that the total white population of the entire territory was not over 300.[1] There was a handful of whites at Saint Michael, but none north of Unalakleet.

Under Russian law, the native peoples who were settled and had adopted the Christian religion were recognized as Russian citizens (mainly southeast Alaskan Indians and Aleuts).[2] Other tribes, which were pagans, were "uncivilized native tribes," without citizenship. The Russians gave no recognition to tribes as domestic nations.

The treaty of cession, therefore, differentiated inhabitants not on the basis of race but on the privileges of Russian citizenship. Under the treaty, those persons who returned to Russia within three years were still Russian citizens; those citizens who remained in Alaska would be permitted to become American citizens; but the "uncivilized tribes will be subject to such laws and

1. Banks 1868, pp. 12–15.
2. Background material for the status of natives is from Cohen 1966, pp. 927–38, and U.S. Court of Claims 1959, pp. 69–99.

regulations as the United States may, from time to time, adopt in regard to aboriginal tribes of that country."[3]

The status of the Bering Strait Eskimos as individuals was clearly "uncivilized," but their status as tribes or sovereign entities was rarely given a thought in the years to come. The whole of Alaska for many years after the purchase was considered no more than a geographical adjunct to the United States. What laws and regulations were adopted were for the benefit of the few white persons south of Saint Michael, or merely for the control of selling liquor and firearms to natives in the vast north.

The administration of Alaska was under the War Department as a military district from 1867 to 1877 and under the Navy from 1879 to 1884, when a civil government was established. The military administration supposedly encompassed the whole of the territory ceded by Russia, but troops were garrisoned only at Sitka, Tongass, and Wrangell. The latter two were abandoned in 1870, Wrangell was reactivated in 1874, but all posts were abolished in 1877.

The Act of July 27, 1868 (15 Stat. 240), extended United States laws regarding navigation and commerce to Alaska and created a customs district. Between 1877 and 1879, when the military troops were taken to Idaho to help quell an Indian uprising, there was no governing authority. The collector of customs was the only man with any legal powers, and he begged that protection against the Indians be sent to Sitka. The British on Vancouver Island were the first to come to the aid of Sitka, sending H.M.S. *Osprey* on 1 March 1879. The revenue steamer *Oliver Wolcott* arrived on 22 March, and the U.S.S. *Alaska* on 3 April. The U.S.S. *Jamestown* took over on 14 June.

After the first rush for gold in the Juneau area in the latter 1870s pointed up the necessity for recording mining claims and providing order for hundreds of miners, Alaska's first nonpartisan convention was held in Harrisburg (now Juneau) in August 1881 with fifteen delegates. The meeting culminated in the drafting of a memorial to the Congress to heed their pleas for laws, and in the election of Mottrom D. Ball as a delegate to Washington to present the memorial. He accomplished little on this, his second, visit to Washington, and Alaska continued under the watchful eye of a ship.

Finally, in 1884, the Organic Act was passed, which provided for civil government in a district designated as a civil, judicial, and land district. Section 8 made Alaska a land district and recognized the mining laws of the United States and title to mining claims, but dashed all hope of legal ownership and title to any lands by the inhabitants. Existing missionary stations among Indian tribes could claim up to 640 acres for their use, and mining laws were "in full force and effect" in the district . . . *"Provided*, That the Indians or other persons in said district shall not be disturbed in the possession of any lands actually in their use or occupation or now claimed by them

3. 40 Congress: 1 session, Sen. Ex. Doc. 17 (serial 1308, p. 3) and 40C: 2s, H.R. Ex. Doc. 177 (serial 1339).

but the terms under which persons may acquire title to such lands is reserved for future legislation by Congress." Twenty-five thousand dollars were set aside for the secretary of the interior to use for the education of children without reference to race, and section 14 brought the act to a close with the prohibition of liquors "except for medicinal, mechanical, and scientific purposes."[4]

In southern Alaska, where almost all of the white population lived (in 1880 there were only seven white persons living at Saint Michael and northward),[5] there was great disappointment because the act provided neither a delegate to the Congress nor a home legislature, and, as one of the United States senators said, it was "a mere shift; it is a mere expedient, it is a mere beginning in what we believe to be the right direction toward giving a civil government and education to Alaska."[6]

The Eskimos north of Saint Michael were noticed in an official sense only in the carrying out of the provisions of the customs act to prohibit the sale of liquor and firearms, and then—with the exception of an abortive attempt to create an Indian agency at Saint Michael in 1873—only after the inauguration of revenue marine patrols in 1880.

The Tlingit and Haida Indians of southeastern Alaska, who had had a long contact with the Russians and various foreign traders, reportedly had objected to the sale of Russian America to the United States on the basis that their fathers had owned all of the land, had allowed the Russians to occupy it for their mutual benefit in trade, and that it was sold without their consent.[7] This awareness of tribal lands being occupied and sold by a foreign power was never voiced by the people of the Bering Strait. With the exception of Saint Michael, no town in the North was a "white town; and when the first teachers and missionaries came to Unalakleet, Golovin, and Wales, they came as individuals taking up residence in an Eskimo town.

The United States government did not make any treaties with the Eskimo or Indian tribes of Alaska, although treaty-making power was vested in the federal government until 3 March 1871. The scattered tribes in the vast land of Alaska did not present a threat needing protection by treaty. Thus, almost from the start of their life under American government, native groups of Alaska were considered to be subjects of the United States without individual tribal autonomy; but the absence of treaties has been misunderstood and sometimes willfully misinterpreted over the years by persons who have claimed that Alaskan natives had no aboriginal title to land because they did not sign treaties with the United States.

4. One of the most tireless workers toward bringing Alaska to the consciousness of people in the United States was the missionary Sheldon Jackson, who was committed to the idea that the native Alaskans were to be civilized by the churches, especially the Presbyterian. Accordingly, he gave 900 talks on Alaska and appeared before committees of the 46th, the 47th, and the 48th Congresses between 1878 and 1884 (Jackson 1886, p. 38).

5. Petroff 1884, p. 11.

6. Quoted in Nichols 1924, p. 76.

7. U.S. Court of Claims 1959, p. 80.

The native as an individual subject, and not as a tribe or domestic nation, was reinforced when sections 20 and 21 of the Trade and Intercourse Act were extended to Alaska. The provisions of the Act of June 30, 1843, "to regulate trade and intercourse with Indian tribes" went into effect on 3 March 1873 to prohibit "the manufacture, introduction, or trading of spiritous liquors in Alaska," and resulted in the only attempt to establish an Indian Agency in Alaska.[8]

Despite the lack of recognition of Bering Strait tribes as sovereign nations, the government of the United States had been slowly developing a concept of Indian sovereignty as domestic nations. This concept, a "legal fiction,"[9] was unique among the powerful nations that had subjugated weaker tribes in their territories, but was of little importance to the Bering Strait tribes until the federal legislation of 1971—far in the future—that settled the aboriginal title to native lands in the whole of Alaska.[10]

Indian title to land and the desire of white settlers to push west and take over Indian lands had been grave issues for many years after the founding of the republic of the United States. One of the architects of the concept of Indian sovereignty was Supreme Court Justice John Marshall, whose opinions in the 1830s formed the basis for the major point of view today by bringing into focus the rights of Indians as nations and land-holding entities. His first opinion concerning this, in 1823, recognized Indian tribes' possessory right in their land, but the ultimate title was in the United States. His second, in 1831, acknowledged the Indian tribes to be "domestic dependent nations," and not "foreign nations," having nevertheless "an unquestionable, and heretofore unquestioned, right to the lands they occupy, until that right shall be extinguished by a voluntary cession to the government."

A third opinion, in 1832, stated the sovereignty of Indian tribes as follows:

> The Indian nations had always been considered as distinct, independent political communities, retaining their original natural rights. . . . The settled doctrine of the law of nations is, that a weaker power does not surrender its independence—its right to self-government—by associating with a stronger, and taking its protection. A weak state, in order to provide for its safety, may place itself under the protection of one more powerful, without stripping itself of its right of government, and ceasing to be a state.[11]

THE LIQUOR TRADE AND FIREARMS AT BERING STRAIT

The first recognition of any governmental responsibility toward Bering Strait tribes occurred only when the Act of March 3, 1873, for the prohibition of liquor, went into effect. The reported excessive use of liquor by

8. Cohen 1966, p. 937; McCoy 1956, p. 350.

9. Cyrus Thomas in Hodge, ed. 1912, p. 803.

10. In December 1971 the Congress of the United States passed legislation that gave all of the native peoples of Alaska a settlement of a billion dollars and title to 40,000,000 acres of land.

11. Marshall's decisions: Johnson and Graham's *Lessee* v. *William M'Intosh* (21 US 543) 1823; *The Cherokee Nation* v. *The State of Georgia* (30 US 1, 5 Pet 1) 1831; *Worcester* v. *The State of Georgia* (6 Peters 515) 1832.

southern Alaskan Indians was the subject of many pleas to obtain legislation for their care, but Secretary of the Interior Columbus Delano said that his department probably could not deal with the natives "prior to some positive legislation bringing them within the recognized jurisdiction of the Office of Indian Affairs."[12] As yet there was no territorial government, and Delano doubted that the Alaskans could be considered Indians since the commissioner of Indian affairs, Francis A. Walker, had said that they were not Indians "in a constitutional sense." Although he agreed that the Alaskan natives deserved attention, he did not want to use existing Indian funds, so he suggested special legislation.[13] No action was taken.

Finally, with the extension of the prohibition of liquor to Alaska, it was hoped that an Indian agent would be named to enforce the legislation; but none was appointed. The secretary did, however, appoint Frederick S. Hall as special Indian agent in April 1873. Hall was permitted to establish his headquarters in Alaska wherever he wished. Choosing Saint Michael, he arrived in June 1873 and remained until the end of summer in 1874, when his agency was abolished.[14]

Hall's sole duty was to ferret out liquor and to apprehend the culprits who sold it to the natives. In Saint Michael he heard that two white men, J. W. Bean and Ivan Kashevnikoff, were manufacturing and selling liquor at Saint Michael and Andreafsky on the Yukon River, respectively. He exonerated Kashevnikoff; and though he could find no evidence against Bean at the time, he eventually learned that he had indeed sold large quantities of liquor to the natives.[15]

Hall found out that the most serious infractions of the law were perpetrated by whalers and Siberian natives who sold liquor to Eskimos north of Unalakleet. He recommended that either a revenue marine patrol be established or that a military post of ten to fifteen men be set up at Saint Michael or Unalakleet. He warned that agents traveling alone—as Americans were wont to do in Alaska—might sustain retribution after confiscating liquor from Eskimos who thought the American government had exhibited no strength, being without warships or large numbers of people. He reported that the Unalit between Pastolik and Shaktoolik had many muskets, repeating rifles, revolvers, and ammunition, and that he was unable to seize liquor from Eskimos at Unalakleet because of their defiance.[16]

During the winter of 1873–74, he heard of liquor along the coast only at

12. Quoted in McCoy 1956, p. 358.
13. Ibid., p. 359.
14. Ibid., pp. 361, 362, 365, 366. Donald R. McCoy has summarized the history of this agency almost entirely from archival and documentary sources.
15. Ibid., p. 362. During the 1879 cruise of the *Rush*, George Bailey heard that Bean had taken a still to Unalakleet, but it was not in operation because the Eskimos, not having the required ingredients for making home-brew, were buying liquor from the traders (Bailey 1880, pp. 16–17).
16. McCoy 1956, p. 363.

Cape Prince of Wales, where the Eskimos bought it from ships. He concluded that there would be little trouble between whites and natives as a result of the natives becoming drunk, but said that if trouble did break out, the liquor traffic at Cape Prince of Wales would be the cause of it.[17]

In 1870 the *Reliance*, under command of Captain James M. Selden, was the first revenue steamer to sail north of the strait; but apparently there was a lapse of nine years before the next cruiser, the *Richard A. Rush*, sailed to the strait. The *Thomas A. Corwin* cruised north of the strait the following year, 1880, and Captain C. L. Hooper recommended that a vessel be sent annually until the trade in contraband goods was halted. The annual cruises were begun the next year, and a large part of our information about northern Alaska during the 1880s and 1890s comes from the revenue steamer reports—printed for the cruises of 1880, 1881, 1884, 1885, and 1889—and from Sheldon Jackson's detailed itineraries of his trips on the *Bear* during the 1890s.[18]

The annual cruise of a revenue steamer was the only visible sign of law and power of the United States government north of the Pribilof Islands until 1897, when the Saint Michael area was declared a military district. One of the principal duties of a revenue cutter was to enforce the ban on selling liquor and breech-loading rifles to natives, but it performed other valuable functions as time went on. It helped out ships in distress and searched for missing vessels; gave passage home to shipwrecked men or impecunious miners; transported teachers and Eskimos to various places; took men of science to the North; performed a large part of the census-taking in 1880 and 1890; and, in the nineties, brought from Siberia most of the tame reindeer for the benefit of the Eskimos.

The cruises of the revenue cutters operated clearly for the benefit of the white man, and during this time the laws of the tribe—not of the United States government—operated for intratribal cases of what would have been breaches of the law in the United States, such as theft or murder. In cases of murder between the two races, as we will see later on, there was little the captain of the cutter could legally do. He could not act as judge, and the judicial aspects of any case had to be disposed of in Unalaska or Sitka, many hundreds of miles away from the Bering Strait.

The first report of a revenue steamer, the *Rush*, north of the Bering Strait

17. Ibid., p. 366.
18. The Logbook of the *Reliance*, U.S. National Archives, RG 26. For the printed reports see G. W. Bailey 1880; Healy 1887, 1889; C. L. Hooper 1881, 1884; and Stockton 1890. The report of the *Corwin* for the year 1883 is deposited in the National Archives, Record Group 26, as a letter, M. A. Healy to the Secretary of the Treasury, dated Saint Michael, 9 August 1883. The report of the *Bear* for 1888 is in a letter, Healy to the Secretary of the Treasury, dated San Francisco, 6 September 1888, Record Group 26. The report of the *Bear* for 1896 is dated Unalaska, 20 September 1896, F. Tuttle to the Secretary of the Treasury, Record Group 26. A handwritten report of the *Bear* for 1887 in the form of a letter is in the Sheldon Jackson Museum: Healy to Secretary of the Treasury, San Francisco, 26 November 1887. The naturalist John Muir also wrote about the 1881 cruise of the *Corwin* (Muir 1917).

revealed that the liquor trade was in full swing. George W. Bailey, skipper of the *Rush*, sailed to Kotzebue Sound in 1879, but turned south when he could find no vessels to search. He reported that the Eskimos had obtained liquor, however, from a number of "whalers" who had left San Francisco "purporting to be engaged in whaling, fishing, and trading," some being simply traders and carrying no whaling or fishing gear at all.[19] Furthermore, three schooners—*General Harney*, *C. M. Ward*, and *Giovani Apiani*—had sailed directly to the Arctic under the Hawaiian flag. "Reliable" natives told Bailey that eleven vessels had sold liquor in the north during 1878, and that thirty barrels had been landed at Cape Rodney. He learned that the schooner *Lolita* had bought 1,600 gallons of rum at the Hawaiian Islands, which were later confiscated at the Pribilofs by the special treasury agent, and that the *Leo*, an American schooner, had taken on 1,247 gallons.[20]

Bailey was the first to report in print the famous "Gilley affair" of 1877 in which a number of Wales Eskimos were said to have tried to seize George Gilley's vessel and in so doing were clubbed and shot to death by the crew. Eskimos in the 1960s had their own versions of what had happened almost a century before, but none coincides with an account told by Gilley himself to Herbert L. Aldrich, a journalist who cruised the Arctic with various whaling ships in 1887. Gilley's own account also differs from Bailey's and C. L. Hooper's, despite their writing only two or three years after the event.

Bailey said that fourteen men and a woman were shot and killed by Gilley's crew; but Hooper said that more than thirty had died, and probably "many more were drowned by jumping overboard." Gilley himself reported that twenty men, including a chief and a subordinate chief, who "had looted Captain Jacobsen's schooner a week before, and tried to take Captain Raven's brig," were killed. All accounts said that the Eskimos were intoxicated.[21] This altercation took place on a vessel which the Eskimos had voluntarily gone to meet several miles out to sea, not on land or near their homes.

Subsequent revenue service cruises reported on the growing liquor trade at Bering Strait. In 1880 Hooper seized from the *Leo* fifty gallons of alcohol sold as "Bay-rum," "Jamaica ginger," "Pain-killer," and "Florida water."

19. Bailey 1880, p. 19.
20. Ibid., pp. 17, 19, 20. Bailey spells the name of this vessel *Loleta*, but other publications use the more common spelling, *Lolita*.
There were only three ways in which the ban on liquor and firearms could be enforced: to bond goods that were to be sold in a foreign country; to prohibit vessels from carrying them from American customs ports; or to confiscate the goods when found in the Arctic. Many ships avoided the customs regulations by loading contraband goods in the Hawaiian Islands, and then would either sell them directly to the Eskimos on the Alaskan coast or to Siberian natives who traded them across the strait to the Alaskans.
21. Gilley's own account is in Aldrich 1889, pp. 143–46. Other accounts are in Bailey 1880, p. 20; C. L. Hooper 1881, p. 20; Jenness 1957, pp. 158–59; and in the Charles Brower manuscript autobiography, pp. 225–26, Stefansson Collection at Dartmouth College.
Gilley, a half-blood Hawaiian, drowned near Sledge Island in August 1900. He was on the *Edith*, which was going to Siberia for trading and prospecting, and was knocked overboard by the boom (*Nome Daily News*, 20 August 1900).

Hooper's interpreter told the Eskimos at Cape Blossom in Kotzebue Sound about this episode, and by the time the *Corwin* had returned to Saint Michael in September the story had preceded them but had become "so exaggerated and overdrawn as to be quite unrecognizable, as it accused us of sinking vessels and shooting down their crews as they attempted to escape over the ice."[22]

Despite Bailey's prediction that the Eskimos wanted the liquor traffic curtailed, Hooper found that the Eskimos were much annoyed at the revenue service's interference during the second cruise of the *Corwin*:

In the vicinity of Kotzebue Sound they were very bitter against us, and, I am informed, openly boasted in their kazhimes that they would capture the vessel and kill all hands if she came again to prevent their getting whisky. On account of these threats, I had some difficulty in obtaining the services of an interpreter at Saint Michael's, the shaman predicting that the Mahlemuts (Kotzebue Sound natives) would not allow the vessel to return if she went among them. They did not, however, attempt to carry their dire threats into execution. On the contrary they *appeared* quite friendly.

Hooper had examined the schooner *Flying Mist* at Saint Michael and passed its cargo of twenty-five gallons of whiskey because it had been given a permit for foreign trade at San Francisco. When he got to Kotzebue Sound, however, he learned that Walker, the skipper, had been selling liquor by the drink—one drink for a fox skin—through which means he later boasted he had "beaten the Government."[23]

During the cruise of the *Corwin* in 1884, Captain Michael Healy said that "the whisky traffic in northern Alaska has almost entirely ceased," but that enforcement could not relax because "some of the masters of the vessels boarded made no secret of having brought large quantities of liquor into the Arctic for trading purposes, but had thrown it overboard before reaching the United States boundary line on learning that a revenue-cutter was in these waters."[24] The biggest problem of enforcement was that the cutter did not arrive until after 1 July, by which time the whalers had already sold liquor to the Eskimos, who then waited until after the revenue steamer had left to trade it among themselves.

Healy relentlessly pursued the culprits and was always concerned about the welfare of the Eskimos who bought the liquor because the usually peaceful, kindly, hospitable persons became "demoniac" from only a small quantity. The young chief of the "Diomedes" had killed two Eskimo men while drunk, and Healy was convinced that "the only trouble that has ever occurred between the whites and natives has been when the latter were under the influence of liquor." Healy said that the Eskimos understood that the cutter had come to suppress the trade and "that no liquor can be got on board

22. C. L. Hooper 1881, pp. 21, 61.
23. Hooper 1884, p. 38.
24. Healy 1889, p. 11.

the *Corwin*, even if they beg for it on their knees, as they have frequently done. When they see our flag they point to it and say, 'Oo-mi-ak'-puck pe'-chuck ton'-i-ka' (no whisky ship). . . ."[25]

Sheldon Jackson, on his first trip to the Bering Strait in the summer of 1890, said that "during the past ten years hundreds of barrels of vile liquors have been emptied into the sea as the result of the vigilance of Capt. Healy . . . who has practically broken up the traffic on this northwest coast." Yet, that very year, he also said that "11 barrels of alcohol and 6 cases of gin were seized upon one schooner and emptied into the ocean," and other ships were seen dumping liquor over the side. Jackson said that the majority of whaling skippers were opposed to trading liquor, "but there are some who believe in it, and boldly say that if the cutter did not come and search them they would engage in it, and that they do engage in it on the Siberian coast, where the cutter has no jurisdiction."[26]

Several Chukchi men were successful liquor traders on the Siberian side. In 1893 one was rumored to have at least 1,000 barrels on hand, another, 60, and a third, 40; and they had "little or no difficulty in shipping it across the Straits [*sic*] and selling it to the natives of Alaska."[27] Some Alaskan Eskimos became active traders, in fixed abodes. Tanena, one of the chiefs at Wales and proprietor of the only saloon in town during the 1890s, was highly successful because of his ability to sell large amounts of liquor without getting drunk himself.

The operation of stills made little headway at Bering Strait after the first attempts at Unalakleet, since liquor could be purchased so easily from ships. Stills were again introduced after silver mining had begun near Golovin and shore whaling stations had been established north of Bering Strait in the 1880s. Except at Wales, their operation was generally not successful. The men of the Omilak mine brought a still for Eskimo use in 1883,[28] but by 1893 Miner Bruce, superintendent of the Teller Reindeer Station, said that he had heard of only a few poorly made stills that concocted a villainous drink from molasses and flour called "tarny uk."[29]

At Wales, however, according to the *Eskimo Bulletin* of 1897, the oldest inhabitants said that never before in their history had a winter "been paralleled for drunkenness, disorder, and bloodshed. Liquor has been distilled in almost every house. . . . Those who had no outfits, borrowed their neighbors'," and others bought a bottle of the rum for a red fox skin.

25. Ibid., pp. 17, 18.
26. Education Report 1893, p. 1274.
27. Letter, J. K. Luttrell to John G. Carlisle, Secretary of the Treasury, dated Unalaska, 29 July 1893, RG 26, Alaska File.
28. Letter, Healy to the Secretary of the Treasury, dated Sausalito, 21 January 1892 (RG 26); Letter, Henry Koenig to Governor Swineford, Rockland, California, 4 December 1888, with comments by Captain Healy.
29. Bruce, in the Third Reindeer Report 1894 (serial 3160), p. 113. Bruce also said that the Eskimos of Port Clarence did not get much liquor from whaling vessels.

Another duty of the revenue cutter was to prohibit the sale or purchase of breech-loading rifles. Guns had been banned by the Russians and early Americans, fearing uprisings among the native peoples; but by the 1880s it was apparent that there was no reason for continuing the ban on the breech-loading rifle. No one who knew at first hand the conditions under which the Eskimos lived looked favorably on the ban. The Eskimos no longer used their native weapons. Muzzle-loading guns, with a charge stuffed down the barrel, were not outlawed, but they had never been efficient, especially in cold weather, and powder was rarely a trade item. Most of the Eskimos had obtained up-to-date guns from whalers, traders, or native Siberians beginning in the middle of the nineteenth century, paying exorbitant prices for both rifles and ammunition. They often paid as much for a small amount of ammunition as they did for a gun.[30]

To both Healy and Hooper, the prohibition of firearms was "a source of great hardship to the natives of Arctic-Alaska. Many had purchased their arms prior to the enactment of the law, and still have them, but can procure no ammunition."[31] During the cruise of the *Corwin* in 1884, Healy said that the latest models of breech-loading rifles were found in Eskimo boats and that white men had no objections to their having them. He recommended the sale of a limited number of rifles for walrus hunting until their sale was unrestricted.[32]

In 1895 William A. Kjellmann, superintendent of the Teller Reindeer Station, said that "the law against the importation of rifles and fixed ammunition does not seem to be of much use in this part of Alaska,'as it is only a dead letter." Indeed, in 1890 at Wales, Thornton had found 67 breech-loading rifles, 46 muzzle-loading rifles, 5 breech-loading shotguns (3 of them double-barreled), 34 muzzle-loading shotguns, and 27 revolvers.[33]

The law of the revenue cutter was on safe ground in matters of liquor and firearms. In others, there was no clear definition of what constituted punishment, or what mechanisms there were for carrying it out. In crimes where only Eskimos were involved, or when Eskimos were killed by white men, American law did not apply (at least not under Captain Healy's jurisdiction, as we shall see in a discussion of law enforcement during the 1890s in the last chapter); but perhaps the circumstances of isolation and patrolling an immeasurable ocean and coastline were justification enough for an arbitrary set of rules and a need to enforce laws of one's own making.

30. Healy 1889, p. 17.
31. C. L. Hooper 1881, pp. 44–45.
32. Healy 1889, p. 17.
33. Report by Kjellmann, "Annual Report Teller Reindeer Station," p. 89 of the Fifth Reindeer Report 1896. His report was written in Norwegian and translated by Rasmus B. Anderson; Thornton 1931, p. 139.

CHAPTER 15

Artifacts, Whaling, and Mining

DURING the 1870s and especially the 1880s, an abundance of reports and travel accounts provided information about Saint Michael and the northward frontier as a prelude to permanent settlement by teachers, missionaries, and miners. From its beginning Saint Michael served as a wilderness center for expeditions as well as a trading post. The Russian-American Company had cooperated with the English and Americans by providing native interpreters and often food and shelter.

After 1870 the Alaska Commercial Company continued the tradition, and Saint Michael was literally the jumping-off-place for expeditions and collecting journeys from the 1870s until the gold rush at Nome. No expedition to the Yukon or to points north failed to stop at Saint Michael.

The Alaska Commercial Company had its beginnings in the Russian-American Company, whose assets had been purchased in 1868 by Hutchinson, Kohl and Company. George R. Adams, formerly of the telegraph expedition, took charge at Saint Michael, where he hired a number of half-blood Eskimos and twenty-one Russians for fur hunting on a year's contract.[1] The next year a fifty-foot stern wheeler, the *Yukon*, was taken to Saint Michael by the company for transportation on the Yukon River. Several Alaska Commercial Company fur traders, formerly of the telegraph contingents, and Charles W. Raymond, U.S. Corps of Engineers, were aboard on its maiden voyage. Raymond reported that a number of small trading vessels had come to Saint Michael since the purchase of Alaska, but all had left, discouraged by the competition of two trading companies, one of which had sold out to the other before the summer of 1869 had ended. A large, well-stocked trading schooner that came in 1869 sold all of its goods to the Alaska Commercial Company.[2]

In 1870 trade goods worth $16,050 were sent to the Alaska Commercial

1. Kitchener 1954, p. 85.
2. Raymond 1870, p. 38.

Company post at Saint Michael, and the Eskimos had one of the largest choices of goods so far: petticoats, hoop skirts, cloth, buttons, beads, American leaf tobacco, flour, seeds, harmonicas, and hardware. That year the company bought out its only rival, Taylor and Bendel, and a former Hudson's Bay Company employee, Louis Le Moult, became the storekeeper.[3] From then until 1892, when a new company, the North American Transportation and Trading Company, was organized, Saint Michael and the Alaska Commercial Company were almost synonymous.[4]

In 1872 François Mercier was chief trader for the company at Saint Michael, and his brother, Moses, was at Fort Yukon. Moses persuaded five men to hire out as company traders on the Yukon, with freedom to prospect. Among them were Arthur Harper, Al Mayo, and Leroy N. McQuesten, who later became famous in the Klondike rush and settlement of interior Canada and Alaska. By 1882 these traders were buying company goods for a special price as independent traders,[5] and several Eskimo men, including Isaac Koliak, were also trading for the company.

A number of expeditions made use of the company's hospitality, among them that of Lieutenant Henry T. Allen. After his remarkable explorations of the Koyukuk, Tanana, and Copper river valleys in 1885, Allen had arrived in Unalakleet via the summer portage from the Yukon. He sent word of his arrival to chief trader Lorenz, who dispatched an umiak "rigged with a single square sail, *a la Mahlemute*" for Allen's transportation to Saint Michael.[6] There the trader made the party comfortable, even letting them use his photographic equipment while awaiting the *Corwin* for the trip home.

Despite the helpfulness of both the Alaska Commercial Company and the Revenue Marine Service in providing transportation to isolated settlements, not all travelers were interested in the Eskimo way of life, and the material culture of the Eskimos between 1875 and 1898 would have been lost to us had it not been for an interest in collecting by a handful of men, among them Miner Bruce, H. M. W. Edmonds, Sheldon Jackson, Johan Adrian Jacobsen, Edward William Nelson, and Lucien McShan Turner.

Saint Michael became the site of a U.S. Signal Service station in 1874, and both Turner, the first signal service officer, and Nelson, who replaced him in 1877, made large ethnological collections for the Smithsonian Institution. By the time Nelson had left Saint Michael in 1881, he had also collected two thousand bird skins and fifteen hundred egg specimens;[7] but it is mainly for his art and artifact collections that he will be remembered. He made trips to

3. Kitchener 1954, p. 87; Raymond 1870, p. 38.
4. Sherwood 1965, p. 147. The Alaska Commercial Co. had the competition of the Western Fur and Trading Co. on the Yukon and Kuskokwim rivers until the AC Co. took over their assets in 1882 (Hooper 1884, pp. 34, 36; Sherwood 1965, p. 45).
5. Kitchener 1954, pp. 148, 150–51.
6. Allen 1887, pp. 112, 113. Sherwood has summarized and discussed the significance of Allen's expedition in *Exploration of Alaska, 1865–1900*, pp. 106–18.
7. Sherwood 1965, p. 94.

the Yukon and to the Kuskokwim in 1878–79. In 1880 he made winter trips to Golovnin Bay and the Yukon, and in 1881, with John Muir, the naturalist, was a passenger on the *Corwin* during its second cruise. Nelson's valuable collections were made even more so by the publication of photographs with careful documentation of many of the artifacts, ceremonial masks, and engraved and sculptured ivory in his *Eskimo about Bering Strait*, and in *The Graphic Art of the Eskimos* by Walter J. Hoffman.

From 1881 to 1883 Johan Jacobsen, collector for the Royal Museum of Berlin, visited the Tlingit Indians and the Eskimos of the Bering Strait area. He had the misfortune to arrive in the Bering Strait area (on 25 July 1882) shortly after the departure of Nelson, who had temporarily cleaned the country of artifacts. Jacobsen's journal, which has never been translated from the German, contains a number of interesting points: (1) observations made during a trip from Saint Michael 900 miles to the east, another to Kotzebue Sound, and a third to a point south of Wales on the coast; (2) a description of a ceremonial feast at Ignituk on the south coast of Seward Peninsula; (3) remarks about Isaac Koliak and his "overpopulated" house at "Orowignarak" (Ukvignaguk, near present-day Isaacs Point) and "Saxo" (Saxy), both of whom had helped members of the Western Union Telegraph Expedition more than fifteen years before.[8]

In 1889 H. M. W. Edmonds went to the Porcupine River as a member of J. Henry Turner's party that was surveying the Alaska-Canada boundary. The party sailed down the Yukon in the summer of 1890 to board the *Bear*; but when they arrived at Saint Michael, the *Bear* had left for the season, and did not return. Consequently, the party remained in Saint Michael, where Edmonds made a fine collection of masks and other artifacts, many of which are deposited in the Lowie Museum of Anthropology, Berkeley, California. In 1898 he returned to Saint Michael and the Yukon as a member of a Coast and Geodetic Survey party, obtained additional ethnological data, and combined it with his data of 1890 in a manuscript about the Eskimos of Saint Michael and vicinity.[9]

Sheldon Jackson's Point Hope and Yukon River masks in the Sheldon Jackson Museum, Sitka, and other artifacts from Seward Peninsula and Norton Sound, also in the National Museum of the Smithsonian, and those of Miner Bruce now in the Field Museum, constitute the last large collections of

8. Jacobsen 1884. Margaret Lantis has summarized in English the Festival of the Dead as reported by Jacobsen in *Alaskan Eskimo Ceremonialism*, pp. 25–27.

9. Edmonds' manuscript was not published until 1966 (see Ray, ed. 1966). The carbon copy of his manuscript, which is now in the University of Washington library archives, is accompanied by forty-nine small photographs. They were supposed to have been printed in the 1966 publication with their original captions, but only thirty-one were finally published. Some of the captions were accidentally switched in the printing, and the monograph acquired two different titles. Biographical information about Edmonds is found in Ray 1966 and Leighly 1969. While looking through material in the Office of Anthropology of the Smithsonian Institution, I recognized an anonymous handwritten notebook of folk tales as belonging to J. Henry Turner, leader of the boundary investigation party. These were published in Ray 1968.

traditional materials before the gold rush. Bruce had acquired his collection mainly at the Teller Reindeer Station, where he was employed during 1892–93; but some, like the Point Hope masks, were gathered when he made a trip to the north in 1897.

Bruce also wrote a small ethnography of the Port Clarence Eskimos in the third reindeer report, and Jackson wrote detailed accounts of his trips on the *Bear* during his annual "inspections" of the schools in northern Alaska, when he collected the artifacts, thus giving us a year-by-year chronology of activities on the west coast of Alaska. The wealth of information about cultural change in all of these various reports and writings, as well as in those of the captains of the revenue cutters and the various teachers and missionaries, can be fully appreciated only by reading each one; but from the aggregate it is possible to discuss the major enterprises that contributed to the formation of the character of Bering Strait culture at the end of the nineteenth century. The principal ones are the whaling and mining activities, discussed in this chapter, and the founding of schools and the reindeer industry, which will be taken up in the next two chapters.

WHALING

Port Clarence, though sheltered and near the strait, was not a port of call for whaling ships during the heyday of sailing ships of the 1850s and 1860s, and the six vessels known to have called there between 1850 and 1854 (only one of them a whaler) is small compared to the total number of vessels supposed to have sailed to the Arctic during that time. ˙

Between 1848 and 1851, 250 ships returned from northern Alaska laden with whale oil.[10] Richard Collinson of the *Enterprise* estimated that in 1850 alone there were 200 ships in the Bering Strait area, and Berthold Seemann, naturalist of the *Herald*, estimated a total of 299 ships with 8,970 sailors.[11] Bancroft, quoting Russian sources, said that the combined Arctic Ocean, Okhotsk Sea, and Bering Sea fleet of 1854 numbered 525 whalers; in 1855 it was 468; and in 1856, 366. These figures seem to be exaggerated, however, because the whalers' shipping list, quoted by Starbuck, gave a much smaller total for a larger area, that "north of 50 degrees north latitude" (near the United States–Canadian border). For 1854 there were 232 vessels; in 1855, 217; and in 1856, 178. By 1862 the number had dwindled to 32, and between 1867 and 1876, the numbers varied from 8 to 90.[12]

During the 1850s and 1860s, before the use of steam vessels, sailing ships went as far north as the ice pack permitted in the spring and returned southward in front of the pack in the fall. The ships rarely anchored near shore on the American side of the strait, but stopped quite often for trading

10. Starbuck 1878, p. 99.
11. Letter, Collinson to Secretary of the Admiralty, 13 September 1850, Admiralty Reports, 1851, 33:217; Seemann 1853, p. 94.
12. Bancroft 1886, p. 584; Starbuck 1878, p. 104.

on the Siberian side despite a Russian ban on trade. In the early days of whaling most of the vessels were strictly work ships devoted to catching whales and turning the blubber into oil on deck. Only when whaling declined during the sixties did whalers turn to two alternatives—trading and walrus hunting—to make a voyage profitable. Sometimes a ship combined all three enterprises.

Independent traders had followed the whalers into the Arctic from the very first with their varied goods, including liquor and firearms. They found places like Port Clarence and Kotzebue Sound, outside the whaling grounds, good trading areas because of Eskimo gatherings. Trading by the whalers was restricted at first to purchase of baleen, when commercial whaling had been poor but Eskimo whaling good. Some whalers sold contraband goods, but the consensus was that the traders were less honest and responsible than the whalers in their dealings with the Eskimos.

Of considerable importance to the Eskimos of northwest Alaska was the whalers' practice of killing walrus for oil and ivory when whaling was not showing a profit. Walrus apparently were first killed for the oil, but later only for the tusks, the rest of the animal being discarded. Walrus were taken in large numbers in several areas—the strait itself, in the lower Bering Sea, and between Point Hope and Point Barrow. One of the first references to the practice of walrus hunting was made by the San Francisco *Weekly Bulletin*, which reported that 50,000 walrus had been taken by the "West Arctic fleet" in 1866; but in 1874 Scammon said, "According to *The Friend*, published at Honolulu, March 1st, 1872, the whalers first began to turn their attention to Walrus-catching about the year 1868." [13] In 1869 the *Whalemen's Shipping List* said, "Owing to the scarcity of whales in the Arctic early in the season, many gave their attention to the capturing of Walrus, and about 4,000 barrels of oil were taken from them." [14]

A comparison with later, and much lower, figures of walrus catches and walrus oil and ivory returns suggests that the 50,000 figure for 1866 was in error as a result of an exaggeration or a misprint for 5,000. Although 50,000 walruses seems unbelievably high (Scammon said that 60,000 walrus had been caught in the five-year period between 1868 and 1872), [15] it conceivably could have been an enormous initial slaughter of an untouched walrus population. Furthermore, ninety-five ships were engaged in whaling during 1866, almost twice as many as in any one year after 1870.

Even if the figure of 1866 was supposed to be 5,000, that in itself would have made considerable inroads into the thousands of walrus that early ex-

13. "Whales and Walrus," Dall scrapbooks, 4:56; Scammon 1874, p. 427. In 1854 the *Phiel* from Honolulu had traded 4,000 pounds of walrus tusks from the Eskimos (see Chap. 11).

14. *Whalemen's Shipping List*, 1 February 1870; "Whales and Walrus," Dall scrapbooks, 4:56. A newspaper report in 1887 said that only 500 pounds of walrus ivory had been taken that year because the whale hunting had been good (*The Weekly Bulletin*, 16 November 1887, Dall scrapbooks, 15:24).

15. Scammon 1874, p. 181.

plorers saw during their voyages. In 1820 Karl K. Hillsen of the *Good Intent* said that he saw an endless ice field stretching from the eastern cape of Saint Lawrence Island to the Bering Strait on which "hundreds of thousands of walrus" were lying.[16] Capturing hundreds in a matter of hours was easy under such circumstances, and fifty-seven years later, in 1877, one skipper, L. C. Owen, said that his crew took 1,600 walrus, 750 in a forty-eight-hour period.[17]

The wanton slaughter of walrus was not lost on many observers. A number of whaling captains abstained from hunting during the early days, and news stories often condemned the taking of walrus by guns as an injustice to the Eskimos, who still killed them with native harpoons.[18] E. W. Nelson estimated "that the number of [walrus] in existence is not over 50 per cent. of the number living ten years ago, and a heavy annual decrease is still going on." It is possible that by the 1870s only one-fourth of the number of aboriginal walrus existed.[19]

Yet even this depletion did not affect the well-being of Bering Strait tribes—not even Wales or King Island, as suggested in Chapter 9. In the 1890s the walrus catch was adequate for comfortable subsistence for the whaling-walrus tribes in conjunction with their large catch of seals, and affected only their trade in surplus walrus skins.[20] This decrease probably had some effect on the numbers of umiaks and kayaks made by other tribes, but there are no comparative figures for a reasonable conclusion.

The killing of walruses by whalers caught the eye and emotions of Captain Michael Healy, and he suggested to Sheldon Jackson, the first agent for education in Alaska, a scheme for importing domesticated reindeer from Siberia to save the "starving Ekimos." Healy's chance remarks resulted in a new industry for which most of the Eskimos had little aptitude, but which played an important part in the history of Seward Peninsula during the 1890s and well into the twentieth century.

The Eskimos of the Port Clarence area did not directly feel the impact of commercial whaling until the steam whaler began to be used for Arctic whaling. The steam whaler permitted many ships to winter together, frozen into the ice, east of Point Barrow, thus necessitating a scheme for getting additional supplies and coal for fuel. In 1884 the Pacific Coast Steam Whaling Company, which owned most of the whaling vessels of the Arctic in the latter part of the nineteenth century, selected a coal-deposit site near that of the Revenue Service's newly established stockpile of coal on Point Spencer.[21]

16. Hillsen 1849, 66:226.

17. *San Francisco Chronicle*, 29 January 1898, Dall scrapbooks, 20:74.

18. "Whales and Walrus," Dall scrapbooks, 4:56.

19. Nelson 1887, p. 270. I have worked out this percentage from receipts of oil and walrus tusks from various sources, in an unpublished paper.

20. A surplus of skins could also have meant increased faction solidarity, especially on King Island, as suggested by Bogojavlensky (1969, p. 244).

21. Healy 1889, pp. 11–12; Healy 1887, p. 13. That same year, the company established its

In the years that followed, dozens of ships anchored
meet the "tender to the fleet," a supply ship that broug.
to vessels remaining in the Arctic over winter and took ι
ivory. Eskimos from the surrounding area came to trade, s
aboard a vessel the entire time it was at anchor, expecting
generally making themselves very much at home. Eskimos alѕ
temporary tent villages for trading as they had done in earlier days
and native trading.

MINING

The first commercial mining venture in northern Alaska began in 1881 on
the Fish River of Seward Peninsula. Little prospecting had been done in the
area after the Western Union people had tried their luck in various streams in
1866 and 1867, but in the summer of 1880 a deposit of galena ore was
accidentally discovered near the Fish River. The San Francisco *Chronicle*
reported the find on 4 December 1880 in an article entitled, "A Silver Mountain," which prophesied that it was "only the beginning of vast discoveries
which will soon be made in Alaska."

According to the story, the deposits were discovered by William P. Gallagher, whose whaling vessel was anchored in Golovnin Bay.[22] Gallagher
was shown heavy pieces of galena by an Eskimo chief who had taken him and
his crew fishing up the Fish River. On Gallagher's return to California, the
Alaska Mining Company was organized, and in 1881 it sent a schooner, the
W. F. March, to Golovnin Bay, where it was wrecked.[23] That year, John C.
Green, one of the stockholders of the company, organized the first mining
district in northern Alaska, the Fish River Mining District, which included
the entire Seward Peninsula. The mine was known as the Omilak mine, from
the Eskimo word *omailak*, meaning "it's heavy."[24]

In 1883 the *Alaska* arrived at Golovnin Bay with twenty men who mined
seventy-five tons of galena ore with considerable help from the Fish River
Eskimos; but the vessel, en route to San Francisco with its cargo and fifteen of
the miners, sank between Saint Lawrence and Saint Matthew islands. The
four men who remained at the mine killed two Eskimos in an altercation,
which will be discussed in the last chapter.

Although a report had been issued that showed there was no continuous
vein of ore, the mine was patented in 1894. The last ore sent to San Francisco

first shore whaling station at Cape Smythe, for year-round occupancy under the direction of E.
P. Herendeen, who had spent two years there with the International Polar Expedition participating in world-wide observations of magnetic and auroral phenomena between 8 September
1881 and 28 August 1883. In 1887 the Pacific Steam Whaling Co. set up a station at Point Hope.

22. San Francisco *Chronicle*, 4 December 1880, Dall scrapbooks, 5:160; San Francisco *Chronicle*,
4 May 1881, ibid., 6:93. There is no Captain Gallagher in whalers' shipping lists for either the east
or the west coasts in 1879 or 1880, so he probably was a trader based in Hawaii or San Francisco.
His full name in not given in the newspaper articles, but is found in Healy 1889, p. 8.

23. A complete account of the history of the Omilak mine is in Ray 1974.

24. From field data.

...s in 1890. From this venture came the first question about individual title and ownership to land, apart from mining claims. John A. Dexter, who was employed at the Omilak mine in 1891, remained in Chinik (Golovin) as a trader. In 1899 he wrote to Sheldon Jackson to inquire whether Mr. Green had "any title for this point of land that I now occupy." Green claimed the land and "a store [storehouse?]," which he had built in 1882 but had not been occupied since 1891. The village of Chinik had grown from a small native village of two houses to one of considerable size due to Dexter's trading post. His holdings in 1899 consisted of a dwelling, 70 by 22 feet, a "store," 16 by 16 feet, a fish house, 12 by 14 feet, a log house, 16 by 20 feet (occupied by his mother-in-law, an Eskimo woman), two small gardens, and "other buildings."[25]

During the 1880s and the 1890s a small amount of prospecting for gold was done around Golovin and on the Fish River by prospectors and missionary-teachers, but the Canadian Klondike rush of 1897, which sent thousands of men and women through Saint Michael and up the Yukon, was indirectly responsible for the discovery of gold on Anvil Creek near Nome in July and September 1898. In September 1897 Daniel B. Libby, who had discovered gold thirty years before on the Niukluk while with the telegraph expedition, got caught up in the excitement of the Klondike rush and organized a mining party to return to the Fish River area.

Adventurers and prospectors were set afire that summer of 1897 when two trading boats returned from the Klondike to Saint Michael loaded with gold. The North American Transportation and Trading Company's *Portus B. Weare* and the Alaska Commercial Company's *Alice* brought jars, bags, and boxes full of gold to be shipped to the outside on the NAT and T's *Portland* and the AC Company's *Excelsior*. As soon as these ships docked in Seattle and San Francisco, respectively, delirium spread over the waterfront, and almost immediately miners, prospectors, adventurers, and malcontents crowded onto all kinds of vessels pressed into service to accommodate them and their "outfits" of food, clothing, and equipment. Saint Michael suddenly became a metropolis: more ships than ever before were built on the ways, and huge buildings—hotels, storehouses, bakeries, and mercantile establishments—sprang from the earth. The men did not fan out into the surrounding country to prospect, as they did later at Nome, because Saint Michael was not considered to be in "mineral country." Therefore, the huge, unruly collection of human beings was contained within Saint Michael itself or confined to the banks of the Yukon. Moreover, Saint Michael, or "Fort Get There," as it was nicknamed by Portus B. Weare,[26] was only a way station on the road to riches. Many persons were stranded in Saint Michael during the fall of 1897; and Sheldon Jackson, who had arrived on the *Bear* on 24 August, said that

25. Letter, Dexter to Jackson, dated Golovin [*sic*] Bay, 10 September 1899, Correspondence MF 137, Presbyterian Historical Society.
26. Curtin 1938, in caption opposite p. 133.

eight or ten ships had come from West Coast ports v,
ters to build river boats, and thirteen more were expe

As all these people were pledged to be taken to the mines this
that there is not only much disappointment but also much irritati.
liable at any moment to break out into open violence.

Among the hundreds now camped upon the beach in tents are all c
best to the lowest; professional men of ability and standing, gamblers a.
roughs, the wealthy and the poor, and the presence of the "Bear" is the on.
on lawlessness.[27]

The confusion and disorder were somewhat alleviated by the establishment of a military reservation, Fort Saint Michael, by executive order on 20
October 1897 with Captain E. S. Walker in charge. One more frustration for
newcomers was added when in only a year's time, or by the end of 1898, all
of the Klondike's richest ground had been staked. But they shortly had new
fields to prospect and to dream about. In the Fish River area John Dexter and
a companion had found signs of gold on the Niukluk five years before Libby's
mining party of 1897. Dexter, unable to continue the mining himself, staked
George Johansen and an Eskimo guide, Andrew Napauk, to expenses for
further prospecting. Johansen and Napauk were joined by two other Eskimos, Tom Quarick and his wife, who lived at a native settlement called
Chauiapuk, about five miles above the mouth of the Niukluk. Johansen
found gold on what was later called Ophir Creek, but inexplicably abandoned his project and went overland to Port Clarence.[28]

When Libby and his party, consisting of H. L. Blake, L. F. Melsing, and
A. P. Mordaunt, arrived at the Fish River in 1897, they employed Dexter's
former guide, Napauk, to help them prospect the Niukluk and the Fish.
They returned to Chinik for the winter, but in April 1898, after finding
abundant gold prospects, built a mining camp with the help of Quarick.
They called the camp Council City, which H. N. Castle, one of the early
attorneys, explained in this way: "Upon whom rests the responsibility of the
name, it is hard to say. . . . It is said that the 'council' [to establish a mining
district] held in Old Tom's igloo coined the name as appropriate to the
assembly which there convened."[29]

News of the Fish River strike spread a considerable distance in a short
time; about four hundred prospectors, many from Saint Michael, spent the
summer in the Golovnin Bay area, and many claims were staked on the Fish
River and its tributaries. By the winter of 1898–99 several mining companies
had been organized and the population of Council was 150.[30] Two of the

27. Letter, Jackson to W. T. Harris, 13 September 1897, U.S. National Archives, RG 75,
letters sent, 17:357–58.

28. Castle 1912, pp. 8–9. Nels O. Hultberg, one of the Swedish teachers and missionaries,
learned of these prospects and urged the Swedish missionary society in 1895 to send a mining
expert to Golovnin Bay.

29. Ibid., p. 10.

30. Ibid., pp. 10–11.

...is in the Council area were owned by Toleef L. Brevig, missionary and superintendent at the Teller Reindeer Station, who reportedly said he would not sell the claims for less than fifty thousand dollars when Captain Cogan of the *Alaska* wanted to purchase them.[31]

At least four separate prospecting trips were made from Council into the surrounding area, one of them resulting in the discovery on Anvil Creek when the prospectors were shown ore by an Eskimo friend of Blake's, "Too rig Luck." By the end of December 1898, Swedish missionaries and prospectors had located 90 out of the 300 claims, and in November and December news of the strike had become common knowledge around Unalakleet and Saint Michael. The latter was full of disappointed and pessimistic Klondikers, although the town itself was booming with 78 military men and 32 transportation companies that supplied goods to the Klondike with a fleet of 60 steamboats, 8 tugs and towboats, and 20 barges. Every day several parties with dog teams and their Eskimo drivers left Saint Michael. One day 40 dog teams were seen along the way, and L. H. French said that within three weeks of the first news, Saint Michael and many small camps nearby were nearly deserted. By the beginning of 1899, 250 persons lived in tents in Anvil City (later called Nome) at the mouth of the Snake River, but news of the strike had not yet gone beyond the boundaries of Alaska. The news shot up the Yukon River from Saint Michael, and during February and March scores of dog teams left the Klondike for the new gold fields.[32]

Mining activities created the most widespread changes in Eskimo life since the beginning of European trade in Siberia. The resulting settlement of the Malemiut traders in foreign Eskimo territory had been a slow process involving only a few native persons over a long period of time. Both the traders and their trade items were readily accepted by the local inhabitants. The loss of walrus and whales in the Bering Strait affected the area only slightly because the Eskimo had depended primarily on other foods as staples. The various expeditions—even the ones that wanted the Eskimos to work—were accepted in a holiday spirit as the Eskimos visited their ships and headquarters. The Eskimos met the newcomers on their own terms.

But mining was in an entirely new sphere. It brought persons interested in exploitation and ownership of large areas of Eskimo land. Up to this time, the Eskimos had usually accepted new ideas and objects voluntarily, but the new mining pursuits suddenly eliminated choices, and the disruption of settlement and subsistence patterns and a new authoritarian government were only a small part of the involuntary changes the Eskimos faced as their land was disturbed and its nonrenewable products extracted without their permission.

31. Dey diary.
32. Blake 1900, p. 2; Carlson 1946, pp. 261, 266, 272; *The Alaskan*, 12 November, 1898; Andrews 1938, pp. 191–92; French [1901], p. iv.

CHAPTER 16

Schools and Missions

THE establishment of schools and the reindeer industry paralleled the beginnings of mining. Most of the teachers and missionaries were also interested in trading and prospecting, although they were supposed to be single-minded and stay with their teaching. But this was hard to do because the schools were hardly schools, and the missions were hardly missions, and life and learning were extremely difficult for both the teachers and the pupils.

Schools and reindeer herding began in only a few settlements during the last part of the century, but almost immediately the entire Bering Strait area was involved, not only through the ambitions of the teachers and administrators of the reindeer business but because the Eskimos themselves began to come from the surrounding areas out of curiosity or to ask that schools be sent to their villages.

Schools and reindeer were not the whole of Eskimo life at this time—subsistence and settlement patterns were still basically the same as before—but their influence was plainly felt, since schools and herds were established in key mainland places: Wales, the largest village; Port Clarence, the whalers' rendezvous; Golovin, in the boundary zone between Yupik and Inupiak speakers; and Unalakleet, the village where three separate tribal groups had lived together since the Russian fur trade began.

These activities of the last decade of the nineteenth century were therefore all-encompassing in a geographical sense and interpenetrated all aspects of culture. A discussion of each area within a chronological scale will bear this out. Attending school and herding reindeer introduced compulsory, repetitive, and sedentary habits, which were foreign to the Eskimos. During earlier expedition days, individual Eskimos had experienced the restrictions the white man imposed on himself and others in various employments, and had not been at all charmed by the experience. He found that school was a dramatic change, and a sudden one; it meant entering a building day after day at the same hour to learn about objects and ideas unconnected with the immediate world, and in a new language.

Schools cannot be discussed apart from missions because all of them, with only the exception of the "reindeer schools," were organized with religion as a foundation. The Russian mission in Saint Michael had little academic instruction and was entirely under the Russian Orthodox Church. Schools north of Saint Michael were supported at first by individual church sects under the guiding hand of Sheldon Jackson, ardent Presbyterian missionary, who had been appointed general agent of education for Alaska on 11 April 1885. The Organic Act of 1884 had provided twenty-five thousand dollars for education in this vast territory, and Jackson, because of his trips to visit the Presbyterian missions and his intense fervor toward civilizing the natives, was deemed the most suitable for—indeed, the only man capable of—carrying out a program of education.

Jackson was not a newcomer to Alaska. In 1877 he accompanied Mrs. A. R. McFarland, who had been sent to Alaska by the Presbyterian Board of Home Missions to take over the school for natives at Wrangell begun by Philip McKay, an educated Tsimshian Indian.[1] By 1881, the board also maintained schools at Sitka and Haines. At that time there were only three other American schools in the territory. These were under the auspices of the Alaska Commercial Company in compliance with terms of their fur-seal lease: one at Unalaska and two on the Pribilof Islands.

Under Jackson's direction, teachers were expected to carry on an active campaign to change the life of the Eskimos because Jackson saw them not as a people with an integrated and workable culture but as barbarians, savages, or an impoverished and almost extinct race, which held distinct promise, however, of quickly learning new ways. He looked upon Eskimo living conditions as being toward the bottom of the scale of human existence; and when he decided to import domesticated reindeer from Siberia as a part of his vigorous program of change and education, he said, "A change from the condition of hunters to that of herders is a long step upward in the scale of civilization."[2]

Owning reindeer was only half the campaign; the other half was converting the Eskimo to Christianity. As late as 1903, Jackson, after an eighteen-year tenure as agent of education, still considered education to be synonymous with religion, and his papers and lectures—in the thousands—emphasized his creed of practical education through the reindeer: "while we offer them Gospel with one hand, we must offer them food with the other."[3]

The early congressional appropriations for schools were too small to satisfy Sheldon Jackson's ambitious plans, so at the outset of his career as general agent he vigorously sought church support. The Moravian missions in Alaska (having established the first school north of the Gulf of Alaska in 1885

1. Hinckley 1972, p. 114; Hulley 1953, p. 233.
2. Education Report 1895, p. 1710.
3. Jackson [1903], p. 57.

at Bethel, eighty miles up the Kuskokwim River) had been Jackson's own idea, and he had personally approached the Moravians about footing the bill. The Swedish schools had his hearty approval, though established by a Swedish society at the suggestion of A. E. Nordenskiöld after his visit to Port Clarence in 1879. But Jackson wanted many, many more missions in the North, so he devised a plan whereby expenses of a school were divided between the Bureau of Education and a church mission.

Mission schools that shared operating expenses with the United States government through a contract were known as "contract schools"; and though they were government schools established for secular education, Jackson demanded that testimonials about Christian activities accompany a teacher's application, and that he be affiliated with a church. No matter how competent an employee was, if he deviated from what Jackson thought was strict Christian living, he was fired.[4]

Jackson's strong advocacy of the marriage of church and state made him many enemies, including almost all government officials in and out of Alaska. Jackson's opponents won the first round when the Congress failed to appropriate money for education in Alaska in 1885; but Jackson continued his fight for funds and missionary teaching in schools, and encouraged sectarianism in every way. The battle between religious and secular education was to rage until Jackson left office in 1907.[5]

Beginning with Governor Alfred P. Swineford's report in 1885, the governors' reports consistently complained about the state of educational affairs in Alaska, particularly that the education agent was never in Alaska, but in Washington, D.C., when school was in session.[6] He was also criticized for not giving the governors information and statistical material, and for not spending time in villages or actually looking at schools while on inspection tours because he lived on the *Bear* during his trips to the Bering Strait. Since the teachers usually came to the steamer to confer with him, he did not have to set foot in a village. In 1896 Thomas Hanna, a Wales teacher, pleaded with Jackson: "If you can at all do come and stay a few days with us. We have so much to tell you. And we need your aid and more so your advice."[7]

Jackson placed little importance on a study program, and from the accumulation of letters and reports from the teachers under Jackson's supervision, one can only conclude that teaching was actually of little interest to him. The results of the first decade of the schools reflected this. The course

4. In 1896, for example, William Kjellmann tried to vindicate Jackson's unjust charges that he drank beer and had done "unnecessary work on Sundays" (letter, Kjellmann to Jackson, Madison, Wis., 10 February 1896, RG 75, letters received).
5. After a special agent, Frank C. Churchill, was sent to Alaska to investigate the schools and the reindeer service in 1906, Jackson was asked to resign; but he did not get completely out of educational matters in Alaska until 1908 (Hinckley 1966, p. 756).
6. For example, see Swineford 1885, p. 6; Swineford 1886, p. 20; Swineford 1887, pp. 26–27; and Knapp 1891, p. 11.
7. Letter, Hanna to Jackson, Cape Prince of Wales, 1 June 1897, RG 75, letters received.

of study in the schools was left up to the teacher, and the best ones found themselves frustrated, not only by lack of direction but by lack of materials with which to work.

SAINT MICHAEL

Saint Michael did not have an American school until after 1900. Before Alaska became a part of the United States the only teaching done by the Russians in this area was in conjunction with missionary work. They had no formal schools. The building of a chapel was not begun at Saint Michael until 1842, but in 1843 and 1844 the priest Gregory Golovin traveled extensively throughout the Yukon area, baptizing eighty-eight men and seventy-five women "from various tribes" of "Norton Sound." [8] Twice during those years, Bishop Innokenty, the head of the church in Alaska, wrote to Adolf Etolin, general manager of the Russian-American Company, for permission to establish a permanent mission in the Yukon region. Finally, on 23 December 1844, Etolin replied that he would grant permission but did not know if the Russian-American Company could help defray expenses. Etolin regarded the duties of this mission as more of a service to the Russians of the Saint Michael–Yukon River area than to the natives, and agreed with Golovin that the best place for headquarters was at the Eskimo village of Ikogmiut (often spelled Ikogmut, later called Russian Mission), where the trader Andrei Glazunov had lived. [9]

On 1 March 1844 Bishop Innokenty sent an order to Priest Golovin to finish building the chapel at Saint Michael, and on 27 December the "Mikhailovsko-Kwihpah" mission was formally dedicated to "spreading God's words among the inhabitants of the Bering Sea coasts and the region of the Kuskokwim River." Bishop Innokenty appointed Jacob Netsvetov as missionary with several assistants. At first the plan was to make Saint Michael their headquarters with an option to move later to Ikogmiut or elsewhere if they wished, but on 30 January 1845 Bishop Innokenty wrote that the mission headquarters were to be located on the Yukon River at 62° north latitude and 161° west longitude (at Ikogmiut) because the river had a much larger population—over 3,500 inhabitants—than Saint Michael. Furthermore, this site was closer to the Kuskokwim River. Netsvetov left Sitka on the *Okhotsk*, arrived at Saint Michael on 9 July 1845, and continued on to the Yukon. In 1850 a parish school was begun at Ikogmiut, and in 1851 a permanent church was finished. Saint Michael, however, had the services of a priest only once a year. [10]

From a travel diary kept by Hieromonk Illarion of the "Kwichpah Mission" between 5 December 1865 and 2 December 1866 we get a glimpse of the procedures of the early-day priests. On 29 May 1866 Illarion found some

8. Alaska History Research Project 1936–38, 1:361.
9. Ibid., pp. 362, 364–66.
10. Ibid., pp. 368–69, 374.

"Native Village, King's Island," 1884. (From Healy 1889, p. 82)

"Natives of King's Island," 1885. (From Healy 1887, following p. 10)

Wales, Alaska, photographed by C. L. Andrews in the mid-1920s. (From the Andrews photograph collection. Special Collections, University of Oregon library)

"Upper Entrance to Eskimo 'Eni' [dwelling] at Cape Prince of Wales," about 1900. (Photograph by Lomen brothers)

Ingalik Indians waiting to be baptized at the mouth of the Innoko River. A group of Malemiut, who were there to buy furs, went shortly thereafter to Ikogmiut and announced that they, too, wanted to be baptized immediately; but Illarion asked them to wait until the next day after they had learned more about the gospel. He baptized all of the Malemiut—twenty-one adults and infants—although he said that living so far from the Russian settlements as they did, they would rarely see a priest. Early in June Illarion traveled to Saint Michael, where he baptized fifty-seven more Eskimos, twenty-one of them Malemiut from Golovnin Bay, who had arrived on the twenty-third, informing Illarion that there were other "Christians" in their villages wanting to be baptized. Being in a hurry to get home, they "gladly consented [on the twenty-sixth] to all the conditions required by the Christian faith."[11] Each convert was given a small gilt cross and other presents.

After Alaska was sold in 1867, the brig *Shelikov* made a last trip to Saint Michael from Sitka to take all church employees to Russia; but Saint Michael was not mentioned in a list of churches, chapels, or clergymen made out for purposes of the transfer in November 1867.[12]

At Saint Michael the chapel continued to be visited only occasionally by a priest. In 1871 Zakhary Belkov, the churchman of "Kwichpah Mission" at Ikogmiut, reported that he had five thousand persons on the church register, although the total population of the entire parish at that time was probably no more than that. By 1880 the number of converts claimed for the entire Yukon–Saint Michael parish appears to have shrunk, for according to the census report for 1880, the priest at the Ikogmiut headquarters claimed only three thousand parishioners, but reported "that he holds 600 more 'nearly persuaded.'" It was said, however, that this priest had very little influence over the people.[13]

In 1884 Consul-General A. E. Olarovsky decided to transfer the mission headquarters from Ikogmiut to Saint Michael because of financial and personnel difficulties. This decision was not popular with some of the Russian church officials who feared they would lose ground to the Jesuits, who were earnestly looking for a location on the Yukon. But Olarovsky was firm in the transfer: "Much to our regret, our missionaries in the North, with very few exceptions, are permeated with the spirit of trade and speculation rather than with their holy duties. The missionary at Ikogmut is one of them, and I consider it desirable and necessary to transfer him to some place where he can be observed and controlled."[14]

11. Ibid., 2:115–17. In 1868 Illarion transferred to Sitka and left for Russia on 30 December 1869 (ibid., 1:218–19). The coincidence of twenty-one persons being baptized in two different places may have been the fault of Illarion's memory, or they may have been the same ones, baptized twice. These Malemiut might possibly have been Isaac Koliak and his people (see Chap. 12).

12. Ibid., 1:185, 317.

13. Ibid., p. 314; Petroff 1880, p. 57.

14. Alaska History Research Project 1936–38, 1:382, 383. Zachary Belkov wrote in his report for 1886 that the reports about his trading operations were untrue.

The order for the transfer and the building of a church in Saint Michael did not come through until the spring of 1886, a timing that interfered considerably with the plans of Octavius Parker, a Protestant Episcopal missionary who had arrived in Saint Michael that summer. Early that year, the Episcopal church had agreed to send a teacher to the Yukon in accordance with the plan of the commissioner of education to establish public schools in the leading population centers of Alaska. Since it was late in the season when the contract was signed (1 July 1886), it was decided to locate the school temporarily at Saint Michael. Housing was scarce, so Parker shared the residence of the agent of the Alaska Commercial Company. He had no place to teach, but attempted a few sessions in the living room.

"To add to his difficulties," wrote Sheldon Jackson, "the priest of the Russo-Greek Church, who had previously been living in the Yukon Valley, removed to St. Michael and opened a school, teaching the natives in the Russian language. This church school, while doing next to nothing for the children, yet through misrepresentation and prejudice kept them away from the Government school [i.e., Parker's classes]."[15] In 1887 Parker moved to Anvik, where he was joined by John W. Chapman, who said that the local agent of the Alaska Commercial Company in Saint Michael had received orders that he was to accord to Parker "every courtesy, but [was] 'not to let him succeed!'" Chapman suspected that this rebuff had stemmed not so much from his being a missionary as from his short stature—like Jackson, who was five feet tall—and that the company "had reason to fear that two men of that calibre and of good intent for the natives would be too many."[16] Chapman had thought of settling down somewhere on the coast, especially on King Island, which had interested him from the first; but he decided to join Parker, who had already purchased buildings, at Anvik.[17]

As early as 1873, the Roman Catholic Church Mission, located on the Mackenzie River in Canada, had sent two priests to establish missions in northern Alaska. One of the priests, a Father Le Corre, was said by Frederick Hall to have begun work in Saint Michael;[18] but the first Catholic mission and school in the Yukon–Saint Michael area was not formally established until August 1888, when a Jesuit priest, Aloysius Robaut, chose the site of present Holy Cross for both a day school and a boarding school operated by several sisters of Saint Ann.[19] In 1896 Jackson reported that the Roman Catholics were "talking of establishing . . . a school at St. Michael," but neither a church nor a school was founded until after 1900.

UNALAKLEET AND GOLOVIN

The first school on the coast north of the Kuskokwim River was established

15. Education Report 1888, pp. 103–4.
16. Education Report 1889, p. 187; Chapman 1948, p. 18.
17. Chapman 1948, pp. 18–19.
18. McCoy 1956, p. 365.
19. Education Report 1894b, 2:875; Hulley 1953, p. 236.

at Unalakleet in 1887 by the Mission Covenant of Sweden. This church is still called the "Swedish Covenant" locally, although the American branch is formally known as the Evangelical Covenant Church of America. After Nordenskiöld returned to Sweden from his visit to Port Clarence in the *Vega*, he brought the need for schools and missions in Alaska and Siberia to the attention of the Swedish organization, then only a few years old. In 1886 the Mission Covenant sent Axel E. Karlson, recently released from a three-year internment in Siberia for proselytizing in Russia, and Adolph Lydell to San Francisco to learn the English language. A year later, Karlson and Lydell boarded a ship, their destination being only "Alaska" since they relied on the revelations of God to show them to their final stations. Lydell was guided to Yakutat while Karlson continued on to Saint Michael, where he met Nashalook (one of Alluyianuk's sons), who invited him to set up his mission in Unalakleet. Shortly after his arrival on 12 July 1887 Karlson learned that three men were plotting his murder, so Nashalook harbored him until the danger had passed. Before winter set in, Karlson had built a house.[20]

He preached that winter throughout the country as far away as Golovnin Bay, but did not teach until 1889, although Jackson reported that Karlson opened his school in September 1887 and had "made good progress during the winter. One boy, who had already learned the Russian language, made such progress through the winter that in the spring he was able to converse in English. Others mastered the alphabet and were able to read intelligently in simple sentences. Special attention is given to the English language."[21] Strangely, Unalakleet church records show that school was not begun for the first time until two years later, on 22 October 1889, when twenty boys and nine girls "all got new names and some clean clothes and promised to wash their faces every morning."[22]

The delay of two years was necessary because one of the Moravian missionaries who had accompanied Karlson north in 1887 said that "he spoke the English language imperfectly."[23] This difficulty also postponed conversions to the new religion, as he had to communicate at first by speaking in Russian, which was translated into Eskimo by an interpreter. Later on, he used English combined with a smattering of Eskimo, "the interpreter filling in" the gaps.[24] The Eskimos themselves said that they were indifferent to Karlson's preaching, and the first conversion did not take place until after several years' labor. Etageak, one of the original converts, said that no one wanted to listen

---

20. Almquist 1962, pp. 18–20.

21. Ibid., pp. 20, 21; Education Report 1889, p. 187. The Bureau of Education report does not list Karlson as a teacher or Unalakleet as a school in the regular lists, although Jackson mentioned Lydell's school at Yakutat in a separate notation (p. 181). This report of the Unalakleet school by Jackson is a mystery since he did not visit Alaska that year and Karlson did not send a report to the bureau.

22. Almquist 1962, p. 21, from Karlson's logbook. Jackson's report for that year said there were thirty-one boys and nine girls (Education Report 1893, p. 1250).

23. Schwalbe 1951, p. 53.

24. Almquist 1962, p. 21.

to Karlson when he began to preach since they "cared only for our own gatherings, plays, and feasts."[25]

Jackson reported that the entire expense of the first year of teaching was borne by the mission, but that "it is proposed that next year the school will be assisted by the United States Bureau of Education" since supervision of the mission had been turned over to the American headquarters of the missionary society. It was not until 1891–92, however, that $1,000 was appropriated ($500 each) for Unalakleet and Yakutat, the church society contributing $7,325.[26]

In 1890–91 school attendance was thirty-six on the first day, but had grown to ninety-six by Christmas. Some of the pupils came from distant villages, and classes in industrial work and sewing were taught in the evenings. The Eskimos asked that branch schools be established in other villages. There were several orphans in the immediate area, so a missionary arrived in the spring of 1891 to take charge of a children's home, which cared for six boys and three girls.[27]

There were no more entries in the education reports for the Unalakleet school until 1893–94, for which there is a two-sentence summary: "The Swedes have established a good school at Golovin Bay, Alaska. This is in addition to their contract schools at Unalaklik and Yakutat."[28]

In 1893–94 the school at Golovin was taught by three persons: N. O. Hultberg, a former iron and woodworker for the Pullman Company and a native of Sweden; his wife; and Frank Kameroff, a native assistant. The site had been selected by August Anderson in the spring of 1892 during a missionary tour of the coast. At Golovnin Bay he "found many Eskimos in poverty and darkness" and when he asked "the natives if they wished to have a school in which their children could learn about God, [they] all answered 'Yes.'" Karlson then went back to the States to raise money for the mission, and returned to Alaska with Hultberg. It is said that Hultberg immediately recognized the harm it would do to take Eskimos away from their hunting and fishing when they were most needed to procure food for the winter, so "as a result of all this he did not enter into his work with the zeal and enthusiasm that he had when he started from the states"; but realizing that he had to stay, he readily began his work in Golovin.[29] He was the first missionary to recognize the value of the gold prospects on Seward Peninsula.

In 1894–95 the school enrollment at Unalakleet was 64, with 4 missionaries. At Golovnin Bay there were 3 missionaries; a native assistant, Kameroff; and 49 pupils. During the winter 20 persons were baptized, the "congrega-

25. Ibid., p. 20.
26. Education Report 1893, p. 1294; Education Report 1895, p. 1747; Education Report 1897, p. 1449.
27. Education Report 1894a, p. 932; Education Report 1898, p. 1625.
28. Education Report 1896a, p. 1468.
29. Education Report 1898, p. 1625; Harrison 1905, p. 219.

tion of converted natives [being] at present 30 in number." A few orphans were still cared for at both stations, and again neighboring villages, including Ulukuk, the Indian village on the upper Unalakleet River, asked for schools.[30]

During this same school year, David Johnson (who later took the surname Elliott), a nineteen-year-old lad who had arrived in Unalakleet in 1891 to teach, and Ojeark Rock, an Eskimo interpreter, traveled to various places along the coast, including Cape Prince of Wales and Kotzebue Sound, where in the summer of 1896 they returned to establish a permanent mission.[31] At that time they were met at Cape Blossom by several skin boats and many Eskimos, Rock's uncle among them. They remained a few months, but the Swedish Society decided that it could not afford such a venture, so it was agreed that the Quakers of the California Yearly Meeting, Society of Friends, from Whittier would establish the mission. They did so during the summer of 1897.[32]

There were four Eskimo assistants in 1895–96 at Unalakleet and Golovin: Frank Kameroff; Dora, a "native nurse"; Rock, the interpreter-evangelist; and Stephan Ivanoff, who, with his wife, had been at a new outstation called Kangekosook, south of Golovin.[33] On 15 July 1896 Sheldon Jackson visited the Golovin school for the first time since it had opened, but remained ashore only a few hours, during which time he was able to stake out "eight or nine acres of ground upon which [the mission] buildings are erected." The problems of land ownership had cropped up again, so that the purpose of Jackson's trip ashore was to assure the mission of its land rights, and not to visit the school. After Jackson's return to Washington, D.C., that fall, the missionaries still worried about title to their land, which Mr. Green, the

30. Education Report 1896b, p. 1428; Education Report 1897, p. 1450; letter, Axel Karlson to Jackson, Unalakleet, 24 June 1895, RG 75, letters received. Five missionaries are listed for Unalakleet, but two of them are the same person, Mrs. Karlson and Miss Swenson, who had become Mrs. Karlson in 1894.

31. Education Report 1896b, p. 1428; Education Report 1897, pp. 1450, 1462; Carlson 1951, p. 15n.

32. Sixth Reindeer Report 1897, p. 28; letter, D. Nyvall to Jackson, Chicago, 3 February 1897, RG 75, letters received. As early as 9 March 1897, Jackson acknowledged receipt of inquiries from the Friends about establishing a station at Kotzebue Sound (letter, Jackson to W. P. Hunnicutt, RG 75, letters sent, 16:117–19). On 22 March 1897, however, Jackson was still not sure whether the Swedish Covenant would also establish a station, because he wrote Charles E. Tebbetts, who had been inquiring for the Friends, that if the Swedish mission decided to go ahead with a permanent station, the "Friends can go to the other [river, i.e., either the Kobuk or the Noatak], or if [David Johnson] reaches there and finds the Friends have occupied a certain territory he will go to some other . . ." (RG 75, letters sent, 16:192–95). The Friends' missionary contingent sailed from San Francisco on 9 June 1897 (Cammack 1899, p. 37).

33. Education Report 1897, p. 1449. Frank Kameroff was listed as being at Koyuk, but nothing was said about it in the text, and it was not mentioned in the years thereafter (p. 1451). Ivanoff had to give up Kangekosook because he was needed at Unalakleet, but he was listed at Kangekosook for the year 1896–97, after which he returned to Unalakleet (Education Report 1898, p. 1616; Education Report 1899, p. 1767).

Omilak miner, also claimed; but Jackson assured them they had nothing to worry about. At the end of the year the missionaries optimistically reported that there had been "a full house every morning [at the Christmas services]. The natives sang, prayed, and testified. Even a young Shuman [medicine man] arose and said that he should not like to be left when the Lord would come." [34]

In 1897 Alice Omegitjoak, who had been educated in the United States, became an assistant at Unalakleet. By 1897, the Golovin mission had two houses, a school, and another native helper, Gabriel Adamson [Adams?]. Forty were enrolled in school, and 35 in church. There were 4 children in the children's home. [35] During the school year of 1897–98, Miss Omegitjoak reported that 14 had died of the "grip" in Unalakleet. Food was scarce, and the teachers at Golovnin Bay "often saw natives chew their skin boats and their shoes in want of food." Many children were fed at the mission. [36]

The year 1898–99 was especially difficult because of illness among the Eskimos and the departure of several missionaries for home, but most of all because of the large number of gold seekers pouring into the area from the Klondike and elsewhere after news of the gold strike near Cape Nome reached into Canada. [37]

CAPE PRINCE OF WALES

Sheldon Jackson, in the capacity of an agent of education, had not yet visited the schools at Golovin or at Unalakleet when he devised a plan to establish three contract schools simultaneously at Bering Strait and northward. His original plan in December 1889 had been to establish only a boarding school at Point Hope, but by March 1890 he had decided to have *three* schools, and in only a few weeks' time had obtained the support of the Congregational church for Cape Prince of Wales, the Episcopalian for Point Hope, and the Presbyterian for Point Barrow. He launched his plan so precipitously that teachers answering his advertisements "for volunteer teachers to go to the barbarous Eskimo of Arctic Alaska" had to leave home in May 1890, only two months after reading the advertisements, which appeared mainly in church publications. Twenty-four persons applied for the jobs, twelve of them women. [38]

34. Letter, Captain F. Tuttle to the Secretary of the Treasury, Unalaska, 20 September 1896, RG 26, Records of the Coast Guard, Alaska File; letter, D. Nyvall to Jackson, Chicago, 3 November 1896, RG 75, letters received; letter, Jackson to D. Nyvall, 10 November 1896, RG 75, letters sent, 14:267–69; Education Report 1898, p. 1625.
35. Education Report 1898, pp. 1616, 1625. Alice Omegitjoak's name as used here is from Almquist 1962, p. 49. Church records at Unalakleet, however, spell it Omekitjoak. Her name is also spelled Omigetjoak, Omekitjook, and Omekejook in various reports.
36. Education Report 1899, p. 1767.
37. Education Report 1900, pp. 1401–2.
38. Education Report 1894a, p. 924; Education Report for 1891, p. 753. A copy of Jackson's advertisement is in Education Report 1894a, p. 924.

In the summer of 1890, when these three schools were established, there were ten contract schools in Alaska, sixteen public schools (all in southern Alaska), ten schools supported entirely by missions, and an undetermined "number of Russo-Greek parochial schools, supported by the imperial Government of Russia." The total school appropriation was fifty thousand dollars for 1889–90.[39]

Jackson chose William T. Lopp and Harrison R. Thornton for the school at Wales, and was present when "the foundations of the first schoolhouse and mission on the Arctic coast of Alaska" were laid on 4 July 1890. Jackson had come north on the revenue cutter *Bear*, but the four teachers (in addition to Lopp and Thornton, one for Point Hope and another for Point Barrow) arrived on the schooner *Jennie*, tender to the whaling fleet. Building supplies for the Wales mission were paid for by the Congregational church of Southport, Connecticut, and the labor of erecting the buildings was supplied free by volunteer carpenters from the whaling ships *Balena*, *Grampus*, *Orca*, and *Thrasher*, and a dozen volunteers from the *Bear*.[40] Within a week, the *Bear* sailed north to build the school at Point Hope, and by 31 July had reached Point Barrow.

The schoolhouse at Wales was built between the two native villages on land claimed by the south village. The teachers' situation was somewhat unpleasant. They knew no Eskimo, and the Eskimos, knowing no English, could not understand why they were there. The teachers had not realized that a certain amount of animosity existed between the two villages, or that there was so much drunkenness. The Wales men often bullied the teachers, who indulgently thought they did it "for the fun of the thing," yet suspected that part of it was instigated by a chief, Elignok (also spelled Alignok), whose eldest son had died at the hands of Gilley in 1877.[41] Resentment over the killings by Gilley still smoldered when the two teachers arrived in Wales. They were young and completely unprepared to live or to teach in an isolated Eskimo village. Lopp was only twenty-six, and Thornton, though thirty-two, had fallen ten years earlier "into . . . a severe depression [from which] it is by no means certain that he ever fully recovered," and having drifted from one job to another, brought to his teaching a belief in strict discipline.[42] It was a perfect setting for tragedy.

Thornton had carried with him a premonition of death before he had ever seen an Eskimo. When he wrote to Jackson on 22 April 1890 about applying for the job at Wales, he asked whether his life would be in "any imminent probable danger."[43] He always carried a revolver around with him in Wales

39. Education Report 1893, pp. 1245–51; Education Report 1897, p. 1440.
40. Education Report 1893, pp. 1260, 1274, 1276. Lopp said that the *Bear* furnished a carpenter and four men (Lopp, diary entry, January 1891, p. 21).
41. *American Missionary* 45 (October 1891):360.
42. Thornton 1931, pp. x, xi–xii.
43. *American Missionary* 47 (October 1893):325.

and was inclined "to be a little imperious in his dealings with the natives," or, as C. L. Andrews said, treated them the way southerners treated the black man at that time.[44] It is not surprising that the Eskimos made him a target for little annoyances.

From the very first the teachers were faced with the conflict between an Eskimo's attendance at school and his participation in activities necessary for survival. This was not to be resolved for many years to come. When school began on 18 August only one-fourth of the villagers had returned from summer fishing, berry picking, and trading. Because of disturbances caused by intoxication and rough behavior, the teachers "taught, ate, worked and slept" for two months "with loaded arms at hand."[45] The teachers had heard of the Gilley affair before leaving home and again at Port Clarence from whalers who also needled the Eskimos with such statements as, "'If we were in your place, we wouldn't allow any damned missionary to settle at Cape Prince of Wales.'"[46] Tension mounted with an epidemic of "grip" or pneumonia from which twenty-six persons died in two months. A shaman attributed it to the presence of the white men, and specifically to pictures drawn on slates, which the children were permitted to take home; but the teachers attributed it to "a cold, wet storm [that] caught the people just as they were preparing to move from their summer tents to their igloos (underground houses) for winter: some of them were in open canoes returning from their summer voyages."[47]

By January 1891 the worst of their fears and dangers were over, and to their surprise the teachers found that their small schoolhouse, which could hold only fifty, was a very popular place. The total enrollment for the year was 304 out of a population of 539,[48] and the average daily attendance of 146 for the last seven months of the year forced them to divide the teaching into morning, afternoon, and evening sessions.

And then, to prevent the children who belonged to the afternoon or evening school from smuggling themselves into the morning session, or the morning children from remaining to the afternoon or evening session, it was found necessary to build two parallel snow walls some distance from the schoolroom door, and when the bell stopped ringing for school the teachers ranged themselves on either side, in order to sift the children that were trying to get into the schoolroom. It was with great difficulty that the pupils were made to understand that it was not proper to talk and laugh and jump over the benches in the schoolroom during school as much as they pleased; nor could they understand why 30 or 40 visitors could not lounge about the room which was needed for those who desired to study.[49]

44. Andrews 1944, p. 52.
45. *American Missionary* 45 (October 1891):359; Education Report 1894a, p. 926.
46. Thornton 1931, p. 57.
47. *American Missionary* 45 (October 1891):360, 361; Education Report 1894a, pp. 926–27.
48. The eleventh census of 1890 gave two different figures for the population of Wales—488 and 652 (Porter 1893, pp. 8 and 158). There is no explanation for the discrepancy.
49. Education Report 1894a, p. 926 (see also Thornton 1931, pp. 52–58).

As if it were not difficult enough to teach under such circumstances, there were other handicaps, too. The observances of various festivals interfered with school activities. After a death, family members did not leave home for ten days except in an emergency, and they could not sing or dance for a year. During the first school year there was only one violation of these rules when a "little fellow held his hand over his mouth to conceal the crime and sang softly to himself."[50]

Keeping regular school hours was difficult for the pupils. There were no clocks, and time for the children was not ordered into strictly divided segments of time, but into irregular parts of a day or night governed by the movements of the family hunting and fishing, or by ceremonial activities that might take up hours, days, or even weeks. Eating and sleeping were fitted in without regard to specific hours, so the result was that attendance, though large for the overall group during the first few years, was often irregular for an individual pupil. Evening sessions were noted not so much for tardiness as for the pupils' absence or drowsiness after a day of arduous seal hunting on the ice when the tired, worn-out hunters found it impossible to keep their eyes open or their chins off their chests in the warm, stuffy room.

On 5 July 1891 Lopp and Thornton met Jackson and the *Bear* at Port Clarence. Eleven whaling steamers and nine sailing vessels were already at anchor when they arrived. Jackson found that the teachers were in good health and was satisfied with their first year's efforts, but added to his report: "They were disappointed, however, in finding that no ladies had been sent up to reinforce their mission." When the *Bear* left Port Clarence for Wales on 7 July, 170 Eskimos were on board and eight umiaks were towed astern. The Eskimos transported in these umiaks all of the 182 tons of the mission's supplies and coal to shore and then carried them to the buildings. The entire village was invited aboard the *Bear*, where they danced to repay the hospitality. The school children were asked to demonstrate their new knowledge, and twelve umiaks raced to shore and back again to the *Bear* for a first prize of three buckets of hardtack, a second prize of two pails' full, and a third prize of one pail.[51]

At the end of summer 1891, Thornton returned to the United States for several reasons. First, he went as an emissary of good will for the Eskimo and to go before the Board of Indian Commissioners to urge complete enforcement of liquor prohibition and killing of walrus by whalers; to repeal the ban on breech-loading rifles; and to support the newly started reindeer project. But he also left because he was afraid to stay.[52]

During the school year 1891–92, Lopp was the only white man in a place where his only English language communicant was a dog that "would obey

50. Thornton 1931, pp. 106–7.
51. Education Report 1894a, p. 941; Lopp diary, December 1892, p. 391.
52. Education Report 1894b, p. 874; Lopp manuscript, 21 March 1933.

commands given in the English language. The loneliness had been so great that Mr. Lopp would visit that dog every day for the companionship of some animal that had once heard the English language."[53] Before being reduced to the companionship of an English-listening dog, he had had the company of Charley Antisarlook and his wife, Mary, a half-blood Russian. But they left after a few months to be with Charley's relatives at Cape Nome in February 1892 after Mary's mother had died in Saint Michael. Both Charley and Mary spoke English and had served as interpreters and helpers for several years on government vessels along the coast. Healy had taken them to Point Barrow several times, once in 1890 as interpreters for the eleventh census.[54] Charley, whose Eskimo name was Anasaluk (usually spelled Antisarlook or Antesilook in government reports) later became famous as the first Eskimo to own a herd of domesticated reindeer, and Mary or Changoonak (whose Russian name was Palasha Makrikoff), was known as "Reindeer Mary" or "Sinrock Mary" after she inherited her husband's reindeer.

During the school year of 1891–92 Lopp reported great progress made by his pupils: "Many of the children mastered the alphabet, learned to spell and pronounce simple English words, read in the first reader, write a neat and readable hand, and sing gospel and patriotic songs." The larger boys and girls learned to make hair seal clothing of American patterns, and prizes were given for "punctuality and diligence."[55]

When Thornton returned in 1892, he brought a wife and another woman teacher, Ellen Louise Kittredge, who became Mrs. Lopp the next month. In the fall of 1892, the original schoolhouse–living quarters was converted into a school when a new house was built a quarter mile away on the outskirts of "A-gen-amete," or the south village on the hill. The new building was used as a dwelling for both families, each having three rooms. Thornton's depression increased, and the Lopps, hoping to resolve their difficulties with the Thorntons, spent three months at Point Hope. The Thorntons often did not teach that winter because of Thornton's depression and worry about his life. As soon as the Lopps left, the number of small annoyances increased. A drunken Eskimo tried to stab him, and after some matches were stolen, Thornton dismissed school for an entire week. He announced in school that "if a native should come to the door after night and refused to give his name [he] would shoot him."[56]

Lopp left Wales and went to the Teller Reindeer Station for the year 1893–94, as he had requested, and the Thorntons were left by themselves. Again, annoyances plagued them, and finally the schoolhouse was broken into and one of the boys expelled from school. After the door of the school

---

53. Education Report 1894b, p. 874.
54. Education Report 1894a, p. 943; Log book, *Bear*, for 4 July 1890, RG 26, U.S. National Archives.
55. Education Report 1894b, p. 874; *American Missionary* 46 (December 1892):386, 388, 390.
56. Lopp diary, 1893.

was broken a second time, Thornton asked Healy to come ashore to warn the villagers about further disturbances and to shoot the guns of the *Bear* to show the power and protection provided by the revenue cutter. On 3 June Thornton wrote to Healy that the schoolhouse had been broken into again, and that if he and Mrs. Thornton did not get adequate protection, they would return to the States. Eleven days later, Lopp wrote to Healy saying that the young thief, Titalk, who had done most of the mischief was "universally hated by the people here." He suggested that he be taken away to school, possibly Sitka, because the old men who customarily punished the younger ones of the village had requested it.

Thornton had trouble with Elignok. On 5 July he wrote to Healy: "Your not taking any action in Alignok's case will leave a woman at the mercy of these savages and in great danger—not to speak of myself. . . . Can you not do or say something to Alignok or the natives generally to show them that we are under your, or U. S. protection?"

On 10 July Healy answered that he would get the Eskimos together and talk to them, "though I doubt the advisability of threatening a whole community in this manner. If your life is in danger I cannot see under what compulsion you are forced to remain here nor can I see any greater danger to you now than during the prolonged absence of Mr. Lopp at Pt. Hope last winter."[57]

After Healy had talked to the villagers and sailed away, Thornton wrote him a letter enumerating occurrences of more desperate acts, and accused Healy of fostering trouble. He said:

> The connection between this act [breaking the schoolhouse door] and your unfortunate lack of fervor and authority to punish offenses against our lives and property . . . seems obvious. The natives are beginning to see that we have no legal protection; it seems reasonable to suppose that such offenses will continue to multiply. . . . If the United States government wishes to civilise the Eskimos, law is as necessary as schools—perhaps, more necessary—and should accompany or precede them.[58]

Having begun his letter on 21 July, he added five postscripts, in which he listed illegal acts committed by the Eskimos. One of 7 August said that "night before last the schoolhouse was broken into again," and his last postscript, dated 18 August, said, "I send this to Port Clarence in case weather prevents your stopping here."

The next day Thornton was dead. About midnight, hearing a loud knock

57. Letters, Thornton to Healy, 3 June 1893; Lopp to Healy, 14 June 1893; Thornton to Healy, 5 July 1893; Healy to Thornton, 10 July, all dated Cape Prince of Wales, RG 26, Alaska File, U.S. National Archives. Titalk had stolen innumerable things from Eskimos, ships, and the school, and "had lost the use of his right arm because he had once stolen tobacco from a King's Island Eskimo" (letter, Lopp to Healy, Port Clarence, 2 September 1893, RG 26, Alaska File).

58. Letter, Thornton to Healy, Wales, 21 July 1893, Sheldon Jackson Museum manuscript collection.

on the front door, he got up from bed, went to the door, and was shot through the unopened panel by a whaling gun. Three young men, including the village troublemaker, ran out into the darkness of night. In the fashion of Eskimo justice, two of the boys were killed by their elders on the beach, stripped naked, and their bodies left for the dogs to eat. The third took to the hills, and returning much later, was taken by his uncle to Thornton's grave on the mountainside and asked how he would prefer to die—by strangulation, stabbing, or shooting. He chose to be shot.[59]

Just before Lopp left Wales, the teachers had published the first issue of the second newspaper of the Bering Strait area, *The Eskimo Bulletin*. Only five issues, each eight by ten inches, were published in all, one a year, the last one in 1902. The first two issues were written by hand and printed on a hectograph machine, and the others, on a printing press donated to the school. The masthead said that it was the "Only Yearly Paper in the World," and had the "Largest Circulation in the Arctic."[60]

School was suspended during 1893–94, but the Lopps returned the year after that. Jackson's report for 1894–95 dwelt mainly on reindeer and religion, although the school had an enrollment of 142 and an average daily attendance of 108. In the fall of 1894, the American Missionary Association received 119 head of reindeer from the government, and David Johnson, the young evangelist from Unalakleet, arrived in the spring of 1895 for revival meetings. No Eskimos had been converted up to 1895, but education was catching on. "Committees from a number of native villages have applied to Mr. Lopp to provide them schools."[61]

The Lopps went on leave during 1895–96, and a minister, Thomas Hanna, and his wife came to the mission. The *American Missionary* had appealed to its readers in 1893 to find a minister for Wales "in accordance with the wise suggestion of Dr. Jackson" because, although "our present excellent missionaries are devoted Christians and experienced teachers, [they] are not ministers." But Thornton and his wife had to spend their year alone at Wales because no suitable minister had been found despite repeated advertising.[62]

59. Education Report 1896a, pp. 1451–52; letter, Lopp to Healy, Port Clarence, 2 September 1893, RG 26, Records of the Coast Guard, Alaska File; *American Missionary* (October 1894): 349. This murder has been summarized in Montgomery 1963, from the standard printed sources.

60. *The Eskimo Bulletin* 3:2. I do not know where a complete set of *The Eskimo Bulletin* exists. There are copies of various issues in the Alaska State Historical Library, the Oregon Historical Society, and the University of Alaska Library. Several copies of the rare volume 1 (apparently consisting of only one page) are in Jackson's scrapbooks in the Presbyterian Historical Society. A news item in the San Francisco *Chronicle* attributed the founding and editing of the first issue of *The Eskimo Bulletin* to Thornton (issue of 3 October 1893, Dall scrapbooks, 20:170). There were three publications incorporating the name Eskimo: *The Esquimaux* of Western Union Telegraph Expedition days; *The Eskimo Bulletin*, and *The Eskimo*, a small leaflet issued at Nome by Walter C. Shields from 1916 to 1918 and by Clarence C. Andrews from 1936 to his death in 1948.

61. Education Report 1896b, p. 1428. Some reports say that 118 reindeer were given (see Chap. 17).

62. *American Missionary* 47 (March 1893):81; 47 (April 1893):114; 47 (July 1893):210.

In 1895 Hanna and his wife arrived, and his report to the Bureau of Education was a gloomy one. He was sent there without any kind of introduction, with no knowledge of the Eskimo language, and no one to initiate him into the difficulties of living in the North, especially in an Eskimo village. Food was scarce, and children had to be absent from school to help with fishing all year. Drunkenness was a problem, and the school windows were broken seven times. Gambling was a popular pastime everywhere, and large quantities of liquor were made in the village for both trade and local consumption.[63]

When the Lopps returned in the summer of 1896 they brought back with them a monument to erect over Thornton's grave. The year 1896–97 was also a discouraging one. Although two sermons were preached every Sunday, and the collection boxes were full of "lead, powder, caps, cartridges, spoons, matches, muskrat, ermine, and squirrel skins," the people of Wales did not prosper as in the preceding years, partly because of widespread drinking and distilling of liquor, which "prevented many from making the most of a favorable wind."[64] The prohibition of hunting on Sunday by the "Christian men" also had a bearing on the rather slim food supply. The teachers reported in the *American Missionary*: "Three of the best days for walrus hunting happened to be three Sundays in June. Some of the canoes got as many as seven big walruses on one Sunday. Our boys did not seem worried because they could not hunt on Sunday" and got only five large and four small walruses all season.[65]

Seven years after the school was founded, Thomas Hanna turned in a school report dated 1 June 1897 which continued to show discouraging progress in Eskimo education. Children still could not report for school in September because of having to stay in their seasonal camps and because Lopp was so busy with the reindeer and the herders and building a new house that he could not begin teaching until December. Hanna felt, moreover, that the kind of education given to the Eskimos was of no consequence to them: "Dear Sir [Jackson], you know too well that there is not at present a single reason to a young man or woman to learn to speak, read, write, and be educated. In fact, such attainment, amongst their own people, is hardly looked upon with favour, and both fathers and mothers make effort to have their boys and girls work and be ever doing something about house or hunting. I say that there must be something done to get better results."[66]

During 1897–98 the Lopps were alone at Wales, but Lopp was away from the village for several months taking the Wales reindeer herd to Point Barrow, where it was supposed that shipwrecked whalers needed food. Educa-

63. Education Report 1897, p. 1435.
64. Education Report 1898, pp. 1621, 1622.
65. *American Missionary* 51 (December 1897):280.
66. Letter, Thomas Hanna to Jackson, 1 June 1897, RG 75, letters received. Hanna had recently come from his native Ireland (letter, Jackson to M. E. Strieby, 31 March 1896, RG 75, letters sent, 13:278–79).

tion at Wales was almost at a standstill during those months, Mrs. Lopp attempting to teach alone, although Jackson had urged her to stay at the Teller Reindeer Station while her husband was away.

During the next year, 1898–99, a small missionary station was started at Mitletok, twenty-five miles northeast of Wales, with a cash contribution of twenty-five dollars from the States and various items like cartridges and lead raised from local Sunday offerings. Sokweena, about twenty years old, and his wife, both of whom had assisted Lopp the year before, were sent to Mitletok as missionaries, the first time that Eskimos were used directly in mission work in the Wales area. (Another man, Elobwok, was assisting at the Wales mission that year.) There were sixteen children of school age at Mitletok and eight or ten young adults who were willing to learn to read. The older people were expected to take an interest in church work. Lopp was able to visit the village only three times during the year, so the children learned only "to spell and write a little, and to sing."[67]

Port Clarence and Eaton Station

The first public school in the Bering Strait area was begun at Teller Reindeer Station and was called "Teller Reindeer Training School, Port Clarence." The teacher, Miner W. Bruce, a former journalist and business lobbyist, had twenty pupils during the first year, 1892–93, but he devoted most of his time to reindeer matters. The school continued each year until the station was closed in 1898–99 and a new reindeer station established at Eaton Station on the Unalakleet River.[68]

Bruce and his assistant, Bruce Gibson, were hired as reindeer superintendents, but were expected to double as teachers; and in a "new and untried" situation it was just about all they could do to keep up with the reindeer and the herders. Bruce began to teach school on 3 November, but discontinued teaching because the schoolhouse was too cold. He reopened school on 6 March, but closed it again on 20 April when all of the pupils left for spring seal and walrus hunting. Neither of the teachers had had time to learn the Eskimo language, and on the first day of school Bruce said that what "few words we did use brought a smile to their faces, and, as a consequence, our vocabulary consisted in a word now and then, interspersed with a half-dozen signs."[69] He said that his pupils were intelligent and inquisitive, but were "easily provoked to laughter, and among themselves are exceedingly talkative."

Jackson had established the school for the education of the herders, but Bruce, in a detailed report, recommended that they not be required to attend

67. Education Report 1900, p. 1389; Education Report 1901, pp. 1755, 1756; *American Missionary* 53 (July 1899):67–68.
68. *The Alaskan*, 18 May 1889 and 5 March 1890; Education Report 1895, p. 1746; Education Report 1900, p. 1378.
69. Bruce 1894, p. 65.

because most of them were older than the children and felt themselves to be a target of ridicule. Besides, they were much too tired in the evening after herding to learn anything. He also recommended that a regular teacher be hired. Bruce's small monograph on the Port Clarence Eskimo, published in the third reindeer report, shows an above-average understanding of the Eskimos in relation to school and herding; but his stay at the Teller Reindeer Station was unfortunately terminated under a cloud of adverse publicity resulting from his own poor judgment and Healy's antagonism in a trading venture.

To make matters worse for himself, Bruce took eleven Port Clarence Eskimos (three men, four women, and four children) and a collection of sleds, dogs, kayaks, and weapons to the United States for exhibition at the Columbian Exhibition in Chicago and various other cities. Healy wrote to Jackson on 30 July 1893: "Had I been in Port Clarence when [Bruce] left there I never would have allowed him to take those natives away, and I hope someone will be thoughtful enough to make him file a bond for their keep while away and to return them to their homes. To have the reindeer project become the father of a Dime Museum is to me a cause of mortification." [70]

At first Bruce publicized this venture as an attempt to induce the Congress to appropriate money for the reindeer industry and to familiarize the people of the United States with "these strange wards" of the government. Although Jackson had dismissed Bruce as reindeer superintendent, he was not loath to appear with him and his troupe of Eskimos before the House Committee on Agriculture on 1 March 1894 to argue for the establishment of four experimental stations in Alaska and for funds to import reindeer. "The hearing closed with a native song, in which all the Eskimos, including the babies, joined so lustily that it could be heard above on the floor of the House." [71]

70. *Alaska Herald*, 8 January 1894; letter, Healy to Jackson, Pt. Barrow, 30 July 1893, Sheldon Jackson Museum Collection.

71. Some of the antics of Bruce's troupe seemed like a carnival as he put them through their paces. "Rina [or Zaksriner, a three-year-old child adopted by Bruce] is . . . remarkably bright, obeying instantly any command of her master. Folding her hands behind her back she will bow forward and rest the top of her head upon the floor, a feat unequaled as a contortion act." They performed for two weeks at Madison Square Garden in New York, and in Washington they attracted a great deal of attention at the Bureau of Ethnology and at the Smithsonian Institution. One of the highlights of their trip was meeting Mrs. Grover Cleveland in a White House tea. Bruce left Rina and her twin sister, Artmarhoke, behind in the United States to be educated until they were sixteen years old. In 1899, when Rina was being scrutinized by anthropologists in New York City, Bruce, then in Seattle, was sent for because she was said to be dying of "the cold." There is no further record of what became of her. During the summer of 1895, Bruce had returned the rest of the Eskimos to their home, bought a lot more trade goods, and established a trading post, Fort Morton, on Kotzebue Sound; but it did not prosper, and apparently existed in name only. (Information about Bruce is taken from newspaper clippings from Sheldon Jackson scrapbooks, 4:41, 42, 44, 45, 46, 141; 24:24, 30, 35, 126; 31:138; and *Alaska Herald*, 8 January 1894; letter, Jackson to Charles Hallock, 2 March 1894, RG 75, letters sent, 8:114; Lopp to Hamilton, RG 75, letters received (received 29 November 1895); "Beth Bell," 1895.

At this time, Bruce sold a large collection of artifacts to the Field Museum of Natural History, having written Jackson in February 1893: "Do you know any one who would like to purchase

During 1893–94 the Lopps were at the reindeer station, and though Mrs. Lopp taught school principally for the herders, "a few children from the outside [availed] themselves of its opportunities," especially to learn to speak English. There were twenty pupils. [72]

In August 1894 Lopp returned to Wales and was succeeded as reindeer superintendent at Teller by William A. Kjellmann, a native of Sweden, assisted by Toleef Brevig, a native of Norway, who had accompanied a Lapp retinue from Wisconsin to the reindeer station (see following chapter). Brevig, a Lutheran minister, had charge of the school, but he had been chosen by Jackson primarily to serve as spiritual adviser to the sixteen Lapps at Teller Station and secondarily to Christianize the Eskimos. Only thirdly was he to teach in the government school. He preached every Sunday morning in the Norwegian language for the Lapps and in the afternoon in English, which he spoke fluently, for the Americans and Eskimos, who listened through an interpreter.

Brevig's earnest wish was to put the shamans out of business and to provide "decent burials" for the Eskimos. Shamanistic ceremonies were still frequent during his first year at the station. He considered above-ground burials to be "heathen," yet it was the only practical solution where the ground was frozen most of the year. Brevig also deplored the leaving of valuable personal belongings with a corpse because the best articles usually showed up later in the possession of a shaman, the only person permitted near the body, although the explanation for the disappearance of good articles and their replacement by worn-out ones was that the site had been visited by a spirit.

After Brevig's arrival, the first Christmas service was expressly for the Lapps and the Norwegians, but Eskimo families had been given a package of flour, beans, and bread the day before. The station was adorned with a Christmas birch tree, which Kjellmann had got from a place he named Birch Hill, fifteen miles southeast of present-day Marys Igloo. [73]

That year the school had a total enrollment of fifty-six, many of whom came from the nearby Eskimo village that had a population of sixty persons under twenty-one years of age. On 11 December not a pupil came to school because of all-day dancing, and in January the school closed when all of the village went to Wales for the messenger feast. Brevig said: "They learned to read in a very short time and likewise also to write. Many of them wrote a very fine hand. All concrete concepts were easy for them, but abstracts were to them a puzzle." [74]

In 1897–98 the school was closed on April first because a shortage of food sent families out on their spring food quest earlier than usual. In the fall of

---

my collection of curios? I have got an excellent lot, and want to dispose of them . . . ." (letter, dated 3 February 1893, RG 75, letters received).

72. Education Report 1896a, p. 1452.
73. Johnshoy 1944, p. 74.
74. Ibid., pp. 35–36; Education Report 1896b, p. 1426.

1897, five of the best pupils were taken on the *Bear* to Seattle where they were sent on to the Carlisle Indian School in Carlisle, Pennsylvania. In 1898 Brevig left for the States and another man was placed in charge of the buildings.[75]

In 1897–98 the site for another reindeer station was chosen on the Unalakleet River. Eaton Station, named after General John Eaton, former commissioner of education, an active Presbyterian, and Jackson's friend, was established in the fall of 1898, when a number of buildings were erected and a school was begun for the eleven children of the Laplanders who had been recruited from Europe to herd the reindeer. Since none of the children could speak English, "Their first lesson was an object lesson, and so was their third and fourth, and so have all their lessons during the whole year," said the teacher, Francis H. Gambell, a medical doctor hired for the Lapp colonists. Eskimos did not live near the station, located about eight miles up the river, but "some have expressed their desire to have their children attend, and probably will move nearer next winter, that their children may come." Eskimos did come to him from as far away as King Island and the Diomedes for medical attention.[76]

Thus, by 1898 schools in conjunction with missions had been started at Unalakleet, Golovin, Wales, and Mitletok; and directly under the Bureau of Education at Teller Reindeer Station and Eaton Station.

The reindeer station schools were established principally for the reindeer herders, and the other schools, for Eskimos. Yet some Eskimos were able to join the herders for their first English lessons. The activities of schools, missions, and reindeer herding in the decade prior to the Nome gold rush were so closely related that all three will be summarized in a résumé in the final chapter.

75. Education Report 1899, p. 1754. It was reported in Education Report 1901 that one of the pupils, Tumasock, had died in Carlisle (p. 1766). Brevig had taught at the reindeer station between 1 July 1894 and 30 June 1898 as a public school teacher, but he returned in 1900 officially as the first Norwegian Lutheran missionary in Alaska, assisted by A. Hovick (Jackson [1903], pp. 57–58). In 1900–1901, Brevig taught school in the headquarters building because the old log schoolhouse was taken to "the new mining town of Teller for the use of the public school started at that place this fall" (Eleventh Reindeer Report 1902, p. 14).

76. Education Report 1900, pp. 1377, 1378, 1405.

CHAPTER 17

The Eskimos and Domesticated Reindeer

ON HIS first voyage to the Arctic in the *Bear* in 1890, Sheldon Jackson looked at the treeless, bleak environment of the Eskimos, the isolated villages, the underground houses that were scarcely mounds in the earth, and the seeming simplicity of life that he interpreted as deprivation, and concluded that the Eskimo race was dying out. His severe cultural shock was reinforced by stories told by Captain Healy and other men of the sea about the decreasing walrus and whales and an increasing drunkenness and wastefulness among the Eskimos. Jackson's judgment was made without knowledge of the real character of Eskimo life or culture. For instance, he did not know that the decrease in whales and walrus affected but a small percentage of the people, and that all Eskimo groups had sufficient alternative sources of food. Nor did he realize that everywhere on the coast the principal mainstays were seal and fish, the oil, flesh, and skin of the seal providing a remarkably well-balanced source of food and clothing. Thus, in 1890 Eskimos were in no greater danger of extinction than generations before when faced with the same monumental forces of nature—erratic hunting seasons, broken ice, storms, early freezes, high winds, and human illnesses. The Eskimos were, in fact, gaining in population at that time. All of the teachers noticed it. Miner Bruce observed during the first year at the Teller Reindeer Station: "[The Eskimos] do not seem to be decreasing in numbers, but, on the contrary, increasing . . . and during the past year there have been in the [Port Clarence] tribes probably twenty births and but four deaths." Lopp and Thornton also noticed the increase. At Wales, "since November 30th [1892] there have been only five deaths from natural deaths and 13 births. So there would seem to be no danger of the Eskimos dying out."[1]

Jackson's solution to what he thought were deplorable poverty, degradation, and ultimate extinction was to inaugurate a new industry, reindeer

1. Third Reindeer Report 1894, p. 75; *American Missionary* 47 (October 1893):324.

herding, which he was convinced would enable the native peoples to become self-sufficient. No matter what Jackson's opponents said about him, they had to admit he was a man of action, as he had already demonstrated with the swift dispatch of teachers to the Arctic in 1890. He launched his reindeer scheme with even greater zeal, though the idea was not originally his own.

The plan of importing Siberian reindeer into Alaska had been cherished by Healy from the time he had adopted it from Charles H. Townsend, the naturalist who had conceived it during the 1885 cruise of the *Corwin* when Healy was skipper. There had, however, been a precedent for even Townsend's plan: in 1880 the Alaska Commercial Company had placed fourteen reindeer from Kamchatka on Bering Island, leased by the company from Russia.[2]

Jackson envisioned an industry far beyond one merely designed to "save" the Eskimos: it would also be the means through which they would be raised from "barbarism to civilization," and prevent their becoming wards of the government. As for the white people, it would solve the transportation problem in the Arctic and increase the population by attracting new settlers.

Lopp and Thornton, the teachers at Wales, independently came up with an idea of importing reindeer for the Eskimos' benefit, planning to ship them from Siberia in skin boats during the summer of 1891.[3] They knew nothing of Jackson's plans, probably because Healy and Jackson had not discussed the reindeer matter until they were homeward bound. Even so, Lopp, who later became an important figure in the reindeer industry, said that Jackson's plan to import reindeer may have rested on merely a quip because "Healy was a critical kidder and told Jackson [that the Eskimos] needed reindeer more than schools."[4]

Once he had decided to buy and import reindeer from Siberia, Jackson lost little time in launching plans to finance the transactions. Shortly after his return to Washington, D.C., Jackson drafted his report of the "destitute condition of the Alaskan Eskimo" and on 5 December 1890 the commissioner of education sent it to the secretary of the interior. On the same day it went to the Senate, and on 19 December Louis E. McComas introduced into the House of Representatives a joint resolution (H. R. 258) providing that the acts establishing agricultural experiment stations in connection with colleges be extended to Alaska, looking forward to purchasing of reindeer as "a part of

2. In 1893 the herd was supposed to have numbered 180 (Education Report 1895, p. 1726).
3. Letter, Lopp to Mrs. Neda Thornton, dated Seattle, 26 March 1930, Lopp Papers, University of Oregon Library; Thornton 1931, p. xvii.
4. "Notes on the Manuscript of Thornton's Book," 3 December 1930, Lopp Papers, University of Oregon Library; handwritten note from Lopp inserted in C. L. Andrews' bound reindeer reports, Andrews Collection, Sheldon Jackson College, Sitka, Alaska. In 1906 Lopp was made superintendent of the Bureau of Education in charge of reindeer in the northern (Alaska) district. In 1908 he was made chief of the Alaska Division and remained there until 1925 when, according to C. L. Andrews, political maneuvers ousted him. Lopp died on 10 April 1939 in Seattle (Andrews 1944, p. 54).

the industrial education of the proposed college."[5] That year the Congress adjourned in February without appropriating any money for the project, although on 20 February Senator Henry M. Teller had moved an amendment to H. R. bill 13462, making appropriations for "sundry civil expenses of the Government," including fifteen thousand dollars for the introduction of reindeer into Alaska.[6]

Jackson's reindeer project had considerable opposition, and his failure to receive financial support and approval was only the first of many skirmishes. A less determined or thick-skinned man would have wilted a thousand times during his affiliation with the project. His opponents said that the scheme would fail for many reasons, especially because of the excessive expense and the fact that the Chukchi could not be persuaded to sell their reindeer. They said, furthermore, that reindeer were not needed in Alaska because the Eskimos were neither starving nor dying out. But Jackson, almost as if he had forgotten the schools he had established the year before, was consumed by the thought of buying reindeer in 1891 and of placing goods for trading on the *Bear*, which was scheduled to sail north from San Francisco in April or May. By that time Jackson was a versatile lobbyist, and putting all of his skills to work, he appealed with great emotion to a sympathetic public for money.[7] He simply was not going to wait another year for congressional aid. The response to his appeals for contributions to the first reindeer fund was not as great as Jackson had hoped, yet in only a few weeks' time he had been promised $2,146, more than enough to buy barter goods for the reindeer; and when the *Bear* sailed from Port Townsend, Washington, both Jackson and the goods were aboard.[8]

Although the Congress had not cooperated with him, various government agencies furnished unlimited support. The commissioner of education authorized his combining the reindeer business with the educational program; the secretary of the treasury (under whom the Revenue Marine Service operated) put the *Bear* at his disposal to transport the deer; and the secretary of state obtained Russian approval for the purchase of reindeer on the coast of Siberia.

A memorandum accompanying the first request for the assistance of Healy and the *Bear* oversimplified what was to be a very difficult and complex business of getting reindeer from Siberia to America. The memorandum said that since Jackson's inspection of the schools of Arctic Alaska would take him near the shores of Siberia, the *Bear* could assist Jackson by purchasing from 150 to 300 head and transporting them "with their keepers over to the island of St. Lawrence [where Jackson had planned to establish a Presbyterian mission and school]. The island [is] only about 40 miles distant from the coast of

5. Education Report 1896b, p. 1438.
6. Ibid.
7. For a discussion of Jackson's lobbying for Alaska see Hinckley 1962, 1965.
8. Education Report 1894a, p. 945.

Siberia [and] it will take but a few hours after the reindeer are loaded to transport them across." The Siberian herders were then supposed to teach "the young men of Alaska the management of the animals."[9]

The pessimists and opponents of Jackson's program were almost vindicated. The reindeer were not bought and transported as easily as anticipated, and the *Bear* spent almost the entire time between the eighth and the twenty-sixth of July attempting to purchase reindeer along the Siberian coast, neglecting its primary duties of helping whalers in distress and of policing the Arctic shores for illegal traffic in liquor and breech-loading rifles. Not until 28 August—a month later—were the first reindeer purchased.[10] Only sixteen reindeer were obtained and placed on Amaknak and Unalaska islands without herders, merely, as Jackson said, "to answer the question whether reindeer could be purchased and transported alive." At the end of two years, all had died.[11]

After Jackson proved that he could buy and transport the reindeer, Lopp and Thornton abandoned their own importing plans, but suggested that one of the Wales Eskimos spend the winter with a Siberian herd to learn herding methods and to pave the way to buy more animals. Healy, whose influence was greatly felt in this project, did not approve, so the plan was abandoned. (Jackson himself said that without Healy's presence on the *Bear* in 1891, "little would have been accomplished.")[12]

Armed with the slight success of sixteen reindeer, Jackson again appealed to the Congress for funds that fall, but the various bills failed to pass the House. Nevertheless, Jackson was again aboard the *Bear* in the summer of 1892, and he bought 171 reindeer in eight separate transactions with the remainder of the 1891 funds.[13] On 4 July the first of many shipments of deer was landed at Port Clarence because it was the only sheltered port in western Alaska. Here the American flag was raised and the Teller Reindeer Station established. In that year Healy again devoted his time to the reindeer project almost to the exclusion of his regular duties. This neglect weighed heavily on Healy's conscience, skilled marine revenue officer that he was, and laid the groundwork for eventual friction between him and Jackson.

Embarking on the third year of buying reindeer, Healy wrote to Jackson, "As Congress has in two sessions refused to appropriate money for transporting domesticated reindeer from Siberia to Alaska, it would seem that the project has not the approval of the Government."[14] In this year, 1894, Healy

9. Third Reindeer Report 1894, pp. 124–25.
10. Education Report 1894a, pp. 941, 953. A typographical error in my original reindeer article gave the date as 21 August (Ray 1965).
11. Education Report 1894a, p. 948; Indian Commissioners, Board of, 1893, p. 152.
12. Letter, Lopp to Mrs. Thornton, Seattle, 26 March 1930, Lopp Papers, University of Oregon Library; Education Report 1894a, p. 946.
13. Some accounts say that 174 were purchased. Twelve deer died of injuries sustained in transit.
14. Letter, Healy to Jackson, San Francisco, 5 March 1893, RG 26, Alaska File. The first ap-

could see that the Siberian herders were reluctant to sell because their monopoly in trading reindeer skins would be broken if the Alaskan Eskimos got live deer to raise. They furthermore wanted to reserve their own reindeer to slaughter for selling skins to passing whalers, keeping the meat for their own use.[15] He was also becoming desperate about his own duties, and writing directly to the commissioner of education, said that "advantage has been taken of our long absence from our own shores by contraband traders to carry on their illicit traffic, and in my opinion it is not wise for the Department to devote so much time to reindeer to the exclusion of our legitimate Revenue Cutter duties."[16]

Other officials censured Jackson's pursuit of the reindeer industry. Governor Lyman E. Knapp said in his report for 1892: "Unfortunately for the educational interests of Alaska, during the past two years the Government day schools in the Territory, have been sadly neglected. It is a source of congratulation, therefore, that it is possible to commend the work of most of the teachers."[17]

In 1892, the first year of the Teller Reindeer Station, four Siberian herders were hired to teach the mechanics of reindeer herding to the Eskimo and the white personnel of the station. The Chukchi herders were not very satisfactory, however. They were sullen, disobedient, and temperamental. During the second year of the station, one of them killed a deer by stamping on its head.[18] Jackson had not, at this time, publicized his original intent of obtaining Laplanders as herders, but even before his first request for funds was turned down in 1891, he had written to a correspondent that "it is our intention to try to secure the services of several young married Laplanders, who would be willing and competent to take charge of the herds and teach the young Eskimos their care and management."[19] Not until the summer of 1894, however, was the first contingent of Lapp herders brought to Alaska.

Meanwhile, in 1892, the first superintendent of the Teller Reindeer Station, Miner Bruce, labored at a job for which he had no training—but then, other candidates for the position had had no experience in reindeer matters, either, and Healy himself had said, "It seems to me that it would not take much of a man to care for the business after all."[20] Bruce and Gibson, his as-

---

propriation for the purchase of reindeer is listed in all of the reports as "1894"; however, it was approved by the 53rd Congress on 3 March 1893, and Jackson reported the expenditures of the summer of 1894 as derived from the six thousand dollars allotted (Third Reindeer Report 1894, p. 21).

15. Education Report 1894a, pp. 947–48; Muir 1917, pp. 128, 215; letter, Healy to Commissioner of Education, San Francisco, 17 December 1894, RG 75, letters received.

16. Letter, Healy to Commissioner of Education, San Francisco, 17 December 1894, RG 26, Alaska File.

17. Knapp 1892, pp. 50–51.

18. W. T. Lopp diary for 1894, Lopp Papers, University of Oregon Library.

19. Letter, Jackson to Paul B. Du Chaillu, 26 January 1891, RG 75, letters sent, 3:97.

20. Letter, Healy to Jackson, San Francisco, 4 April 1892, Presbyterian Historical Society, MSJ 137.

sistant, had charge of the four Chukchi herders; four Eskimo apprentices, two from Cape Prince of Wales and two from Sinramiut on the north shore of Port Clarence; and Charley Antisarlook, who was hired at fifty dollars a year.[21] The running of the reindeer station was necessarily makeshift because instructions left by Jackson contained no more information about the caring of reindeer than Bruce or Gibson themselves knew.

Apprentices drawn to the reindeer station during the first several years were either young men interested in the comforts of a mission or those enamored by the prospects of a different kind of life. But soon even these atypical Eskimos found that hunting and fishing were more to their liking after all and they neglected their herding. Jackson's repetitious writing about "raising" the Eskimos from hunters to herders was without knowledge of the real nature of Eskimo life; and contrary to what Jackson supposed, becoming a herder was in no way felicitous, since such sedentary work was in opposition to all normal inclinations. The role of a hunter was not "lower" or less profitable than that of a herder; indeed, in an Eskimo's own culture it was "higher" and more rewarding.

When William Kjellmann, a Norwegian expert on reindeer affairs, arrived at the station in 1894, he learned that the apprentices thought of herding as a pastime rather than as an occupation and that, having herded the deer so close to the station during the two years before his arrival, the young Eskimo men looked upon the station, rather than the herd, as their "home."[22] Kjellmann said that unless a herder thought of reindeer camps as headquarters, the industry would not succeed; but he was unable to make the apprentices understand that they were to remain at a reindeer camp and "not run away from the herd every other day to see what is being done at the station." If they were to become real herders, said Kjellmann, the reindeer had to take precedence over everything else: "Living in camps and moving [is] a matter which is absolutely necessary for every reindeer herder. . . . Any person who desires to become the owner of reindeer must first become a nomad." And the Eskimos, although they lived in seasonal camps throughout the year, were not nomads.

Of the thirteen apprentices under contract that year, only three or four began to take a real interest in traveling with the herd. Kjellmann found that the least cooperative and least interested apprentices were those who had come from mission stations. Yet Jackson originally planned that the various mission stations would furnish apprentices, who would eventually take over the proposed mission herds. Kjellmann also realized that the most skillful hunters would not make the best herders, and that the best hunters would by

21. Third Reindeer Report 1894, pp. 35, 72.
22. Kjellmann's name is spelled both Kjellman and Kjellmann in various reports. The letterheads for his Madison, Wisconsin, fish business and his own signature on copies of letters in the National Archives indicate that two n's are correct. Arestad also says that Jackson misspelled Kjellmann's name by omitting one of the final n's (Arestad 1951, p. 215*n*).

choice and necessity continue to live near traditional hunting and fishing grounds, with no need for the reindeer. Furthermore, he thought that Eskimos who had been caribou hunters would make the best herders. In other words, then, reindeer herding would not suit the coastal Eskimo, or at least not the ones best adjusted to their own culture.

It was clear that the majority of Eskimos were not interested in the reindeer, but rewards of reindeer as payment for herding were made to entice them into the program. During the first few years only the very young were attracted: most were mere boys; after two years, of the seventeen apprentices, only six were over twenty and none was over thirty.[23] Some of the herders fell into their jobs because of the novelty of it, or for the free room and board offered, or because a relative lived nearby; they were not drawn by a desire to learn the reindeer business. One of these misfits was Soovawhasie from Cape Nome, who was discharged as "utterly unfit" for herding, the Eskimos themselves predicting a great future for him as a shaman; yet he was named by Jackson as co-owner, along with Antisarlook, in the official loan agreement for the first native-owned reindeer herd in Alaska.

The wages (payment in reindeer) to apprentices changed annually during the first few years, being raised and lowered at whim. The payments varied from ten reindeer to be paid at the end of two years to eighteen female and two male deer for five years' work. One of the more complicated proposals was to work for two reindeer to be paid at the end of the first year, five for the second, and ten at the end of the third and every year thereafter. This method of delayed payment, said Healy, was beyond Eskimo comprehension, and the indecisiveness on the part of those in charge of reindeer affairs indicates that they, too, were aware of the unsatisfactory payments.[24]

As if troubles with the Siberian herders and Eskimo apprentices were not enough, friction was commonplace among those in charge of the reindeer program and the schools during the first few years. Every year brought its slate of charges and countercharges of illegal trade, misconduct, and petty annoyances. Not a person escaped being either the accused or the accuser.

In 1892 Jackson wrote the Reverend M. E. Strieby of the American Missionary Association that Lopp was planning to resign because of difficulties with Thornton at Wales, and hoped that a new reindeer station could be located at Shishmaref Inlet. So at this time, without even having received a report of the station's first year's work, Jackson had already decided that Lopp was to take over a position not yet vacated. Lopp said, "Jackson refused [to let me go to Shishmaref Inlet], saying that if I would serve a year at Port Clarence with Bruce, he would then let us have a herd. He wanted me to take Gibson's position." Healy, however, had decided that both Bruce and Gib-

23. Fourth Reindeer Report 1895, p. 72.
24. Third Reindeer Report 1894, p. 89; letter, Healy to Jackson, San Francisco, 25 January 1893; RG 26, Alaska File; Sixth Reindeer Report 1897, p. 110; Ninth Reindeer Report 1900, p. 159.

son were to be fired, and Lopp was then put in charge of the station by Jackson despite the fact that when he had wanted to have a herd at Shishmaref, "Dr. Jackson informed me he couldn't trust me with a new herd."[25]

Lopp's year at the station was more or less a repetition of the station's first year: the Siberian herders were unsatisfactory, the herd had a successful fawning season, and several more apprentices from different tribes arrived at the station, creating friction among the herders—an aspect that Jackson had not anticipated. Said Lopp, "We think we can see indications of tribal jealousy arising, which in another year might result in something serious."[26]

During the summer of 1894, after Lopp had left the station to return to Wales, and William A. Kjellmann, the third superintendent, had arrived, rumors spread that the Eskimos were not going to own herds of reindeer after all. Two events substantially contributed to this belief. One was the arrival of Lapland families at the station in July 1894 with contracts stipulating that they were to have all of the reindeer they required for food and clothing. Up to that time, no Eskimo had been permitted to kill a reindeer. The other was an outright gift of 100 reindeer to the Congregational mission by the government in August 1894 when Lopp returned to Wales, in accordance with Jackson's plan to supply missions with deer. Lopp took 118 reindeer, including eighteen that belonged to the Wales herder.[27]

The hiring of Kjellmann and the Laplanders was speedily accomplished after the Teller herd had survived its first winter in Alaska. This convinced Jackson that the reindeer scheme was a resounding success, but he was equally convinced that it would continue to thrive only if the herds were taken care of by Laplanders. He advertised for Lapp herders who lived in the United States; but not finding any that he thought were suitable, he sent Kjellmann, who had been living in Madison, Wisconsin, to Lapland to hire herders with one thousand dollars obtained from private donors.[28] After long and difficult negotiations, Kjellmann persuaded six families and a bachelor to return with him to Alaska on a three-year contract.[29] The Eskimos thronged to the ship anchored in Port Clarence to watch them disembark, and seeing the Lapps' peaked caps and boots with turned-up toes, one of them exclaimed, "Well, well! these are the people we have seen on our playing cards for all these years."[30]

25. Letter, Jackson to M. E. Strieby, 31 December 1892, RG 75, letters sent, 5:240–41; "Notes for Mrs. Neda S. Thornton 3-21-33," Lopp Papers, University of Oregon Library; "Notes on the Manuscript of Thornton's Book," 3 December 1930, Lopp Papers, University of Oregon Library.
26. Fourth Reindeer Report 1895, p. 72.
27. Fifteenth Reindeer Report 1906, p. 14. Some of the tables give 119, as in the Fifth Reindeer Report 1896, p. 15.
28. Third Reindeer Report 1894, p. 17.
29. Names of the families are given in the Fifth Reindeer Report 1896, p. 47.
30. Ibid., p. 99.

The presence of the Lapps created a few changes at the station and the nearby Eskimo village of Sinramiut. First of all, the Eskimos adopted skis and the Lapp fur shoes, which continued to be made by Eskimo seamstresses for many years as "Lapp boots." Its sole and toe curved upward, the tip of the boot originally equipped with a hook to keep the foot in the ski. The square Lapp hats with four peaks were worn for a while, but soon went out of style. Other innovations adopted by the Eskimos were the Lapp method of tanning leather and skins, and Lapp fishing tackle.

During the year Kjellmann scouted for new pasturage and herding locations. Prior to his coming, the grazing of reindeer within only a three-mile radius of the station had destroyed all of the lichen cover. He traveled as far away as Golovnin Bay, but did not visit the new herd at Wales under Lopp's care. In 1894–95 this station had five Eskimo herders, ages fourteen to nineteen, and one Siberian herder, all of whom had been at Teller with Lopp the year before.

Discontent among the Eskimo herders had developed before the Laplanders arrived and the Congregational mission received a herd. Lopp had advised Jackson at the beginning of his one-year stay at the station in 1893 that "it would be a good plan to give or loan Charley [Antisarlook] and three or four more herders about 20 deer each, so that they could put them together and have a herd of about 75 or 100 deer. . . . I think it important to do something like this next year. One real example of a man like Charley at the head of a herd of deer would do much towards educating the people up to the advantages of becoming deermen."[31]

Thus, after the Wales mission had received a free herd, and the Lapps had arrived to look after the animals originally destined for the Eskimos, Jackson decided to loan 100 reindeer to Antisarlook. Jackson, reporting the loan, said that "the Eskimo have been so little accustomed to assistance from the whites that they have been somewhat skeptical concerning their being permitted to ultimately own the reindeer. As evidence of good faith [Charley and several apprentices were loaned a herd.]"[32] Despite hundreds of press releases and reports written by Jackson, and his verbal promises to the Eskimos that his original reason for importing reindeer was to keep them from starving, few Eskimos, even apprentices, had reindeer meat in their diet, and were not to have for many years to come. Rations at the station did not include meat for herders and apprentices, though it did for the Lapps, and Eskimos were reprimanded and made to pay fines of furs whenever they killed an animal for their own use. The weekly ration for an Eskimo herder during 1894–95 consisted of white man's food, fish, and seal oil, but no reindeer meat.

This attitude took on an even more incredible turn when, in 1897, five years after the first reindeer were landed at Port Clarence, Jackson urged

31. Letter, Lopp to Jackson, Teller Reindeer Station, 2 September 1893, in Third Reindeer Report 1894, p. 135.
32. Fifth Reindeer Report 1896, p. 15.

Captain Francis Tuttle of the *Bear* to arrest some Eskimos who had killed reindeer, to "put them in irons, and keep them awhile on board, giving them as much of a scare as it is possible. We must do something to cause them to leave the reindeer alone: if the first offenses are punished it will deter others from interfering with the reindeer."[33]

Antisarlook was chosen to receive the first reindeer herd because he was the most mature Eskimo around the station, was a willing worker, was eager to cooperate, and could speak English. When employed as a herder he had preferred to work for cash, and though offered a gift of fifteen reindeer for working another year at the station, he elected to undertake the risks involved in Lopp's suggested loan of 100 deer, which would ultimately, with luck, result in his private herd. In January 1895 Charley chose 115 reindeer from the Teller herd, fifteen of which already belonged to him and his brothers as apprenticeship payment. On 5 September 1894 Antisarlook signed the agreement with his brothers, Iziksic, Koktowak, Iuppuk, and Soovawhasie. The deer were to be delivered on 1 January 1895, and after five years Antisarlook was to return 100 head of reindeer, seventy-five of them females, to the government. No bearing female was to be killed during the five-year period.[34] Antisarlook had almost sole control of his herd, although his training had been sketchy. A Laplander helped him only in moving his reindeer to the Sinuk River and at fawning time in April. After locating his herd at Sinuk, however, he often neglected it to go seal hunting and fishing. When he and two brothers died in the measles and pneumonia epidemic of 1900, Mary, his wife, inherited the herd.[35]

Dividing the reindeer into small herds was an example of the ignorance under which the industry struggled during the first few years, since it is now accepted that the most efficient and profitable herds do not number less than one thousand or more than thirty-five hundred reindeer.[36] After reindeer were taken from Teller to Wales in 1894, only 389 reindeer were left in the government herd. On 4 January 1895, thirty-seven days before Antisarlook chose his deer, there were 379; by 1 April the number had been reduced to 260.[37]

During 1894 the personnel of the Teller Reindeer Station expanded considerably. Besides Kjellmann, new personnel consisted of T. L. Brevig as schoolteacher; Jens C. Widstead, Kjellmann's brother-in-law, as assistant superintendent; and Thorvald K. Kjellmann, Kjellmann's father, as mechanic. The principal difficulty during the year was antagonism between the Laplanders and the Eskimo apprentices. The Eskimos apparently had

33. Ibid., p. 72; letter, Jackson to Tuttle, 22 April 1897, RG 75, letters sent, 16:393.
34. Fourth Reindeer Report 1895, p. 84.
35. Mary Antisarlook Andrewuk died in Unalakleet on 22 November 1948.
36. Lantis 1950, p. 42. Jackson himself mentioned that even the Chukchi recognized the value of large herds: "Families own from 1,000 to 10,000 deer. These are divided into herds of from 1,000 to 1,500" (Education Report 1893, p. 1293).
37. Fifth Reindeer Report 1896, p. 55.

been led to believe that they were superior to the Lapps in reindeer matters and that the Lapps had no reason to be in Alaska in the first place. These attitudes were partly attributable to Healy's views on the reindeer industry and the Eskimo. The commissioner of education said in 1896: "I am afraid that Mr. Lopp was prejudiced last year by something that Captain Healy told him in regard to the Laplanders. Captain Healy could endure the natives well enough but he could not endure immigrants."[38]

Kjellmann worked at reconciliation all year and toward the end was able to say that "the relations very rapidly improved. . . . The apprentices, at least most of them, have long since discovered their inferiority and seen how much they have to learn from these people. We have now reached a point where no apprentice undertakes to do anything before he has consulted one of the Lapps, so far as the languages make it possible."[39]

Unfortunately, disagreement between Healy and Kjellmann resulted in Kjellmann's resignation in 1895, although his official reason for leaving was his wife's health. Kjellmann's place as superintendent was taken by Widstead, but his lack of experience, and eventual friction with Brevig, reduced his efficiency and productivity.[40] When Kjellmann returned as superintendent in the summer of 1896 (Healy was no longer on the *Bear*, having been court-martialed earlier that year), there were 1,175 reindeer in Alaska. Although this was near the lowest efficient number for a herd, the deer were divided into four herds—Antisarlook's, with 218 reindeer; the Wales herd with 168; a new herd at Golovnin Bay, 130; and the main Teller herd.[41]

Before Jackson gave 100 reindeer to the Congregational mission in 1894, he had also written the "Swedish Church" at Golovnin Bay, the Roman Catholic mission on the Yukon River, and the Presbyterian on Saint Lawrence Island that he planned to loan them the same number; yet the total reindeer in Alaska at that time—the winter of 1893–94—was only 221.[42] Eventually, Jackson hoped to supply reindeer to every mission station in the tundra country of Alaska. A third herd was not separated from the main one, however, until January 1896, when 130 reindeer (thirty of them belonging to Eskimo apprentices) were sent to Golovnin Bay for the Swedish Covenant and the Episcopalian missions. Although the latter was at Anvik on the Yukon, only fifty were given to each because there were not enough to fulfill the original promise of 100. This loan created dissatisfaction, especially in

38. Letter, W. T. Harris to Rev. C. J. Ryder, 14 May 1896, RG 75, letters sent, 14:18.

39. Fifth Reindeer Report 1896, p. 65.

40. Letter, Widstead to Hamilton, Madison, Wisconsin, 17 September 1896, RG 75, letters received; Widstead to Hamilton, Madison, 18 December 1896, ibid.

41. Sixth Reindeer Report 1897, pp. 13, 53, 57. In a letter from Jackson to Harris, dated Unalaska, 19 September 1896, Jackson said that the number of domesticated reindeer in Alaska was 1,091 on 1 July (RG 75, letters received).

42. Third Reindeer Report 1894, pp. 18, 31; *The American Missionary*, 1894, p. 186; Board of Indian Commissioners, *Proceedings*, 1893, p. 144.

view of the gift of 100 to the Wales mission.[43] In answer to the complaints, Jackson wrote the Reverend D. Nyvall of the Covenant Mission early in 1897: "With regard to the number of reindeer given at the time the distribution was made by Mr. Hamilton, there was an epidemic in the herd and under the circumstances it was thought unsafe to send more than fifty away. So that Mr. Hultberg has no reason to be dissatisfied. The Government was under no obligation to let him have any particular number, if any at all, but as a matter of favor spared him all [possible]."[44]

The idea of introducing reindeer had taken place in a highly charged, emotional atmosphere, and undoubtedly its original purpose was to benefit the Eskimos; but faced with the problems of raising money to buy the animals, Jackson added another hard-cash purpose for doing so: industrial development of the country. Publicly, at least, it appears that Jackson was not completely honest in his original plan of devoting all of the reindeer to the Eskimo, because even before he had purchased the sixteen expendable reindeer in 1891 he had sent a letter to the president of the Tacoma, Washington, Chamber of Commerce, urging his support of the pending congressional appropriations. In the entire letter there is not a whisper that the reindeer were being bought for the Eskimo. Instead, Jackson said, "the introduction of domesticated reindeer from Siberia into Alaska . . . will build up a new industry and greatly add to the commerce of the Puget Sound ports as well as to that of the whole Pacific coast."[45]

Once the program was underway, Jackson held no steadfast course toward the goal as originally conceived, that is, for the exclusive interests of the Eskimo people. In 1895, in the fifth reindeer report, Jackson was thinking not of food for the Eskimos but of food for the vast non-Eskimo world, "tons of delicious ham and tongues. . . . Surely the creation of an industry worth from $83,000,000 to $100,000,000, where none now exists, is worth the attention of the American people."[46] As gold continued to be found in various parts of Alaska toward the end of the nineteenth century, Jackson bent his ideas to keep pace with the changing country in regard to the white people.

Another indication of Jackson's indecision as to who would eventually benefit from the reindeer was his intention of bringing a large contingent of Laplanders to Alaska after the contracts of the original group of 1894 expired. In 1897 Jackson said that "the pressing need of the hour is more reindeer and more Lapps," and that the Laplander will "teach us and our Eskimos their method of transportation . . . to get to the valuable gold fields in the mountains and streams."[47]

Jackson had been corresponding actively with Kjellmann about a proposed

43. Sixth Reindeer Report 1897, pp. 103, 105–7.
44. Letter, Jackson to Nyvall, 2 April 1897, RG 75, letters sent, 16:253–54.
45. Letter, Jackson to President, Chamber of Commerce, Tacoma, Wash., dated Washington, D.C., 29 January 1891, RG 75, letters sent, 3:122.
46. Fifth Reindeer Report 1896, pp. 16–17.
47. Seventh Reindeer Report 1898a, pp. 17, 50.

colony of Laplanders to be brought to Alaska. Kjellmann said that "the first colony [of Lapps] should consist of about fifteen families, together with some youths; in all, about fifty persons. A school must be established, and other socially binding institutions. The colony must be formed with the greatest prudence and foresight, that there may be no conflicting powers within the colony."[48]

Subsequently, Kjellmann was sent to procure the colonists, leaving Dr. A. N. Kittilsen, a physician, in charge of the Teller Reindeer Station. After Kjellmann's return, a new official station, Eaton Station, was located on the Unalakleet River.[49]

The Lapp herders of 1894 had been paid in cash and board and room, not reindeer; but when Kjellmann got to Norway to gather up families for the second contingent, he found that they would not consent to go to Alaska unless they were paid in reindeer. A total of 113 Laplanders, Finlanders, and Norwegians, which contained sixty-three herders, arrived in 1898, when there were only 2,062 reindeer in Alaska.[50] Had they been paid even a reasonable number of reindeer each year, all, except those already owned by Eskimos, would quickly have fallen into their hands. The majority of the immigrants, however, returned home or went to the gold fields shortly thereafter.

One of the most ludicrous aspects of this immigration was the accompanying shipment of 538 reindeer steers to feed the "suffering miners of the Yukon," a situation that developed after Kjellmann was commissioned to hire the Lapland herders. When news had come from the upper Yukon that men were starving, the first effort by the United States government to come to their aid was to borrow back Charley Antisarlook's 100 reindeer loaned him in 1895, almost three years short of the time he should have returned them according to his contract.[51] He was left with only a few deer during an especially hard winter, but, ironically, even the remaining few were "borrowed" to feed the "starving whalers" at Point Barrow later in the year.

After Antisarlook's deer were driven to Saint Michael in the fall of 1897, destined for the starving miners, it was decided that a thousand-mile trip to the upper Yukon was out of the question, so the Congress was prevailed upon to authorize two hundred thousand dollars for the purpose of importing the Laplanders and their reindeer, and to send Jackson to Lapland to meet Kjellmann.[52] The importation was widely ridiculed in the press (for ex-

48. Sixth Reindeer Report 1897, p. 118.

49. Jackson said that "the reindeer station has not been moved but another station has been established at Unalaklik . . ." (letter, Jackson to C. B. Kittredge, 6 January 1899, RG 75, letters sent, 21:263–64).

50. Tenth Reindeer Report 1901, p. 12; Education Report 1899, p. 1776; Eighth Reindeer Report 1898b, p. 39. There were 78 Lapps, 25 Norwegians, and 10 Finns.

51. Letter, Jackson to the Secretary of the Interior, 15 November 1897, RG 75, letters sent, 18:65–68.

52. Eighth Reindeer Report 1898b, p. 32.

ample, "Dr. Jackson's Wild West Show Arrives in New York") from beginning to end, especially after it was learned that almost half a year had passed from the time the first alarm went out from the Yukon to the actual arrival of the animals in the mountains. Worst of all, there had been no need for the reindeer, as the miners had gotten along very well on local food—which was very fortunate indeed, since on 6 May 1898, when the deer finally arrived near their destination, only 228 out of the original 539 were alive.[53]

During the same fall, reports came of another crisis, this time involving "starving whalers." The crews of several whaling ships, which had been caught in the northern ice pack, were living in the refuge station at Point Barrow. Jackson again turned to reindeer as the solution and borrowed all of Lopp's animals at Wales and all of those remaining to Antisarlook. The "starving" whalers had actually been well supplied with food from their own ships' stores and Eskimo hunters, who sold them caribou and other wild game.[54] But in December Jackson had persuaded the Treasury Department to send the *Bear* as far north as possible into the Bering Sea where Lieutenants D. H. Jarvis and E. P. Bertholf and Surgeon S. J. Call could begin their overland journeys to the north. From Nelson Island at the edge of the ice pack, Bertholf set out with dogs and sleds loaded with food supplies, and Jarvis and Call, to borrow the reindeer.

Jarvis found the task of asking Antisarlook for his herd disagreeable.

> I had looked forward to this day [19 January] so long that now it had come I almost shrank from the task it brought. . . . He and his wife were old friends, and I knew I would receive a hearty welcome, but how to induce them to give up their deer and convince them that the Government would return an equal number at some future time, was quite another matter. These deer were their absolute property. The Government had only a few weeks before taken from Artisarlook [*sic*] the original number it had loaned to him because of his good service and character, and had left him the increase, which were now his. . . . He and the people gathered about him, were dependent upon the herd for food and clothing.
> I explained to him carefully and particularly what the deer were wanted for. . . . He and his wife, Mary, held a long and solemn consultation, and finally explained their position. They were sorry for the white men at Point Barrow, and they were glad to be able to help them; they would let me have their deer, which represented their all, on my promise of return, if I would be directly responsible for them. . . . I readily agreed to this. . . . They were poor except for the deer herd, which was all they had to depend upon.[55]

At that time, there were only 1,466 reindeer in Alaska, but 448, or almost one-third of them, were taken to save whalers, not Eskimos. Only 382 of the

53. Ibid., p. 43. The headline appeared in the *Morning Oregonian*, 1 March 1898. An account of the drive is given in Arestad 1951, translated from an article in Norwegian by the leader, Hedley E. Redmyer.

54. Eighth Reindeer Report 1898b, p. 29: "During the latter part of November . . . the natives were able to procure for the use of the community 12,604 pounds of deer meat [caribou], 8,692 pounds of fish, and 2,506 pounds of wild fowl." Only 180 reindeer were killed for food.

55. *Report of the Cruise of the U.S. Revenue Cutter Bear and the Overland Expedition* . . . 1899, pp. 50–51.

combined herds of Lopp's and Antisarlook's reindeer reached Point Barrow, having traveled about seven hundred miles from Cape Prince of Wales (or eight hundred miles from Cape Rodney) between 19 January and 29 March. Because there had been ample food, only 180 reindeer were killed for the 130 whalers, the rest of the animals being reserved to start herds at Point Barrow and Point Hope.[56]

56. Ibid., pp. 84, 86; Eighth Reindeer Report 1898b, p. 29. Antisarlook was repaid.

By 1900 Jackson was openly advocating non-native ownership of reindeer, and was negotiating with at least two persons interested in investing money in private herds. In 1902 the Russian government stopped the exports of domesticated reindeer, and a small shipment of 30 concluded the importations into Alaska, bringing the official total to 1,280 reindeer, although the yearly purchases added up to a bigger total. In 1902 there were 5,148 reindeer in Alaska, or approximately 1 reindeer for every 2½ Eskimos, which had cost the government $133,000. In 1903 there were 6,505 reindeer in eleven herds at nine stations. Over the years 500 reindeer had been loaned to five Laplanders, but none to Eskimos after Antisarlook's loan. Only 25 Eskimos were serving a five-year apprenticeship more than ten years after the first reindeer were landed at Port Clarence (letter, Jackson to Brynteson, 6 February 1900, RG 75, letters sent, 25:76; letter, Jackson to William Bergstrom, 28 March 1900, RG 75, letters sent, 25:352–53; Twelfth Reindeer Report 1903, pp. 11, 19, 52; Thirteenth Reindeer Report 1904, p. 17).

At one time there were about 600,000 reindeer in Alaska (Lantis 1950, p. 33). In the 1930s, legislation put ownership of reindeer back into the hands of the Eskimos after a white corporation had purchased reindeer in 1914. The industry declined tremendously during the 1940s. In 1964 there were only 38,000 reindeer in 16 herds, and in 1971 there were 27,399. The largest herd was the Kakaruk herd of Teller with 4,878 reindeer using a range of 1,300 square miles (Bureau of Indian Affairs, 1971, p. 4).

"Group of Kiñugumut [Wales people] from Port Clarence," about 1881. (From Nelson 1899, pl. 1)

Houses on Little Diomede Island, about 1928

A woman from Little Diomede Island, about 1902

CHAPTER 18

Bering Strait Culture, 1867–98

Intertribal Relations, Settlements, and Subsistence

From the beginning to the end of this period, intertribal relations and tribal movements remained stable with the exception of the Malemiut, who moved ever farther afield. Warfare had ceased, although folk takes about raids and conflicts were still very common.

Demographic patterns, too, were stable, but population was increasing toward the end of the century. Kauwerak was the only large village that was abandoned during this period, apparently some time after Jacobsen's visit in 1882. Contributing to its abandonment was the movement of caribou herds southward and eastward. The Eskimos continued, however, to cling to a native diet, even at Saint Michael, where they bought a few staples like sugar, flour, molasses, tea, and tobacco from the store, and which the people farther north got from trading ships.

Up to the very end of the nineteenth century, most Eskimos lived in their traditional wood and turf houses, but a number of aboveground houses had been built here and there, especially in Saint Michael. Three were built in Wales alone in 1896.[1] The criticism leveled at the white man's "drafty" houses seems out of line in view of the drawbacks of the underground houses, which, the early observers unanimously agreed, were dark, freezing at floor level, stuffy, smoky, and contributed to universal respiratory disorders, chronic coughing, and eye diseases.

By 1898 in Saint Michael the caches set up on posts were disappearing, and with the coming of large numbers of white men, they had to be locked, or the goods moved to the safety of Eskimo dwellings.[2]

1. *The Eskimo Bulletin* 3 (July 1897).
2. Ray, ed. 1966, p. 51. Information about the Saint Michael area is also found throughout Nelson's *The Eskimo about Bering Strait*, and most of the information corroborates statements made herein.

CLOTHING AND ART

The Eskimos used a great deal of cotton material in their clothing during this period, and were buying an odd assortment of new garments. At Port Clarence in 1887, Herbert L. Aldrich reported that one woman had a "regular dress" and a pair of corsets, which she later threw away as "no good." Cotton material was especially sought for parkas to be worn over fur garments, but cloth was popular for all purposes. In 1882 at Ignituk, cloth made up 80 percent of the European goods distributed at a feast for the dead. These included twenty pieces of cloth, twenty yards of colored cotton material, twenty cotton shirts, and twenty underpants. (Non-native goods made up one-seventh of all gifts.) [3]

By 1898 almost everyone wore cloth breeches and trousers, and some shirts, and it was immaterial to the wearers that their clothes were made from mattress ticking or cloth bags imprinted with "Dried Peaches" or "Finest Sperry's Flour." [4] Cotton clothes usually went unlaundered and eventually became stiff with grease. At various places a few persons had begun to use soap for cotton garments and personal cleanliness, but lice were still thick in their fur clothes and hair. Hats and caps were covering more heads than ever before, but even the Eskimos at Saint Michael clung to their gutskin parkas and grass socks in their boots.

The gold seekers who swarmed through Saint Michael in 1897 demanded such large quantities of native fur clothing that the trading companies imported deerskins and other furs from the United States for the Eskimo seamstresses. An Eskimo trader returning from Saint Michael to Wales in 1898 reported that skin clothing was bringing fabulous prices, and H. M. W. Edmonds said that the high prices had induced the Eskimos to part with their best clothes despite the fact that some of the Eskimos still dressed in a "very dandified manner in fine furs." [5]

Tattooing was still popular, but some of the girls in the Port Clarence area were not marked in 1887 because the Eskimos who had sailed on ships reported that this was not the style in San Francisco. Men also began to discard their labrets; very few young men wore them in 1887 at Port Clarence, but in 1893 a Wales man had made some new ones from Dr. Driggs' glass bottle stoppers. (At the same time, a woman had a new pair of earrings made of safety pins.) Turquoise-colored trade beads were said to be worn in 1887 as amulets. [6] This may explain why various dolls and figurines used by shamans have eyes made of these costly beads.

The curio business was flourishing by the early 1880s. The King Islanders had heard of Edward Nelson's collecting, and made objects especially to trade to him. One of the most popular souvenir items at both Port Clarence

3. Jacobsen 1884, pp. 263–64.
4. Aldrich 1889, p. 64; *The Eskimo Bulletin*, March 1893 and June 1895; Ray 1966, pp. 34, 36.
5. The above information is from *The Eskimo Bulletin*, July 1898; Ray 1966, pp. 34–35, 39, 66.
6. The above information is from Aldrich 1889, pp. 69, 166; *The Eskimo Bulletin*, March 1893.

and Saint Michael was the ivory pipe, either carved with multiple figurines in imitation of their old carvings or engraved with graphic scenes as on their earlier drill bows.[7]

Edmonds said, "Everyone [in Saint Michael] attempts to make a curio, but few are very good artists. Those that are, are so skillful that they may live off the proceeds of their workmanship and are often very rapid as well as artistic. A few cuts of an etching tool will often, in not more than a couple of seconds, mark out the figure of an animal on ivory." Masks, which formerly were held very sacred, and often destroyed after a ceremony, were copied and sold to the relic hunters in the 1890s.[8]

HOUSEHOLD UTENSILS, WEAPONS, AND TRANSPORTATION

The Eskimos preferred metal utensils for cooking, but wooden dishes for serving and eating. (At Port Clarence in 1879, Nordenskiöld also found Eskimos using coconut shells brought from the tropics by traders.)[9] Metal tools were used almost exclusively for work in ivory and wood, but ivory tools for fur and sewing.

Guns had supplanted all other weapons for land hunting; steel traps were almost universally used, though native snares for smaller animals like squirrels and ptarmigan were still preferred. The harpoon and other native implements for catching sea mammals had not yet been replaced by those of foreign manufacture.

The umiak and the kayak were used as much as ever, but the umiak had been provided with oars and a steering oar. Miners' abandoned wooden boats on the Yukon River were appropriated by Eskimos, and by the mid-1890s at Saint Michael a few enterprising Eskimos were building schooners for trading and fishing. The first skis were introduced to the Saint Michael area by the J. Henry Turner party in 1890 and by the Laplanders at Port Clarence in 1894.

In 1882, although seal oil lamps were still widely used in the underground houses, Jacobsen observed that most of the lamps at the Ignituk men's house were made from old frying pans. In 1879 matches were used only occasionally, but by 1898 they had supplanted the bow drill and flint and tinder.[10]

PATHOLOGY

H. M. W. Edmonds, who was a medical doctor, said, "Sickness is very common among these people [around Norton Sound] and as a consequence there used to be many doctors."[11] In the 1890s, because of better observers, like Edmonds, and a steadier firsthand contact with Eskimos, there was greater opportunity to observe health conditions. Among the older people,

7. Aldrich 1889, p. 75; Hoffman 1897; Nordenskiöld 1882, p. 577; Ray 1969.
8. Ray 1966, pp. 83, 84.
9. Nordenskiöld 1882, p. 574.
10. Jacobsen 1884, p. 262; Nordenskiöld 1882, p. 756; Ray 1966, p. 53.
11. Ray 1966, pp. 29–31.

lung trouble was a common cause of death, but among the general population, pneumonia was first. Bronchitis was also widespread. Rheumatism, skin troubles of all kinds—ulcers, eczema—and syphilis were prevalent. Eye troubles, common among those living in the native houses, included conjunctivitis, corneal affections, and opacities, according to Edmonds. He said that even with a difficult birth, a woman rarely called a physician (there were several in Saint Michael by 1898), and there seemed to be growing difficulties in confinements. "Humpbacks, victims of hip disease, undeveloped lower jaws, and ill shaped bodies are frequent," but the crippled and abnormally formed babies were quickly disposed of. Infanticide was still very common.

At Wales the teachers also reported the prevalence of pneumonia and bronchitis. In October and November 1890, twenty-six persons died of pneumonia, but there were only four deaths the rest of the year. The teachers attributed the pneumonia to exposure during a storm as they were preparing to move into their semisubterranean homes for the winter.[12]

In October 1894 at Oowoodlawok, north of Wales, four Eskimos died of pneumonia, which was thought by the Eskimos to have been caused "by having hewn drift wood too soon after netting a white whale." In the fall of 1897, eleven persons from King Island died in "an epidemic" and in two weeks' time in the spring of 1898 fifteen Wales Eskimos died of an "epidemic form of bronchitus [*sic*]." Fourteen died of "grip" in Unalakleet in 1897–98.

Accidental deaths contributed to a high mortality rate. Between 1881 and 1891, sixteen men were carried off on floating ice at Wales and never seen again; in 1891, three were carried off, but rescued.[13]

From observations beginning from the time of Cook, one point cannot be overlooked: before any large numbers of white men had come to the area the Eskimos were unresistant to respiratory diseases, which with the probable exception of accidents, thus constituted the most common cause of death. The causes for the highest mortality then were essentially the same as in the 1970s.

THE ESKIMO AND THE WHITE MAN

The teachers at Wales deliberately made changes in cultural mannerisms, although the Eskimos had unconsciously borrowed from whalers, traders, and members of the various expeditions for some time all along the coast. At Port Clarence in 1867 the telegraph men said that the Eskimos were sometimes seen sitting on a chair with their feet propped on the table in good American style. At Wales the teachers taught the Eskimos how to shake hands and campaigned against the wearing of labrets and wolf tails. The teachers also gently derided a facial gesture like a snarl or a sneer that ac-

12. *The American Missionary* 45 (October 1891):360, 361; *The Eskimo Bulletin*, June 1895 and July 1898.
13. *The American Missionary* 45 (1891):368.

companied the saying of the word meaning no (pronounced "no-may") and saw it disappear.

In the 1890s the school pupils sang American songs and hymns (to the accompaniment of an organ at Wales), and in the Saint Michael area they had learned to play the accordion and to sing many popular melodies and dance western dances. The custom of nude dancing by women was "falling out of custom near white settlements."

As early as 1890, the Wales teachers planned to have the Eskimos go into the business of making curios to send out to the States—sealskin thong hammocks, boots and gun covers for sportsmen, deerskin sacks for invalids—and of salting ducks for ships. The teachers were also going to act as an employment agency to get jobs for Eskimos on ships. But none of these ambitious plans materialized. During the school year 1892–93 the teachers taught knitting and planned to build a wash house for the community, which would also serve as a workshop, study, and gymnasium.[14]

From 1884 on, whalers employed many Eskimo men and women as cabin boys (an Eskimo surname at Nome was Cabinboy), harpooners, hunters, and seamstresses. Henry Elliott said that whalers had taken Eskimos to Hawaii beginning in 1865,[15] and after the steam whaling ships came to Port Clarence in 1884, a handful of Eskimo men had an opportunity to see San Francisco.

Some of the Eskimo women willingly became sailors' lovers or wives of the officers, especially when the ship wintered over at Herschel Island. Many an Eskimo woman hoped for a permanent place in her "husband's" affections when he promised to return later to take her to the "States," which he rarely did. A few names of whaling men still survive among the Alaskan Eskimos, and in the Port Clarence area several Eskimos acknowledge their parentage from the steam whaling days. By 1898 Edmonds said that the part-blooded Eskimos outnumbered those considered to be full-blooded at Saint Michael.

Eskimo villages became havens for deserters from ships. In Wales the teachers had to take care of three deserters in 1890. In that same year the teachers said they had heard of only two or three instances of prostitution of local natives by ships' sailors and officers, the reputation of the Wales people (after the Gilley affair) keeping ships "away somewhat."

Polygyny was still common in the entire area, but the first marriage between Eskimos, performed by a preacher, took place at Wales on 30 September 1894. Netaxite and Kungik presented two white fox skins to T. L. Brevig of Port Clarence as a fee. The second marriage, at Port Clarence, united Tautook, one of the herders, and Nazooka on 29 February 1895.[16]

Begging was so widespread that travelers tried not to stay in a village very

14. The above information is from *The American Missionary* 45 (October 1891):366–67, and 47 (October 1893):323, 325; Ray 1966, pp. 85, 86; Thornton 1931, pp. 32, 35.

15. Elliott 1886, p. 247.

16. *The American Missionary* 45 (October 1891):360, 361, 365; *The Eskimo Bulletin*, June 1895; Johnshoy 1944, p. 94.

long because of it. Jacobsen, Edmonds, and Nelson all spoke about the continuing persistence in begging, which was found wherever the Eskimo had had a great deal of contact with whites. Furthermore, Edmonds said that by 1898 thievery by "bad Eskimos" had become quite common around Saint Michael.[17]

DISCUSSION: PRELUDE TO THE TWENTIETH CENTURY

Until the 1890s the Bering Strait area was a pioneering country of white males—explorers, traders, scientists, and adventurers—in a native population, and until the establishing of missions and schools there were few white women or families. Only in 1897 did women come in any numbers to the booming Klondike port of Saint Michael. Unlike the pattern of settlement in the western continental United States, the white men at Bering Strait did not create their own towns or homesteads in Indian country, but became inhabitants of Eskimo villages. Even Saint Michael, the only permanent "white" town before Nome, was but a short distance from an Eskimo settlement. If a man were single, he usually married an Eskimo woman and reared a family. If a married man, he and his family remained an island of whiteness in the Eskimo community. Until the gold rushes, no white woman went alone to this area unless attached to a mission or school.

Two important differences stand out in the changes of the 1890s. One was the directed change of schools, missions, and reindeer herding. The other was the sudden incursion of many non-natives during the gold rushes into Saint Michael and Nome, each area receiving from ten to twelve times the population of the entire Bering Strait in the space of a year. During the twentieth century this centralized the population in urban centers at the expense of the smaller villages, which, however, continued in existence into the 1970s.

For many years non-native material culture was interwoven with the native in a rather well-balanced way. Tools and many other European-type goods were so well stabilized by the latter part of the nineteenth century that they were little different from those elsewhere in the western world. But Eskimo acquaintance with law enforcement, education, reindeer herding, and the Christian religion were comparatively recent, and were just beginning to find an integrated place in Eskimo life by the time of the gold rush.

The sphere of law was considerably different from the other three in that it had become an amalgam of both American and Eskimo law by the turn of the century, a situation that did not endure beyond the gold rush and the extension of mining and land laws to the Bering Strait area. Until the Klondike rush and the establishment of a military encampment at Saint Michael in 1897, the only evidence of law and the sovereignty of the United States north of the Aleutians was the annual journey of a single revenue cutter during the three months of summer. At the most, it stopped only once or twice at a vil-

---

17. Jacobsen 1884, pp. 230, 277; Nelson 1899, p. 295; Ray 1966, p. 72.

lage so that the prevailing law continued to be Eskimo law, which was so clearly seen in the punishment decreed at Wales for the murderers of H. R. Thornton in 1893. Until Thornton's death, Eskimo-European conflicts were solely with men of exploring expeditions in a territory over which no firm sovereignty of any nation had been established. By the 1890s, as schools, reindeer herds, missions, and many white men arrived to occupy the lands permanently, the subject of law and punishment for crimes other than the selling of liquor and contraband firearms became extremely important.

It was tacitly understood that in the case of murders among their own people the Eskimos could mete out punishment under traditional law, which was usually banishment from the village or killing of the murderer by the elders. But in offenses against the white man, it was difficult to bring the offender to justice. Captain Healy, for example, was constantly faced with the problem of what to do with Eskimos who had broken an American law in a place where jails and magistrates were a thousand miles away. When Thornton once asked Healy to arrest a father and son who had shot at him, Healy said that if Thornton would make an affidavit that he had been shot at, he would arrest them and take them to Sitka; Thornton and his witnesses, however, would also have had to go along, requiring an absence of possibly one or two years away from home. In this case, Thornton decided not to make the affidavit, but asked Healy to arrest them, nevertheless.

"Captain Healy asked where he should take them," reported Sheldon Jackson. "He could not leave them on the coast to starve. If he did so he would be tried for kidnapping. He could not take them to San Francisco, for there was no one to meet the expenses." [18]

The subsequent murder of Thornton by three young Eskimo men illustrated both the impotency of American patrols and the effectiveness of native law at this time. The relationships between white men and Eskimos hinged on personal ethics and Eskimo codes rather than on American enforcement. In Wales the leading men were confident of their superiority over the white men and appeared to stand in awe only of the revenue cutter, especially when Captain Healy shot his twenty-pound howitzer over the water to show the power of the ship. [19]

The morning after the murder, the Eskimos took Mrs. Thornton to the Teller Reindeer Station because the *Bear* was at Point Barrow. When the *Bear* returned the following week, not a person walked about the village or came out to the ship. The next morning two officers found Thornton lying in the house, and a note from Mrs. Thornton telling of her whereabouts. The *Bear* then went to the reindeer station for her and Mr. Lopp to close up the

---

18. Board of Indian Commissioners, *Proceedings*, 1893, p. 90. Jackson said in a letter that the natives were so hostile to Thornton that he heard the Eskimos ask Healy to take him away, and Jackson himself asked Thornton not to remain that winter at the Cape (Jackson to Strieby, 4 October 1893, RG 75, letters sent, 6:331–32).

19. *The American Missionary* 45 (October 1891):358–59.

buildings; but the Eskimos, who had come out of hiding by that time, would not go aboard because they had heard the rumor that Healy was going to kill everyone in the village. This, of course, was an extension of what action might be taken under native law, but it also arose from the complications of communication. Despite three years of schooling, Eskimos used English so rarely that the man who most likely would have taken Mrs. Thornton to Port Clarence had to remain in Wales because he was "the only one who could talk English" to Captain Healy.[20]

When Healy went ashore he turned the rumors to good advantage and told the Eskimos that the teachers had asked him to spare them because they had already avenged Thornton's death by killing the murderers. If they had not, wrote Mary Healy, who often accompanied her husband, "he said he would have done so, and would not have left a single one of their people alive, and that he would have followed them north and south, over mountains and sea until everyone of them was killed or afraid to say they were of Cape Prince of Wales."[21]

Healy had capitulated, at least figuratively, to the Eskimo form of justice when it came to dealing with the murder of a white man; but at the same time, he tried to enforce a concept of American law by appointing native "policemen" at the schools, ostensibly to monitor school attendance but, according to Lopp, actually "to take care of drunken natives." At Wales, Healy appointed ten policemen, and at the Teller Reindeer Station, four. Kjellmann discharged the four at Teller in 1894, saying that they were not needed to protect the station personnel, although Thornton had been murdered at Wales only the year before. Furthermore, the policemen had been uncertain as to what constituted their duties. At one time they were asked to track down two deserters from an American whaling ship, but could not understand why. At another, a "policeman" knew what kind of justice was required when a neighbor robbed him—he killed him.[22]

Healy's arbitrariness in matters of justice had also been evident earlier in the disposition of the case in which two Eskimos were killed during the winter of 1883–84 at the Omilak mine near Golovin (Chapter 15). Immediately following the incident Healy called it justifiable homicide "for breaking, entering, and robbing the company's storehouse because the Eskimos had been considered desperados by their own people."[23] But eight years later (before Thornton's murder, however) Healy, apparently angry at

20. Letter, Lopp to Mrs. Thornton, Seattle, 13 March 1935, Lopp papers, University of Oregon Library.
21. Third Reindeer Report 1894, p. 139.
22. Fifth Reindeer Report 1896, pp. 84–85; Education Report 1894a, p. 941; Lopp diary, December 1892, p. 391. Er-a-hĕ-na, as chief of police at Wales, received a uniform cap and three sacks of flour. His assistant, Kitmeesuk, two sacks and a uniform cap. The other eight, Tiongmok, Ootiktok, Teredloona, Kalawhak, Weahona, Wĕakīseok, Kartayak, and Maana, each got a uniform cap and one sack of flour.
23. Healy 1889, p. 9.

John Green's insistence on having the revenue cutter help in his private affairs, said that the Eskimos were murdered deliberately and that the mine's employees had "invaded the homes of the Indians and violated their marital relations. The Indians expostulated with them whereas these law abiding men of whom Mr. Green speaks angered by the suggestion that the Indian had any right they were required to respect, took 12 rifles, loaded six, distributed the twelve among their number, selected two prominent Indians, and cowardly murdered them."[24] (One Eskimo tradition gives a third explanation that they were murdered because they complained about the white man taking their land, but this appears to be a tale that grew out of the Alaskan Indian land claims discussions of the 1960s, and was not an issue at the time. Thus, we do not know exactly why the Eskimos were killed.)

Unlike law enforcement, which was a gradual working out of both native and non-native solutions, education, reindeer herding, and Christianity entered their lives rather suddenly. In reindeer herding the Eskimos dealt with an animal similar to the caribou, but the methods of management and utilization were quite foreign. The reindeer industry soon became marked by divisiveness stemming from distrust, broken promises, and friction created by various circumstances ranging from using the old enemies of the Eskimos, the Chukchi, as herders, and putting together jealous men of different tribes, to discord among the whites responsible for the program.

Generally, the decade of teaching was wasted, and the most that can be said about the success of an alien educational system was that the Eskimo children (and some adults) had made an attempt to speak the English language; had become acquainted with English symbols and materials; and had been permitted to indulge in their fondness for drawing. But progress was slow, not only because the teachers seemed to have little time to devote to their pupils but because the Eskimo way of life itself was an impediment, especially when the family left the main village for seasonal camps in the fall and the spring, and often took time out for winter ceremonials. The observance of certain taboos also kept attendance down. School sessions were further curtailed at Wales and at the reindeer station by personal problems of the teachers and the emphasis on reindeer business rather than education, and at Unalakleet and Golovin by the importance placed on religion.

The biggest hurdle that faced all the teachers from the very beginning was the inability to communicate with their pupils, a problem that had not been resolved by the end of the century. Each school year most of the pupils had to relearn English because Eskimo was spoken at home in the winter and in camp during the summer. Before going to their posts in the North, the teachers had not been taught the Eskimo language or a method of learning it efficiently. At Golovin and Unalakleet, moreover, the first teachers could

24. Letter, Healy to Secretary of the Treasury, dated Sausalito, Calif., 21 January 1892, RG 26, U.S. National Archives.

scarcely speak English. Some Eskimos had learned an English trade jargon on board ship, and quite a few at Saint Michael spoke English well enough to act as fairly good interpreters.

If the teachers' enrollment and attendance records are correct, the educational program reached a much larger percentage of the population than did the reindeer program, despite Sheldon Jackson's pursuit of his reindeer plans at the expense of education. The reindeer industry was unsuccessful in the early years mainly because the Eskimos did not like to be restricted to a life completely dependent on one activity or source of food. They wanted variety. Attending school was a restriction of a sort, but the schoolroom was warm, and though unfamiliar discipline was brought to bear, the pupils learned that the teachers were considerably permissive in both their conduct in the schoolroom and in adapting school sessions to the yearly round of activities. In spite of the poor showing at the beginning, schools and education were becoming a positive force in Eskimo culture by the turn of the century.

The turbulence in Wales that led to Thornton's death and to the suspension of school for a year contrasted to the more ostensibly peaceful behavior at Golovin and Unalakleet, but even there the missionaries said that there were no converts during the early years. Toward the end of the decade, however, there was a surge of interest in Christianity, brought about mainly by the conversion of several young Eskimo men who learned to speak English and who acted first as interpreters and later as preachers.

The Eskimos accepted the new religion for many reasons, among them, a new-found freedom from fear both in the present and after death. The unknown became more tolerable through a knowledge of Christ, and Christian teachings permitted them to set aside fear of their own shamans and the many mysteries of the universe. At places like Unalakleet and Golovin, and later, Teller, where the new religion was totally fundamental, Christianity was adopted with considerable frustration on the part of many because they could not reconcile giving up many cherished activities like dancing, mask-making, festival giving, and even card playing, drinking, and smoking, which they had already learned from the whites. Yet in a strangely ambivalent manner the church services and assemblies provided by the missionaries fulfilled some of the original functions of their earlier gatherings.

A positive factor in the acceptance of the new religion was the constant breaking of taboos by the white man without retribution from the spirits, although this refusal to comply with taboos in the very early days may also have made the Eskimos reluctant to act as guides. Those Eskimos who became "Christians" did not observe many of the taboos, and some of the younger women began to sew during the prohibited time after beluga and whale hunting. But it seemed that having given up the old taboos, they merely took on new ones. Yet their acceptance of the sacrifices and abstinences required for rewards in Christianity was because their own religion was based on prohibitions, particularly in connection with subsistence activities. Many actions were curtailed altogether during whale or caribou hunting season. In the case of salvation through Christ, however, abstinence took on a unique aspect. The various taboos and practices connected with food getting, the weather, and personal safety in the traditional culture were geared to the well being of the entire community. In Christianity, they were designated for the individual, and the idea of a personal commitment to a being that marked every sparrow's fall was highly attractive to the individualistic and independent Eskimo, whose own wishes had usually been submerged traditionally to that of the group.

The shamans' own actions belied the effectiveness of their own cures. They soon began to obtain their medicine from the teachers along with the ordinary people. A few villagers began to believe that Christ was more effective than a shaman, and according to Lopp, "many of the people believe in [the shaman] only when it is convenient."[25] Eskimos turned to admire Christ's miraculous powers that seemed even greater than their own shamans' trips to the moon or recovery from seemingly mortal wounds. For the most part, Jesus was thought of as a super shaman who had performed far more superlative feats and had effected far greater cures than their own shamans. Moreover, he offered them a peaceful life in eternity based on how they lived rather than on how they died, as in their own religion.

Although the specter of hell with its threatened punishments was always present, it was preferable to famine or death in the present life, which could occur because of a broken taboo or rule under the old religion. Thus, at least one burden was lifted from the Eskimo conscience—his actions under Christianity could not be blamed for the catastrophes of the present; yet he could, with his own will, make a place for himself in an afterlife of peace and beauty.

We come now to 1898. During the next two years more than thirty thousand persons—at least seven times its population—would overrun Seward Peninsula. From the reconstruction of this history it is apparent that on the eve of the gold rush the Eskimos were so far acculturated to the western life style that their own culture can no longer be discussed mainly in terms of traditional content, but in terms of adaptation and acceptance of large parts of American culture. The popular notion that Eskimos lived in an aboriginal condition at the end of the nineteenth century, awaiting their first foreign ideas, is far from accurate. Even at the first meetings with Europeans their material culture already contained European objects. Economic adjustments that had been developing since the 1780s had interpenetrated all aspects of their life, including intertribal affairs, and had prepared the foundation for changes during the twentieth century. The direction taken in this respect was a matter of degree, not kind.

25. *The American Missionary* 46 (December 1892):388, 390, 391; 47 (October 1893):323, 324; *The Eskimo Bulletin*, July 1897; Jacobsen 1884, p. 277.

The meeting of the Eskimos with the outside world was, up to the time of the gold rush, a gradual and obviously satisfactory one. From the first knowledge in Siberia that people lived in a land to the east to the beginning of the twentieth century 250 years later, it is apparent that most of the changes were adopted voluntarily, the Eskimos having exercised their own choices in trade, liquor, law enforcement, reindeer herding, religion, and even in education at its beginning. The voluntary sexual liaisons were an extension of their own cultural behavior, and the kinship system was so constructed that children born of such unions were easily absorbed into the system or put to death. Liquor, like tobacco before it, was used not only as a stimulant but as a palliative for the numerous cultural restrictions imposed on their behavior, and then, in a never-ending circle, as justification for the feelings and actions thereby released. A point that must not be overlooked is that the Eskimo drank excessively from the first sip of liquor, which was at a time in history when he felt no stress from a "clash" of cultures. He drank because he liked what it did to him. From the time liquor was first obtained—at Kotzebue Sound and at the Bering Strait—there would be no white man living permanently in the area for forty years, and no permanent "white" settlement would be established for almost fifty.

Toward the end of the nineteenth century the Eskimos were increasing in population. Warfare had stopped—the white man's presence had ended intertribal wars—and the mere appearance of the revenue cutter with its awesome potentialities was enough to considerably dampen even the thought of vengeance killings and the blood feud. No longer did inhabitants of a village live in fear of raids—or complete annihilation, as the folk tales often related—and they could travel wherever they wished without danger of being killed. By this time the white man had made no great demands. He was a trader of goods that were desired and needed, and he brought himself, as an individual. With the exception of a few tons of galena ore near Golovin he had taken little from the land. He had purchased furs, but the Eskimos considered themselves well paid in return. Whales and walrus were taken from the sea, but at the Bering Strait it affected surplus commodities more than subsistence.

Very little has been written about the reception of the white man as a permanent resident of Eskimo territory, but in most cases he was looked upon as a welcome addition to the community. The Eskimo woman welcomed him as a mate, and the Eskimo man, as a producing member. (Antagonism developed only when the newcomers were obviously spongers.) When a white man remained, he became a member of the Eskimo community. If he married an Eskimo woman, his children were looked upon as Eskimo; and though he usually did not learn the language, he often preferred to adopt Eskimo values and way of life. Even the few teachers and missionaries with their own families at the widely separated villages were residents of Eskimo communities. There were no Indian reservations to dramatize a difference in race or culture. Life resolved culturally and genetically to the Eskimo. This was the character of Bering Strait culture as the twentieth century approached, and to which many would nostalgically look back as a meeting of the best of two worlds.

Appendix

In the following list of informants the names appearing in Group I are those of persons with whom I have worked somewhat extensively, whereas those in Group II are the persons whom I have interviewed more briefly. Where possible, I have given the date of birth, or an approximation, and the date of death if the person is no longer living. The dates in parentheses following the names indicate the years during which I conducted my interviews.

Group I

Anawrok, Mrs. Nannie (Deliluk), b. 1892, Egg Island; d. 1968 (1964)

Atchak, Benjamin Gladstone, b. 1898, Golsovia; d. 1969 (1964, 1968)

Atchak, Mrs. Benjamin (Mattie Joe), b. 1901, Hooper Bay (1968)

Charles, Mischa, b. 1896, Mountain Village; d. 1973 (1964)

Charles, Mrs. Mischa (Louisa Kotongan), b. 1896, Cape Darby (1964)

Degnan, Mrs. Frank (Ada Ryan), b. 1910, Unalakleet (1964, 1968)

Fagerstrom, John, b. 1902, Golovin (1968)

Fagerstrom, Mrs. John (Minnie Curran), b. 1902, Okpiktulik (1964, 1968)

Gonangan, Myles, b. 1896, Unalakleet; d. 1967 (1964)

Gonangan, Mrs. Myles (Marion Nashalook), b. 1891, Unalakleet; d. 1971 (1964)

Johnson, Alexander (Alec), b. 1890, Andreafski; d. 1969 (1968)

Johnsson, Mrs. Eric (Margaret Johnson), b. 1897, Unalakleet (1964–68)

Kakaruk, John E., b. 1906, d. 1965 (1964)

Kakaruk, Mrs. John E. (Ruth Noonesaluk), b. 1905 (1964)

Katchatag, Mrs. Thora (Thora Ekootak), b. 1893, Unalakleet (1964, 1968)

Kazingnuk, Michael, b. ca. 1890, Big Diomede Island; d. 1966 (1961)

Kotongan, John, b. 1898, Norton Sound (1968)

Kotongan, Mrs. John (Hazel Mullock), b. 1908, Unalakleet(?) (1968)

Kotongan, Mrs. Elmer (Ruth Asicksik), b. 1927 (1968)

Mayokok, Robert, b. 1903, Wales (1961, 1964, 1968, and in intervening years in Seattle)

Miyomic, Alec, b. 1874(?), Klikitaruk; d. 1968(?) (1964)
Moses, James Kivetoruk, b. 1902, near Cape Espenberg (1964, 1968)
Moses, Mrs. James (Bessie Ahgupuk), b. 1907, Shishmaref (1964, 1968)
Nanouk, Peter, b. 1904, Unalakleet (1968)
Nanouk, Mrs. Peter (Martha Isaac), b. 1909, Unalakleet (1964, 1968)
Omelak, Mrs. Rosie, b. 1903, Herschel Island (1961)
Oquilluk, William, b. 1896, Point Hope of Kauwerak parents; d. 1972 (1961)
Pikonganna, Aloysius, b. 1909, Sinuk River of King Island parents (1961)
Punguk, Edwin, b. 1892 or 1893, Fish River (1968)
Sagoonik, Simon, b. 1877, Cape Nome; d. 1967 (1964)
Savok, John, b. 1880, d. 1965 (1961)
Savok, Mrs. John (Lily Ekak), b. 1893, Buckland River (1961, 1968)
Sockpealuk, Silas, b. 1920, Shaktoolik (1968)
Sockpealuk, Mrs. Silas (Lucy Sookiayak), b. 1930, Shaktoolik (1968)
Soxie, Mrs. Harry (Carrie Deliluk), b. 1891, d. 1964 (1964)
Toshavik, Shafter, b. 1882, Stebbins; d. 1973 (1968)
Willoya, Mrs. Mike (Emma Haggerty), b. 1900, Port Clarence (1961, 1964, 1968)

Group II

Ailak, Sam (1961)
Amahsuk, Rita (1961)
Anungazuk, Toby, b. 1916, Wales (1968)
Brown, Tom, Sr., b. 1913, Solomon (1968)
Degnan, Frances (1968)
Degnan, Frank, b. 1901, Saint Michael (1964)
Foster, Mrs. Maggie (1964)
Horen, Topsy (1961)
Jackson, Mrs. June Jorgenson (1960s, Seattle)
Kakaruk, David, b. 1898 (1964)
Karmun, Daniel (1964)
Katexac, Bernard, b. 1924, King Island (1968)
Kenick, Jacob, b. 1886, Golovnin Bay (1968)
Kugzruk, Mrs. Ahvrena, b. 1879, Wales (1964)
Moses, Mrs. Maude, b. 1894(?), Cape Darby (1968)
Moto, Taylor, b. 1910 (1964)
Nagozruk, Arthur, Sr., b. 1890, Wales (1968)
Nagozruk, Mrs. Arthur, Sr., (Lucy) (1968)
Nakarak, Mrs. Andrew (Ida Takak) (1968)
Natungok, Mrs. Dora, b. 1905, Wales(?) (1968)
Olson, Martin, Sr., b. 1927, White Mountain (1968)
Ootenna, George, b. ca. 1876, Wales; d. 1971 (1968)
Paniptchuk, Reuben, b. 1889, Egg Island (1968)

Paniptchuk, Mrs. Reuben (Catherine Anasukak), b. 1898, Buckland River (1968)

Ramsey, Mrs. Mabel, b. 1893(?), d. 1969 (1968)

Sarran, Eugene (1964)

Seelkoke, Buster, b. 1912, Wales (1968)

Seetot, Elmer, b. 1915, Teller Mission (1964)

Soosuk, Lars, b. 1921, Unalakleet (1968)

Takak, Carl, b. 1891, Shaktoolik; d. 1968 (1968)

Takak, Mrs. Carl (Agnes Deliluk), b. 1897, Unalakleet (1968)

Tiulana, Paul, b. 1919, King Island (1961)

Tokeinna, Mrs. Katie, b. 1904, Wales (1968)

Weyapuk, Mrs. Carrie, b. 1914, Wales (1968)

I am also grateful for the help of Bert Bell, Floyd Singyke, Nellie David, who are now dead, and Sammy Mogg, in supplying village names and other information before I began my research on settlement patterns. Nellie, whose own Eskimo name was Kauwerak, gave me my first lessons in speaking the Kauwerak Eskimo dialect.

References Used

(The following publications do not constitute an exhaustive listing of works on the Bering Strait area between 1650 and 1898, but are those used for this study or are directly related to important topics.)

Adams, George R.
  1865–67   Diaries, dated 26 September 1865 to 23 March 1866; and 1 October 1866 to 8 October 1867. E. S. Hubbell Collection, University of Washington library.
Alaska History Research Project
  1936–38   "Documents Relative to the History of Alaska." University of Alaska. 15 manuscript vols. (The University of Alaska Library has all 15 vols.; the Library of Congress has vols. 1–11, 14, and 15, and has vols. 12 and 13 on order.)
Aldrich, Herbert L.
  1889   *Arctic Alaska and Siberia; or Eight Months with the Arctic Whalemen.* Chicago and New York: Rand, McNally.
Allen, Henry T.
  1887   *Report of an Expedition to the Copper, Tananá, and Koyukuk Rivers . . . in the year 1885.* Washington, D.C.
Almquist, L. Arden
  1962   *Covenant Missions in Alaska.* Chicago: Covenant Press.
The American Missionary
  1890–1901 Vols. 44 through 55, with the exception of vol. 52 (1898). The American Missionary Association. (Information about the Wales area is in the form of reports written by W. T. Lopp or H. Thornton.)
Andrews, C. L.
  1938   *The Story of Alaska.* Caldwell, Idaho: Caxton Printers.
  1944   "Wm. T. Lopp." *Alaska Life* 7 (no. 8):49–54.
  n.d.   Manuscript notebooks, Sheldon Jackson College, Sitka, Alaska.
Antropova, V. V., and V. G. Kuznetsova
  1964   "The Chukchi." In Levin and Potapov, eds. 1964, pp. 799–835 (based on data from G. I. Mel'nikov).

Archiv für Wissenschaftliche Kunde von Russland. See Erman, A.

Arestad, Sverre
    1951   "Reindeer in Alaska." *The Pacific Northwest Quarterly* 42 (no. 3):211–23 (translation and editing of an account by Hedley E. Redmyer printed in *Skandinaven*).

Baikaloff, Anatole V.
    1950   "Notes on the Origin of the Name, 'Siberia.'" *The Slavonic and East European Review* 29 (no. 72):287–89.

Bailey, George W.
    1880   *Report upon Alaska and Its People; the Cruise of the Richard Rush in 1879.* Washington, D.C.: U.S. Government Printing Office.

Bailey, Thomas A.
    1934   "Why the United States Purchased Alaska." *The Pacific Historical Review* 3 (no. 1):39–49.

Bancroft, Hubert Howe
    1885   *History of California*, vol. 2: *1801–1824*. San Francisco.
    1886   *History of Alaska 1730–1885.* New York: Antiquarian Press (1959 reprint of original edition).

Banks, N. P.
    1868   *Treaty with Russia.* 40C:2s, HR Report no. 37 (serial 1357).

Beaglehole, J. C., ed.
    1967   *The Journals of Captain James Cook on his Voyages of Discovery*, vol. 3: *The Voyage of the Resolution and Discovery, 1776–1780.* Cambridge: Published for the Hakluyt Society, Cambridge University Press.

Bear. See United States Treasury Department 1899.

Beechey, Frederick W.
    1831   *Narrative of a Voyage to the Pacific and Beering's Strait.* London: 2 vols. Henry Colburn and Richard Bentley.

"Bell, Beth"
    1895   "Alaska and the Alaskans." *The Northwest Magazine* (St. Paul) 8 (no. 9):19.

Belov, M. I.
    1956   *Arkticheskoe moreplavanie s drevneishikh vremen do serediny XIX veka* [Arctic voyages from the earliest times to the middle of the twentieth century]. Istoriia otkrytiia i osvoeniia severnogo morskogo puti, vol. 1. Moscow.

Berkh, Vasilii N.
    1823a   *Khronologicheskaia istoriia otkrytiia Aleutskikh ostrovov* [Chronological history of the discovery of the Aleutian Islands]. St. Petersburg.
    1823b   *Khronologischeskaia istoriia vsiekh puteshestvii v severnyia poliarnyia strany* [Chronological history of all voyages to the Arctic], vol. 2. St. Petersburg.
    1938   "The Chronological History of the Discovery of the Aleutian Islands." Works Progress Administration, manuscript (translation, by Dimitri Krenov, of 1823a).

Bernardi, Suzanne R.
    1912   "Whaling with Eskimos of Cape Prince of Wales." *The Courier Journal* (Louisville, Ky.), 20 October, pp. 1, 2.

Black, David
1970 "Saint Herman of Alaska." *Alaska* 36 (no. 11):14–15, 55.
Blake, H. L.
1900 *History of the Discovery of Gold at Cape Nome.* 56C:1s, Sen. Doc. 441 (serial 3878).
Blashke, E. L.
1848 "Neskolko zemechanie o plavanii v baidarkakh i o Lisevskikh Aleutakh" [Some notes about sailing in baidarkas and about the Fox Island Aleuts]. *Morskoi sbornik* 1:115–24.
Blomkvist, E. E.
1951 "Risunki I. G. Voznesenskogo" [Drawings of I. G. Voznesenskii]. *Sbornik Muzeia Antropologii i Etnografii*, vol. 13, pp. 230–303. Moscow and Leningrad: Akademia Nauk SSSR.
1972 "A Russian Scientific Expedition to California and Alaska, 1839–1849." Translated by Basil Dmytryshyn and E. A. P. Crownhart-Vaughan. *Oregon Historical Quarterly* 73 (no. 2):101–70.
Board of Indian Commissioners. *See* Indian Commissioners, Board of
Bockstoce, John R.
1973a "Aspects of the Archaeology of Cape Nome, Alaska." Ph.D. dissertation, Oxford University, England.
1973b "A Prehistoric Population Change in the Bering Strait Region." *Polar Record* 16 (no. 105):793–803.
Bogojavlensky, Sergei
1969 "Imaangmiut Eskimo Careers: Skinboats in Bering Strait." Ph.D. dissertation, Harvard University.
Bogojavlensky, Sergei, and Robert W. Fuller
1973 "Polar Bears, Walrus Hides, and Social Solidarity." *The Alaska Journal* 3 (no. 2):66–76.
Bogoras, Vladimir G.
1904–9 *The Chukchee.* Memoirs of the American Museum of Natural History, vol. 11, pt. 1: *Material Culture* (1904); vol. 11, pt. 2: *Religion* (1907); vol. 11, pt. 3: *Social Organization* (1909).
Brevig, T. L. *See* J. Walter Johnshoy
Bronshtein, Y., and N. Shnakenburg
1941 "Zapiski Doctora K. Merka—uchastnika ekspeditsii Billingsa-Sarycheva, v 1785–1792 gg" [Notes of Dr. K. Merck, participant in the expedition of Billings-Sarychev, from 1785 to 1792]. *Sovietskaia arktika*, no. 4, pp. 76–88.
Brooks, Alfred H., George B. Richardson, Arthur J. Collier, and Walter C. Mendenhall
1901 *Reconnaissances in the Cape Nome and Norton Bay Regions, Alaska, in 1900.* Washington, D.C.: U.S. Geological Survey.
Brooks, Jerome E.
1937 *Tobacco: Its History Illustrated by the Books, Manuscripts, and Engravings in the Library of George Arents, Jr.*, vol. 1: *1507–1615.* New York: Rosenbach.
1938 *Tobacco: Its History Illustrated by the Books, Manuscripts, and Engravings in*

the Library of George Arents, Jr., vol. 2: *1615–1698*. New York: Rosen-bach.

Brower, Helen. *See* Masterson, James R., and Helen Brower.

Bruce, Miner
  1894   "Report of Miner Bruce, Teller Reindeer Station, June 30, 1893." *Report on Introduction of Domesticated Reindeer into Alaska*, pp. 25–121. U.S. Bureau of Education, whole no. 215. Washington, D.C.: U.S. Government Printing Office.

Bulkley, Charles L.
  1865–67   "Journal, Russo-American Telegraph Expedition, 1865–1867." Man-uscript journal, original at the Portland Library Association (Oregon); microfilm at the University of Washington library.

Burch, Ernest S., Jr.
  1970   "The Eskimo Trading Partnership in North Alaska: A Study in 'Bal-anced Reciprocity.'" *Anthropological Papers of the University of Alaska* 15 (no. 1):49–80.
  1971   "The Nonempirical Environment of the Arctic Alaskan Eskimos." *Southwestern Journal of Anthropology* 27 (no. 2):148–65.
  1974   "Eskimo Warfare in Northwest Alaska." *Anthropological Papers of the University of Alaska* 16 (no. 2):1–14.

Burch, Ernest S., Jr., and Thomas C. Correll
  1972   "Alliance and Conflict: Inter-Regional Relations in North Alaska." In *Alliance in Eskimo Society*, edited by Lee Guemple. Proceedings of the American Ethnological Society, 1971, Supplement, pp. 17–39.

Bureau of Education Reports. *See* Education Reports

Bureau of Indian Affairs, Juneau area office
  1971   *Report, Annual Land Operations* (mimeographed).

Burney, James
  1819   *A Chronological History of North-Eastern Voyages of Discovery; and of the early eastern navigations of the Russians.* London.

Bush, Richard J.
  1872   *Reindeer, Dogs, and Snow-shoes: A Journal of Siberian Travel and Ex-plorations Made in the Years 1865, 1866, and 1867.* London: Sampson Low, Son, and Marston.

Cammack, Irvin C.
  1899   "Report of Superintendent of Mission Work." Official minutes, California Yearly Meeting of Friends Church, pp. 35–39. Whittier, Calif.

Campbell, John M., ed.
  1962   *Prehistoric Cultural Relations between the Arctic and Temperate Zones of North America.* Arctic Institute of North America Technical Paper no. 11.

Carlson, Leland H.
  1946   "The Discovery of Gold at Nome, Alaska." *The Pacific Historical Review* 15 (no. 3):259–78 (reprinted in Sherwood, ed. 1967, pp. 353–80).
  1947a   "The First Mining Season at Nome, Alaska—1899." *The Pacific Histori-cal Review* 16:163–75.

1947b   "Nome: From Mining Camp to Civilized Community." *Pacific Northwest Quarterly* 16:233–42.

1951   *An Alaskan Gold Mine: The Story of No. 9 Above.* Evanston, Ill.: Northwestern University Press.

Castle, N. H.

1912   "A Short History of Council and Cheenik." *The Alaska Pioneer* (Nome, Alaska) 1 (no. 1):8–14.

Chapman, John W.

1948   *A Camp on the Yukon.* Cornwall-on-Hudson, N.Y.: Idlewild Press.

Chard, Chester S.

1967   "Arctic Anthropology in America," in Gruber 1967, pp. 77–106.

Chernenko, M. B.

1957   "Puteshestviia po chukotskoi zemle i plavanie na Aliasku kazachego sotnika Ivana Kobeleva v 1779 i 1789–1791 gg. [Travels to the land of the Chukchi and voyage to Alaska by the Cossack sotnik (leader of a hundred men) Ivan Kobelev in 1779 and 1789–1791]." *Letopis severa* 2:121–41.

[Chimmo, William] (published anonymously)

1860   *Euryalus; Tales of the Sea, a Few Leaves from the Diary of a Midshipman.* London: J. D. Potter.

Choris, Ludovik

1822   *Voyage pittoresque autour du monde.* Paris.

Clark, M.

1902   *Roadhouse Tales; or Nome in 1900.* Girard, Kan.: Appeal Publishing Co.

Cochrane, John Dundas

1824   *Narrative of a Pedestrian Journey through Russia and Siberian Tartary . . . 1820, 1821, 1822, and 1823.* London: John Murray.

Cohen, Felix

1966   *Federal Indian Law.* New York: Association on American Indian Affairs (reprint of original edition, 1958, published by the U.S. Government Printing Office).

Collier, Arthur J. *See* Brooks, Alfred H., et al.

Collins, Henry B.

1937   *Archeology of St. Lawrence Island, Alaska.* Smithsonian Miscellaneous Collections 96 (no. 1). Washington, D.C.: Smithsonian Institution.

Collinson, Richard

1889   *Journal of H. M. S.* Enterprise *on the Expedition in Search of Sir John Franklin's Ships by Behring Strait, 1850–55.* Edited by Major-General T. B. Collinson. London: Sampson Low, Marston, Searle, and Rivington.

Cook, James, and James King

1784   *A Voyage to the Pacific Ocean*, vols. 2 and 3. London: W. and A. Strahan. (Vol. 2 was written by Cook, vol. 3 by King.)

Correll, Thomas C. *See* Burch, Ernest S., Jr., and Thomas C. Correll

Coxe, William

1787   *Account of the Russian Discoveries between Asia and America.* 3rd ed. London.

Curtin, Walter R.

1938   *Yukon Voyage.* Caldwell, Ida.: Caxton Printers.

Curtis, Edward S.
1930   *The North American Indian*, vol. 20. Cambridge, Mass.: The University Press.

Dall, William H.
1870   *Alaska and Its Resources*. Boston: Lee and Shepard.
1873–98   Scrapbooks of newspaper clippings, 29 vols. Smithsonian Institution Libraries.
1877   "On the Distribution and Nomenclature of the Native Tribes of Alaska and the Adjacent Territory." In *Tribes of the Extreme Northwest*. Contributions to North American Ethnology 1:1–40. Washington, D.C.
1881   "Notes on Alaska and the vicinity of Bering Strait." *The American Journal of Science* 21 (whole no. 121, 3rd ser.):104–11.

Dey, Robert L.
1898   "Diary of a trip to Kotzebue Sound, Alaska, per Bark Alaska, B. Cogan, Captain, April 28, 1898." Manuscript diary, collection of E. B. Joiner, Kotzebue, Alaska.

Divin, V. A.
1971   *Russkie moreplavaniia na Tikhom Okeane v XVIII veke* [Russian sea voyages to the Pacific Ocean in the eighteenth century]. Moscow: "Mysl."

Dumond, D. E.
1965   "On Eskaleutian Linguistics, Archaeology, and Prehistory." *American Anthropologist* 67 (no. 5, pt. 1):1231–57.
1969   "Prehistoric Cultural Contacts in Southwestern Alaska." *Science* 166:1108–15. Rejoinders by Jean S. Aigner, William S. Laughlin, Robert F. Black, and Dumond in *Science* 171 (1971):87–90.

Edmonds, H. M. W. *See* Dorothy Jean Ray, ed. 1966

Education Reports (usually submitted under the name of Sheldon Jackson)
1888   "Report of the General Agent of Education in Alaska." In *Report of the Commissioner of Education* [hereafter cited as *RCE*] *for 1886–87*, pp. 101–11. Washington, D.C.: U.S. Government Printing Office.
1889   "Alaska." In *RCE for 1887–88*, pp. 181–94. Washington, D.C.: U.S. Government Printing Office.
1891   "Report of the General Agent of Education for Alaska." *RCE for 1888–89* 2:753–64. Washington, D.C.: U.S. Government Printing Office.
1893   "Education in Alaska." In *RCE for 1889–90* 2 (whole no. 199):1245–1300. Washington, D.C.: U.S. Government Printing Office.
1894a   "Report on Education in Alaska." In *RCE for 1890–91* 2 (whole no. 208):923–60. Washington, D.C.: U.S. Government Printing Office.
1894b   "Report on Education in Alaska." In *RCE for 1891–92* 2 (whole no. 212):873–92. Washington, D.C.: U.S. Government Printing Office.
1895   "Report on Educational Affairs in Alaska." In *RCE for 1892–93* 2 (whole no. 218):1705–48. Washington, D.C.: U.S. Government Printing Office.
1896a   "Report on Education in Alaska." In *RCE for 1893–94* 2 (whole no. 222):1451–92. Washington, D.C.: U.S. Government Printing Office.
1896b   "Report on Education in Alaska." In *RCE for 1894–95* 2 (whole no. 227):1425–55. Washington, D.C.: U.S. Government Printing Office.

1897 "Report on Education in Alaska." In *RCE for 1895–96* 2 (whole no. 234):1435–68. Washington, D.C.: U.S. Government Printing Office.

1898 "Report on Education in Alaska." In *RCE for 1896–97* 2 (whole no. 239):1601–46. Washington, D.C.: U.S. Government Printing Office.

1899 "Report on Education in Alaska." In *RCE for 1897–98* 2 (whole no. 258):1753–71. Washington, D.C.: U.S. Government Printing Office.

1900 "Report on Education in Alaska." In *RCE for 1898–99* 2 (whole no. 261):1373–1402. Washington, D.C.: U.S. Government Printing Office.

1901 "Report on Education in Alaska." In *RCE for 1899–1900* 2:1733–62. Washington, D.C.: U.S. Government Printing Office.

1902 "Report on Education in Alaska." In *RCE for 1900–1901* 2 (whole no. 288):1459–80. Washington, D.C.: U.S. Government Printing Office.

1903 "Report on Education in Alaska." In *Annual Reports of the Department of the Interior for the Fiscal Year ended 30 June 1902*, vol. 2: *Report of the Commissioner of Education* 2:1229–56. Washington, D.C.: U.S. Government Printing Office.

Efimov, Aleksei V.

1948 *Iz istorii russkikh ekspeditsii na Tikhom Okeane . . .* [From the history of Russian expeditions to the Pacific Ocean . . .]. Moscow.

1949 *Iz istorii velikikh russkikh geograficheskikh otkrytii . . .* [From the history of great Russian geographical discoveries . . .]. Moscow.

1950 *Iz istorii velikikh russkikh geograficheskikh otkrytii . . .* [From the history of great Russian geographical discoveries . . .]. Moscow.

Efimov, Aleksei V., ed.

1964 *Atlas geograficheskikh otkrytii v Sibiri i v severo-zapadnoi Amerike XVII–XVIII vv.* [Atlas of geographical discoveries in Siberia and northwestern America in the seventeenth and eighteenth centuries]. Moscow: Akademiia Nauk SSSR.

Eide, Arthur Hansin

1952 *Drums of Diomede.* Hollywood, Calif.: House-Warven Publishers.

Elliott, Henry W.

1877 "Ten Years' Acquaintance with Alaska: 1867–1877." *Harpers New Monthly Magazine* 55:801–16.

1886 *Our Arctic Province.* New York: Chas. Scribner's Sons.

Erman, A.

1851 "Expedition der Sloop Blagonamjerenny zur Untersuchung der Küsten von Asien und Amerika jenseits der Beringsstrasse, in den Jahren 1819 bis 1822." *Archiv für Wissenschaftliche Kunde von Russland* 9:272–94.

The Eskimo Bulletin

1893–1902 Vol. 1 (1893), edited by Harrison Thornton; vols. 2 (1895), 3 (1897), 4 (1898), and 5 (1902), edited by W. T. Lopp.

The Esquimaux

1867 (Newspaper published at Port Clarence, Russian America, and Plover Bay, Siberia. Editor, John J. Harrington. Turnbull and Smith Printers, San Francisco.)

Evans, A. N., ed.

1905 *The Midnight Sun*, vol. 1, no. 3, in Sheldon Jackson scrapbook 26.

Farrar, Victor J.
1937   *The Annexation of Russian America to the United States.* Washington, D.C.:
        W. F. Roberts.
Farrelly, Theodore S.
1944   "A Lost Colony of Novgorod in Alaska." *Slavonic and East European
        Review* (American Series, vol. 3, no. 3) 22 (no. 60):33–38.
Fedorova, Svetlana G.
1964   "K voprosu o rannikh russkikh poseleniiakh na Alaske" [Concerning
        the question of early Russian settlements in Alaska]. *Letopis severa*
        4:97–113.
1971a   "Issledovatel Chukotki i Aliaski kazachii sotnik Ivan Kobelev" [Ex-
        plorer of Chukotka and Alaska, Cossack Sotnik Ivan Kobelev]. *Letopis
        severa* 5:156–72.
1971b   *Russkoe naselenie Aliaski i Kalifornii* [The Russian population of Alaska
        and California]. The N. N. Miklucho-Maclay Institute of Ethnog-
        raphy. Moscow: Akademiia Nauk SSSR.
1973   *The Russian Population of Alaska and California* (translation of 1971b).
        Kingston, Ontario: Limestone Press.
Firth, Edith G.
1963   *The North West Passage 1534–1859: A Catalogue of an Exhibition of Books
        and Manuscripts in the Toronto Public Library.* Toronto.
Fisher, Raymond H.
1943   *The Russian Fur Trade 1550–1700.* University of California Publications
        in History, vol. 31. Berkeley: University of California.
1956   "Semen Dezhnev and Professor Golder." *Pacific Historical Review*
        25:281–92.
1971   *Records of the Russian-American Company, 1802, 1817–1867.* National Ar-
        chives Microfilm Publications, Pamphlet Describing M11.
        Washington, D.C.: National Archives and Records Service.
1973   "Dezhnev's Voyage of 1648 in the Light of Soviet Scholarship." *Terrae
        Incognitae* (Amsterdam), vol. 5.
Foote, Don Charles
1964   "American Whalemen in Northwestern Arctic Alaska." *Arctic An-
        thropology* 2 (no. 2):16–20.
1965   "Exploration and Resource Utilization in Northwestern Arctic Alaska
        before 1855." Ph.D. dissertation, McGill University.
Forster, Johann Reinhold
1786   *History of the Voyages and Discoveries Made in the North.* London. (Transla-
        tion from the original German.)
French, L. H.
[1901] *Seward's Land of Gold.* New York: Montross, Clarke and Emmons.
Fuller, Robert W. *See* Bogojavlensky, Sergei, and Robert W. Fuller
Gibson, James R.
1968–69 "Sables to Sea Otters." *Alaska Review* 3 (no. 3):203–17.
1969   *Feeding the Russian Fur Trade.* Madison: University of Wisconsin Press.
Giddings, James Louis
1964   *The Archeology of Cape Denbigh.* Providence, R.I.: Brown University
        Press.

1967   *Ancient Men of the Arctic*. New York: Alfred A. Knopf.

Giddings, James. L., et al.
1960   "The Archeology of Bering Strait." *Current Anthropology* 1 (no. 2):121–38.

Gilbert, Benjamin F.
1965   "The Confederate Raider *Shenandoah.*" *Journal of the West* 4 (no. 2):169–82 (reprinted in Sherwood, ed. 1967, pp. 189–207).

Golder, Frank A.
1914   *Russian Expansion on the Pacific 1641–1850*. Cleveland, Ohio: The Arthur H. Clark Co.
1917, 1937 *Guide to Materials for American History in Russian Archives*. Carnegie Institution of Washington Publication 239, vols. 1 and 2. Washington, D.C.: Carnegie Institution of Washington.
1920   "The Purchase of Alaska." *The American Historical Review* 25 (no. 3):411–25.
1922, 1925 *Bering's Voyages*. 2 vols. New York: American Geographical Society.

Governor of Alaska, Report of. *See* Lyman E. Knapp; and Swineford, A. P.

Great Britain. Parliament. House of Commons. Sessional Papers, accounts and papers. Arctic Expeditions.
1847–48   Vol. 41, no. 264: "Instructions to Lieut. (now Commander) Thomas E. L. Moore . . . and to Captain Kellett, dated 3 January 1848 and 13 December 1847."
1849   Vol. 32, no. 188: III. "Expedition to Behring's Straits." No. 7. "Henry Kellett to The Secretary of the Admiralty, 25 November 1848, Mazatlan," pp. 16–18; V. "Further Instructions to Captain Kellett, of Her Majesty's Ship 'Herald,'" pp. 24–26.
1850   Vol. 35, no. 107: No. 2 "Narrative of the Proceedings of Captain Kellett, of Her Majesty's Ship 'Herald,' and Commander Moore and Lieutenant Pullen, of Her Majesty's Sloop 'Plover,' through Behring's Straits, and towards the Mouth of the Mackenzie River," pp. 9–44. No. 7 (B. 2): "Copy of a Letter from Captain Sir W. Edward Parry to the Secretary of the Admiralty, dated 2d December 1849," pp. 75–77. No. 7 (E): "Copy of a Letter from Captain Sir George Back to the Secretary of the Admiralty, dated 1st December 1849," pp. 80–81. No. 8** (C.): "Memorandum by Dr. Sir John Richardson," pp. 91–94.
1851   Vol. 33, no. 97: No. 3 (L.): "Copy of a Letter from Captain Collinson, C. B., to the Secretary of the Admiralty, dated 13 September 1850, Port Clarence," pp. 14–16. No. 4 (A.): "Narrative of the Proceedings of Captain Henry Kellett, of Her Majesty's Ship, 'Herald,' from May 1849 to October 1850," pp. 19–25. No. 4 (B.): "Narrative of the Proceedings of Commander T. E. L. Moore of Her Majesty's Ship 'Plover,' from September 1849 to September 1850," pp. 28–34.

Great Britain. Parliament. House of Commons. Sessional Papers, accounts and papers. Further Correspondence and Proceedings Connected with the Arctic Expedition.
1852   Vol. 50, no. 1449: Part VI. "Proceedings of Her Majesty's Ship, 'Enterprise,' Captain Collinson, C. B." No. 2: "Abstract of the Information obtained by Commander Moore relative to White Men and Ships

having been seen by Natives in the Polar Sea." No. 5: "Captain Collinson to the Secretary of the Admiralty, 23 Dec. 1850." No. 7: "Letter to Captain Moore informing him of his Promotion, and conveying Approval of his conduct while in command of H. M. S. 'Plover.'" No. 8: "Mr. Edward Adams, Assistant Surgeon, to Captain Collinson, 10 July 1851." No. 10: "Further Proceedings of Captain Collinson, C. B." Enclosure 1 in No. 10. "Captain Moore's Report of his proceedings, dated 30 April 1851, Grantley Harbour," pp. 201–3. Enclosure 6 in No. 10: "Lieutenant Barnard to Commander Moore, dated 1 Jan. 1851, Kalishka Fishing Station," p. 206. Enclosure 7 in No. 10: "Lieutenant Barnard to Commander Moore, 3 January 1851, Kalishka," pp. 206–7. Enclosure 9 in No. 10: "Mr. Adams to Commander Moore, dated 26 Feb. 1851, Michaelowski redoubt," pp. 207–8. Enclosure 14 in No. 10: "Lieutenant Cooper to Commander Moore, dated 17 March 1851, Gariska [Kalishka]," pp. 211–13. Enclosure 15 in No. 10: "Journal of a journey from Gariska, Russian fishing station, Norton Sound, to H. M. S. Plover, in Grantley Harbour, Port Clarence, performed by Mr. Thomas Bourchier, Acting Second Master," pp. 213–15.

1852–53   Vol. 60, no. 82 (Continuation of Arctic Papers, Session 1852): "Proceedings of Captain Thomas Moore . . . in the Vicinity of Behring's Straits, during the winter of 1851–52." No. 36: "Letter from Captain Moore to the Secretary of the Admiralty; dated Her Majesty's Ship 'Plover,' Port Clarence, 1 July 1852," pp. 42–43. No. 39: "Letter from Commander Maguire to the Secretary of the Admiralty, Port Clarence, 20 August, 1852," pp. 45–47.

"Proceedings of Captain Charles Frederick [of the Amphitrite] . . . on a Visit to Behring's Straits and the Vicinity. . . ." No. 42: "Letter from Captain Frederick to the Secretary of the Admiralty, 13 October 1852, San Francisco," pp. 60–62.

Great Britain. Parliament. House of Commons. Sessional Papers, accounts and papers. Papers Relative to the Recent Arctic Expeditions in search of Sir John Franklin.

1854   Vol. 42, no. 1725: XI. "Orders to, and Proceedings of, Commander Henry Trollope, Her Majesty's Discovery Ship 'Rattlesnake.'" No. 7: "Reporting Proceedings, September 1, 1853," pp. 153–55. No. 8: "Letter from Trollope, Port Clarence, 11 September 1853," pp. 155–56. XII. "Report on the Proceedings of Her Majesty's Ship, Amphitrite, Captain Frederick." No. 1: "Report of Proceedings," pp. 156–58.

1854–55   Vol. 35, no. 1898: "Further papers relative to the recent Arctic Expeditions in Search of Sir John Franklin."

"From Captain Houstoun to the Secretary of the Admiralty, 'Trincomalee,' San Francisco, September 20, 1854," pp. 859–60.

"Proceedings of Her Majesty's Discovery Ship 'Rattlesnake,' Commander Henry Trollope. Commander Trollope to the Secretary of the Admiralty, July 6, 1854, Port Clarence," pp. 861–68. Enclosure 1: "Journal Kept by Commander Henry Trollope, during a trip from H. M. Sloop Rattlesnake in Port Clarence to King-a-ghee, a village four or five miles round Cape Prince of Wales. January 9, 1854–January 27, 1854," pp. 868–79. Enclosure 2: "Orders to and Proceedings of Mr.

Gilpin, Clerk, H. M. S. 'Rattlesnake,'" p. 879. Enclosure 3: "Mr. Gilpin's Journal," pp. 880–81. Enclosure 4: "Orders to and Proceedings of Mr. Hobson, Mate, H. M. S. 'Rattlesnake,' and Mr. Bourchier, Assistant Master," pp. 881–82. Enclosure 5: "Memorandum, March 21, 1854," pp. 882–83. Enclosure 6: "Journal of the Proceedings of Mr. W. R. Hobson (Mate) and Party under his Charge, whilst Travelling from Port Clarence to Chamisso Island, and Returning to the ship, Between February 9 and March 27, 1854 (inclusive)," pp. 884–98. "Observations on the Western Esquimaux and the Country they inhabit . . . by Mr. John Simpson . . . ," pp. 917–42.

1856 Vol. 41, no. 2124: "Further Papers relating to the recent Arctic Expeditions. Proceedings of the Second United States' Arctic Expedition in search of Sir John Franklin and his Companions, under the command of Lieutenant Kane." No. 58: "Lieutenant Bedford Pim to the Secretary of the Admiralty," pp. 69–78. Inclosure 3 in No. 58: "Copy of the Journal of Lieutenant Bedford Pim . . . from the 10th of March till the 29th of April, 1850," pp. 75–78.

Grekov, Vadim L.
1960 *Ocherki iz istorii russkikh geograficheskikh issledovanii v 1725–1765 gg.* [Essays from the history of Russian geographical explorations, 1725–1765]. Moscow: Izdatelstvo Akademii Nauk SSSR.

Grinnell, Joseph
1901 *Gold Hunting in Alaska.* Chicago: David C. Cook Publishing Co.

Gruber, Jacob W.
1967 *The Philadelphia Anthropological Society: Papers Presented on Its Golden Anniversary.* New York: Columbia University Press.

Gruening, Ernest
1954 *The State of Alaska.* New York: Random House.

Hammerich, L. L.
1958 "The Western Eskimo Dialects." *Proceedings*, International Congress of Americanists, 32nd Congress, Copenhagen, 1956, pp. 632–39.

Harrington, John J. See *The Esquimaux*

Harrison, Edward S.
1905 *Nome and Seward Peninsula.* Seattle: The Metropolitan Press.

Hawkes, Ernest W.
1913 *The "Inviting-In" Feast of the Alaskan Eskimo.* Canada Department of Mines, Geological Survey, Memoir 45. Anthropological Series, no. 3. Ottawa: Government Printing Bureau.

Healy, Michael A., et al.
1887 "Report of the Cruise of the Revenue Marine Steamer Corwin in the Arctic Ocean in the year 1885." 49C:1s, H. Ex. Doc. 153 (serial 2400). Washington, D.C.

1889 "Report of the Cruise of the Revenue Steamer Corwin in the Arctic Ocean in the year 1884." 50C:1s, H. Miscel. Doc. 602 (serial 2583). Washington, D.C.

Heinrich, Albert C.
1960 "Structural Features of Northwestern Alaskan Kinship." *Southwestern Journal of Anthropology.* 16:110–26.

1963   "Eskimo Type Kinship and Eskimo Kinship." Ph.D. dissertation, University of Washington.

1972   "Divorce as an Alliance Mechanism among Eskimos." In *Alliance in Eskimo Society*, edited by Lee Guemple. Proceedings of the American Ethnological Society, 1971, Supplement, pp. 79–88.

Hillsen, Karl K.

1849   "Puteshestvie na shliupe 'Blagonamerennyi' dlia izsledovaniia beregov Azii i Ameriki za Beringovym prolivom s 1819 po 1822 god" [Voyage of the sloop Good Intent to explore the Asiatic and American shores of Bering Strait, 1819–1822]. *Otechestvennyia zapiski* (series 3) 66 (pt. 8):213–38; 67 (pt. 8):1–24, 215–36.

Hinckley, Ted C.

1962   "Sheldon Jackson, Presbyterian Lobbyist for the Great Land of Alaska." *Journal of Presbyterian History* (March), pp. 3–23.

1965   "Publicist of the Forgotten Frontier." *Journal of the West* 4 (no. 1):27–40.

1966   "The Presbyterian Leadership in Pioneer Alaska." *The Journal of American History* 52 (no. 4):743–56.

1972   *The Americanization of Alaska, 1867–1897*. Palo Alto, Calif.: Pacific Books.

Hinz, John

1944   *Grammar and Vocabulary of the Eskimo Language*. Bethlehem, Pa.: The Society for Propagating the Gospel, The Moravian Church (second printing, 1955).

Hodge, Frederick Webb, ed.

1912   *Handbook of American Indians North of Mexico*. Bureau of American Ethnology, bulletin 30, pt. 2.

Hoffman, Walter J.

1897   "The Graphic Art of the Eskimos." U.S. National Museum, Annual Report for 1895, Washington, D.C., pp. 739–968.

Holmberg, Henrick J.

1855   *Ethnographische Skizzen über die Völker des Russischen Amerika*. Helsinki: H. C. Friis.

Homann, Erben

1759–[84] *Atlas geographicus maior exhibens tellurem seu globum terraqueum in mappis generalibus & specialibus per Iohannem Baptistam Homannum ejusque heredes editis.* (Copy in Library of Congress, map division.)

Hooper, C. L.

1881   "Report of the Cruise of the U.S. Revenue-Steamer Corwin in the Arctic Ocean, November 1, 1880." Treasury Department document 118. Washington, D.C.

1884   "Report of the Cruise of the U.S. Revenue Steamer Thomas Corwin, in the Arctic Ocean, 1881." 48C:1s, Sen. Ex. Doc. 204 (serial 2169), Washington, D.C.

Hooper, William H.

1853   *Ten Months among the Tents of the Tuski*. London: John Murray.

Hopkins, David M., ed.

1967   *The Bering Land Bridge*. Stanford, Calif.: Stanford University Press.

Howay, F. W.
1931   "A List of Trading Vessels in the Maritime Fur Trade, 1795–1804." *Transactions*, The Royal Society of Canada, 3rd series, vol. 25, section 2, pp. 117–49.

1932   "A List of Trading Vessels in the Maritime Fur Trade, 1805–1814." *Transactions*, The Royal Society of Canada, 3rd series, vol. 26, section 2, pp. 43–86.

1933   "A List of Trading Vessels in the Maritime Fur Trade, 1815–1819." *Transactions*, The Royal Society of Canada, 3rd series, vol. 27, section 2, pp. 119–47.

1934   "A List of Trading Vessels in the Maritime Fur Trade, 1820–1825." *Transactions*, The Royal Society of Canada, 3rd series, vol. 28, section 2, pp. 11–49.

Hrdlička, Aleš
1930   "Anthropological Survey in Alaska." *Forty-sixth Annual Report of the Bureau of American Ethnology (1928–29)*, pp. 29–374.

1944   *Alaska Diary, 1926–1931*. Lancaster, Pa.: The Jaques Cattell Press (second printing).

Hughes, Charles C.
1960   *An Eskimo Village in the Modern World*. Ithaca, N.Y.: Cornell University Press.

Hulley, Clarence C.
1953   *Alaska 1741–1953*. Portland, Ore.: Binfords and Mort.

Indian Commissioners, Board of
1893   *Twenty-fourth Annual Report, for the year 1892*. Washington, D.C.

1894   *Twenty-fifth Annual Report, for 1893*. Washington, D.C.

Innis, Harold A.
1956   *The Fur Trade in Canada*. Toronto: University of Toronto Press.

Irving, W. N.
1971   "Recent Early Man Research in the North." *Arctic Anthropology* 8 (no. 2): 68–82.

Ivashintsov, G.
1849   "Russkiia krugosvietnyia puteshestviia" [Russian round-the-world voyages]. *Zapiski gidrograficheskago departamenta* (St. Petersburg), 7:1–116 (the article is continued in vol. 8). In vol. 7 are the following topics: "Lieut. Kotzebue (Brig Riurik), 1815–1818," pp. 53–68; "Kap. Bellinshauzen i Lieut. Lazarev Shliupy Vostok i Mirnyi, 1819–1821," pp. 92–105; "Kap. Vasiliev i Shishmarev (Shliupy Otkrytie i Blagonamyrennyi), 1819–1822," pp. 106–16.

Jackson, Sheldon
1886   "Report on Education in Alaska." 49C:1s, Sen. Ex. Doc. 85 (serial 2339).

1888–1903   *See* Education Reports
1894–1908   *See* Reindeer Reports
[1903]   *Facts about Alaska, Its People, Villages, Missions, Schools*. Pamphlet issued by the Woman's Board of Home Missions of the Presbyterian Church in the United States of America. New York.

n.d. Scrapbooks and Correspondence. Presbyterian Historical Society, Philadelphia, Pa.

Jacobi, A.
1937 "Carl Heinrich Mercks Ethnographische Beobachtungen über die Völker des Beringsmeers 1789–91." *Baessler-Archiv* 20 (pt. 3–4):113–37.

Jacobsen, Johan Adrian
1884 *Capitain Jacobsen's Reise an der Nordwestküste Amerikas, 1881–1883.* Edited by A. Woldt. Leipzig.

James, James Alton
1942 *The First Scientific Exploration of Russian America and the Purchase of Alaska.* Northwestern University in the Social Sciences, no. 4, Evanston and Chicago: Northwestern University.

Jenness, Diamond
1928 "Archaeological Investigations in Bering Strait, 1926." *Annual Report for 1926*, National Museum of Canada, Bulletin 50. Ottawa.
1957 *Dawn in Arctic Alaska.* Minneapolis: University of Minnesota Press.
1962 *Eskimo Administration: I. Alaska.* Arctic Institute of North America, Technical Paper no. 10.

Johnshoy, J. Walter
1944 *Apaurak in Alaska.* Philadelphia, Pa.: Dorrance and Co.

Josephson, Rhea, and Dorothy Jean Ray
1971 "Translation of Vasilii Berkh's and Karl K. Hillsen's Accounts of the Shishmarev-Vasiliev Expedition to the Arctic, 1819–1822." Typescript in the Dartmouth College Libraries.

Kashevarov, Aleksandr F.
1840 "Obozrenie beregov Severnoi Ameriki, ot mysa Barrova, sovershennoe russkoiu ekspeditsieiu v 1838 godu" [Survey of the coast of North America to Cape Barrow accomplished by the Russian expedition in 1838]. *Syn otechestva*, pt. 1, pp. 127–44.
1845 "Otryvki iz dnevnika korpusa flotskikh shturmanov poruchika A. F. Kashevarova, vedennogo im pri obozrienii poliarnogo berega Rossiiskoi Ameriki, po porucheniiu Rossiisko-Amerikanskoi kompanii v 1838 g." [Excerpts from the diary of Naval Lieutenant A. F. Kashevarov, written during his survey of the polar coasts of Russian America on behalf of the Russian-American Company in 1838], reprinted from the newspaper *Sankt-Peterburgiskiia viedomosti*, nos. 190, 191, 192, and 195, 1845.
1879 "Zhurnal vedennyi pri baidarnoi ekspeditsii, naznachennyi, dlia opisi severnago berega Ameriki, 1838 goda iiulia s 5-go po 6-oe chislo sentiabria togo-zhe goda" [Journal of a baidar expedition, intended for a survey of the northern coast of America from July 5, 1838, to the sixth of September of the same year]. *Zapiski po obshchei geografii* 8:275–361.

Keithahn, Edward L.
1963 *Eskimo Adventure.* Seattle: Superior Publishing Co.

Kennan, George
1902 *Tent Life in Siberia and Adventures among the Koraks and Other Tribes in Kamtchatka and Northern Asia.* New York: Putnam. (Original edition published in 1870.)

Khromchenko, Vasilii S.

1824   "Otryvki iz zhurnala plavaniia g. Khromchenki, v 1822 godu" [Excerpts from the journal of the 1822 voyage of Khromchenko]. *Severnyi arkhiv*, pt. 10, pp. 254–76, 303–14; pt. 11, pp. 38–64, 119–31, 177–86, 235–48, 297–312.

1973   *See* VanStone, James W., ed. 1973

King, James. *See* Cook, James, and James King

Kitchener, L. D.

1954   *Flag over the North*. Seattle: Superior Publishing Co.

Knapp, Lyman E.

1891   *Report of the Governor of Alaska for the Fiscal Year 1891*. Washington, D.C.: Goverment Printing Office.

1892   *Report of the Governor of Alaska for the Fiscal Year 1892*. Washington, D.C.: U.S. Government Printing Office.

Kotzebue, Otto von

1821a   *Puteshestvie v Iuzhnyi okean i v Beringov proliv dlia otiskaniia sievero-vostochnago morskago prokhoda, predpriiatoe v 1815, 1816, 1817 i 1818 godakh . . . na korablie Riurikie*. Vol. 1 (three volumes, 1821–23, and atlas).

1821b   *A Voyage of Discovery, into the South Sea and Beering's Straits . . . in the years 1815–1818*. 3 vols. London: Longman, Hurst, Rees, Orme, and Brown.

Krause, Aurel

1956   *The Tlingit Indians: Results of a Trip to the Northwest Coast of America and the Bering Straits*. Translated by Erna Gunther. American Ethnological Society Monograph 26. Seattle and London: University of Washington Press. (Originally published as *Die Tlinkit-Indianer*, Jena, 1885.)

Kuznetsova, V. G. *See* Antropova, V. V., and V. G. Kuznetsova

Lafortune, Bellarmine

n.d.   "History of the Mission of King Island." Manuscript journal of a Jesuit priest. Original journal at Gonzaga University; copy at Saint Joseph's Church, Nome, Alaska.

Lantis, Margaret

1947   *Alaskan Eskimo Ceremonialism*. American Ethnological Society Monograph 11. Seattle and London: University of Washington Press.

1950   "The Reindeer Industry in Alaska." *Arctic* 3 (no. 1):27–44.

Lantzeff, George V.

1943   *Siberia in the Seventeenth Century: A Study of Colonial Administration*. University of California Publications in History, vol. 30. Berkeley and Los Angeles.

Lantzeff, George V., and Richard A. Pierce

1973   *Eastward to Empire*. Montreal and London: McGill-Queen's University Press.

Larsen, Helge, and Froelich Rainey

1948   *Ipiutak and the Arctic Whale Hunting Culture*. Anthropological Papers, American Museum of Natural History, vol. 42. New York: American Museum of Natural History.

Laufer, Berthold
  1924a   *Introduction of Tobacco into Europe.* Anthropology Leaflet 19, Field Museum of Natural History, Chicago.
  1924b   *Tobacco and Its Use in Asia.* Anthropology Leaflet 18, Field Museum of Natural History, Chicago.
Lazarev, Aleksei P.
  1950   *Zapiski o plavanii voennogo shliupa Blagonamerennogo v Beringov proliv i vokrug sveta dlia otkrytii v 1819, 1820, 1821 i 1822 godakh vedennye gvardeiskogo ekipazha leitenantom A. P. Lazarevym* [Notes on the voyage of the naval sloop Blagonamerennyi (Good Intent) into the Bering Strait and round the world for discoveries, in 1819, 1820, 1821, and 1822, kept by the guards' Lieutenant A. P. Lazarev]. Moscow: Gosudarstvennoe izd-vo geograficheskoi literatury.
Leighly, John
  1969   "[Letter about H. M. W. Edmonds]." *Anthropological Papers of the University of Alaska* 14 (no. 2):85–89.
Levin, M. G., and L. P. Potapov, eds.
  1964   *The Peoples of Siberia.* Chicago: The University of Chicago (translated from the Russian edition of 1956).
Longworth, Philip
  1970   *The Cossacks.* New York: Holt, Rinehart and Winston.
Lopp, William T.
  1890–1901 See *The American Missionary*
  1893–1902 See *The Eskimo Bulletin*
  1893–1931 Lopp papers and diaries. University of Oregon Library, Eugene.
Lopp, William T., and Mrs. Lopp
  1892–93   Diary, 25 September 1892 to 2 July 1893. C. L. Andrews collection, Sheldon Jackson College, Sitka, Alaska.
Loyens, William J.
  1964   "The Koyukon Feast for the Dead." *Arctic Anthropology* 2 (no. 2):133–48.
Luthin, Reinhard H.
  1933   "The Sale of Alaska." *Slavonic and East European Review* 16:168–82 (reprinted in Sherwood, ed. 1967, pp. 233–51).
Lutz, Bruce
  1969   "Archaeological Investigations near Unalakleet, Alaska." *Expedition* 11 (no. 2):52–54.
McCoy, Donald R.
  1956   "The Special Indian Agency in Alaska, 1873–1874: Its Origins and Operation." *Pacific Historical Review* 25 (no. 4):355–67.
Mackenzie, Alexander
  1801   *Voyages from Montreal on the River St. Laurence through the Continent of North America to the Frozen and Pacific Oceans; in the Years 1789 and 1793.* London.
Markov, Sergei
  1948   *Podvig Semena Dezhneva* [The feat of Semen Dezhnev]. Moscow.
Masterson, James R., and Helen Brower
  1948   *Bering's Successors, 1745–1780.* Seattle: University of Washington Press.

Mayokok, Robert
    1951   *Eskimo Customs.* Nome, Alaska: Nome Nugget.
    1959   *True Eskimo Stories.* Sitka, Alaska: Sitka Printing Co.
Mendenhall, Walter C. See Brooks, Alfred H., et al.
Merck, Carl H. See Bronshtein, Y., and N. Shnakenburg; and Jacobi, A.
The Midnight Sun. See Evans, A. N., ed.
Montgomery, Maurice
    1963   "The Murder of Missionary Thornton." *Pacific Northwest Quarterly* 54
            (no. 4):167–74.
Morris, William G.
    1879   *Public Service and Resources of Alaska.* 45C:3s, Ex. Doc. no. 59 (serial
            1831).
Muir, John
    1917   *The Cruise of the Corwin.* Boston and New York: Houghton Mifflin Co.
Müller, Gerhard
    1758a   "Opisaniia morskikh puteshestvii po Ledovitomu i po Vostochnomu
            moriu s Rosiiskoi storony uchinennikh" [Description of maritime
            travels to the Arctic and Eastern oceans from Russian foreign en-
            deavors]. *Ezhemesiachnyia sochinennia i izvestiia o uchenykh delakh* 1:99–
            120, 195–212, 291–325, 387–409; 2:9–32, 99–129, 195–232, 309–36,
            394–424.
    1758b   *Sammlung Russischer Geschichte*, vol. 3. Saint Petersburg.
    1761   *Voyages from Asia to America.* Translated by Thomas Jefferys. London.
            (This is vol. 3 of *Sammlung Russischer Geschichte*.)
Murray, Alexander H.
    1910   *Journal of the Yukon 1847–48.* Edited by L. J. Burpee. Publications of
            the Canadian Archives, no. 4. Ottawa: Government Printing Bureau.
Nelson, Edward W.
    [1877–81]   "List of Ethnological Specimens Obtained in Alaska with Notes."
            Manuscript, U.S. National Museum Archives.
    1887   *Report upon Natural History Collections Made in Alaska between the years
            1877 and 1881.* No. 3, Arctic Series of Publications, issued in connec-
            tion with the Signal Service, U.S. Army. Washington, D.C.
    1899   *The Eskimo about Bering Strait.* Bureau of American Ethnology, Annual
            Report, vol. 18, pt. 1. Washington, D.C.
Nichols, Jeannette P.
    1924   *Alaska: A History of Its Administration, Exploitation, and Industrial De-
            velopment during Its First Half Century under the Rule of the United States.*
            Cleveland, Ohio: The Arthur H. Clark Co.
Nordenskiöld, A. E.
    1882   *The Voyage of the Vega round Asia and Europe.* Translated by Alexander
            Leslie. New York: Macmillan.
Ogloblin, N. N.
    1890   *Semen Dezhnev (1638–1671 gg.)* Saint Petersburg. (Offprint of an article
            first published in *Zhurnal Ministerstva Narodnago Prosveshcheniia*, De-
            cember 1890.)

Okun, S. B.
1951   *The Russian-American Company.* Translated by Carl Ginsburg. Cambridge, Mass.: Harvard University Press.

Oquilluk, William A.
1973   *People of Kauwerak: Legends of the Northern Eskimo.* Alaska Methodist University Book Publication, no. 17 *Alaska Review.*

Oswalt, Wendell H.
1953   "Recent Pottery from the Bering Strait Region." *Anthropological Papers of the University of Alaska* 2 (no. 1):5–16.
1962   "Historical Population in Western Alaska and Migration Theory." *Anthropological Papers of the University of Alaska* 11 (no. 1):1–14.
1967   *Alaskan Eskimos.* San Francisco, Calif.: Chandler Publishing Co.

Pallas, Peter S.
1781, 1783 *Neue nordische Beyträge zur physikalischen und geographischen Erd- und Völkerbeschreibung, Naturgeschichte, und Oekonie,* vols. 1 and 4. Saint Petersburg and Leipzig.

Petroff, Ivan
1880   *Population and Resources of Alaska.* 46C: 3s, H.R. Ex. Doc. 40 (serial 1968).
1884   "Report on the Population, Industries, and Resources of Alaska." In *U.S. Tenth Census,* Department of the Interior, Census Office, Washington, D.C.

Pierce, Richard A.
1968   "The Russian Period of Alaskan History." In *Frontier Alaska,* pp. 63–73. Anchorage: Alaska Methodist University Press.
1973   *See* Lantzeff, George V., and Richard A. Pierce

[Polonskii, Aleksandr S.]
1850   "Pokhod geodezista Mikhaila Gvozdeva v Beringov proliv, 1732 goda" [Expedition of geodesist Michael Gvozdev to the Bering Strait, 1732]. *Morskoi sbornik* 4:389–402.

Porter, Kenneth W.
1930a   "Cruise of Astor's Brig Pedler, 1813–1816." *Oregon Historical Quarterly* 31 (no. 3):223–30.
1930b   "John Jacob Astor and the Sandalwood Trade of the Hawaiian Islands, 1816–1828." *Journal of Economic and Business History* 2 (no. 3):495–519.
1931   *John Jacob Astor, Business Man.* 2 vols. Cambridge, Mass.: Harvard University Press.
1932   "More about the Brig Pedler, 1813–1816." *Oregon Historical Quarterly* 33 (no. 4):311–12.

Porter, Robert B.
1893   "Report on Population and Resources of Alaska." *Eleventh Census, 1890.* Washington, D.C.: U.S. Government Printing Office.

Potapov, L. P. *See* Levin, M. G., and L. P. Potapov, eds.

Price, Jacob M.
1961   *The Tobacco Adventure to Russia.* Transactions of the American Philosophical Society, n.s. vol. 51, pt. 1. Philadelphia, Pa.: American Philosophical Society.

Rainey, Froelich. *See* Larsen, Helge, and Froelich Rainey

Rasmussen, Knud
1941   *Alaskan Eskimo Words.* Edited by H. Ostermann. Report of the Fifth Thule Expedition 1921–24, vol. 3, no. 4. Copenhagen: Gyldenalske Boghandel, Nordisk Forlag.

Ray, Dorothy Jean
1961   *Artists of the Tundra and the Sea.* Seattle and London: University of Washington Press.
1964a   "Kauwerak, Lost Village of Alaska." *The Beaver*, Outfit 295, Autumn, pp. 4–13.
1964b   "Nineteenth Century Settlement and Subsistence Patterns in Bering Strait." *Arctic Anthropology* 2 (no. 2):61–94.
1965   "Sheldon Jackson and the Reindeer Industry of Alaska." *Journal of Presbyterian History* 43 (no. 2):71–99.
1967a   *Eskimo Masks: Art and Ceremony.* Photographs by Alfred A. Blaker. Seattle and London: University of Washington Press.
1967b   "Land Tenure and Polity of the Bering Strait Eskimos." *Journal of the West* 6 (no. 3):371–94.
1968   "St. Michael Eskimo Myths and Tales." *Anthropological Papers of the University of Alaska* 14 (no. 1):43–83.
1969   *Graphic Arts of the Alaskan Eskimo.* U.S. Department of the Interior, Indian Arts and Crafts Board, Native American Arts 2. Washington, D.C.: Indian Arts and Crafts Board.
1971a   "Eskimo Place-Names in Bering Strait and Vicinity." *Names* 19 (no. 1):1–33.
1971b   *See* Josephson, Rhea, and Dorothy Jean Ray
1974   "The Omilak Silver Mine." *The Alaska Journal* 4 (no. 3):142–48.
1975   "Early Maritime Trade with the Eskimo of Bering Strait and the Introduction of Firearms." *Arctic Anthropology* 12 (no. 1):1–9.
n.d.   "The North Alaskan Eskimo: The Bering Strait." *The Handbook of North American Indians*, vol. 5 (forthcoming).

Ray, Dorothy Jean, ed.
1966   "The Eskimo of St. Michael and Vicinity as Related by H. M. W. Edmonds." *Anthropological Papers of the University of Alaska*, vol. 13, no. 2.

Raymond, Charles W.
1870   *Youkon River and Island of St. Paul.* 41C:2s, HR Ex. Doc. 112 (serial 1417).

Reindeer reports (usually prepared by Sheldon Jackson)
1894   "Report on Introduction of Domesticated Reindeer into Alaska" (third report, 1894). 53C:2s, Sen. Ex. Doc. 70 (serial 3160).
1895   "Report on Introduction of Domestic Reindeer into Alaska" (fourth report, 1894). 53C:3s, Sen. Ex. Doc. 92 (serial 3280).
1896   "Report on Introduction of Domestic Reindeer into Alaska" (fifth report, 1895). 54C:1s, Sen. Doc. no. 111 (serial 3350).
1897   "Report on Introduction of Domestic Reindeer into Alaska" (sixth report, 1896). 54C:2s, Sen. Doc. no. 49 (serial 3469).
1898a   "Report on Introduction of Domestic Reindeer into Alaska" (seventh report, 1897). 55C:2s, Sen. Doc. no. 30 (serial 3590).

1898b   "Report on Introduction of Domestic Reindeer into Alaska" (eighth report, 1898). 55C: 3s, Sen. Doc. no. 34 (serial 3728).

1900   "Ninth Annual Report on Introduction of Domestic Reindeer into Alaska" (report for 1899). 56C:1s, Sen. Doc. no. 245 (serial 3867).

1901   "Tenth Annual Report on Introduction of Domestic Reindeer into Alaska" (report for 1900). 56C:2s, Sen. Doc. no. 206 (serial 4043).

1902   "Eleventh Annual Report on Introduction of Domestic Reindeer into Alaska" (report for 1901). 57C:1s, Sen. Doc. no. 98 (serial 4230).

1903   "Twelfth Annual Report on Introduction of Domestic Reindeer into Alaska" (report for 1902). 57C:2s, Sen. Doc. no. 70 (serial 4422).

1904   "Thirteenth Annual Report on Introduction of Domestic Reindeer into Alaska" (report for 1903). 58C:2s, Sen. Doc. no. 210 (serial 4599).

1906   "Fifteenth Annual Report on Introduction of Domestic Reindeer into Alaska" (report for 1905). 59C: Sen. Doc. no. 499 (serial 4931).

1908   "Sixteenth Annual Report on Introduction of Domestic Reindeer into Alaska" (report for 1906). 60C:1s, Sen. Doc. no. 501 (serial 5239).

Richardson, George B. *See* Brooks, Alfred H., et al.

Rudenko, S. I.

1961   *The Ancient Culture of the Bering Sea and the Eskimo Problem.* Translated by Paul Tolstoy. Arctic Institute of North America. Anthropology of the North: Translations from Russian Sources, no. 1. Toronto: University of Toronto Press.

Samoilov, Viacheslav A.

1945   *Semën Dezhnev i ego vremia* [Semen Dezhnev and his times]. Moscow.

Samwell, David

1967   "Some Account of a Voyage to South Sea's in 1776–1777–1778." In Beaglehole 1967, pp. 989–1300.

Sarafian, Winston L.

1970   "Russian-American Company Employee Policies and Practices, 1799–1867." Ph.D. dissertation, University of California, Los Angeles.

Sarychev, Gavriil A.

1806–7   *Account of a Voyage of Discovery to the Northeast of Siberia, the Frozen Ocean, and the Northeast Sea.* 2 vols. London.

1952   *Puteshestvie flota kapitana Sarycheva po sieverovostochnoi chasti Sibiri, Ledovitomu moriu i Vostochnomu okeanu . . . s 1785 po 1793 god.* [Voyage of Captain Sarychev to the northeastern part of Siberia, the Arctic Ocean, and the Eastern Ocean . . . from 1785 to 1793]. Moscow. (Reprint of the original Russian with annotations.)

Sauer, Martin

1802   *An Account of a Geographical and Astronomical Expedition to the Northern Parts of Russia . . . in the Years 1785 etc. to 1794.* London: T. Cadell.

Scammon, Charles M.

1874   *The Marine Mammals of the Northwestern Coast of North America, Described and Illustrated; Together with an Account of the American Whalefishery.* San Francisco, Calif.

Schwalbe, Anna B.

1951   *Dayspring on the Kuskokwim.* Bethlehem, Pa.: Moravian Press.

Schwatka, Frederick
  1885   *Report of a Military Reconnaissance in Alaska, Made in 1883.* Washington,
              D.C.: U.S. Government Printing Office.
Searby, Harold W.
  1968   *Climates of the States: Alaska.* U.S. Department of Commerce.
              Washington, D.C.: U.S. Government Printing Office.
Seemann, Berthold
  1853   *Narrative of the Voyage of HMS Herald; During the Years 1845–51, under the
              Command of Captain Henry Kellett.* Vol. 2. London: Reeve and Co.
Semenov, Iurii N.
  1944   *The Conquest of Siberia: An Epic of Human Passion.* Translated from the
              German by E. W. Dickes. London: George Routledge and Sons.
Seward, William H.
  1868   *Russian America.* 40C:2s, H.R. Ex. Doc. no. 177 (serial 1339).
Sherwood, Morgan B.
  1959   "George Davidson and the Acquisition of Alaska." *Pacific Historical
              Review* 28:141–54 (reprinted in Sherwood, ed. 1967, pp. 253–70).
  1965   *Exploration of Alaska, 1865–1900.* New Haven, Conn.: Yale University
              Press.
Sherwood, Morgan B., ed.
  1967   *Alaska and Its History.* Seattle and London: University of Washington
              Press.
Shishmarev, Gleb S.
  1852   "Svedeniia o chukchakh Kapitana Shishmareva 1821 goda" [Captain
              Shishmarev's observations of the Chukchi in 1821]. *Zapiski Gidro-
              graficheskago Departamenta* 10:178–200.
Shnakenburg, N. *See* Bronshtein, Y., and N. Shnakenburg
Slovtsov, Petr A.
  1886   *Istorichesko obozrenie Sibiri* [Historical survey of Siberia]. 2nd ed. Saint
              Petersburg (first edition, 1838).
Smith, Fred M.
  1865–67   Manuscript diary dated 26 August 1865 to 22 March 1867. Charles S.
              Hubbell Collection, Manuscript collection, University of Washington
              library.
Sobranie sochinenii vybrannykh iz mesiatsoslovov na raznye gody [Collection of extracts
from Mesiatseslov (an almanac) for various years]
  1790a   "Izvestie o Chukotskom Nosie" [Information about Cape Chukchi],
              4:226–36.
  1790b   "Perechen iz dnevnoi zapiski kazacheva sotnika Ivana Kobeleva,
              posylannago 1779 goda v martie miesiatsie iz gizhiginskoi krieposti v
              Chukotskuiu zemliu" [Sequences from the daily notes of Cossack *sotnik*
              Ivan Kobelev, settled in 1779 in March at the Gizhigi fort on Chukchi
              Peninsula], 5:369–76.
[Sokolov, Aleksandr P.]
  1851   "Pervyi pokhod Russkikh k Amerikie 1732 goda" [First expedition of
              the Russians to America in 1732]. *Zapiski Gidrograficheskago De-
              partamenta*, 9:78–107.

Starbuck, Alexander
    1878   "History of the American Whale Fishery from its Earliest Inception to the Year 1876." In *Report of Commission of Fish and Fisheries for 1875–76.* Washington, D.C.: U.S. Government Printing Office.

Stefansson, Vilhjalmur
    1921   *The Friendly Arctic.* New York: Macmillan.

Stockton, Charles H.
    1890   "Arctic Cruise of the U.S.S. Thetis in 1889." *National Geographic Magazine* 2 (no. 3):171–98.

Sumner, Charles
    1867   *Speech of Hon. Charles Sumner of Massachusetts on the Cession of Russian America to the United States.* Washington, D.C.: Congressional Globe Office.

Swineford, A. P.
    1885   *Report of the Governor of Alaska to the Secretary of the Interior, 1885.* Washington, D.C.: Government Printing Office.
    1886   *Report of the Governor of Alaska for the Fiscal Year 1886.* Washington, D.C.: U.S. Government Printing Office.
    1887   *Report of the Governor of Alaska for the Fiscal Year 1887.* Washington, D.C.: U.S. Government Printing Office.

Taggart, Harold F.
    1954   "Journal of Wm. H. Ennis." *California Historical Society Quarterly* 33 (no. 1):1–11; 33 (no. 2):147–68.
    1956   "Journal of George Russell Adams." *California Historical Society Quarterly* 35 (no. 4):291–307 (abridged version of original diary).

Thomas, Benjamin P.
    1930   *Russo-American Relations 1815–1867.* Johns Hopkins University Studies in Historical and Political Science, series 48, no. 2. Baltimore, Md.: The Johns Hopkins Press.

Thornton, Harrison R.
    1931   *Among the Eskimos of Wales, Alaska.* Baltimore, Md.: The Johns Hopkins Press.

Tikhmenev, Petr A.
    1861–65   *Istoricheskoe obozrienie obrazovaniia Russiisko amerikanskoi companii.* Saint Petersburg (the original of the translation below).
    1939–40   "The Historical Review of the Formation of the Russian-American Company and Its Activity up to the Present Time." Translated by Dimitri Krenov. Two parts, typewritten copy in the University of Washington library.

Tompkins, Stuart R.
    1945   *Alaska: Promyshlennik and Sourdough.* Norman: University of Oklahoma Press.
    1955   "After Bering: Mapping the North Pacific." *British Columbia Historical Quarterly* 19 (nos. 1 and 2):1–55.
    1968   "Another View of Russian America. A Comment." In *Frontier Alaska*, pp. 75–88. Proceedings of the Conference on Alaskan History, 8–10 June 1967. Anchorage: Alaska Methodist University Press.

United States Court of Claims
1959   The Tlingit and Haida Indians of Alaska . . . v. The United States. No. 47900, decided 7 Oct. 1959.
United States Senate
1867   *Message from the President of the United States (Treaty of purchase)*. 40C:1s, Sen. Ex. Doc. no. 17 (serial 1308).
United States Treasury Department
1899   *Report of the Cruise of the U.S. Revenue Cutter Bear and the Overland Expedition for the Relief of the Whalers in the Arctic Ocean, from November 27, 1897 to September 13, 1898*. Treasury Department document no. 2101. Washington, D.C.
VanStone, James W.
1959   "Russian Exploration in Interior Alaska." *Pacific Northwest Quarterly* 50 (no. 2):37–47.
1960   "An Early Nineteenth-Century Artist in Alaska." *Pacific Northwest Quarterly* 51 (no. 4):145–58 (see also Choris 1822).
1967   *Eskimos of the Nushagak River: An Ethnographic History*. Seattle: University of Washington Press.
1970   "An Introduction to Baron F. P. von Wrangell's Observations on the Eskimos and Indians of Alaska." *Arctic Anthropology* 6 (no. 2):1–4.
VanStone, James W., ed.
1973   "V. S. Khromchenko's Coastal Explorations in Southwestern Alaska, 1822." Translation by David H. Kraus. *Fieldiana Anthropology*, vol. 64, Field Museum of Natural History, Chicago.
Van Valin, William B.
1944   *Eskimoland Speaks*. Caldwell, Ida.: Caxton Printers.
Vevier, Charles
1959   "The Collins Overland Line and American Continentalism." *The Pacific Historical Review* 27:237–53 (reprinted in Sherwood, ed. 1967, pp. 209–30).
Von Wrangell. *See* Wrangell, Ferdinand P. von
Western Union Telegraph Company
1865–67   Wemple papers relating to the Russian-American telegraph project. 1865–67. Photostats of the originals in the library of the Western Union Telegraph Co., 433 manuscript leaves. Northwest Collection. University of Washington library.
Whalemen's Shipping List (New Bedford, Mass.) 1843–1914
Whymper, Frederick
1869   *Travel and Adventure in the Territory of Alaska*. New York: Harper and Brothers.
Wickersham, James
1927   *A Bibliography of Alaskan Literature, 1724–1924*. Miscellaneous Publications of the Alaska Agricultural College and School of Mines, Cordova, vol. 1.
Wrangell, Ferdinand P. von
1839   *Statitische und ethnographische Nachrichten über die Russischen Besitzungen an der Nordwestküste von Amerika*. Saint Petersburg.

1840   *Narrative of an Expedition to the Polar Sea in the years 1820, 1821, 1822 &* *1823*. Edited by Major Edward Sabine. Translated by Mrs. Sabine. London.

1970   "The Inhabitants of the Northwest Coast of America." Translated by James W. VanStone. *Arctic Anthropology* 6 (no. 2):5–20.

Yefimov. *See* Efimov, Aleksei V.

Zagoskin, Lavrentii A.

1956   *Puteshestviia i issledovaniia leitenanta Lavrentiia Zagoskin v russkoi Amerike v. 1842–1844 gg.* (reprint of 1847 edition published by the State Publishing House of Geographic Literature, Moscow).

1967   *Lieutenant Zagoskin's Travels in Russian America 1842–1844: The First Ethnographic and Geographic Investigations in the Yukon and Kuskokwim Valleys of Alaska.* Edited by Henry N. Michael. Translated by Penelope Rainey. Arctic Institute of North America. Anthropology of the North: Translations from Russian Sources, no. 7 (Russian edition, 1956). Toronto: University of Toronto Press.

Index